Discovering God's Word

◆ AN INTRODUCTION TO SCRIPTURE ◆

Marilyn Gustin, Ph.D.

Benziger Publishing Company

Mission Hills, California

Cover Photo by Tim Fuller

Ainari/Art Resource 64, 153; Bill Aron/Photo Edit 21; Art Resource 10, 14, 168, 62, 67, 77, 86, 87, 90, 116, 239; Leslye Bordon/Photo Edit 257; Robert Brenner/Photo Edit 11; Bidgeman Art Library/Art Resource 18, 28; Buck Campell/FPG International 122; Comstock 274; Culver Pictures 19, 45, 149, 248; Dennis MacDonald/Photo Edit 242, 273; Mary Kate Denny/Photo Edit 223, 277; Ectra/Photo Edit 185; Myrleen Ferguson/Photo Edit 200, 206, 280; FPG International 210; Tony Freeman 8, 132, 278; Giraudon/Art Resource 150, 224, 230, 264; Jeff Isacc Greenberg/Photo Edit 212; Jewish Museum/Art Resource 44, 120; Lessing/Art Resource 6, 20, 29, 41, 48, 56, 80, 94, 105, 118, 156, 162, 190, 191, 235, 254, 255, 268, 272; Stephen McBrady 4, 5, 281; Stephen McBrady/Photo Edit 188, 194r; National Museum of American Art/Art Resource 197; National Portrait Gallery/Art Resource 180; Richard Nowitz 16, 23, 25, 26, 38, 101, 123, 133, 139, 175, 193, 198, 258, 259; Alan Oddie/Photo Edit 275; Photo Edit 36, 138; Zev Radovan 52, 70, 72, 82, 95, 98, 100, 114b, 130, 216, 241, 260; Scala/Art Resource 22, 27, 30, 39, 43, 47, 54, 57, 61, 83, 96, 103, 104, 106, 112, 121, 135, 143, 144, 151, 157, 172, 179, 181, 194L, 196, 199, 205, 215, 218, 219, 221, 232, 238, 243, 244, 250, 251, 262; Rhoda Sidney/Photo Edit 148, 170; Taposchaner/FPG International 228; Tate Gallery/Art Resource 176, 183; Vanni/Art Resource 114t, 146, 237, 271; Wayne State University/Archives of Labor and Urban Affairs 276; Wide World Photos 60, 74, 76, 81; David Young-Wolff/Photo Edit 92, 140, 160, 161, 186, 270

Scripture passages are taken from *The New American Bible with Revised New Testament,* copyright ©1988 by the Confraternity of Christian Doctrine, Washington, D.C. All rights reserved.

Excerpts from *Vatican Council II, The Conciliar and Post Conciliar Documents,* Austin Flannery, O.P., ed., ©1975, reprinted with permission of Costello Publishing Co., Inc., Northport, NY 11768.

High School Consultant
John Allen, MA
Notre Dame High School, Sherman Oaks, CA

Censor Librorum
The Reverend Michel J. St. Pierre

Imprimatur
The Most Reverend Kenneth A. Angell, D.D.
Bishop of Burlington
Given at Burlington, Vermont on the 24th of January, 1994.

The nihil obstat and imprimatur are official declarations that a book or pamphlet is free of doctrinal or moral error. No implication is contained therein that those who have granted the nihil obstat and imprimatur agree with the contents, opinions, or statements expressed.

Send all inquiries to:
BENZIGER PUBLISHING COMPANY
15319 Chatsworth Street
P.O. Box 9609
Mission Hills, California 91346-9609

ISBN 0-02-662334-X (Student's Edition)
ISBN 0-02-662335-8 (Teacher's Wraparound Edition)

Printed in the United States of America

    4 5 RRW 99 98 97 96 95

Table of Contents

What Is the Bible?

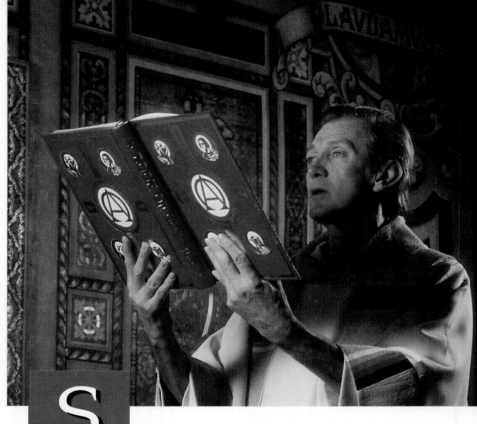

Legend

- ● General History
- ● Biblical History
- ● Jewish History
- ● Books written

Shannon walked into the first religion class of the year a little worried; she knew nothing about the Bible. Would she end up behind everyone else and feel left out? Nervously, she pulled her Bible out of her book bag, waiting to see what would happen.

Mr. Martinez introduced himself to the class, took roll, and then said, "Let's get started right away." He handed Shannon's friend, John, an open Bible and asked him to read aloud from the Gospel of Matthew. After helping John find the right page, Mr. Martinez waited.

"Take this and eat it, this is my body," John read.

Mr. Martinez interrupted, "Anybody recognize those words?"

Hands shot up immediately, including Shannon's. "The priest says those words at Mass," she said.

"Very good," Mr. Martinez replied, smiling. "Let's try something a little more difficult." He handed the Bible to Sophia and asked her to read the marked passage. Sophia read about two people named Moses and Aaron who went to talk to somebody called the pharaoh. "Anybody know what a pharaoh is?" Mr. Martinez asked.

Suddenly Shannon remembered studying Egypt in middle school. "The king of Egypt," she said.

"Excellent!" responded Mr. Martinez. "I wanted to make a point with these questions. I wanted to show you that you all know more about the Bible than you think. Shannon, here, is already on her way to being a Bible expert!"

Shannon smiled and felt her nervousness going away. "Maybe the semester won't be so bad after all," she thought.

Whether you're aware of it or not, you probably already have some knowledge of the Bible that you learned from church and from school. In this book, you will build upon what you already know, and also learn to understand the Bible in a variety of new ways. In the process, you will also discover that the Bible is a book that can entertain you, educate you, inspire you, and most importantly, involve you in a conversation with God, who speaks through its pages.

Whether or not you establish a conversation with God during this course of study is up to you. As with any relationship, developing a closeness and dialogue with God requires a great deal of effort and attention. The more time you spend speaking with God, the better able you will be to communicate with God. The more time you spend reading the Bible in order to understand God's word, the better able you will be to understand it.

Getting Started

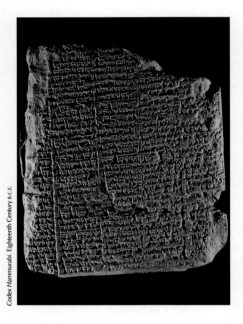

Codex Hammurabi. Eighteenth Century B.C.E.

Within each chapter of this book there are two sections. The first section provides the background you need to understand a part of the Bible. It always illustrates how God's Word has been shaped by the circumstances in which it was written.

For both sections in each chapter, you'll be given a set of "learning objectives." These identify what you should know by the end of the section. In this first section of the book you will consider how the Bible is organized, how it came to be written, and why there is diversity in the Bible.

Learning Objectives for Section One

By the end of this section, you will be able to:

- Explain the difference between the two testaments.
- Look up Bible references by chapter and verse.
- Define "canon" and "oral tradition."
- Explain why there is diversity in the Bible.

◆ Introducing the Bible

As you would with any book, you need to know your way around the Bible to make the best use of it. First, however, you need to decide that learning about the Bible is worth doing. As you'll see, there are a variety of reasons why learning more about the Bible is a valuable thing for you to do.

Why Study the Bible?

There are several reasons why knowledge of the Bible should be important to you.

1. The Bible is a unique place to meet God. Through prayer and reflection, you can grow in your appreciation of what God has to say to you.
2. The Bible is the "book of the Church." It tells the story of the people of God, and therefore connects us to our ancestors in faith.
3. The Bible can help you solve the problems you meet in ordinary life, especially ethical and moral dilemmas. The Bible presents ways that other people in God's family were confronted with problems, the choices they made, and the results of those choices.
4. Because the Bible is so often used in social debate today, a familiarity with Scripture will help protect you from being manipulated by politicians and people using the Bible to accomplish their own ends.
5. Because the Bible is cherished by many different religions, knowing the Bible helps us build relationships with people of other faiths.
6. Bible study builds solid academic skills. It requires you to learn to read literature carefully, and to place it in historical context.

LEARN FROM THE MAP

Ancient Israel

Once in each chapter, you'll have a chance to explore the geography of the Bible. Here, you see ancient Israel, the land that was promised by God as part of the Covenant. Take a minute now to become familiar with the lay of the land. Notice how small the area is—so much history in so little space! Using the scale given, can you figure out how long Israel is?

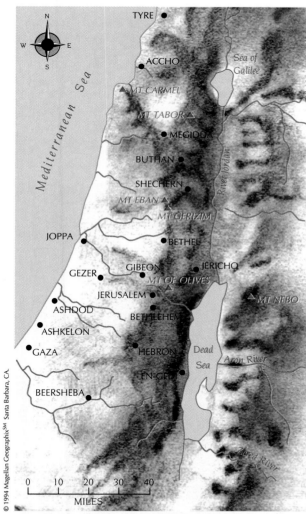

Area: *Approximately 8,000 square miles*
Elevation–Highest Point: *3,962 feet*
Lowest Point: *1,292 feet below sea level*
Physical Features: 1) *Coastal Plain—117 miles along Mediterranean Coast;* **2)** *Western Mountains—extending from Galilee to Jerusalem;* **3)** *Negev—the triangularly shaped southern half of the country;* **4)** *Rift Valley— the land along the Jordan River*

How the Bible Is Organized

There are two main divisions in the Bible: The Old Testament and the New Testament. The word "testament" means "covenant." The theme of the Covenant between God and humanity is central to both sections of the Bible. The Bible is, in fact, the story of God's Covenant with humanity. In the Covenant, God offers to bless and protect us in exchange for obedience to the path God marks out for us.

The Old Testament   The first two-thirds of the Bible is the story of ancient Israel. It begins with the creation of the universe and follows the story through the rise and fall of the Israelite kingdom. The Old Testament is divided into four sections:

- **Pentateuch.** This section includes the first five books of the Bible, called "Torah" by the Jews. These books include the stories of the creation of the world and of the nation of Israel, as well as the law given by God to the Israelites.
- **Historical Books.** These books tell the story of the nation of Israel from the Hebrew's entry into the promised land until the Exile.
- **Writings.** This section includes religious poetry and essays about God's relationship with humanity.
- **Prophets.** These are the words of the people God inspired to present messages to Israel.

You'll learn from the Old Testament that God chose Israel to be a special nation. God made a Covenant with Israel: if Israel would accept God's law, God would bless and protect it. The Old Testament tells the story of Israel's struggle to be faithful to the Covenant, and to understand the God who had chosen it.

Most of the books of the Old Testament are also sacred to Jews, who call their collection the "Tanakh." A few books from the ancient Greek version of the Old Testament are accepted by Catholics, but not by Jews or some other Christians, who accept only the books from the ancient Hebrew version. The list of accepted books in the Bible is called the "canon."

The New Testament   Christians believe that through Jesus, God made a new Covenant with humanity. Based on the earlier Covenant with Israel, this new arrangement invites all humanity to become part of God's Chosen People through faith in Jesus.

The New Testament consists of:

- **Gospel accounts.** Four collections of stories and sayings of Jesus.
- **Acts of the Apostles.** The story of the early Christian Church after the Ascension of Jesus.
- **Letters.** Letters written by early Christians that show us the problems and concerns of the early Church.
- **Revelation.** A book which offers comfort to oppressed Christians, promising future salvation.

How the Bible Was Written

The stories now found in the Bible were told for many centuries before they were written down. They were memorized by professional storytellers and passed along by word of mouth. This is called the "oral tradition."

Eventually, people preserved these traditions in writing. The earliest writings probably date from 1000 B.C.E. For the most part, we don't know who the authors were, because ancient people weren't interested in the identity of the author. For them, the content mattered, not who wrote it. As a result, different works by different authors often got combined into new works, a process called "editing."

The Old Testament was reedited and put into its final form after the destruction of the nation of Israel by the Babylonians in 587 B.C.E. The priests who put it together wanted to make sure that the sacred traditions of the nation didn't perish.

The New Testament was written during a much shorter period of time, approximately a hundred years: 40–110 C.E. It, too, began with oral stories about Jesus, and then was put on paper to preserve these traditions for later generations. For a while, the Church argued over which books should be in the New Testament, reaching a general consensus around 300 C.E. The Bible was finalized only at the Council of Trent in 1543.

Diversity in the Bible

As we've seen, the Bible is not one big book, but a collection of smaller books. The Bible is, in fact, a small library: 73 separate titles, with 46 in the Old Testament and 27 in the New Testament. The word "bible" comes from a Greek term which means "the books."

As you would expect to find in any library, there are many different kinds of writing in the Bible.

in the Spotlight

Biblical Languages

"In the Spotlight" is another feature that will appear in each chapter. This "In the Spotlight" deals with the languages of the Bible.

The ancient Israelites spoke *Hebrew,* and most of the Old Testament is written in this language. Around 500 B.C.E., however, they started to speak *Aramaic,* another Middle Eastern language, and some portions of the Bible were written in it. Finally, after 300 B.C.E., Greece dominated the Middle East, and a few Old Testament books were written in that language.

The New Testament was written entirely in Greek. The early Christians lived in the eastern Roman empire, where Greek was the international language. Although Jesus knew Greek, his primary language was Aramaic, since he was a part of Jewish culture. There are also some hints that he may have known Latin.

Think of the Bible as a library with many different types of books to explore.

Scripture Workshop

Chapter and Verse

Twice in every chapter, you'll find a "Scripture Workshop." These exercises are intended to give you hands-on experience in working with the Bible.

In order to use the Bible, it is important to be able to look up references in the way they are usually given. For example, Chapter 10, verses three to five of the First Book of Kings would be written like this:

1 Kings 10:3–5

When searching for a biblical reference, first locate the book, then turn to the chapter. Most Bibles put the chapter numbers as headings on each page. Make sure you are at the beginning of the chapter. Then, search for the first verse listed in the reference. Read the *passage* through the last verse listed.

Finding Bible passages can be fun. How fast can you look up these references? Write the first word of each passage. Then read the completed sentence.

_____	_____
Tobit 8:6	Genesis 31:15
_____	_____
Hebrews 4:12	Proverbs 29:17

The Bible in Context

Dating History

"The Bible in Context" will examine specific biblical issues in detail. This one describes how dates are identified in this textbook.

Traditionally, dates were given using B.C., meaning "before Christ," and A.D., meaning "anno Domini" (Latin for "in the year of the Lord"). These abbreviations have been in use since the Middle Ages.

Although these abbreviations work as well as anything else for dividing time, they are specifically Christian designations. Jews, Muslims, and members of other religions based on the Bible may feel uncomfortable referring to the "year of the Lord," when they do not share the belief that Jesus is the Lord of humanity.

For that reason, biblical scholars have substituted the terms B.C.E., meaning "before the common era," and C.E., meaning "in the common era," as a neutral means of dating historical events.

---

many subjects. These are not "contradictions," but simply different human beings responding to their experience of God in different ways. Consider this example: A newscaster reports, "An earthquake struck Northern India killing over 20,000." A person who survived the quake said, "Buildings fell around our heads. Why did God save my family instead of my neighbors'?" The same truth, different expressions.

The Bible records the efforts of many holy people, who, over thousands of years, attempted to express the truth about God. Those efforts have to be read in the light of much study and prayer before we can come to our own conclusions about their meaning.

Stories and histories, legends and myths, poetry, songs, wise sayings, prophecies, laws, letters—all of these types of writing are included in Scripture. Although at times the Bible may seem like a slow-moving sermon or history book, it's really a record of the ways people in ancient Israel experienced God. The Bible is actually alive with the excitement and astonishment they felt.

Because the Bible is a "library" consisting of different books, written by different people at different times and in different styles, it is hardly surprising that these books exhibit different points of view on

Have You Considered?

These questions appear regularly throughout the chapter to help you think about the issues raised in that part of the book.

1. Which reason for studying the Bible seems most important to you? Why?
2. Why do you suppose Jews don't like to use the term "Old Testament" to refer to their Scriptures? What does this phrase suggest which they might find objectionable?
3. If there are many different people who contributed to the Bible at different times, why does it follow that we should expect to find different points of view?

Understanding the Bible

Playfair Book of Hours, St. Jerome in his Study, Fifteenth Century.

The second section in each chapter of this book focuses on a specific part of the Bible, and studies how that part helps you learn about God and yourself. In order to do this, it applies what you learned in the first section.

In the first section you learned about what the Bible is, how it came to be written, and how knowing how to read the Bible can be an asset for you. In this section you will come to understand the Bible as the story of human salvation. The Bible is God's Word, inspired through human authors and revealed over many centuries.

Learning Objectives for Section Two

By the end of this section, you should be able to:

- Define "salvation history" and "religious truth."
- Explain what is meant by the phrase "Word of God."
- Explain the idea that the Bible is "revealed" and "inspired."
- Discuss why the Bible is the Church's book.

◆ Biblical Truths

Both through study and prayer, our goal is to understand the truth of the Bible. The word "truth," however, can be used in many different ways. What are the different kinds of truth found in these statements:

- "My mother loves me."
- "2+2=4"

The first statement is just as true as the mathematical equation but you can prove that "4" is the answer to the math problem using logic. Could you prove your mother's love in this way? The point is, two statements can both be true, but in different ways. In this section, you will learn what the statement "the Bible is true" means.

The Bible Is a Book of Religious Experience

The Bible does not pretend to be based on totally objective history. The biblical writers and editors wanted to use history to teach about God. When they wrote about the past, therefore, they had several preconceived notions about what had happened. They believed that the most important goal was understanding God, not objectivity about the past.

In our day, we think of historical truth in scientific terms: "What are the facts about how something happened in the past?" But ancient history-writers conceived of truth differently. They thought of history in moral terms, and a historian's job was to assign credit and blame for the events of the past. The specific details of what happened were not very important.

They wrote with what we would call a "bias," that is, an idea of why things happened based on a careful judgment. A history lacking such a bias would, by their standards, be considered incomplete.

Salvation History

The nature of ancient history-writing means that the biblical authors were interested not so much in

Learning about the Bible requires effort on your part, just as you must study to master mathematics.

history itself, but how the events of the past could be seen in relation to their faith. For them, all of history was religious history.

Religious history is often referred to as *salvation history*. The history of salvation recounts God's un-ending love for the Chosen People. The Bible constantly reminds us of how God is with us. The history of salvation is fulfilled in the life, death, and resurrection of Jesus Christ.

Religious Truth

From a strictly factual standpoint, one part of the Bible may not agree with another part. There are instances of geographical error and numbers are often used as symbols. For example:

- In Mark's Gospel account, the author explains how Jesus traveled south from Galilee to Jerusalem through Tyre and Sidon. These two cities, however, are actually north of Galilee, and therefore Mark's geography is confused.
- Numbers were certainly used differently than they are today. In the Bible, numbers are often exaggerated or used as symbols, rather than used literally. The Book of Exodus says that 600,000 men left Egypt when Moses led the Jewish slaves to freedom. But if there really had been that many Israelites in Egypt, they could have conquered Egypt rather than flee from it. Since women and children accompanied

Scripture Workshop

Historical Dates

The Bible's focus on religious history often means that minor historical details are left out or confused. The following exercise will illustrate this point.

Open your Bible to Chapter 2 of Matthew. Keep that place, and also turn to Chapter 2 of Luke. Both Gospel accounts tell the story of the birth of Jesus. Now, answer the questions below:

1. According to Matthew, who was king when Jesus was born?
2. According to Luke, who was the governor when Jesus was born?

We know from historical records that Herod the Great died in 4 B.C.E., while Quirinius was not sent to Syria until 6 C.E. Knowing this, is it possible that both Matthew and Luke could be right?

When we get to the New Testament, you'll see that both Matthew and Luke have reasons for dating the birth of Jesus as they do, but these reasons have to do with religious truth, not historical fact.

People of Note

Saint Augustine

"People of Note" will appear in the second section of each chapter. It will focus on some person (or group of people) important for understanding the Bible.

Though a brilliant man, Augustine had lived a carefree life. He enjoyed a good party, and he lived with his mistress for 16 years. Prior to becoming a bishop and great thinker in the Church, Augustine converted to Christianity with the help of the Bible.

In July of 386, Augustine heard a voice cry out, *"Tolle, lege,"* which means, "take and read." Augustine randomly opened the Bible to the Book of Romans. He read:

Let us throw off the works of darkness and put on the armor of light; let us conduct ourselves properly as in the day, not in orgies and drunkenness, nor in promiscuity and licentiousness, not in rivalry and jealousy. But put on the Lord Jesus Christ, and make no provision for the desires of the flesh.

Romans 13:12–14

Augustine was to turn to the Bible as his source of inspiration for the rest of his life. Reflecting on Psalm 36 Augustine wrote, "There is obviously some kind of blissful vision reserved for us; . . . It is for this that our hearts are being trained in all the hardships and trials of this life. . . . you are being schooled for a wonderous destiny." For Augustine, the Bible was the text for this school.

---

the men on their journey, a conservative figure would put the total number at 1,500,000. Such a multitude would have difficulty being fed by all the fields and pastures in the promised land, let alone the desert they crossed!

The reason for these "inaccuracies" is that biblical authors were mainly concerned with presenting religious truth about God and God's relationship with them.

Biblical authors also knew that what they understood could be expressed in ways other than factual reporting, such as poetry and tall tales. For example, the account of Jonah being swallowed by a big fish (Jonah 2:1–2) seems unlikely to be fact, though many ancient people believed in the mysteries of the deep. But it does communicate in a very dramatic way the truth of God's persistence and saving power.

Religious truth—the truth of God's love and care for humanity—is preserved in the Bible, whether buried beneath factual inaccuracies or not.

The Bible and the "Word of God"

The Bible is often called the "Word of God." This phrase refers, first of all, to the experience of people in the Old Testament, to whom God spoke quite directly. God placed the Word, or message, into the hearts and minds of those who heard it and felt it. They, in turn, passed it along to others in their preaching and writing. By passing on God's Word,

"the works performed by God in the history of salvation . . . clarify the mystery" (*Dei Verbum*, #2).

The Bible Is Revealed

Revelation means "the uncovering of something that was previously not known." From a personal standpoint, such a revelation may simply come from a thought that pops into your head or the reception of some words of advice from another.

Revelation can come directly from God. Married people often reflect back on how it was "revealed" to them that a person they were dating was the "right one" for them. God is certainly revealed to us in such personal ways. God speaks to us in personal revelation—sometimes even directly—through our relationships, our daily experiences, natural and historic events, and in prayer.

The Bible is a book of such revelations. Although we can never be completely sure if a personal revelation comes to us from God, we are sure that the Bible is a direct communication of truth from God. Our certainty comes from the tradition of the Church, as well as the evidence of the millions of lives over time which have been touched and healed by prayerful reading of Scripture.

The divine revelation, as presented in the Bible, continues to have power today. The message of the Bible is not limited to a certain time or to a select few.

The Bible Is Inspired

When we say the Bible is inspired we mean that it was written by human authors under the **guidance and protection** of the Holy Spirit. Catholics believe that the Holy Spirit teaches "that truth which God, for the sake of our salvation, wished to see confided to the sacred Scriptures" (*Vatican* II, Dei Verbum, III.11).

Because the Scriptures were written by humans, they contain all the biases, mistakes, and points of view common to people of a particular time in history. But, because they are also divinely inspired, the writings of the Bible are free from error involving anything that God wanted to express.

Exactly how inspiration works is not fully known. But through our own experiences, we can gain some idea of how God's Word is communicated through the written words of Scripture.

Have you ever been called to the front of the classroom to give an oral presentation? Even though you may have spent hours and hours preparing, you were still nervous and not sure of what you would say and how you would say it. As you relaxed and your presentation went on, you were amazed at how easily the words came out. You might ask, "Is *this really me* speaking?" That's an example of how inspiration operates.

Jesus explained inspiration in more detail just prior to his arrest. Speaking to his disciples, he said:

> When they lead you away and hand you over, do not worry beforehand about what you are to say. But say whatever will be given to you at that hour. For it will not be you who are speaking but the Holy Spirit.
>
> Mark 13:11

Have You Considered?

1. What would be a helpful definition of the term "Word of God"?
2. How is religious history different from other forms of history?
3. What different kinds of truth are there? For example, how is moral truth (how you know something is right or wrong) different from scientific truth?

Spiritual Reflection

Praying with the Bible

Praying with Scripture has been mentioned several times in this chapter. Here's a way to begin:

- Find a place where you can be alone for a while, without any time limit, uninterrupted and quiet.
- Settle yourself comfortably and become very still. Breath softly.
- After you are relaxed, open your Bible to Psalm 103. (Psalms can be found almost in the middle of your Bible; look it up in the table of contents.)
- Pray in your own words. Ask the Lord to be with you and to help you be aware of God's love.
- Think about the words as you read the psalm very slowly. Let yourself **feel** their meaning.

- When one line seems finished to you, go quietly to the next and repeat what you have just done.
- Pray for as long as you feel good about what you are doing. (You don't have to pray the whole psalm, or you could repeat it several times.)
- When you are finished, take two extra moments to thank God for this quiet time. Thank God for the qualities described in this psalm. Ask God to help you remember what you have prayed. Then, take a deep breath, get up, and go your way!

Q/A

Section One

1. What does "Tanakh" mean?
2. What is the meaning of the term "covenant"?
3. What is the difference between the Old and New Testaments?
4. Describe the process known as "the oral tradition."
5. Define the term "canon."
6. Why is there diversity in the Bible?
7. List four reasons to study the Bible.

Section Two

1. Define the term "salvation history."
2. Define the term "religious truth."
3. How is the Bible a book of revelation?
4. Explain how the Bible is divinely inspired.
5. Why are there inaccuracies in the Bible?
6. Who was Saint Augustine and what was his connection with the Bible?

BIBLE ACTIVITY

1. Open your Bible to Chapter 5 of the prophet Isaiah (find it in the table of contents if you need to). Look at the verse numbers in this chapter. What do you notice? Based on what you now know about how the Bible was put together, what problem do you think the publisher of this Bible was trying to correct?

2. Read Chapter 5 of Genesis. Notice the ages of the people in this chapter. Based on what you learned in this chapter, do you think these ages should be taken literally? If not, what do you think the author might have intended to symbolize by using such high numbers?

Loeb ben Elhanan, *Hebrew Prayerbook*. Eighteenth Century.

GLOSSARY

- **Canon:** The list of books accepted for the Bible.
- **Inspiration:** The idea that God assisted the authors in writing the Bible.
- **Old Testament:** The first two-thirds of the Bible which tells the story of ancient Israel's covenant relationship with God.
- **Oral Tradition:** The process of storytelling and word of mouth circulation that occurred before any of the biblical books were written down.
- **Pentateuch:** First five books of the Bible.
- **Religious Truth:** The truth of what the Bible tells us about God's love and desire for our well-being.
- **Revelation:** The idea that the Bible shows us something of God.
- **Salvation History:** The idea that God is involved with the events of history, directing them for our salvation.
- **Tanakh:** Word used by Jews to refer to their holy Scriptures.
- **Testament:** Another word for "covenant," which refers to a promise made by God to humanity.
- **Word of God:** A term for the Bible; it refers to the inspiration of the biblical authors by the Holy Spirit.

UNDERSTANDING MORE ABOUT:

Ancient Manuscripts

This is the final feature you'll find in each chapter. It's a chance to introduce some issue or aspect of Bible studies that will help in your understanding the Bible.

All the books of the Bible were written before printing presses, so copies were made by hand. A handmade copy of something is called a "manuscript."

Biblical scholars translate the Bible from ancient manuscripts. This process is complicated, however, by four facts about ancient Hebrew manuscripts: (1) they have no punctuation, (2) they are written entirely in capital letters, (3) no spaces are placed between letters, and (4) Hebrew was written without vowels until about 700 C.E.!

How can anyone read such a mess? Actually, it's not as hard as you may think. Try this one for starters:

YOUCANREADTHIS.

When written in your native language, you can generally recognize the different words and easily decide where punctuation should go. Now try this one without vowels:

THBBLSGDBK.

For people who study the Bible, it takes years to acquire the kind of familiarity with the original languages needed to make translations easily. Even then, there are cases where it's difficult to tell what is meant. Try this:

GODISNOWHERE.

Did you get "God is now here" or "God is nowhere?" In cases such as these, biblical scholars have to trust their skill and instincts, as well as the context in which the phrase appears.

By the way, the answer to the example above without vowels is "The Bible is a Good Book."

The Original Covenant

Chapter Listings

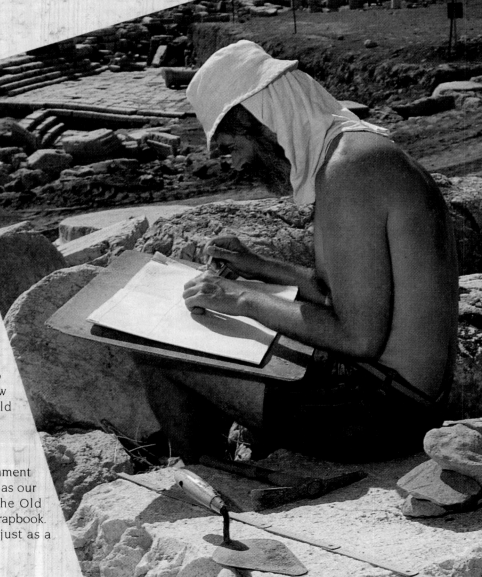

The first part of the Bible is called the "Old Testament." The word "testament" means "covenant." In this case, covenant refers to the special, unbreakable agreement between God and humanity. The Old Testament is the story of God's original Covenant made with Israel. Catholics consider this part of the Bible to be "Scripture," or "holy writings," just as much as the New Testament. In order to understand it, there are a few basic things about the Old Testament you should know.

A Family Story

The stories in the Old Testament are about the people we look to as our ancestors in faith. As such, the Old Testament resembles a family scrapbook. It contains historical records, just as a scrapbook might have birth certificates and wedding licenses. The Old Testament also has essays and stories, like a scrapbook might have letters and other writings. The Old Testament has no photographs, of course, but it does have vivid descriptions of people, so real you can almost see them. The Old Testament also has its share of legends and tall tales, like exaggerated stories about family members.

When you read a scrapbook, you expect to see something different on every page. You will also find many different kinds of writing in the Bible. You shouldn't expect everything to read the same way or share exactly the same ideas, just as you wouldn't expect that from a scrapbook.

Finally, just as you wouldn't hold a scrapbook to the same standards of historical and scientific accuracy as you would a textbook, you should expect to find factual mistakes and exaggerations here and there in the Old Testament. The authors, inspired by God, were trying to tell their family story, not write an error-free research paper.

Why the "Old Testament"?

Why is the first part of the Bible called the "Old" Testament? Christians use this word to signify that God has made a more recent covenant with humanity through Jesus, which is described in the "New" Testament. Jews, however, believe that the first covenant is still in effect. They don't think of it as "old," since to them there isn't a "new" one. For this reason, Jews don't use the term "Old Testament" for their Scripture. They call it the "Tanakh," a Hebrew word which stands for the three parts of the Jewish Bible: law, prophets, and writings.

The Old Testament has four basic divisions:

1. The Pentateuch (Greek for "five books") are the first five books in the Old Testament: *Genesis*, *Exodus*, *Leviticus*, *Numbers* and *Deuteronomy*. Judaism knows these five books as the "Torah." Sometimes Jewish people refer to their whole Bible as "Torah."

2. The Historical Books are *Joshua* and *Judges*, books which tell of Israel's entry into the promised land and her first years there; *Samuel*, *Kings*, and *Chronicles*, records of the rise and fall of the monarchy of Israel; *Ezra* and *Nehemiah*, stories of the return to Jerusalem after 538 B.C.E. and the rebuilding of the nation and the Temple; and *Maccabees*, the story of Jewish rebellion against Greek influences.

3. The Wisdom Books include the *Psalms*, *Job*, *Ecclesiastes*, *Proverbs*, *Wisdom*, *Sirach*, and *Song of Songs*. These books suggest how people should live, and why there is evil in the universe. They are reflections about life, justice, choice and behavior, and love. They are collections of advice, reflections and sayings about love, human as well as divine.

4. Prophets include the three major (or longer) prophetic books and the twelve minor (or shorter) books. The major books are *Isaiah*, *Jeremiah*, and *Ezekiel*. *Daniel* includes legends and predictions, visions and symbols. If the reader understands the historical situation in which each prophet lived, he or she can then understand the meaning of the prophecy offered in the books.

Why Read the Old Testament?

Since the Catholic Church teaches that we have a new Covenant with God through Jesus, you may be wondering why we bother with the Old Testament at all. Although it is a logical question, there are several reasons why neglecting the Old Testament would be a tragic mistake.

1. The Second Vatican Council (1962–65), declared that the Old Testament has permanent value and is an important witness to God's revelation.
2. The actions and attitudes of our ancestors in faith can be examples for us.
3. Reading the Old Testament prepares us to understand the New.
4. The Old Testament forms a link between the three major western religions: Christianity, Judaism, and Islam.
5. The final reason for studying the Old Testament is because it introduces us to the story of salvation.

By reading the Old Testament, we are able to locate ourselves as members of a faith community involved in an ongoing relationship with God. We can face the challenges life gives us, knowing that God has a plan for our salvation. We can face the future with confidence, anchored in a covenant relationship that spans 3,000 years, and that is founded upon God's ultimate gift: the power of love.

CHAPTER 2

Moses and the Covenant

1450 **1450 B.C.E.**
- Beginning of Hittite Empire

1304–1237
- Reign of Ramses II in Egypt

1300 **1300**
- Mycenaean-Minoan culture begin civil wars

1300–1280
- Likely date for the Exodus

1288
- Battle of Kadesh; Egypt and the Hittites make peace

1250
- Greek settlers found a colony in Etruria (Italy); basis for Etruscan civilization
- Tribal life in Canaan; Judges

1212
- Merneptah stele, commemorates victory of Egypt over Israel

1200 **1200**
- Migration of "Sea Peoples" into the Middle East—later called Philistines

1000
- Exodus story first written

550 **550**
- Book of Exodus completed

Legend
- General History
- Biblical History
- Jewish History
- Books written

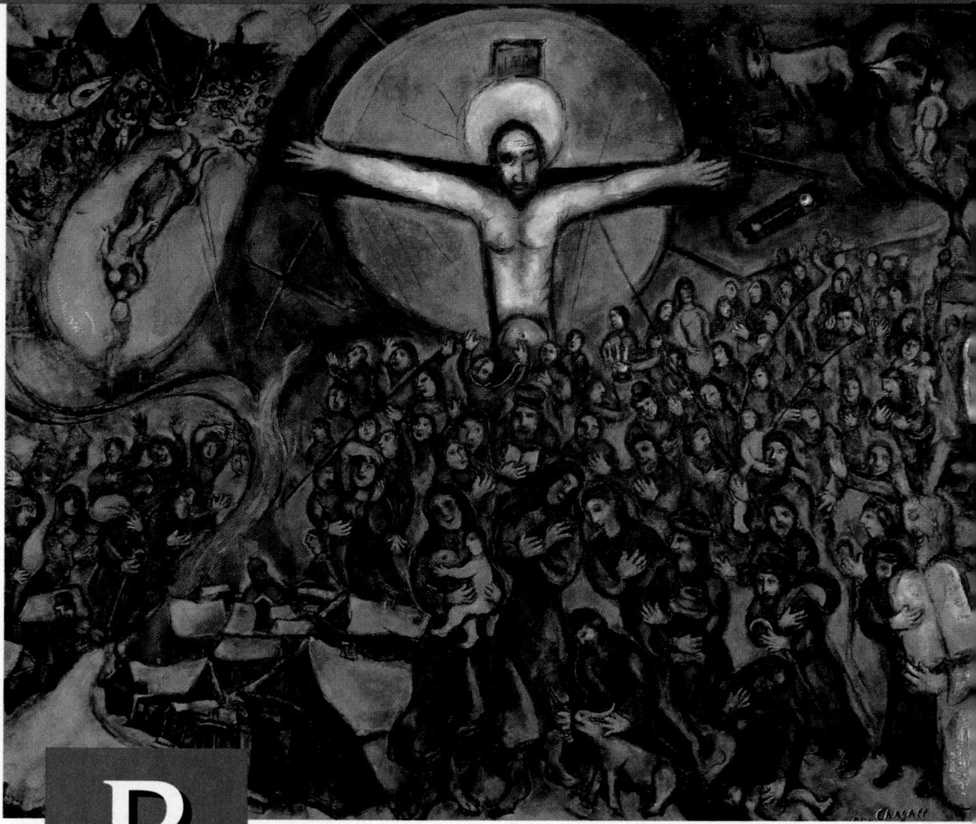

Chagall, *Exodus.* Twentieth Century.

Relationships with people you love are different from relationships with people in movie theaters or video arcades. When you buy a movie ticket or change a dollar for video game tokens, you form a "contract" with the owner of the theater or arcade. Your ticket or token entitles you to a service, namely a movie or video game. If the machine breaks down or the game doesn't work, you get your money back. You also hold the owner responsible if anything happens to you or your possessions while you're on the premises.

With people you love, you have a different kind of relationship, one we call a "covenant." Let Karen, age 26, explain. She recently married Patrick, her college boyfriend. Here's what she has learned about a covenant relationship after 11 months of marriage:

I have found that one of the strengths of our relationship is freedom. My goal has always been to study law. Patrick knew that our finances would be tight while I went to law school and yet he supported me in all ways. Through our relationship, I feel like I am blossoming into the person that God intends for me to be.

Our marriage grows, in part, due to the support we receive from our family, friends, and Church. To have the people we love and care about at our wedding to share and witness our love was a great gift.

Most importantly, God is a part of our relationship. The faith that Patrick and I share has been the foundation of our marriage. Most nights we talk about our day and then we pray together before going to sleep. We believe that our marriage is modeled on the relationship that God has had with humanity since the beginning of time.

God's faithfulness throughout history is an inspiration to us. We expect to receive many blessings in married life, especially children. We know that our love will survive and last forever!

Loving Relationships   Contracts are legal agreements which protect rights. They are written in technical language that can feel very cold. Covenants, however, bind people together in a warm, loving relationship. Although you can form a contract just by buying a ticket, a covenant takes a lot of time, effort, and trust to build.

In this chapter, you will read about how God began the Covenant with the people of Israel. This Covenant is still alive today in the lives of Jews and Christians throughout the world. You will also see how God built a relationship with the Hebrew people, freeing them from slavery in Egypt and leading them safely across the desert to the promised land. We call this event the "Exodus" (exit) from Egypt. Finally, you will discover how God cemented the Covenant by giving the Israelites the law through their great leader, Moses.

The story of the Exodus has been expressed in many artistic media, including this filmed version called The Ten Commandments.

Forming a Covenant

Egypt, Akhnaton Worships Aton. Fourteenth Century B.C.E.

One of the most important themes in the Old Testament is the special relationship that exists between God and the people of Israel.

This special relationship did not happen immediately. The people of Israel grew into it over the course of many hundred years. Yet, from the beginning of the Covenant, God's love for the Hebrew people is clearly evident. Before looking at the story of how this Covenant began, we will consider how people living in the ancient world would have understood the idea of a "covenant." In addition, we will find out who the ancient Hebrews were and how they thought about God.

Learning Objectives for Section One

By the end of this section, you will be able to:

- Explain the idea of God's "election" of Israel.
- Describe the variety and elements of ancient covenants.
- Compare the Bible to writings from a similar time and place.
- Define "monotheism" and place it in its historical context.

◆ A Covenant People

For Jews, the most important story of the Tanakh is found in the Book of Exodus. *Exodus* comes from a Greek word meaning "to exit." The story of the Hebrews' exit and liberation from slavery in Egypt is told in chapters 1–15 of the Book of Exodus. It is the story of how, from all the people on earth, God chose the Hebrews, offering them freedom from slavery, rules to live by, and the blessing of a permanent homeland.

Election

The covenant agreement in the Book of Exodus is understood as a fulfillment of the promises made to the Hebrews' ancestors, particularly the patriarch, Abraham. The agreement also made new promises, since the land of Canaan, which had first been promised to Abraham, would be a lasting gift from God to the Hebrew People. You will study more about Abraham in Chapter 4.

The Covenant bound the people in a loving relationship with God. They were a people especially chosen from among all the other races and nations on earth. They had been "elected" by God, not because of anything that they had accomplished, but because of God's love for them:

It was not because you are the largest of all nations that the Lord set His heart on you and chose you, for you are really the smallest of all nations. It was because the Lord loved you and because of His fidelity to the oath He had sworn to your fathers.

(Deuteronomy 7:7–8)

The election of the Hebrew people reveals most clearly God's saving power. God freely chose the Hebrews because God loved them, and for no other reason. Think about that for a moment; what does it mean that someone is chosen strictly out of God's love? What would it mean to you to know that God will love you and be with you no matter what you may do? Such an act of generous love is hard to understand, yet that is how God is.

The Bible in Context

The Sh'ma

The Covenant between God and the Hebrews, described in the Book of Exodus, remains the basis of life for modern Judaism. Today's Jews stand in a tradition that is over 3,200 years old!

Jews have a special prayer which expresses this relationship with God, called the "Sh'ma" (from the Hebrew word meaning, "hear.") The first line reads: "Sh'ma Yisrael: Adonai Elohenu Adonai Echad!" ("Hear O Israel: The Lord our God, the Lord is One!") The words of the prayer are taken from the Book of Deuteronomy.

According to the Jewish "rabbis," or teachers, when Jews say the first verse of this prayer, they renew their acceptance of the Covenant. This act is called "accepting the yoke of the kingdom of Heaven." Traditionally, Jews cover their eyes when saying the first verse, and stretch out the word "echad" ("one") as they think about God's oneness.

Another custom related to this prayer is the *Mezuzah,* a container with a scroll inside with the words of the Sh'ma written on it. Jews place the Mezuzah on their doorposts, because the last line of the Sh'ma instructs them to keep the words of the prayer "on the doorposts of your house and upon your gates." (Interestingly, the Mezuzah is always hung at an angle. It seems that two great rabbis in the Middle Ages argued over whether the Mezuzah should be placed horizontally or vertically. Eventually, they reached this compromise.)

These customs, and many others like them, remind the Jews of their special relationship with God, formed by the Covenant of Exodus.

Covenants in the Ancient Middle East

The ancient Israelites who wrote the Book of Exodus needed a set of terms to describe this special relationship between God and Israel. The closest parallel they could find was the treaties formed between two nations. Therefore, they used the language and even the format of international treaties to describe the bond that existed between God and Israel. They called this agreement a *"b'rith,"* or "covenant," the same word they used for alliances between groups and nations.

Most of our information about these ancient treaties comes from the study of the Hittite Empire (1400–1200 B.C.E.; the area is now part of modern Turkey), although other nations of that time also made formal agreements with covenants. (The Hittite covenants were based upon the code of law developed in Babylon.)

In form, the covenant treaty consisted of three parts: (1) the agreement itself, (2) witnesses, and (3) a ritual act. The witnesses were not only other humans, but also the Hittite gods.

The two sides bound themselves to their agreement through an act of ritual. For example, they would kill an animal, cut it in half, and walk between the halves. This ritual symbolized that they should be killed and cut into pieces if they broke their word. For a description of a similar ritual involving Abraham, see Genesis 15.

Each year Jewish families remember God's Covenant with them by celebrating Passover with the Seder meal where the story of the rescue from Egypt is remembered.

Scripture Workshop

Elements of the Vassal Treaty

The vassal treaty:

- Described the greatness and kindness of the king.
- Listed rules and regulations.
- Named the witnesses and enforcers of the treaty.
- Identified the blessing and curses that would follow either obedience or disobedience.

To become familiar with this format, do the following:

1. Find each of the four elements of the vassal treaty in Deuteronomy 5:1–33. This passage is a version of the giving of the Ten Commandments to Moses.
2. List the verse numbers where each of the elements occur.
3. Write 1 or 2 sentences for each, explaining how you recognize these particular elements in the verses.

Over time, two major types of covenants became prevalent in the ancient Middle East. One was a *parity treaty*, an agreement entered into by equal parties. A second type of covenant was a *vassal treaty*, that is, a powerful king would gain power over a weaker one.

The Covenant given by God to the Hebrews was a very formal treaty. It was not an agreement between equals. It was more like the agreement between a conquering king and his new subject. Therefore, it was closest in form to the vassal treaty. Yet, this Covenant agreement was also quite different from any other that existed at that time.

Have You Considered?

1. Which do you think is more rare, contracts or covenants? Why?
2. Which type of covenant (parity treaty or vassal treaty) does a marriage most closely resemble? Explain your answer.
3. The Bible says that God chose the Hebrews to make them into a special nation. Do you think that God continues to choose people today for special purposes? Explain your answer.

These lion gates continue to guard the remains of the Hittite city of Hattusas, the ancient capital of the Hittite empire. The Hittite nation lasted from the sixteenth to the seventh century B.C.E.

For the Hebrew people who followed Moses out of Egypt, the destination was the land of Canaan.

◆ The Early History of the Chosen People

Most scholars agree that the people of God did not think of themselves as a nation until after they had made it out of Egypt and into the promised land. In other words, they did not become a nation until after the Exodus. Before this time, they existed as various tribes and clans who shared a language and some cultural traditions. In order to understand the importance of the Exodus, we need to look at this earlier period.

The Hebrews

Before you continue, take a moment to understand a few names.

- **An "Israelite"** was someone who was a citizen of the nation of Israel. Since Israel did not exist as a nation until after the Exodus, there were no "Israelites" in Egypt.
- **A "Hebrew"** was someone who spoke the Hebrew language and was born into the Hebrew culture. This cultural group was organized into tribes, shared a language and traditions (including stories and songs), served as slaves in Egypt, and formed the basis for the nation of Israel.
- **The word "Semite,"** is often used in place of the word "Hebrew." Semite, however, refers to a much larger group of people that includes Hebrews, Arabs, Canaanites, Babylonians, Assyrians, and other people who live in Palestine and Mesopotamia. Each of these peoples speaks a related language.

The Hebrews probably were originally a group of "nomads," people who wander around following a flock or herd of animals rather than living in one settled location. They roamed the Middle East, merging with various groups as they went along. Eventually, they became farmers and settled down.

The Hebrews probably came to Egypt, along with many other smaller cultural groups, attracted by the higher standard of living to be found there. Over time, these groups were reduced to slavery. In the next section, we will take up the story of the Exodus, as God delivers the Hebrews from their slavery and leads them to a homeland.

LEARN FROM THE MAP

The Ancient Middle East

Notice that ancient Israel was near to several larger, more powerful empires. Through trade, immigration, and political ties, Israel's culture was strongly influenced by the cultures of these surrounding nations. Each time Israel was conquered, its culture and religion was affected. For this reason, it's not surprising that the biblical authors modeled their description of the relationship between God and Israel on the covenant formulas used by surrounding nations to make treaties.

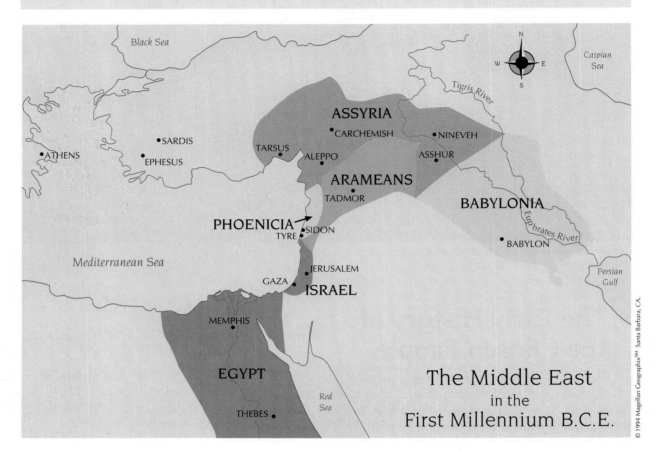

The Middle East
in the
First Millennium B.C.E.

© 1994 Magellan Geographix℠ Santa Barbara, CA.

How the Israelites Thought about God

The Israelites were unusual in the ancient world because their Covenant said that they worshipped only *one* God, although all of the surrounding cultures worshipped a wide variety of gods and goddesses. Moses may have recognized that this Yahweh whom he worshipped exclusively was the only God, but that's not true for the rest of the Hebrews. The Bible records an ongoing battle that raged over the people's worship of many gods, even in the Sinai while on the Exodus!

There is a major difference between the idea that Yahweh is the first among many gods, and the idea that Yahweh is the **only** God. It took the Hebrew people many years to come to this complex understanding. Their awareness grew with experience and especially with the insights of the prophets.

Moses told the people that the God who delivered them from Egypt and the Sinai was "a jealous God," who insisted that they "have no other gods besides Me." This God was different from the gods worshipped by other people. This God demanded an exclusive right to the people's allegiance. This teaching, however, did not deny the *existence* of other gods. It was, instead, the first step toward that realization.

Toward Monotheism Belief in the existence of only one God is called *monotheism*. Ironically, the foundations of monotheism may have begun in Egypt itself.

From 1364–1347 B.C.E., the Egyptian pharaoh was Akhenaton. Unlike his forefathers, he worshipped only one god, the Solar Disk or Sun God. Akhenaton's name means "Glorious Spirit of Aten," referring to the sun god, Aten. He forced this belief on the nation and did his best to eliminate all other religious views. After his death, Egypt returned to the practice of worshipping many gods (*polytheism*). During his reign, however, the Israelite slaves in Egypt would certainly have been exposed to Akhenaton's monotheism. We know that they were moved by Akhenaton's religious poetry, because his "Hymn to the Sun" influenced many of the psalms.

The Hebrew Difference The Hebrews did not simply take over Akhenaton's ideas, however. Always when the Hebrews (or Israelites) were influenced by religious ideas other than their own, they reshaped them to express their unique experience and understanding of God. Even in the beginning, they did not see Yahweh as part of nature, as Egyptian myth tended to do. Yahweh was, instead, separate from and above nature.

Nomadic people still wander across the Middle East, leading their animals to water and better pastures. Their lives have changed little over the centuries.

in the *Spotlight*

The Armarna Letters

There are very few records outside the Bible that help us understand these events which happened over 32 centuries ago. Within the last 100 years, however, archaeologists have discovered a series of writings which are as old or older than the Bible, and which help us understand the Bible in new ways.

One such text is a collection known as the Amarna letters, which date from the time of the pharaoh Akhenaton (between 1400 and 1350 B.C.E.). In several of the letters, the rulers of Palestine and Syria write to the pharaoh in Egypt, asking for military assistance. Wandering groups of attackers called the *'Apiru'* were attacking small walled cities and could not be defeated.

Some scholars have suggested that these 'Apiru' are the same as or related to the 'Ivri', or 'Hebrews.' It's not really certain that these two people are the same group, but it does show that many peoples were wandering in search of a home at the time the Israelites made their journey from Egypt into the Promised Land.

Today, belief in the existence of only one God is so common that it may be hard to imagine anything else. But in the time when Israel was finding its identity as a people, monotheism would have been almost unimaginable.

Yahweh demanded exclusive worship and loyalty of his people, who were not inclined to speculate about (for them) all the details of divine nature. They wanted to know whose power was available to them and how they should live in relationship with that god. For the early Israelites, Yahweh was the one.

Have You Considered?

1. Why do you think the Hebrews could not form a nation while living as slaves in Egypt? What prevented this from happening?
2. The Amarna letters and the religious policies of Akhenaton help us understand the historical context of the Bible. Give an example of how knowing the context of something today helps you understand it.
3. What difference does it make whether there *is* only one God or if there were many gods, but you worshipped only one?

Israel Becomes a Nation

Few characters in the Bible rival Moses in importance:

- He was the person who introduced the Hebrews to Yahweh and served as God's voice.
- He was the leader who brought the Hebrews out of slavery in Egypt to freedom in the promised land of Israel.
- He was the one who received the Law, the code which God gave to the people of Israel as a sign of their election.

In this section, we'll see how God forms Israel into a nation.

Learning Objectives for Section Two

By the end of this section, you will be able to:

- Describe the importance of Moses in the story of Israel.
- Explain the idea of "formation" and how the wilderness experience of Israel was as an example of formation.
- Identify the Ten Commandments and explain their significance.

◆ The Story of Moses

The witness, mediator, and key figure in the covenant between God and the Hebrews was Moses. Even today, Moses is generally considered the most important figure in Jewish history. Moses is the person appointed by God to deliver the Hebrews from slavery in Egypt and to lead them to the promised land of Canaan. Most importantly, Moses was the one who received the Law from God and promised obedience on behalf of the people. In this way, it was Moses through whom the Covenant between God and Israel was made. The story of the Covenant, therefore, begins with his life story.

Moses' Birth and Early Years

According to the story in the Book of Exodus, the pharaoh began to fear the Hebrews because

> *the more they were oppressed, the more they multiplied and spread.*
>
> (Exodus 1:12)

The Pharaoh issued an edict (royal order) to kill all the baby Hebrew boys in order to stop the Hebrew population from growing.

Exodus tells how the infant Moses was spared when his mother set him afloat in the Nile River in a basket made of papyrus. He was found by a royal princess and his life was spared. The name Moses is similar to an Egyptian word, *Mosheh*, which means "to draw out."

The story of Moses' rescue is the type of story that is quite common in ancient literature. It was a sign of divine favor when a child survived a brush with death in order that he might grow into a great leader and deliverer of his people. Early Christians even had a similar story about Jesus (see *Matthew* 2).

As a young man, Moses was forced to leave Egypt because he killed an Egyptian who was striking a Hebrew. When the event became known, Moses fled for his life to Midian, an area including the eastern side of the Sinai peninsula. There, Moses was taken into the clan of the priest, Jethro, given a wife, and became a shepherd.

It was while Moses was living in the desert of Midian that the knowledge of the "greatness and kindness" of Yahweh was revealed to him.

"I Am Who I Am"

God's introduction to Moses and the Hebrew people is described in Exodus 3:1–4:17. In the desert Moses encounters a burning bush that is not consumed by the fire. From this bush Moses hears the voice of God.

The story of the burning bush reveals God's concern and action on behalf of the Hebrew People. God has seen their suffering in Egypt, and God intends to deliver them from slavery. God tells Moses that he will be the one to lead the Hebrew people out of Egypt. Moses' first response is to refuse:

Who am I that I should go to the Pharaoh and lead the Israelites out of Egypt?

(Exodus 3:11)

God answers: "I will be with you" (*Exodus* 3:12).

Moses then attempts to find out God's name. To most ancient people, a person's name was the expression of who he or she was. Names were not given by accident, a name expressed a person's character. Parents carefully named their children. After major events, people would often adopt new names to reflect who they were now. In addition, ancient magic spells were based on the power of knowing the secret names of angels and spirits. For a Hebrew to know someone's name, therefore, meant that he or she held some type of power over the other.

God refuses to be possessed. Instead of giving a name to Moses, God says, "I am" or "I am who I am."

What does the artist, Raphael, do to capture God's power in the burning bush?

Scripture Workshop

The Burning Bush

The scene where Moses encounters God in the burning bush is called a "theophany," an appearance by a god to a human being. This experience is the key to Moses' later life and accomplishments. It is also the beginning of God's explicit action in the history of the Hebrew people. Read Exodus 3:1–4:17, where this story is told. Answer the following questions:

1. What did Moses see? What would you think of such a sight?
2. What did the voice in the bush say to Moses? List five separate points.
3. How did Moses react? (3:11, 4:1 and 4:10–14) Was his reaction justified?
4. Who was Aaron? What was his function to be?
5. What does God give Moses to take with him? What is Moses to do with God's gift?

The Hebrew word for "I am" is YHWH. (Remember, in Hebrew only consonants were written.) Today we write this Hebrew word "Yahweh."

From this statement, Moses learns that the essence of God is *being*. Whatever is, exists because of God. God brings all things to be. The name "I am who I am" also says that this God cannot be controlled by Moses or any other creature. Instead, it is Yahweh who will be in control. The Hebrews will learn time and time again that it is Yahweh who saves them, when God is ready to save them. Yahweh will not be forced into acting.

In the Jewish tradition, the name of God is so sacred that it is not to be spoken aloud. Conservative and Orthodox Jews today maintain the tradition of not pronouncing or even writing the name of God at all. This tradition springs from the idea that the name of God should not be manipulated for human purposes for any reason.

The Liberation from Egypt

There once was a fish who swam in a different direction from the other fish in her school. Another fish questioned her. "Where are you going?"

Poynter, *Israel in Egypt.* Nineteenth Century.

The Hebrew people were the slaves of the Egyptians, and provided the manual labor for building cities for Ramses II.

The counter-cultural fish responded, "Leave me alone. I am looking for the ocean."

"Ocean? You are swimming in the ocean at this very moment," the other fish said.

"This is not the ocean. This is only water," the first fish responded, and continued on her way.

The point of the story is that sometimes we may have trouble recognizing or seeing something clearly, even though it is right before our eyes. This failure to see clearly was the problem the Pharaoh had with Moses' and Aaron's demand from Yahweh to "Let my people go to worship me in the desert" (*Exodus* 7:16).

Several times, Moses brought God's word to Pharaoh, commanding him to let the Hebrews go. Each time, Pharaoh refused, and so God sent down a series of "plagues." In spite of the plagues—water filled with blood, influx of frogs, flies, and gnats—that befell Egypt, Pharaoh remained stubborn and refused to release the Hebrews from slavery.

While these plagues did not convince Pharaoh or Egypt of God's power, they do reveal to us Yahweh's authority over all people, events, and gods, along with Yahweh's determination to deliver the Hebrews to freedom. God was drawing the Hebrews into a new venture that would be forever binding. The plagues were signs to Israel of God's commitment to them. Through the plagues, Israel learned that God can be trusted.

Final Plague

The final plague is known to us as the "death of the first born":

At midnight the Lord slew every first-born in the land of Egypt, from the first-born of Pharaoh on the throne to the first-born of the prisoner in the dungeon, as well as all the first-born of the animals.

(Exodus 12:29)

Whereas the first-born of the Egyptians were killed, the lives of the Hebrews were spared because of their participation in the rituals of an ancient festival known as the *Pesach.* (Originally a celebration of the birth of the new lambs in spring.)

Following God's command, the Hebrews, on the night of the tenth plague, smeared the blood of slaughtered lambs over their doorposts. Putting blood on the doorpost was an ancient practice to avert evil and call down divine protection.

Seeing the blood on the lintel and the two doorposts, the Lord will pass over that door and not let the destroyer come into your houses to strike you down.

(Exodus 12:23)

The results of this final plague were devastating: the first-born children of the Egyptians died while the first-born children of the Hebrews lived. Following the finality of the tenth plague, the Hebrews were permitted to leave Egypt.

Their departure from Egypt was accompanied by amazing events: a pillar of cloud and fire led their way through the desert, (*Exodus* 13:21), and the Reed Sea parted and drowned the pursuing Egyptian army (*Exodus* 14:19–28).

Today, the Jewish feast of Passover celebrates when the Lord "passed over" their homes. It is one of the most holy festivals of the Jewish year. The ritual meal which Jews eat on this night is called the "seder."

Moses introduced the Hebrews to the "God of your fathers, the God of Abraham, the God of Isaac, the God of Jacob" (*Exodus* 3:15). The Exodus from Egypt proved to the Hebrews that Yahweh was indeed their God and that they were Yahweh's People.

Their joy is expressed by the hymn Miriam sang after the Hebrews crossed the Reed Sea to the freedom of a new life in the desert:

I will sing to the Lord, for He is gloriously triumphant; horse and chariot He has cast into the sea. My strength and my courage is the Lord, and He has been my savior.

(Exodus 15:1–2)

The story of the Hebrew's salvation from Egyptian slavery demonstrates the power of Yahweh. The Hebrews were powerless; their deliverance was accomplished by the deeds of Yahweh alone. The story of Yahweh's compassion, guidance, and deliverance shaped the Hebrew people into God's people.

Have You Considered?

1. Moses was called by God for a special and unique task. What does it mean to be called by God today? What might a person be called to do?
2. From God's point of view, explain to Moses why you refuse to reveal more of your identity.
3. Describe an event when you had difficulty recognizing something that was "right before your eyes."

◆ The Making of the Nation

When Moses brought the Hebrews out of Israel, they brought with them all their differences. The common experience of slavery in Egypt had made them one people, but they were not yet a nation.

The bond between Yahweh and the Hebrews was further formed in the desert wilderness. After leaving Egypt, the Hebrew people crossed to the other side of the Reed Sea. Their journey was long and difficult. Though their exact route cannot be determined, they eventually reached Mount Sinai, where God's Law was given to them.

Years in the Desert

A prophecy recorded in the Book of Hosea sums up Yahweh's relationship with the Hebrews in this opening stage of their desert journey:

When Israel was a child I loved him, out of Egypt I called My son.

(Hosea 11:1)

The Sinai Desert is a wild and barren land. The Hebrews' journey through it could not have been easy.

Raphael, *Water from the Rock.* Sixteenth Century.

Through the able leadership of Moses, God freed the Hebrews from slavery and formed a Covenant with them.

Yahweh molded the Hebrews by teaching them discipline and trust, in much the same way that a parent molds the behavior of a young child.

The Bible says the journey in the desert took 40 years. Why did it take so long? Not because the distance was long; it wasn't, as you can see at a glance on your map. The number 40 probably stands for a generation, not an exact length of time. This number suggests that:

- Most of the adults who had lived in Egypt died in the desert.
- Many of the people who eventually entered the promised land were born in the desert.

Whether it was 40 years or a generation, it's clear that the journey took a long time to complete; much longer than the distance involved warranted. Exodus makes it clear that the journey was long because Yahweh was forming the Hebrews into a new people focused on the life God wanted to give them.

So, in the beginning years of the desert experience, the Hebrews were like babies who needed a new kind of care, new obstacles to overcome, and new challenges to strengthen them. Gradually, the character of this people was oriented to their identity as the people of Yahweh.

Yahweh Provides

The Hebrews persevered for a long while in the desert because they believed that the experience was a transition to a better life to come. Yahweh had promised them freedom and a land that they could call their own. Nevertheless, they had to survive while in the desert. It was in that experience of day-to-day living that they learned total dependence on Moses—and Yahweh.

The major hardships of the desert were a lack of food and water, and the threat of attack by enemies. In each of these cases, Moses provided the leadership necessary for the Hebrews to move forward, while God provided the food, water, and protection.

The People Are Hungry   The people complained to Moses and Aaron about their hunger and thirst. God told Moses: "I will now rain down bread from heaven for you" (*Exodus* 16:4). This bread, known as manna, supplemented a diet of quail meat.

Although these events are presented in the Bible as supernatural miracles, there are possible natural explanations for them:

- **Manna.** The term is connected with the Hebrew expression for "What is this?" It may refer to the small honeydew pellets that are produced by the excretions of scale insects that suck the sap of the tamarisk plant. It is often found in the morning hours before it is eaten by ants, and it resembles white bread.

- **Birds.** There is an annual migration of birds from Europe to the south in September and October. During this time, quail fly over the Sinai Peninsula in great numbers. When they lie down to rest, they can easily be gathered for food.

The People Are Thirsty   When the people were thirsty, Moses prayed to God, who told him, "Strike the rock, and the water will flow from it for the people to drink" (*Exodus* 17:6). Moses did this in the presence of the Hebrew leaders and water flowed readily.

Actually, this event can also be explained by natural causes. When water flows slowly it often leaves lime deposits. Sometimes, water flows so slowly through certain kinds of rocks that large lime deposits form, blocking the flow of water completely.

A person familiar with the desert, as Moses was, would have learned how to recognize such places. When he knocked off the lime deposit, the water would run freely once again. To people unacquainted with desert life (such as the Hebrews out of Egypt), this "miracle" would surely seem extraordinary!

The People Are Attacked   While traveling, the Israelites were attacked by a people from southern Palestine called the *Amalekites*. Moses inspired the Israelites to do battle. The story is told in Exodus 17:8–13. While his assistant, Joshua, led the fight, Moses stood on a hill with his arms outstretched to heaven. Moses' witness provided inspiration and helped to lead Israel to victory. Moses built an altar there in remembrance. Unlike the examples mentioned above, there are no natural occurrences to explain this phenomenon.

Through these actions, Moses and God won greater respect and trust from the people. God's hand was seen in every occurrence. The people had gained more strength and a faith to follow.

The Giving of the Law at Mount Sinai

Recall the four elements of a vassal covenant mentioned earlier:

1. The greatness and kindness of the king is highlighted.
2. Rules and stipulations are included.
3. Witnesses and enforcers of the treaty are stipulated.
4. Blessings and curses are stated dependent on how the rules of the covenant were followed.

By the time the Israelites reached Mount Sinai, Yahweh was ready to enter into the Covenant with them. But this relationship would not be a covenant of parity, as equals trade favors between themselves. Yahweh's power and faithfulness were proved to the Hebrews in the Exodus from Egypt and through their time in the desert. Now, the Hebrews would be offered a chance to become a Covenant people, Yahweh's chosen ones for all time.

When they arrived in the desert of Sinai, Moses went up to the mountain to speak with God. These were Yahweh's words:

You have seen for yourselves how I treated the Egyptians and how I bore you up on eagle wings and brought you here to myself. Therefore, if you hearken to my voice and keep my covenant, you shall be My special possession, dearer to Me than all other people, though all the earth is mine.

(Exodus 19:4–6)

While God made the Covenant with Moses, the Hebrew people were ordered to remain at the foot of the mountain with only Moses and Aaron climbing to the top. Sinai was "wrapped in smoke, for the Lord came down upon it in fire" (Exodus 19:18). Yahweh then delivered the Law to Moses and Aaron for the sake of all the people.

The Ten Commandments

The heart of the Covenant is known as the *Decalogue* or *Ten Commandments*. They parallel the elements of the vassal treaty. First the announcement on the king's qualifications to receive homage:

I, the Lord, am your God, who brought you out of the land of Egypt, that place of slavery.

(Exodus 20:2)

Next, the rules and stipulations. In vassal covenants, the first condition was always a pledge of loyalty to the king. The first condition of Israel's Covenant is no different:

You shall not have other gods besides Me.

(Exodus 20:3)

In the Book of Exodus, three chapters of lesser regulations follow the Decalogue. Most of these later laws reflect the circumstances after the Hebrews had settled in Canaan. According to Jewish tradition, there are 613 commands in the law.

While in the Hittite vassal treaties the gods themselves often served as witnesses to the agreement, here the Hebrew people are referred to as witnesses, as are heaven and earth:

He summons the heavens from above, and the earth, to the trial of His people: "Gather My faithful ones before Me, those who have made a covenant with Me by sacrifice."

(Psalm 50:4–5)

Hittite treaties concluded with a list of blessings and curses that spelled out the consequences of faithfulness or disobedience to the covenant. In the Ten Commandments, there is a suggestion of punishments after the second and fifth commandments. For example, after the fifth commandment, the ruling is "For the Lord will not leave unpunished him who takes His name in vain" (Exodus 20:7).

The account of the giving of the decalogue in Deuteronomy Chapter 11 (a companion story to the one in Exodus), describes a ceremony of pronouncing blesses and curses, exactly as performed in the vassal treaties.

A Covenant People

When Moses came down from Mount Sinai, he heard the people make the pledge: "We will do everything the Lord has told us" (Exodus 24:3). According to the narrative:

People of Note

Joshua and Aaron

Joshua was Moses' assistant for politics and military battles. He is introduced in Scripture rather suddenly as a military leader in the first battle against the Amalekites (*Exodus 17:8–14*). In Numbers 11:28, it says that Joshua had been Moses' aide since his youth and that his father's name was Nun.

These few points are all that is known about Joshua's early life. Eventually, this man would become Moses' successor. When the time came for scouts to be sent to spy on the Promised Land, it was Joshua who led the first mission.

Frequently mentioned in the Pentateuch, Moses' older brother Aaron was the first priest of Israel, made one through the anointing of Moses (see: *Leviticus 8:1–8*). Aaron also filled other important roles in the Exodus and in the acceptance of the Covenant at Sinai. When Moses did not believe he was capable of speaking to the people, God made Aaron spokesman.

It is Aaron's role as priest that is of most lasting importance to the people of Israel. Centuries later, Israel's priests would become the political as well as religious rulers. This was the case in the time of Jesus.

- Moses arose early the next morning and wrote down all the words that God had spoken to him.
- He then built an altar at the foot of the mountain, with twelve pillars to represent the twelve tribes of Israel.
- Young men were sent out to offer the blood of young bulls as peace offerings to God.
- Moses took a cup filled with half of the blood and sprinkled it on the altar.
- Moses read from the Covenant and splashed some blood on the people, saying: "This is the blood of the Covenant which the Lord has made with you in accordance with all these words of His" (*Exodus 24:8*).

The ratification, or approval, of the Covenant in blood was very significant to the Hebrews. Because blood was what sustained life, a sacrificial offering of blood was thought to have the power to bind two parties together. The Israelites now shared a common life with God. They became blood brothers and sisters and established lasting family ties with Yahweh.

An Unworthy People   Of course, the fact that the Hebrews had a covenant with God did not mean that they somehow became perfect. Far from it. In fact, even while Moses was on Mount Sinai, they demonstrated their weakness and fear.

The Book of Exodus says that Moses was on Mount Sinai with Yahweh for 40 days receiving the Law. (Note that the number 40 is used here once again. What do you think this might mean?) While he was away, the people began to question whether Moses was ever going to return, and to doubt his leadership. They resolved to continue their journey without him, and decided to fashion images of God to carry with them as they moved forward.

The story tells us that they melted the gold they had taken with them from Egypt, known as the "spoils of Egypt," and used it to fashion a golden calf. The "golden calf" was probably an image of a bull that was commonly used in ancient Middle Eastern religions to represent powerful male gods. The same image was later used by the kings of the Northern Kingdom of Israel when they set up shrines to compete with the Temple in Jerusalem.

Moses Loses His Temper   When Moses returned, he was astonished. After only a few days without him to remind them, the Hebrews had abandoned Yahweh. Moses expressed his anger over this behavior by smashing the tablets of the Law. Although new tablets would be fashioned, and the Covenant sealed, Moses' action marked the beginning of Israel's struggle to become faithful.

This story shows us how difficult it often is to see God's involvement in our lives in the "heat of the moment." Lost in the desert, eager to reach their new home, the Hebrews behaved like spoiled children. They lost patience when they couldn't see immediate results or didn't receive what they wanted. Impatience is a powerful temptation we experience any time we find circumstances pressing down around us.

God's Involvement

The most important thing that the Hebrews learned through their experience of election, deliverance, and covenant was that Yahweh wanted to be involved in their lives. From all of their experiences, the Hebrews learned that God was not far away. Rather, they learned that God was a present, creative power who guided the affairs of nations, and showed deep care and concern for each individual person.

The Israelites marveled at God's involvement with their lives. They wondered why they had been chosen. The only answer they found was that Yahweh had freely chosen them. They had done nothing to merit the gift of the Covenant. In this favor, they discovered God's great mercy. They had been given a special relationship with God.

In the Covenant relationship, the Hebrews became Yahweh's special people. They acquired an identity in Yahweh's love for them and in God's wonderful deeds on their behalf. They were offered God's constant protection and were invited to always remain close to God. That they remained free to act against God's law is a part of the story.

From the first communication to Moses, Yahweh had promised them "a good and spacious land, a land flowing with milk and honey" (*Exodus* 3:8). In response, the people were to follow God's commands gratefully. The Hebrews had every reason to hope: Yahweh was their God and a land would be given to them.

The Old Testament recognizes God as the initiator of a kind, cherished relationship, and the one who was always faithful to that relationship, even when people did not respond with equal fidelity or love. Because people had lots to learn about love, God also taught them by discipline and consequences, just as good parents must sometimes teach their immature children.

The Old Testament traces God's invitation to eternal love that is open to all who wish to belong to the covenanted people.

Have You Considered?

1. How do scientific explanations threaten the idea that it was Yahweh who cared for the Israelites in the wilderness?
2. Explain how the wilderness experience was a time of "formation." Why is character so often formed through difficult situations?
3. The Israelites had to "ratify" the covenant with God. How can we indicate our acceptance of the Covenant today?

Spiritual Reflection

Praying with Exodus

Choose readers. Conduct this prayer service with your classmates on the theme of covenant and the sharing of God's Word.

Reader 1: Yahweh instructs us through the Living Word of Scripture. Let us prepare to receive God's Word by reciting from Psalm 18:

All: I love You, O Lord, my strength, O Lord, my rock, my fortress, my deliverer. My God, my rock of refuge, my shield, the horn of my salvation, my stronghold! Praised be the Lord, I exclaim, and I am safe from my enemies.

Reader 2: A reading from the Book of Exodus.
(Read Exodus 19:1–8. In this reading, the Bible tells us that the Israelites are the Chosen People.)

Reader 2: Let us respond from Psalm 99.

All: The Lord is king; the peoples tremble; he is throned upon the cherubim; the earth quakes. The Lord in Zion is great, He is high above all peoples. Let them praise your great and awesome name; holy is He!

Reader 3: A reading from the Book of Exodus.
(Read Exodus 24: 1–8. In this reading, the Bible tells us that Moses read the book of the Covenant to the Israelites, who promised to be obedient to Yahweh.)

Reader 3: Let us respond from Psalm 117.

All: Praise the Lord, all you nations; glorify Him, all you peoples! For steadfast is His kindness toward us, and the fidelity of the Lord endures forever.

CHAPTER 2 REVIEW

Q/A

Section One

1. How is a covenant different from a contract?
2. What were the differences between a parity treaty and a vassal treaty?
3. How was the covenant God made with the Hebrews like a Hittite vassal treaty?
4. What is the meaning of election?
5. Who were the 'Apiru'?
6. What is the difference between an Israelite and a Hebrew?
7. Define "monotheism."
8. Who was Akhenaton and what is his significance to the Bible?

Section Two

1. Define "formation." How is the experience of the Hebrews in the wilderness an example of this?
2. What are the possible natural explanations for the miracles of the manna, the quail, and the rock water? What is meant by the number 40, as in "40 years in the desert," and "40 days on Mount Sinai"?
3. Who was Joshua? Who was Aaron?
4. How were the Hebrews spared the final plague, the death of the first-born?
5. What is one example of how the Hebrews were dependent on Yahweh in the desert?
6. What is the first commandment of the Decalogue?
7. Who were the witnesses of the covenant between Yahweh and the Hebrews?
8. How was the Covenant ratified?

BIBLE ACTIVITY

Pick two of the following references, read them, and answer the questions. Together, these references narrate the deliverance from Egypt.

1. Exodus 5:1–8:11
   a. Describe the work of the Hebrews in Egypt.
   b. How did Moses react? How did the Lord react?
   c. What magic did Moses perform? What did the Egyptian magicians perform?
   d. What are the first plagues?
   e. Could Moses do anything the Egyptian magicians couldn't?
2. Exodus 8:12–10:29
   a. What plagues does the Lord send by Moses' staff?
   b. What effect do the plagues have on Pharaoh?
   c. Who are the two main opponents seen in these stories?
3. Exodus 11:1–13:16
   a. What was the point of the death of the first-born Egyptians?
   b. Compare 12:1–27 with the rest of the passage. What changes if you leave this part out?
   c. List the similarities and differences in comparing 12:1–27 with 13:1–16.
4. Exodus 13:17–15:21
   a. Who arranged for the Egyptians to pursue the Hebrews?
   b. What exaggerations do you find in these stories? List specific verses and give reasons for your choices.
   c. How did the Hebrews escape from the Egyptian army?

GLOSSARY

- **Armarna letters:** Letters from the princes of Palestine to the Pharaoh that describe a nomadic people that could be the Hebrews.
- **Contract:** A legal agreement establishing rights and responsibilities between two or more people.
- **Covenant:** A bond which unites two or more people in a loving relationship.
- **Decalogue/Ten Commandments:** The ten rules which form the basis of the Law.
- **Deliverance:** The act of God in freeing the Hebrews from captivity.
- **Election:** The idea that God has freely chosen to establish a covenant with the Hebrew people.
- **Exodus:** The Hebrew slaves leaving captivity in Egypt for freedom in the promised land.
- **Hebrews:** A group of nomadic peoples who settled in Egypt and later formed the nation of Israel; part of the "Semitic" cultural group.
- **Israelites:** The nation of people living in Israel under the covenant formed on Mount Sinai.
- **Parity treaty:** An ancient treaty made between two parties of equal social standing.
- **Manna:** A food which the Israelites found in the wilderness while traveling to the promised land.
- **Monotheism:** Belief in only one god.
- **Moses:** The leader chosen from birth to bring the Hebrews out of Egypt and into the promised land.
- **Passover:** The Jewish feast celebrating the "passing over" of their people by God on the night of the final plague in Egypt.
- **Pharaoh:** The king of Egypt.
- **Ratification:** The people's acceptance of the covenant given by God.
- **Theophany:** An appearance by a god to a human being.
- **Vassal treaty:** An ancient treaty made between two parties, one of which was more powerful or from a higher social class than the other; most often it was a treaty between a stronger king and a weaker one.
- **Yahweh:** A Hebrew expression which means "I am who I am;" it was the answer Moses received when he asked God's name.

UNDERSTANDING MORE ABOUT:

Different Bible Translations

As you learned in Chapter 1, the various books of the Bible were written in different languages, generally Hebrew for the Old Testament and Greek for the New Testament. Since you're now reading the Bible in English, you may wonder about how the translations happened.

Actually, there are many different English translations of the Bible. The most popular of all time has been the King James version, produced for James I of England in 1611. This translation is regarded as a masterpiece of English literature, rivaling Shakespeare in beauty of expression.

Because of conflict between Catholics and Protestants, however, Pope Paul V forbade Catholics to read this translation made for a Protestant King. Instead, Catholic scholars translated the Douay-Reims version, named for the towns in France where the translation was produced.

Despite the beauty of their language, both of these translations were made before modern biblical scholarship, and were therefore based on poor-quality manuscripts. Both Catholics and Protestants have since produced more accurate translations today.

The translation used in this book is called *The New American Bible*. The NAB is the translation approved by the American bishops for use in Catholic Churches. Protestant scholars worked with Catholics in putting it together, however, just as Catholics helped prepare the *Revised Standard Version*, the most commonly-used Protestant Bible translation.

Generally, Catholics and Protestants may use one another's Bibles today without fear of "getting something wrong." Differences of opinion, where they exist, are about how to interpret passages, not about what they actually say.

David, Dedicated to Yahweh

Legend

- General History
- Biblical History
- Jewish History
- Books written

I n your many roles as a son or daughter, a friend, a student, and as a member of various clubs and organizations, you have already experienced many different styles of leadership. See if you can identify the leadership styles in the following examples.

- Sixth months before high school graduation, John's family moved 1500 miles to a new city. Although the family protested, his father said **he** would make the final decision.
- Adela loved being in Mr. Birmbaum's third period math class. Though he assigned homework, he never checked it! "High school students are responsible adolescents. If they don't understand a problem they can ask for help. I am not going to play policeman," he said. Adela used her freedom to skip homework assignments

regularly. Then, reality struck when she did poorly on Mr. Birmbaum's very difficult tests. Adela's grades sunk lower than ever before. Now she wished that Mr. Birmbaum had **forced** her to work.

- Down by 15 points at half-time, Wayne thought that Coach Klemm might really explode in the locker room. Instead, Coach simply noted a few points that needed improving, saying calmly, "If we can cut the lead in half by the start of the fourth quarter we can win." Then, he surprised Wayne and the other players by asking for their opinions. "What do you think we are doing wrong? How can we improve?" At first, the players didn't comment, but then, one by one, they began to suggest how they could play better.

How did these examples of leadership differ? How would you describe these forms of leadership? For the first example, did you choose hard-handed ruler? Dictator? "Do as I say" leadership is all too common. Mr. Birmbaum, in the second example, held people accountable for making responsible choices and bearing the consequences of their own behavior. How did you describe the final example? The coach offered his own opinions and then let the players share theirs. This is known as shared leadership.

Consider the following questions:
- How important is leadership to the success of an activity?
- Are there times when the leader is more important than the members of a group?
- What makes for a good leader?
- From your experience, how are leaders chosen by a group? Why does the group choose the leader that it does?

As you can see, there are a lot of pieces that go into being a leader. Think of these issues as you read about Israel's changing leadership.

A Time of Development

As the Hebrews moved from the desert to their promised land of Canaan, they were clearly under the leadership and rule of Yahweh. As they formed into a nation, they experimented with new forms of leadership.

In Chapter 3, you will see how Israel developed from a loosely confederated people into a unified nation under various types of leaders: from Moses' successor, Joshua, to the military leaders, (the Judges) and to the kings, Saul and David.

Dictators and rulers, hands-off and shared leadership. As you read about the leaders of Israel, take note of how they made use of various leadership styles. How can each be an effective form of leadership? How did each shape the future of the nation?

Israel Enters the Promised Land

The books of Joshua, Judges, 1 and 2 Samuel, and 1 and 2 Kings record ancient Israel's national history. For this reason, they were very important to later generations of Israelites, who looked to them for inspiration and comfort. To understand them, we need to look at the circumstances in which they were written. Because they open with the entry into the promised land, we also need to see how that entrance happened in order to follow the rest of the story.

Learning Objectives for Section One

By the end of this section, you will be able to:

- Explain the importance of the Deuteronomic history.
- Explain the difference between ancient and modern styles of writing history.
- Describe how the Israelites gradually occupied Canaan.
- Recognize the structure of the tribal system in ancient Israel and describe how it worked.

◆ The Deuteronomic History

The events described in Joshua, Judges, and 1 and 2 Samuel took place between the years 1,200–900 B.C.E., although these books were not finalized until several hundred years later. To understand their message, we need to take a closer look at the circumstances in Israel when they were written into their final form.

We will see in Chapter 7 that around 587 B.C.E., the Babylonians became a strong military power in the Middle East, defeated the Israelites, and took them into "exile." This means that they took the Israelites as prisoners and forced them to live in Babylon. They destroyed all that the Israelites had built: the homes, businesses, and places of worship. This was a terrible blow to their faith because they believed they were God's Chosen People. How could God allow such a horrible thing to happen?

The authors and editors of Joshua, Judges, 1 and 2 Samuel, and 1 and 2 Kings thought they had the answer. This disaster had happened not because God forgot about them, or because God was not powerful enough to protect them, but because Israel had sinned and violated the Covenant. This understanding would explain how Israel could be the Chosen People and still suffer such a humiliating defeat.

The writers of these books drew on the memories of the various tribes and smaller groups that had come together to make up the nation of Israel, and put together its history. The writers designed this history to show that Israel's punishment in the exile was deserved because of its misbehavior, and that God is never unfaithful to the Covenant made with Moses. Even in the Exile, if the people were to turn their backs on their sinfulness, God would restore their hopes.

This understanding of Israel's history is what we see in Joshua, Judges, 1 and 2 Samuel, and 1 and 2 Kings. It's called the "Deuteronomic history" because the authors felt that Israel had sinned by not obeying the laws found in Deuteronomy.

The Bible in Context

Developing Traditions

The Deuteronomic history contains stories, legends, and historical records from a variety of Israel's ancient tribes and clans. How were all of these traditions combined into one?

Such a historical collections of stories is actually not so unique. The United States, for example, has a single history, yet, in the beginning, there were thirteen colonies with separate backgrounds and separate histories. People had come to the New World from different countries for different reasons. Later, the French traditions of the Louisiana Territory, as well as the Spanish traditions that had developed in the Far West, were added to the history of America.

In the same way, Israel's history is the collected stories of many different people who shared a common belief in God and an acceptance of the Covenant.

Ancient vs. Modern History

The history of Israel was not invented. The Deuteronomic historians (or "D") drew on much older sources in order to compile their history. They used the official records written down during the time when Israel had strong kings. For other periods, such as the time of Joshua and the Judges, they relied primarily on stories passed down by word of mouth.

The Deuteronomic account is historically accurate in general and can often be confirmed by sources outside the Bible. There are places, however, where mistakes were made, the roles of certain people are exaggerated, or the significance of events are either over emphasized or down-played. In other words, there are places where this record is not accurate by modern historical standards.

Like all ancient historians, the Deuteronomic authors did not view their task as "getting all the facts straight." This is a very modern idea. Instead, they felt their job was to communicate the meaning of their history, what it was "all about." In so doing, they felt free to edit their sources to make their point.

This approach to history is one of the basic differences between ancient and modern historians. Today, historians are criticized if they are inaccurate about dates and places. In the ancient world, historians were given a great deal of liberty with such matters. Their purpose was to explain what it all meant, what the inner purpose of the past had been.

By these standards, the Deuteronomic history is excellent history indeed.

As we read these books, then, we should not be surprised to see minor contradictions or misrepresentations of what "actually happened." These are to be expected because of the very nature of ancient history. Focus, instead, on the message the Deuteronomic authors try to communicate; it is their understanding of God's faithfulness to the Covenant made with Moses and ratified by the people of Israel.

Have You Considered?

1. Name an example of how the circumstances in which a book, movie, or television show is put together influence its message.
2. How can a story be made-up and yet still be true? Give an example with your answer.
3. The Deuteronomic historian's answer to the question "Why does God allow bad things to happen to people?" was that the people sinned. What's your answer to that question? Include the reasons for your answer.

Bust of Thucydides. Fifth Century B.C.E.

Ancient historians like the famous Greek Thucydides, shown here, had a different approach to history than do modern historians.

◆ The Entry into the Promised Land

The point made at the beginning of Joshua is clearly that Yahweh continued to lead the Israelites to the land that was promised to them even after Moses' death. Yahweh said to Moses' aide, Joshua: "As I promised Moses, I will deliver to you every place where you set foot" (Joshua 1:3). The Book of Joshua presents a record of Yahweh's faithfulness to this promise.

Joshua

In many ways, Joshua himself is portrayed as the ideal leader of Israel, one who keeps God's law in its entirety. In so doing, Joshua was promised that Yahweh would be with him "by day and by night." Yahweh told him: "Do not fear or be dismayed, for the Lord, your God, is with you wherever you go" (Joshua 1:9).

In the book that bears his name, Joshua is portrayed as a great general and military leader. Today, a statue of Joshua stands outside West Point, the Army's military academy, in recognition of his great leadership.

Israel's entry into the promised land is pictured as one great victory after another. Probably the best-known of these battles was at the city of Jericho.

When the Israelites attacked Jericho, Yahweh directed them to circle the city seven times as the priests led the Ark of the Covenant before them. According to Joshua, the priests blew the ram's horn after the seventh time around, and the walls of the city crumbled. The Israelites swarmed in and captured the city.

This episode is told in highly dramatic fashion by the Deuteronomic historian. It illustrates the author's total confidence that Joshua's victories happened through the power of Yahweh.

The Archaeological Record While the fall of Jericho's walls makes an interesting story, archaeological evidence suggests that the Deuteronomic historians may have exaggerated how things actually happened. While the land of Canaan was eventually won by the Israelites, the events of the conquest were far more complicated and took a much longer time than the first 12 chapters of Joshua suggest. Even though all the details of the settlement of Canaan are not known, a general picture can be pieced together.

in the Spotlight

Canaan

You may have noticed that we have used a variety of words to refer to the land where the Hebrews settled: Israel, Canaan, Palestine. All three of these terms refer to basically the same territory, a stretch of land along the eastern coast of the Mediterranean Sea. Generally, we call this place "Canaan" before the kingdom of Saul, "Israel" after that. "Palestine" refers to the whole territory after the kingdom of Israel split apart in 922 B.C.E. After that date, only the northern portion of the territory should technically be called "Israel."

The Situation in Canaan In Canaan, around 1200 B.C.E., when the Hebrews first entered the land, cities were self-governed; there was no national or larger government. They made their own laws and fought their own battles. The territory of a city also included the farmlands surrounding it, that were worked by the city's inhabitants.

Cities often fought among themselves for control of territory and resources such as water and wood. This conflict between cities explains why Canaan was so vulnerable to attacks by the Hebrews: it was divided against itself. In addition to this disunity,

- **There was no standing army.** Most Canaanites were farmers and traders, becoming soldiers only when necessary to defend their town.
- **Alliances between cities were rare,** and the defeat of a city was generally ignored by its neighbors.

This disunity also helps to explain why Canaan was so often ruled by foreign powers such as Egypt, the Hittites, and the Philistines.

The Canaanites did share a common fertility religion. This means that their myths and rituals were concerned with keeping the land and animals fertile, so that crops would grow and herds would have offspring. But even though the Canaanites held certain religious attitudes in common, there was wide variation in their practical understanding of religion, which intensified the disunity of their community and political habits.

A Gradual Conquest

Over a period of time, small groups of Israelites won small battles in the hills of Canaan. Military

Scripture Workshop

Renewing the Covenant

The people of Israel renewed the Covenant with God regularly. It was not enough for the Israelites to express belief in the power of goodness of Yahweh. They also had to express their commitment to live as God directed. The Book of Joshua captures the power of this ceremony and its importance in the life of Israel.

Read about the annual Covenant renewal ceremony in Joshua 24:1–28. Compare this with Joshua 8:30–35. Then answer these questions:

1. What mighty deeds of Yahweh were retold at the ceremony?
2. What were the requirements for new members?
3. How did the people respond?
4. What, besides Covenant renewal, was done on that day?

individual towns and settlements as they were able in order to gain land on which to settle.

As they were victorious in these battles, additional towns and territories came under their control and the total number of people belonging to the people of Israel increased. Within a few years, the Hebrews were able to put together a large, well-trained, and battle tested fighting force that was able to defeat larger settlements in battle.

Pledging Allegiance to the Covenant   Not all of Israel's success came about through battle. Some opposing clans and towns probably joined with the Hebrews voluntarily because of the special covenant relationship they had with Yahweh. These people would hear of the Hebrews' deliverance from the Egyptians and the stories of God's love and care for them in the desert.

All who joined the Israelites did so by pledging their allegiance to Yahweh and by promising to keep the Covenant. For a town to join the already covenanted clans was a big step. It required the approval of all the clans when they gathered together at an annual, solemn ceremony in which the

successes in the hill country gave the core group of Hebrews a foothold in the new land. However, their first expedition could not have taken them much further than the rugged mountains for these reasons:

1. **The Egyptians controlled the major cities in the plains.** The Hebrew warriors were no match for the powerful Egyptian army.
2. **The Hebrews were guerrilla fighters.** They took advantage of the rough terrain to overcome their limited wood and stone weapons and their lack of horses. In the wide open areas of the plains, they were at a disadvantage.
3. **The Philistines.** A people who lived in the southwest coastal area—had iron tools, iron weapons, and they also used chariots. They held a long-lasting monopoly on the making of iron. The use of chariots with iron armoring and the use of iron tools became part of Israel's culture only in the time of King David.

Growing Town by Town   Israel could not have put together a large military effort. They did not have iron weapons and did not have a standing army. The Israelites did, however, continue military attacks on

Philistine spearhead, Twelfth Century B.C.E.

The Philistines used their control of iron making technology to build a strong army.

members renewed their allegiance to Yahweh. The new members would also recite these pledges. This ceremony occurred, at least for a while, in the town of *Shechem*. Eventually, Shechem became the religious center of the Covenant confederation. By joining the Covenant, people became "children of Israel," or Israelites. In time, no distinctions were made between those who professed the Covenant early and those who came to it later. Their common Covenant brought them a common historical tradition—roots for all of them together.

Twelve Tribes

As more groups joined or were conquered by Israel, a tribal system developed. There were ten northern tribes, the most powerful of which were *Ephraim and Mannaseh*. The two southern tribes were *Judah and Benjamin*.

Only commitment to the Covenant and Yahweh's leadership held these 12 tribes together. Each of the 12 tribes lived independently of the others, each had its own territory, life, and form of government. There was no one political system that united them, only the Covenant. It would be as if there were no federal government in the United States, only states.

They did, however, come to each other's aid in times of military crises. The tribes would band together to face the common enemy as needed. Afterwards, they would go their separate ways.

This sense of tribal independence never left the Israelites. As we shall see, it is a major reason why the unified kingdom of Israel lasted only 100 years.

Have You Considered?

1. Why do you suppose the Deuteronomic historian placed such emphasis on Joshua's military success? When are you tempted to over-emphasize your own accomplishments?
2. When Europeans colonized the Americas, many looked to the Book of Joshua to justify their behavior. How does this illustrate a possible misunderstanding of the idea that someone is "chosen" by God?
3. At first, the United States tried a system of government similar to that used by the 12 tribes. Under the Articles of Confederation, each state was almost totally independent from the others. Why do you think this system was abandoned? What would the problems with it be?

LEARN FROM THE MAP

Israel's Twelve Tribes

Each of the 12 tribes had its own territory, as shown here. In addition, each tribe had its own collection of traditional legends and songs. Eventually, many of these legends and songs were combined into historical works such as the Deuteronomic history and into collections of reflections and observations like the Proverbs. Consult Joshua 13–21 to see how the land was divided between the tribes.

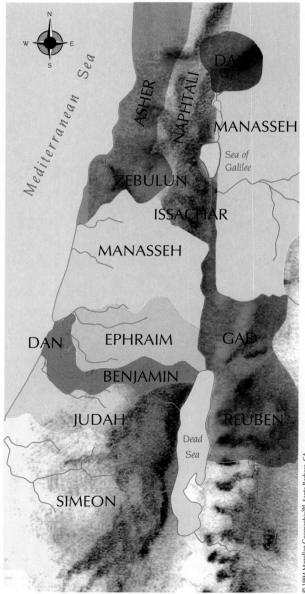

© 1994 Magellan Geographix℠ Santa Barbara, CA.

Israel Gets a King

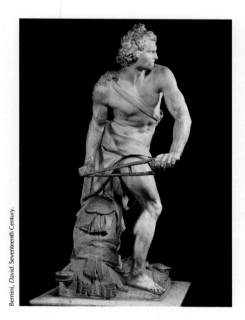

Bernini, *David*, Seventeenth Century.

After the Hebrews moved into Canaan, each tribe went its own way, with its own laws and leaders. From time to time, a crisis would come along that required several tribes to work together. When that happened, God would inspire a temporary military leader called a "judge," to lead the tribe. Over time, however, the Israelites decided they didn't like this system, and they asked Samuel for a king. This began the monarchy that produced Israel's most famous leaders: Saul, David, and Solomon. We'll follow this amazing story in this section.

Learning Objectives for Section Two

By the end of this section, you will be able to:

- Define: judge.
- Explain the meaning of theology and how it is used in the Book of Judges.
- Identify: Samuel, Saul, David.
- Describe God's Covenant with David.

◆ The Judges

In ancient Israel the word "judge" meant something quite different from how the term is used today. In modern times, a judge is someone who rules in a court of law. When you hear the word judge you may imagine a person dressed in a black robe and called "your honor."

That's not what the word meant for the Israelites. For them, a judge was someone inspired by God to lead them in battle and govern them afterwards. In the Book of Judges we hear the stories of these inspired leaders.

Theological Ideas in Judges

A "theology" expresses one's understanding of God. In writing the Book of Judges, the Deuteronomic historians were clearly guided by certain beliefs about God and the Covenant. The writers make the following theological points:

- When Israel followed Yahweh and the Covenant, she lived in peaceful prosperity.
- When Israel lost the awareness that Yahweh, and only Yahweh, was in charge, suffering followed (usually at the hands of a foreign group that would threaten an Israelite area or town).
- The people would cry out to Yahweh for help, and help would be granted.
- After their rescue, they would resume their careful practice of the Covenant, at least for awhile.

This pattern which the Deuteronomic historian saw as prevalent during the time of the judges (B.C.E. 1200–1120) is summarized as:

1. Sin
2. Punishment
3. Repentance
4. Deliverance

The theology here is very simple: when Israel obeys the demands of the Covenant, God keeps it safe; when Israel disobeys, it suffers disaster.

Tissot, *Jael Smote Sisera and Slew Him*, Nineteenth Century.

The Book of Judges retells the brave deeds of the Hebrew people as they fought to survive. This picture shows an event recorded in Judges 4:17–22.

Charismatic Leadership

When a tribe was faced with attack, the spirit of Yahweh would "fall upon" an individual, making that man or woman strong and full of initiative. That person would then rally soldiers from the nearby covenanted clans to help defeat the invader. These individual leaders, given their strength from Yahweh, are called the judges.

The style of leadership common to the judges is sometimes called "charismatic leadership." "Charismatic" means "empowered by the spirit." Today, we use this word to refer to any leader who has the power to move and inspire his or her followers to action.

Lessons Learned from the Judges

One lesson that can be learned from the Book of Judges is that our lives are better when we remember God and obey the teachings of the Covenant. It is not that God punishes us when we fail to live up to our promises, but rather that every action in life brings with it definite consequences. Actions that take people far from God have terrible consequences. But every time this happened to a clan in Israel, they were rescued from the crisis by Yahweh.

The Book of Judges also teaches the lesson that the people God chooses will often be the unexpected choice. One of the most powerful and important judges, Deborah, was a woman. She led Israel into battle when all the male generals lost their nerve. It may have shocked many Israelites to hear that Deborah (and not a man) was giving the orders. But then again, since Yahweh was in charge, whomever Yahweh chose would be followed into battle.

Each of the stories of the judges tells how Yahweh acted on behalf of the people. Each time some of the Israelites were in trouble because of their disobedience, Yahweh inspired a judge who saved them and led them to victory. Through each battle, Yahweh was with the people. Again and again, the Covenant with Yahweh was strengthened by God's faithfulness and the people were once again drawn to repentance and prayer, deliverance and victory.

Have You Considered?

1. Share an example of how a charismatic leader can lead people into a situation against overwhelming odds. The example may be historical or from current events.
2. How has God's faithfulness been revealed in your lifetime? Explain.
3. Describe an experience, similar to that of Deborah, where prejudice against a certain group has been challenged by dramatic action from a member of that group.

Careers of the Judges

When you look at this chart, do not imagine that these careers should be added together or that they are in sequential order. Each judge's work (and the length of success) was for a certain local group—a clan within Israel—sometimes enlarged by contributions of warriors from other local clans. Later, when the stories were collected, they were all recognized to be Israelite judges, from whom all Israel had benefited and learned.

Name	Reference	Success	Result
Othneil	Judges 3:7–11	Defeated King of Aram	40 years of peace
Ethud	Judges 3:12–30	Defeated 10,000 Moabites	80 years of peace
Shamgar	Judges 3:31	Slew 600 Philistines	Unknown
Deborah and Barak	Judges 4:1–5:31	Defeated Canaanite army	40 years of peace
Gideon	Judges 6:1–8:35	Defeated legions of Midian	40 years of rest
Tola	Judges 10:1 and 2	Unknown	Led for 23 years
Jair	Judges 10:3–5	Unknown	Led for 22 years
Jephthah	Judges 11:1–12:7	Slew Ammonites, Amorites	Led for 6 years
Ibzan	Judges 12:8–10	Unknown	Led for 7 years
Elon	Judges 12:11–12	Unknown	Led for 10 years
Abdon	Judges 12:13–15	Unknown	Led for 8 years
Samson	Judges 13–16	Slew Philistines	Led for 20 years
Samuel	1 Samuel 1and 25:1	Anointed Kings of Israel	Saul and the monarchy

◆ A King Is Anointed

Against enemies such as the Philistines, with their trained army, iron weapons, and chariots, Israel's way of waging war—a charismatic leader calling fighters together in a time of need—was not effective. Lacking a central organization, the Hebrews were no match for its neighboring nations, each ruled by a king.

Samuel

In approximately 1040 B.C.E., Samuel, the most influential of the judges, led the forces of Israel. Samuel was also a prophet. Samuel lived in Ramah, where he led a group of prophets dedicated to protecting Israel's traditional worship against pagan practices. Some of the elders (leaders) of Israel came to Samuel, asking him to anoint a king.

The Only King of Israel   Samuel was not enthusiastic about the requests for a king. Yahweh was the one and only King of Israel for Samuel. For the people to want a human king seemed, to Samuel, a direct rejection of God. Yahweh had brought the people into the land and protected them in times of threat. Why should the people now reject Yahweh's protection and promise? Didn't they know that an Israelite king would be a tyrant, just like the neighboring kings?

Samuel warned them that any king he might appoint would:

- Take your sons and assign them to his chariots and horses.
- Set them to do his plowing and his harvesting.

Samuel, portrayed here in the movie, King David, was the last judge of Israel.

Scripture Workshop

Birth Stories

As you learned when you studied about the life of Moses, ancient literature concentrated much attention on the events surrounding a great leader's birth. The more unique the events surrounding a birth, the greater the leader. This is seen once again in the stories of the judges. Look up Judges 13:1–25 and 1 Samuel 1:1–28. The first reading is the story of the birth of Samson, and the second is the story of the Birth of Samuel.

1. Make a list of all the elements the two stories have in common (include at least five items).
2. How do these two stories differ? Make another list and include at least three differences.
3. Answer this question: Why do you suppose the Bible so often includes a story about the miraculous birth of an important character?

- Use your daughters as ointment makers, as cooks, and as bakers.
- Take the best of your fields, tithe your crops, and give the revenue to his eunuchs and his slaves.

When this takes place, you will complain against the king whom you have chosen, but on that day the LORD will not answer you.

(1 Samuel 8:10–18)

The people refused to listen and persisted with their demands:

There must be a king over us. We too must be like other nations, with a king to rule us and to lead us in warfare and fight our battles.

(1 Samuel 8:19–20)

There is an old saying, "Be careful when you ask God for something, for your wish might be granted." That is, you might get more than what you expected or wanted. That's exactly what happened to Israel in this case; God responded,

Grant the people's every request. It is not you they reject, they are rejecting me as their king. As they have treated me constantly from the day I brought them up from Egypt to this day, deserting me and worshipping strange gods, so do they treat you, too.

(1 Samuel 8:6–9)

Samuel then ordered the men of Israel to report back to their own cities. The people of Israel had made their decision, they would have a king. The period of direct rule of Israel by Yahweh and through the judges was at its end. Today, historians question whether charismatic leadership could have continued to be successful in Israel. Most likely, Israel would never have achieved power and stability as a nation without a monarchy. Their society was simply not unified enough under the judges.

It is not known if Samuel's warnings of the corruptness and ineffectiveness of a monarchy were his own, or those of later editors who had experienced the effects of the monarchy. Regardless, the *ideal ruler* for Israel is clearly identified by the Deuteronomic historian as Yahweh.

King Saul

Saul was the king first chosen and anointed by Samuel as "commander over the Lord's heritage" and governor of Israel (*see* 1 Samuel 9–10). After leading the Israelites to a military victory over the Ammonites (1 Samuel 11), the people acclaimed Saul their ruler.

Saul was truly a tragic person (some people think that he was the inspiration for Shakespeare's "King Lear"). He was known as a handsome man, courageous, yet modest, and willing to admit his faults. He was, however, emotionally unstable. Apparently, he suffered terrible mood swings.

People Are Alienated   Saul alienated the people close to him, including Samuel. Although Saul was a religious man, he did not appreciate the importance of religion. Twice, he disobeyed direct instructions from Samuel, and in so doing he offended God's prophet.

As Saul lost favor with Samuel and Yahweh because of his odd behavior, the spirit that had "rushed upon him" at his anointing, turned dark. Saul became even more depressed and moody. His fears of losing the kingship dominated his decisions. His response to seemingly unimportant matters bordered on craziness. Needless to say, his court and his army both began to lose their trust in his leadership.

To his credit, Saul kept his faith in Yahweh. When a battle turned against him, Saul would suspect that he or one of his men had done something to displease God. Nevertheless, Saul learned the hard way that Yahweh shaped the course of history and demanded absolute faithfulness from those who followed the Covenant.

A Difficult Challenge   Saul was faced with a difficult task: to form a nation out of the loosely united tribes of Israel. People who had previously gathered only for religious ritual and for self-defense now were being asked to give up their tribal independence, form a standing army, pay taxes, and pledge allegiance to a king. Adding to Saul's other problems, he was attempting this while trying to fight off a powerful Philistine army.

Saul's fall from favor with Samuel (1 *Samuel* 15) foreshadows the trouble the nation would always have between political and religious leadership. Although Saul was the anointed king, Samuel still was the religious leader in Israel. When Saul failed to follow Samuel's instructions, he offended God by claiming power that was not properly his. Samuel had told Saul he must destroy his enemies completely, but Saul saved some treasure and spared the life of the king. As a result, Samuel rejected Saul. He said,

I will not return with you, because you rejected the command of the LORD and the LORD rejects you as king of Israel . . . The LORD has torn the kingdom of Israel from you this day, and has given it to a neighbor of yours, who is better than you.

(1 Samuel 15:26–28)

Saul's days as king were numbered.

Have You Considered?

1. Why do you suppose that religious and political leaders, such as Samuel and Saul, so often find themselves fighting with each other?
2. Put yourself in the position of one of the ancient Israelites. Do you think you would have wanted a king?
3. One of Saul's problems was insecurity about his position as king. Discuss an example of how insecurity can prevent us from making the right choices in difficult situations.

Rosa, Saul and the Witch of Endor. Seventeenth Century.

After Samuel's death, Saul asked a witch at Endor to call forth his ghost (1 Samuel 28:8–25).

◆ David: The Beginnings

David is the central character in the Deuteronomic history, and one of the most important figures in the entire Bible story. It was during David's rule that Israel truly became a nation. Under David, Israel secured peace with its neighbors and the nation prospered. The story of David is found in 1 and 2 Samuel.

Introducing David

David is introduced in three separate stories.

1. **1 Samuel 16:1–3.** David is first introduced during Samuel's visit to the sons of the shepherd, Jesse. Samuel said: "Do not judge from his appearance . . . Not as man sees does God see, because man sees the appearance but the Lord looks into the heart" (1 *Samuel* 16:7).

2. **1 Samuel 16:14–23.** David is brought to King Saul at Gibeah with the reputation of a gifted musician. Saul was "tormented by an evil spirit" and David was asked to play his harp to soothe the pain of his headaches.

   David is known as a musician—he is credited with composing some of the psalms—and he also is recognized as a great military leader. He may well have developed some of his military skills while serving as Saul's armor-bearer.

3. **1 Samuel 17:1–18:5.** The third story is the famous incident with the Philistine, Goliath, and the slingshot.

   Although the story may be legendary, there's nothing impossible about it; the slingshot was an accepted weapon of war, and in the right hands, it could be deadly. This story details the first of many military triumphs for David. Because of his success, the people exalted him over Saul: "Saul has slain his thousands, and David his ten thousands" (1 *Samuel* 18:7).

There are some inconsistencies in the David and Goliath story, however. For one, Saul had to ask who David was, although David had already been introduced to Saul in the earlier story (not to mention that 16:21 has Saul being very fond of David). Also, the story reports that "David took the head of the Philistine and brought it to Jerusalem" even though Jerusalem was not yet an Israelite city (1 *Samuel* 17:54). Finally, in 2 Samuel 21:19, another Israelite soldier, Elhanan, is said to have killed Goliath.

What are we to make of the contradictions in this story? Remember what you learned about the nature of ancient history. Because David had become a great king and Israel a great power, legends of his early strength would have been quite common. It would have certainly been possible for David, the famous and revered leader, to be credited for a lowly soldier's actions. The Deuteronomic historian is interested in the meaning of the story, that as a young man David showed the qualities that would make him a great king, even if the facts aren't quite accurate. To ancient peoples, this was how history should be written.

David's Early Career

However David is introduced, he is always pictured as being intensely loyal to King Saul, the anointed one of Yahweh. And although Saul is shown to be jealous of David and his popularity, David is never shown wavering in his respect for Saul.

David must have been a person of considerable political importance, for he married Saul's daughter, Michal, and he formed a lasting friendship with one of Saul's sons, Jonathan. Lofty accomplishments for a lowly shepherd!

Rembrandt, *David Playing the Harp before Saul.* Seventeenth Century.

David is remembered also for his love of music.

David was undoubtedly an important military leader in his own right. He most certainly had men who followed his leadership, and, probably, he was actively involved in politics, no matter how innocent the Bible makes him out to be. Saul, for all of his moods, was still an intelligent leader. Saul certainly considered David a political rival, because he openly declared war on David, driving him into hiding.

David with the Philistines   David found shelter from Saul among the Philistines, in the "cave of Adullam." He was quickly joined there by a loyal group of his own followers, "all those who were in difficulties or in debt, or who were embittered, and he became their leader" (1 *Samuel* 22:1–2). Like Robin Hood in the Sherwood Forest, David formed these men into a superior fighting force.

Faced with Saul's hostility, David approached A*chish*, the Philistine king. He offered the king the services of his army and pledged to be Achish's vassal. Not only would David bring Achish the loot from his raids against the Amalekite villages in southern Palestine and the Negeb, but he would also strengthen Achish's position against Israel. David insisted, however, that he would not fight the Israelites directly. In short, David cut a deal with the Philistines to protect himself against Saul.

David Prepares   By helping the Philistines, David and his army brought relief to the southern tribes, especially Judah, from the constant attacks they had faced from the Amalekites. David divided the loot, sharing with the people of Judah, gaining their gratitude and earning their trust. The people later rewarded David's generosity by making him king.

Saul and his son Jonathan were eventually killed in a battle with the Philistines at Gilboa. Afterwards, David moved to the town of Hebron, where the leaders of Judah came to him and declared him the king over the tribes living in southern Canaan.

Have You Considered?

1. What characteristics of leadership do you recognize in David? What kind of a leader would David have been?
2. David has been described as a resourceful person. In what ways do you find him to be resourceful?
3. It is possible that the story of Goliath had nothing to do with David, who was added to the story later as his popularity grew. Why do you think people like stories about the courage and goodness of their leaders? What other examples can you think of that fit this pattern?

◆ David Becomes King

David made Israel into a true power in the Middle East, and the kingdom would never again be as united as it was at the height of his rule. Forever after, when Israelites thought of their "glory days," it was David they remembered. Most importantly, David received a promise from Yahweh that a descendant would rule Israel forever.

David did not come to power miraculously, and he was not a perfect model of holiness. David's story is another example of how Yahweh chooses to work through imperfect human beings to achieve divine goals. In the end, however, David overcame his temptations and limitations to provide the classic model of a king who was faithful to God.

David Takes Over

Although accounts vary at times, 1 and 2 Samuel provide a fascinating story about the death of Saul, and about David becoming king. Here are the highlights as the Bible tells the story:

1. **The Philistines attack Israel** and kill Jonathan and several of Saul's other sons (1 *Samuel* 31:2).
2. **Saul is wounded** and begs for someone to kill him. When no one will, Saul falls on his own sword and kills himself. The Philistines find the body, mutilate it, and show it for all to see (1 *Samuel* 31:3–10).
3. **David learns of Saul's death.** 2 Samuel begins with David's hearing of Saul's Death. Here again we have a contradiction, because the messenger reports that he killed Saul "for I knew that he could not survive his wounds" (2 *Samuel* 1:10).
4. **David pays tribute to Saul and Jonathan** in 2 Samuel 1:17–27. David then is "anointed king of the Judahites" (2 *Samuel* 2:1–7) and "spent seven years and six months" (2 *Samuel* 2:11).
5. **Saul's son Ishbaal is made king** over the rest of Israel ruling for two years (2 *Samuel* 2:10).

   There followed a long war between the house of Saul and that of David, in which David grew stronger, but the house of Saul weaker.

   (2 Samuel 3:1)

   Finally, Abner, Ishbaal's general, changes allegiance. He tells David, "Make an agreement with me and I will aid you by bringing all Israel over to you" (2 *Samuel* 3:12). Before he can complete the deal, Abner is murdered by David's general, Joab (2 *Samuel* 3:12–39).

People of Note

David and Bathsheba

Despite his greatness as a king, David was not a perfect person. Through much of his life he was troubled. The best example of this was his affair with Bathsheba.

One day, while David was standing on the roof of the palace, he saw a woman sunbathing. He was filled with lust for her, and he immediately sent someone to find out who she was. It turned out that she was the wife of Uriah, a Hittite who fought in David's army. Even though she was married, David decided to have an affair with her.

Before long, Bathsheba was pregnant. To conceal his crime, David tried to get Uriah to have intercourse with Bathsheba so he would think the child was his. Uriah, however, refused, because he didn't want to relax while his troops were still in combat. Thus, David felt he had no choice: he had Uriah killed in the next battle.

The prophet Nathan then approached David. He told him a story of a rich man who had stolen and killed the only lamb belonging to a poor servant. David said the rich man should be killed, and Nathan responded, "You are the man!" David wept with sorrow and begged forgiveness.

This story shows us that everyone, even God's anointed ones, experience weaknesses and temptations.

---

6. **Ishbaal gave up hope** when he heard of Abner's death. Ishbal was himself soon murdered by his own followers. (2 *Samuel* 4).

7. **David was now king of all Israel.**

   After this, *"When all the elders of Israel came to David in Hebron, King David made an agreement with them there before the Lord, and they anointed him king of Israel."*

   (2 Samuel 5:3)

He had proved himself in battle and had been accepted by the elders of the tribes. He had mourned the deaths of Saul, Jonathan, Abner, and Ishbaal. Now that he was king, however, David's problems really began. If he were to have a nation to rule, he first had to defeat the mighty Philistine army with its iron weapons and chariots.

David Builds a Strong Monarchy

The days of charismatic leadership—as in the time of the judges—ended completely when David took power. David came to power with an army of loyal soldiers hardened by their days among the Philistines. He had the blessing of the leaders of Israel to gather a more powerful army and use it to defend Israel. David took control of Israel's future and built it into a powerful nation. He was God's anointed and he would rule!

Military Victories The Philistines presented David with an immediate military problem:

   When the Philistines heard that David had been anointed king of Israel, they all took the field in search of him.

   (2 Samuel 5:17)

When David asked about the feasibility of battle Yahweh responded: "Attack, for I will surely deliver the Philistines into your grip" (2 *Samuel* 5:18). And attack David did. In two decisive battles, David's army drove the Philistines out of central Palestine and back to their territory on the southern plain. They would never again pose a major threat to Israel's security.

Statesmanship David next turned his attention to administering the unified nation. He moved the capital city from Hebron to Jerusalem. Jerusalem had been an independent Canaanite city, without allegiance to any tribe or to the Israelite covenant before David captured it (2 *Samuel* 5:6–9).

Jerusalem was centrally located to both the northern and southern halves of Israel, and, because it was built on a hill surrounded by three valleys, it was easily defended. Jerusalem came to be known as the "City of David," which is literally true. Jerusalem was captured by David and was never tribal property.

With relative peace at home, David expanded the kingdom. He conquered the territories of Edom, Moab, and Ammon. David also formed many alliances with other rulers, including one with Phoenicia that would last for centuries and greatly benefit Israel's economic life.

Religious Leader As a religious leader, David was very influential. Jerusalem became both the nation's political capital and its religious center. The Ark of the Covenant had been hidden for more than 20 years in fear of losing it to the Philistines. David brought it to Jerusalem with great celebration. David, who was

   girt with a linen apron, came dancing before the Lord with abandon, as he and all the Israelites were bringing up the Ark of the Lord with shouts of joy and to the sound of the horn.

(2 Samuel 5:14)

David had a special tent built, like the one that the Israelites believed had housed the Ark in the Sinai desert. Priests were appointed to serve in the sacred tent and oversee sacrifices and liturgies.

David also made a valuable contribution to liturgical music. Besides composing music himself, he encouraged choral music (songs sung by choirs) and hired musicians to perform it. He supported public worship of Yahweh and enriched it in every way he could, leaving a lasting legacy.

One thing that David did not do was to build a permanent temple for the Ark. Religious habits are slower to change than others, and the people were used to the Ark as a mobile symbol. The prophet Nathan discouraged him, reporting God's words that it would be David's son "who shall build a house for My name" (2 Samuel 7:13).

God's Covenant with David

From the experience of the Exodus, to the giving of the Covenant to Moses, to the military leadership of the judges, the Israelites understood that all leadership came from Yahweh. David took his place alongside Moses as a recipient of Yahweh's Covenant.

Under King David, a theology developed which said that the king ruled as God's appointed. Further, the Israelites believed that God had made a covenant with David which promised that David and his descendants would sit on the throne of Israel forever. As David himself said,

Is not my house firm before God? He has made an eternal covenant with me, set forth in detail and secured. Will He not bring to fruition all my salvation and my every desire?

(2 Samuel 23:5)

When the Israelite kingdom had been destroyed in the time of the Deuteronomic historian, the people questioned whether or not God had broken this promise. The Deuteronomic historian responded that God's word was unbreakable, and that in the future God would establish a "Son of David" on Israel's throne forever. Today, Christians see that promise fulfilled in the reign of Jesus.

Have You Considered?

1. When Abner decided to double-cross Ishbaal, David went along with the deal. Was he wrong to do so? Why or why not?
2. The ancient Israelites believed that God selected the king, and that political power came from God. How could this belief lead to abuses of power from corrupt leaders?
3. Read through the list of David's accomplishments above. Which do you consider to be the greatest? Why?

Spiritual Reflection

Praying the Psalms

Many of the psalms are attributed to David. Some of the psalms seem especially appropriate to David's life. Today, we continue to use the psalms in our public prayer. The response to the first reading at Mass is usually taken from the Book of Psalms. Develop your own psalm response to be used at liturgy. Follow these directions:

- Read Psalms 14, 15, and 16 in their entirety.
- Choose the psalm that appeals to you the most.

- Reflect on the words of the psalm in writing.
- Quietly pray, using the words of the Psalm to guide your thoughts.
- When you have prayed as long as you feel comfortable, use David's words in Psalm 16:8–11 as a promise to the Lord and as a thanksgiving.

Q/A

Section One

1. What is the Deuteronomic history? Under what circumstances was it written?
2. What answer does the Deuteronomic history give to the question of why God would allow bad things to happen to the Chosen People?
3. What is the difference between ancient and modern approaches to writing history?
4. Define the following terms: Canaan, Israel, Palestine.
5. Why might Joshua be described as the "ideal leader of Israel"?
6. What are some reasons why Israel's initial military action in Canaan could not have taken them much farther than the southern hill country?
7. What was the system of government for the 12 tribes? What were the weaknesses in this system?
8. How did a clan join the Israelite covenant faith?

Section Two

1. Who were the judges and what was their role in Israel?
2. What are the four phases of Israel's behavior during the time of the judges?
3. Define: charismatic leadership, theology.
4. What is the basic theological idea in Judges?
5. Why did the Israelites want a king? How did Samuel respond to their request?
6. What was the significance of establishing Jerusalem as the capital city of the new nation?
7. What contributions did David make as a religious leader?
8. What was God's covenant with David?

BIBLE ACTIVITY

1. Read Judges 2:1–4 and Judges 3–4. Outline the four-fold pattern of sin, punishment, repentance, and deliverance as seen in these passages.
2. Read and summarize Joshua's final plea to the Israelites in Joshua 23, identifying his major concerns for Israel.
3. Write a dramatization of Samuel's call as described in 1 Samuel 3:1 and 21. Include these characters: narrator, Samuel, Eli, Yahweh.
4. Report on these incidents from Saul's life: (a) Saul is anointed by Samuel (1 Samuel 10:1–10), (b) Saul turns away from God (1 Samuel 15:22–35), and (c) Saul is jealous of David (1 Samuel 18:6–15).
5. Form debate panels to take positions on the different forms of leadership modeled in this chapter. Each group should defend one form of leadership as the ideal.

These ruins are believed to be the remains of King David's tomb.

GLOSSARY

- **Ark of the Covenant:** A portable shrine originally constructed in the Sinai desert, believed to contain the tablets of the Law; a symbol of God's presence.
- **Canaan:** The area around the Jordan River and the Dead Sea. This is the term used before David's kingdom.
- **Charismatic leader:** A person upon whom the spirit of the Lord had come with power, thus enabling him or her to be a successful military leader and judge.
- **Confederation:** A league or alliance. In Israel, the confederation was based on the Covenant.
- **Deuteronomic History:** The history of Israel, written in 587 B.C.E., that includes the books of Joshua, Judges, 1 and 2 Samuel, and 1 and 2 Kings.
- **Israel:** The term used for the promised land (Canaan) after the kingdom is formed. Also used for the Northern Kingdom after 920 B.C.E.
- **Judah:** The southern part of Canaan.
- **Judge:** A charismatic leader and dispenser of justice among the Israelites from about 1200–1030 B.C.E.
- **Palestine:** Another term for the promised land, used to refer to the entire territory after the split between Israel and Judah.
- **Philistines:** A people who came from the Aegean area to the coast of Palestine around 1100 B.C.E.; rivals of Israel for control of the land of Canaan.
- **Theology:** The study of God. When talking about people's theology, the term refers to their ideas about God.
- **Tribe:** A group of people united by family ties and common interests; ancient Israel was divided into 12 tribes.
- **Vassal:** One who holds land given by a superior (e.g., a king), and who fights and/or farms for him in return.

UNDERSTANDING MORE ABOUT:

The Deuteronomic History

The Deuteronomic history received its name because its authors believed Israel had sinned by not following the laws in the Book of Deuteronomy. "Deuteronomy" is a Greek word meaning "second law." The fifth book of the Pentateuch, Deuteronomy has that name because it is a second version of the laws found in Exodus.

In 2 Kings 22, the Deuteronomic historians describe the reign of Josiah, one of the descendants of King David. The historians say that King Josiah found a book of law in the Temple while it was being renovated. The king was devastated, because he realized that the nation had not obeyed the laws of God as set forth in this book. Many scholars believe this book to be Deuteronomy.

About 100 years later, the Deuteronomic historians, living in exile, examined the history of Israel. The theme of their work was that Israel's disregard for the Law grew steadily worse after King David, until God allowed them to be defeated and humiliated. Through the promise of the Covenant with David, however, the Deuteronomic historians held out hope that things would improve and God would rebuild the people.

CHAPTER 4

Genesis: At the Beginning

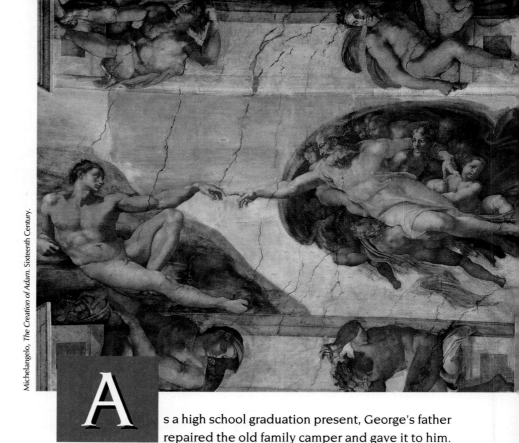

Michelangelo, *The Creation of Adam*. Sixteenth Century.

As a high school graduation present, George's father repaired the old family camper and gave it to him. Soon after graduation, George and his two older brothers took off from San Pedro, California, for a cross-country trip to New York state.

The drive took almost two weeks. The brothers camped at some pretty remote places along the way. They were able to take only two showers during the entire trip. The worst part about it was that none of them knew how to cook anything but scrambled eggs. Needless to say, they were all happy when they reached their Uncle Antonio's house in the Little Italy section of Manhattan. George thought, "A warm shower, a great Italian meal, and then . . . check out the night life in New York!"

After supper, Uncle Antonio had other plans. "Boys, boys, I have some things to show you and some things to tell you," he said.

The old man pulled out a worn photo album and an envelope of other equally tattered papers.

"This is our family story," he began, extending some old, faded photographs. "Here I am with your father and our parents at Ellis Island. We were so frightened; we were only babies, your father and I. He was three and I was six when we came here. The boat ride from Italy seemed to last a year, although it really only took ten days. Your grandmama and grandpapa were strong. When many of their friends fled back to their homeland because of the crowded living conditions here in the city, they decided they could make a better life for their children here. They would never have made it without their great trust in God to provide. Look here. This one shows the fish market where we worked and lived. At first the smell of fish was everywhere. But, as we got used to it, the smell didn't bother us. Did your father ever tell you about the first time he met your mother? Look, here are some of the love letters he wrote to her from the war."

George's brothers squirmed anxiously. George knew they were thinking about having fun in Times Square. George waved them on. "You guys go party without me. I'm a little tired. Besides, these stories are interesting!"

His uncle smiled and went on with his stories.

Cherished Family Stories

During George's visit to his uncle's home in New York he discovered a universal truth: people in all times and places have cherished their family story. It gives them some perspective on what's happening in their own lives. Being in touch with their roots gives people a better foundation for living in the present, because it helps them answer one of the basic human questions: "Who am I?"

People have always searched to discover their origins far beyond their own memory. The question "How did we begin?" comes up in every culture and in every generation. You may also be interested in your own origins: Where did you come from? Where did your parents, grandparents, and great-grandparents live and what did they do? How did your family customs get started?

The Israelites asked these same questions. Much of their early history was unknown. In order to explain their origins—and the origins of humankind—they developed more of their family story. In this chapter, you'll learn about that story as it's presented in the Book of Genesis.

Myth, Legend, and Story

Babylonian, *Goddess Gula with Her Dog*, Fourteenth Century B.C.E.

In Chapter 3, you studied a part of the Israelites' family story, the Deuteronomic history. But this part of the story wasn't enough. The Israelites wanted to examine their story as far back as the beginning of humanity, and also to their beginnings as a people. Of course, no historical records exist from that far back in time. The Israelites had to develop other kinds of stories about these ancient events. For the beginnings of humanity, they used the type of story called a myth, and for their origins as a people, they used legends. First, meet the people responsible for these stories: the authors of the Book of Genesis.

Learning Objectives for Section One

By the end of this section, you will be able to:

- Compare and contrast the three authors of Genesis.
- Explain the four functions of myth.
- Compare and contrast different ancient Middle Eastern "creation myths."
- Explain the nature of a legend.

◆ The Authors of Genesis

The Book of Genesis, as it is in the Bible, was finalized relatively late in the history of the Old Testament. It was probably finished a little later than the Deuteronomic history, sometime during the Babylonian Exile after 587 B.C.E. The Exile was a national disaster, so catastrophic that it threatened to bring Israel's family story to an end. This threat to the survival of the nation created an intense interest in the beginnings of the story.

The Book of Genesis was put together by people who combined and edited earlier sources in an effort to keep the nation together. By rallying its members around the story of their roots the writers and editors of Genesis hoped to help the exiled Israelites feel proud about who they were; they wanted the people to know their ancestors and to see God's blessings from the beginning of time. These efforts brought them a deeper understanding of God and God's purposes for the world and for humankind.

Sources

In modern times, we have a concept called "plagiarism." We regard it as immoral (not to mention illegal) to use someone else's words as our own. In the ancient world, however, this concept did not exist. *Scribes,* the people who were responsible for copying and taking care of a culture's literature, felt free to take the words of one author, mix them with those of other authors, to produce a new book, without giving credit to anyone.

Using written works in this way was accepted in the ancient world because people felt that literature belonged to the whole culture, not simply to the person who had produced it. An original work is known as a *"source."* Often books were produced by combining several original sources together. In most cases, the original authors have not been credited with their work.

Since most biblical books have more than one source, we often find different points of view and different versions of the same event repeated within the text. Two or more sources have been combined into one version. This mixing of sources allows the insights and wisdom of many different people to contribute to the contents of the Bible. Nowhere is this variety more evident than in the first 11 chapters of Genesis.

The Three Sources

The earliest writings in Genesis come from three sources, or authors.

- **"J" Source.** The largest source is known as the *Yahwist* source. This author referred to God by the name "Yahweh." The Yahwist source is commonly referred to as "J" because in German (the people who first suggested this theory were German), J is the first letter of the name of God, Yahweh. The Yahwist author probably worked in the court of King David (1020–970 B.C.E.).

- **"E" Source.** The second early source is called the *Elohist*, derived from the way the author refers to God. "Elohim" is the generic Hebrew word for God. The Elohist source is found in bits and pieces throughout the Book of Genesis. It is known commonly as the "E" source. It is most likely that the "E" author wrote in the time of Solomon.

- **"P" Source.** Genesis was put into its final shape and form by the priestly authors. These authors are known as the "P" source. The priestly authors

The Bible in Context

Writing in the Ancient Middle East

When the authors of the Bible sat down to write, they couldn't simply boot up their word processors and type. The technology of writing then may have been primitive compared to our modern instruments, but the techniques developed by ancient people were fascinating.

The earliest writings—*cuneiform*—are dated prior to 4000 B.C.E. in Mesopotamia. Cuneiform writing was done with a wedge-shaped stylus (needle) on clay tablets. The tablets were then baked to make them hard so that they couldn't be erased. Cuneiform was a common form of writing for many centuries.

In Egypt, *hieroglyphs,* or picture writing was developed around 3000 B.C.E. The Egyptians wrote on *papyrus,* a kind of paper manufactured from the leaves of the papyrus plant. Strips would then be cut and glued together to form a scroll. The fibers of the plant provided horizontal lines to guide a scribe's writing.

Another common writing surface was stone, used for official decrees of the king and for national records. Animal skins, especially leather, were also used. For everyday needs, people would use easily erased wax tablets. In general, however, ordinary people didn't know how to write. When they needed something written, they would usually pay a highly respected "scribe,"—a professional trained to write and read well—to do the writing for them.

God's act of creation is celebrated in the Book of Genesis. It is a time of perfection and beauty, peace and harmony.

LEARN FROM THE MAP

Abraham's Journey

Many of the legends in Genesis concern Abraham, the person looked upon as the "father" of the Hebrew people. Originally from Ur in Mesopotamia, Abraham migrated into Canaan somewhere around 1800 B.C.E. in response to an invitation from God. Using the map's scale of one–quarter (1/4) inch equals 60 miles, calculate the approximate distance of this journey.

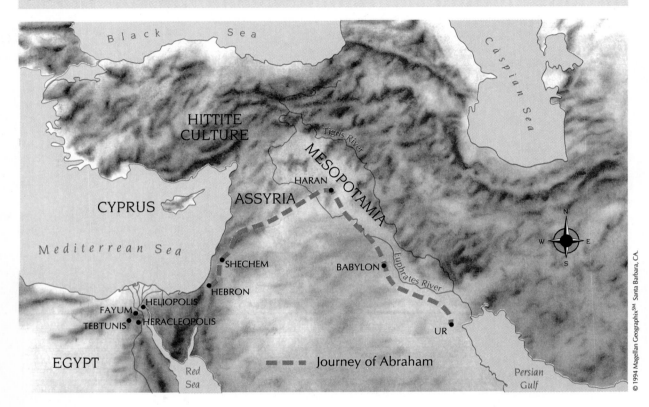

Journey of Abraham

© 1994 Magellan Geographix℠ Santa Barbara, CA.

added to the "J" and "E" sources to give the story its final form.

How can you tell the material added by "P"? Look for:

- Chronological information, lists, and family trees.
- Laws like those having to do with the Sabbath and circumcision.
- Definitions of covenant, as in those between God and Noah or God and Abraham that can be understood only in the light of the Covenant given to Moses.

In the first eleven chapters of Genesis, the two main sources are the Yahwist and the Priestly writers (the Elohist references begin with Chapter 12). These chapters attempt to tell the story of creation and to answer some of the basic questions that the people of God had about their past.

Have You Considered?

1. Have you ever worked on a group project? What was it like putting all your contributions together? How might your experience be similar to how biblical books such as Genesis were put together?
2. List some advantages (at least three) that might result from having more than one author's point of view represented in the Bible.
3. The Babylonian exile, when the "P" source put Genesis together, was a time of great pain for Israel. Why do you suppose interest in their nation's past was so strong for the people at this time? Why do people in general find comfort in the stories about where they came from?

◆ Mythology and Genesis

The first part of Genesis (chapters 1–11) are stories from the "J" and "P" authors about the origins of humanity. These are mythological stories rather than historical accounts, and therefore they're called "creation myths." To appreciate the beautiful stories "J" and "P" have contributed to Genesis, it's first necessary to focus on what's meant by the term "myth."

What Is a Myth?

A myth is an imaginative story which embodies the beliefs and values of a group of people. Myths tell about a culture's gods and heroes, and are usually set far back in the past, often at the beginning of time. These stories are not meant to be taken as historical records. Instead, myths communicate ideas and beliefs in story form.

A common misconception is that a myth is a story without truth. Some people fault myths for not having the same kind of truth found in historical, mathematical, or scientific works. This complaint misses the point. A myth contains a different kind of truth; it conveys meanings which are truthful, but which may or may not have a basis in historical fact.

The Earth Mother   Let's take an example. Native American creation myths often tell of an "earth mother" who gave birth to all living things at the beginning of time. Is this story true? Well, if by "true" you mean was the earth mother a historical or scientific fact, then probably not. But since the earth provides the food and water all things need to survive, don't we depend on it for our very lives as we do our mothers? Isn't it true that without the earth, nothing could exist? In this sense, then, the myth speaks a powerful truth.

This example shows the nature of myth. Myths are symbolic stories and can be understood in many ways. The purpose of a myth is to reveal many meanings, many levels of understanding through a simple story. Myths point beyond the obvious to more inward or spiritual realities.

Truths for Understanding God   In Genesis, the creation myths found in chapters 1–11 are full of important truths for understanding God, God's plan for humanity, and our common destiny. Sometimes, however, these truths get lost when people try to read Genesis as if it were a history or science book.

People who argue "creationism" (God created all things as stated in Genesis) over the science of evolution, are misreading the Genesis story. Their argument is based on a mistake. Myth doesn't try to tell us "what actually happened." It uses stories to communicate ideas. Genesis is not interested in the scientific facts of creation, as long as we recognize that God is the Creator.

All Cultures Have Myths   All cultures have their own myths. Through myths, people learn about values, beliefs, and experiences. Myths, likewise, help individuals to find out how they fit into the group.

---

in the *Spotlight*

Middle Eastern Creation Myths

Myths about the beginning of the world and of humanity are called "creation myths." As you've learned, all cultures have myths, and the ancient Middle East was no exception.

Here are summaries of two creation myths from ancient Middle Eastern cultures. See how many similarities you can spot with the creation mythology in Genesis.

The "Enuma Elish" (Babylonian):

Marduk, a fierce warrior, fights with the goddess Tiamat for rule over the other gods. Marduk, who controls the winds, fills Tiamat with air and stabs her with his spear. After his victory, Marduk is the supreme god. He then orders a rival's throat slit. From the blood of his opponent, Marduk has human beings created. He decreed that humans are to serve as the slaves of the gods. Marduk was celebrated as a king who rules over the kingdom of heaven.

The Epic of Gilgamesh (Babylonian):

The hero Gilgamesh is one-third human and two-thirds divine. Nevertheless, he is a mortal man. He decides, therefore, to go on a quest for immortality. He searches for and finds Utnapishtim, a human being who survived a great flood by riding on a boat. The gods are so upset that a mortal has survived their flood, they turn Utnapishtim and his wife into immortals! Utnapishtim tells Gilgamesh where he can find the plant that will give him eternal life. Gilgamesh finds the plant, but he is so tired from his journey that he decides to sleep before he eats it. While Gilgamesh sleeps, a serpent steals the plant, and, therefore, denys Gilgamesh eternal life.

The most important beliefs of a culture or religion are included in these creation myths.

Myth fulfills four functions:

1. **Theological.** Myths tell us what God is like and how God relates with us.
2. **Cosmic.** Myths tell us how the world works and what its purpose is.
3. **Social.** Myths tell us how society should be organized and who should be in charge.
4. **Ethical.** Myths tell us what values human beings should have and how we should behave.

When myths are read or told, it is up to the individual listener to find the particular meaning in the story. If one is only interested in the literal facts of the story, the deeper significance of the myth is often missed or misunderstood.

The Oral Tradition

For generations, Israel's myths were kept orally—stories that were told and re-told, passed along from an elder to a younger person, and cherished for the understanding and stability they provided to the community. The passing of knowledge in this way is known as the *oral tradition.*

Eventually, by the time of King David, the nation of Israel had progressed to where it could capture the oral tradition in writing. "J" was the first author to write a creation myth based on the oral tradition. Later, "P" did the same thing. The fact that these stories survived so long in the memories of the people is proof of how important they were. Like all creation myths, they helped the people maintain their identity.

Have You Considered?

1. Given what you know about mythology, should "creation by God" be taught as a rival scientific theory to the hypothesis of evolution in science classes? Why or why not?
2. What was the main way the Israelites altered and changed the form of myths found in other ancient Middle Eastern cultures?
3. In this chapter, we said that all cultures have myths. What is an example of myth in American culture? Do you think this myth captures some truth? Why or why not?

◆ Legend and Genesis

Myth is not the only style of writing that "J" and "P" used to tell the family story of Israel. In Genesis 12–50, they move from telling the story of the creation of the world to telling the story of the Hebrew people's beginnings. To do that, they used the form of writing known as "legend."

What Is a Legend?

Babe Ruth was one of the greatest baseball players of all time. A famous story about the Babe illustrates the nature of a legend. According to the story, the Babe visited a dying boy in a hospital and promised to hit a home run for him in that day's game. During the game, the Babe stepped up to the plate, pointed to the outfield bleachers, and then hit the ball exactly where he had pointed. This homer is known as Babe Ruth's "called shot."

Babe Ruth is a legendary hero. While Ruth's records are factual, stories are told to emphasize his performance that may go beyond what actually happened.

This story illustrates the nature of a legend in two ways:

1. **It has been told and re-told countless numbers of times.** For those who hear the story, it helps bind them in a "family" of baseball fans by connecting them to the game's past.
2. **It may or may not be true.** There were no TV cameras present at that game, radio recordings are inconclusive, and people who were there are unsure about what happened.

A "legend," therefore, is an unverifiable story about some famous person or event of the past. Although legends are generally about actual, historical individuals, the purpose of the story is not to provide fact. Instead, legends illustrate principles and beliefs mixing fact with fiction.

The legends in Genesis are of this sort. The characters in these legends were real people: Abraham, Isaac, Jacob, and Joseph all really existed. There's no way to know, however, whether the specific stories told about them actually happened. Certainly there's some historical truth in these legends. The purpose of these legends, however, is not to record details accurately, but to connect the Israelites to their origins and their relationship with God.

Sagas

The specific kind of legend used in Genesis is called a *saga*. A saga is a tale—with both elements of legend and history—that describes a famous person of the past.

The sagas in Genesis 12–36 center primarily on three characters: Abraham, Isaac, and Jacob. From Genesis 37–50, the focus shifts to Joseph. Scholars disagree about exactly how much of these stories is legend and how much is based on historical truth, though they all agree that the stories contain a mixture of both. It is likely that the stories of Abraham, Isaac, and Jacob are part of Israel's earliest oral traditions.

Customs and legal items mentioned in these sagas date them to a definite time in history: between 1900 and 1700 B.C.E.

Have You Considered?

1. Give another example of a "legend" as defined in this section. How do you suppose this story got started?
2. Do you think it matters how much historical truth a legend contains? Why or why not?

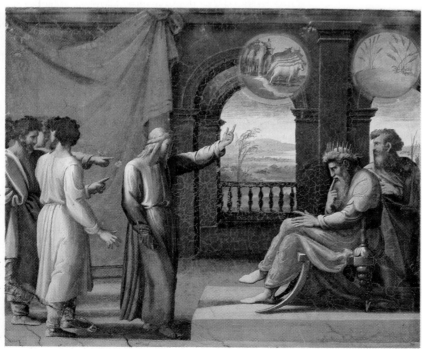

Raphael, *The Story of Joseph.* Sixteenth Century.

The saga of Joseph serves as a transition from the patriarchal legends and the Exodus.

Israel Explores Its Roots

Bible of Souvigny, *Descendants of Abraham.* Twelfth Century.

Now that you know about myths and legends and who wrote the ones in Genesis, you're ready to encounter the stories themselves.

As you read through them, remember the four functions of myth, and ask:

1. What does this story tell me about God?
2. What does it tell me about the world?
3. What does this story tell me about my society, based on how it got started?
4. What does it tell me about how I should behave?

Learning Objectives for Section Two

By the end of this section, you will be able to:

- Compare and contrast the "J" and "P" creation stories.
- Discuss the following stories: Cain and Abel, The Flood, The Tower of Babel.
- Identify Abraham, Sarah, Isaac, Jacob, Esau, Joseph, and the 12 sons of Jacob.

◆ Creation Myths in Genesis

The earliest myths in Genesis were written by the Yahwist; the later materials were added by the Priestly writers. Remember that the Yahwist wrote under King David (approximately 1000 B.C.E.) while the Priestly authors wrote at the time of the Exile (around 550 B.C.E.).

Using the story forms of the Creation and the Flood common to the mid-East, the Israelite myths highlight Yahweh's presence in the world's beginnings and in the fall of humanity. The nature of God is revealed as just and forgiving. These two themes of creation and redemption found in the myths of Genesis 1–11 are repeated often through the rest of Hebrew Scripture.

The "J" Story

The Yahwist creation story in Genesis 2:4–4:16 describes both the creation of the world and of human beings. The Yahwist creation story also introduces a longer narrative that includes sections on the fall of humankind from grace and the loss of the privileges of paradise.

Imagine along with the writer of the story:

- Yahweh is intimately involved with creation— "hands on," so to speak.
- The first event is the creation of humanity: " . . . the Lord God formed man out of the clay of the ground and blew into his nostrils the breath of life, and so man became a living being" (*Genesis* 2:7).
- Everything else—the garden, and all other living things—was created for the man's benefit.

- God brings all the living creatures before the man to be named.
- When a suitable mate for the man is not found among the other animals, Yahweh created woman.

What do you notice about this story? What image of God does the writer offer us: an all-knowing, distant deity or one who is actively involved in creation and who learns by doing?

As you read the creation story, notice that God, at first, thinks the garden and other living things will make the man happy. Only when God finds out this was wrong is woman created. This is a very different understanding of God than that held by the "P" authors, as you will discover.

The "P" Story

The "P" story (*Genesis* 1:1–2:3) stands on its own. There is no doubt here that God is in control and that God knows what's what.

- God first creates the environment, and then its inhabitants, all in six days. An impressive feat, an act of a powerful God.
- Human beings are created last, the climax of all that went before: "God created man in His image; in the divine image He created him; male and female He created them" (*Genesis* 1:27).
- Because human beings are made like God in a mysterious and powerful way, they are responsible for the rest of creation.

The style of the Priestly authors follows a precise pattern in which the works of the three first days establish the conditions for the last three. Read Genesis 1:1–31 and look for this pattern:

- The created light of the *first day* is given form in the sun and the moon of the *fourth day*.
- The sea and sky of the *second day* are the habitats of the fish and birds of the *fifth day*.
- The earth and its vegetation created on the *third day* provide a home and food source for the animals and people of the *sixth day*.

This pattern was similar to a primitive three-tiered understanding of the universe—heavens above, earth below, and waters underneath.

In the Priestly story, Yahweh is understood to be in complete control of creation. Nothing happens that is not part of the divine plan. Also, Yahweh creates with the purpose of creating humankind in the divine image. You can notice here the differences between the Yahwist and Priestly understanding of God.

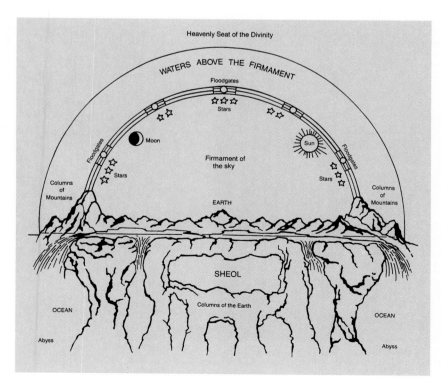

This illustration depicts the structure of the world as seen by ancient peoples. Compare this model to the story in Genesis 1–2:3.

"P" finds significance in the seventh day, on which God rested. The Sabbath was very important for the Priestly writers. During the Exile, when the other leaders of the nation had been killed or scattered, priests were charged with preserving the religious traditions of Israel. One of the most important traditions was the Sabbath ("seventh day") rest. Work was not permitted on the Sabbath. By placing this tradition in the creation story, Yahweh is proclaimed the originator of the Sabbath and its rules.

Have You Considered?

1. How do you think the "J" and "P" stories differ on the theological function of myth? Which appeals to you more, and why?
2. Both the "J" and "P" stories suggest that humanity is "in charge" of creation. What kind of responsibility for the earth do you think this responsibility means we should have?
3. The "P" authors placed the Sabbath rule in their creation story, to make sure that people continued to obey the rule. Which function of myth was "P" using here? How do you know?

◆ The Fall

Just as all cultures have creation myths, they also have a story about what has "gone wrong" in human life; about how the perfection of creation has become messed up. And as their creation stories differ, so do their explanations about the cause of humanity's problems.

For example, the Babylonian epic, Gilgamesh, tells how human beings lost the chance to live forever. In this story, it is the failure to consume a life-giving substance that results in the loss of immortality. Notice the similarity with the "tree of life" in Genesis 2:9 and the "tree of the knowledge of good and evil" in Genesis 2:16.

Adam and Eve

Although there are similarities between Genesis and other mid-eastern fall myths, the Yahwist story of the fall is radically different from any other story.

- *Adam* ("man") and *Eve* ("mother of all living") are symbols of humankind.
- The garden of Eden is paradise, the perfect and free state where the relationship between God

Perugino, *Expulsion from Paradise*. Fifteenth Century.

Adam and Eve's expulsion from Paradise demonstrates the consequences of sin.

and humans could be exactly as it was intended. What happens in the garden is symbolic of the events of human history.

- The responsibility for the fall belongs to man and woman together. They made the moral choice to disobey the rules of creation, so they bear responsibility for the fall and for the introduction of sin into the world.

Themes Presented

Genesis 3 develops four themes—awareness, choice, consequences, and mercy—and suggests that they are representative of the human condition.

1. **Awareness.** In their original state in the garden of Eden, Adam and Eve had no awareness of good and evil. It was only through disobedience that Adam and Eve gained this awareness

2. **Choice.** After choosing evil, Adam was afraid (*Genesis* 3:10). His act created a fear that he had never felt before. As a result, he did not want to bear responsibility for his own choice.

3. **Consequences.** The consequences of the wrong choice (*Genesis* 3:14–19) imposed by Yahweh meant that the necessary elements of life (childbirth, marital relationships, work) would from then on be mixtures of beauty and pain, desire and conflict.

4. **Mercy.** In Genesis 3:21, the Lord makes clothes for Adam and Eve. This act of mercy showed that though God is bound to respect the necessary consequences of human choice, God would not abandon humankind. Rather, Yahweh continued to care for them, even though they were no longer able to live in Eden and were barred from the "tree of life"—a symbol for immortality.

Social Function of the Fall

Remember that one of the functions of myth is to describe what society is like, and point out what it should be like. The story of the fall illustrates clearly this social function of myth.

In Genesis 3:16, Yahweh speaks to the woman, and says "Yet your urge shall be for your husband, and he shall be your master." This verse suggests that in a marriage, the husband will rule over the wife. The ancient Israelites lived in a society in which women were under the authority of men, so this verse was an accurate reflection of their social situation.

What people often fail to notice, however, is that Genesis 3:16 doesn't say this inequality is how life is supposed to be. Notice that Yahweh is speaking after the fall. In other words, God is saying that the present relationship of men over women is a consequence of sin, not part of the divine plan. According to the story, therefore, inequality between men and women is sinful.

This observation illustrates an important lesson about reading the Bible: make sure to read verses in context, so you can make good decisions about what they mean.

The Pattern Repeats Itself

Three other stories—part of the Yahwist's creation narrative—repeat and emphasize the continuing pattern of sin in the world.

Cain And Abel (*Genesis* 4:1–16)   Cain's sin of murdering his brother follows a pattern similar to his parents' sin. An awareness develops in Cain that he wants what God has refused him: a praise greater than was given to his brother Abel. Cain's choice—murder—is a violation of God's will. The consequences for his sin are even greater for Cain than they had been for Adam and Eve. He is driven from the community. Still, God's mercy abounds. Yahweh placed a mark—a sign of grace—on Cain so that he would not be killed in his wanderings.

The Tower of Babel is a symbol for us. When we try to reach God without God's help, our efforts end in failure.

The Flood (*Genesis 6:5–9:17*) The "P" and "J" versions of this story are woven together. Once again, it is "man's wickedness on earth" (6:5) that causes the ensuing destruction of the flood. God's mercy is experienced through Noah. In a binding, everlasting covenant, Yahweh promises "that never again shall all bodily creatures be destroyed by the waters of a flood; there shall not be another flood to devastate the earth" (9:11).

The Tower of Babel (*Genesis 11:1–9*) The story of humankind's desire to "build a city and tower with its top in the sky, and so make a name for ourselves" (11:4) is the last of the Creation narrative stories detailing the effects of humankind's fall. The decision to build a tower is seen to anger God, perhaps because of its arrogance and lack of humility.

Yahweh's decision to "scatter them all over the earth" (11:9) explains how the earth became populated with different races, nations, and languages.

Insight for Today

Test question

These stories of humanity's sin and fall from grace help to explain why life is such a mixed bag of beauty and pain, delight and struggle, goodness and evil. They communicate how the relationship between God and humans was meant to be good and close, but that somehow human beings misunderstood and disobeyed the only limit God made for them. This disobedience and its motive changed all of life.

Today, every person lives with the consequences that result from the first act of disobedience. Human nature was changed by it. Since every human has this nature, everyone lives in and with the same conditions. This common condition is what the Catholic Church calls "original sin."

Test question

Although the stories about the fall emphasize humanity's sinfulness and the consequences for that sin, they do not end there. The authors of Genesis were interested in showing God's saving action, not humanity's sinful behavior. If the tragic condition of the world was the author's concern, the Bible would end there. But it doesn't. By showing us the mess that humanity made of God's creation Genesis points out the simple truth that it is God who saves. The authors of Genesis, whether Yahwists or Priestly, leave no doubts that God has never abandoned us, even when we have made incredibly stupid decisions. God has never abandoned us! Think about it.

Scripture Workshop

Detailing the Flood

Read the story of the flood from Genesis 6:5–9:17. You will notice that events are repeated and that details do not agree. The evidence shows that two sets of traditional stories about the flood—Yahwist and Priestly—have been combined into one story.

As you read the story of the flood, find the answers to these questions:

1. Why did God flood the earth?
2. Why did God spare Noah?
3. A cubit is roughly 18 inches in length. In feet, how long was the ark? How wide? How high?
4. What directions does God give Noah in 6:19–20? How do these instructions differ from 7:2–3? What do you think explains these different instructions?
5. How long did the flood last? You can determine this by adding up the days mentioned in chapters 7 and 8.
6. How does Noah determine that the flood has subsided and that it's safe to leave the ark?
7. After the flood was over, what was Noah's first act on newly dried land?
8. What was God's promise to Noah after the flood?
9. What is God's sign of faithfulness after the flood?

Have You Considered?

1. In this section, Adam and Eve were described as "symbols" of humanity. Even if the story of Adam and Eve is not historically accurate, what truth does the myth of the fall communicate? How does it do so?
2. How does freedom play a part in each story of humanity's fall?
3. What are the implications in the statement that "God has never abandoned us"? How does that change how you think about God?

◆ Legends of the Patriarchs

Beginning with Chapter 12, the stories in Genesis shift in focus. No longer concerned with the origins of the universe and humanity, these stories tell of the beginnings of a specific culture—the Hebrews, who in time were to become God's chosen people.

In telling the story, "J," "P," and "E" (The Yahwist, Priestly, and Elohist sources) focus on specific individuals: Abraham, Isaac, Jacob, and Joseph. These people are called the "patriarchs," or "ruling fathers."

The Book of Genesis describes Abraham as the father of Isaac, who is the father of Jacob, who in turn is father to twelve sons; these will become the 12 tribes of Israel. What are the implications of this story?

This arrangement was probably a device invented by the authors to include the traditions of several originally separate tribes. Recall that in the period of the Judges, many small clans joined the Covenant with Yahweh to become "the people of Israel." Each group brought their own traditions with them. Those traditions became part of Israel's accepted history. Because Israel later came to understand itself as one people, the biblical writers made these various traditions of Abraham, Isaac, and Jacob into one family story.

In these collected traditions, the Israelites felt themselves to be connected to the past. Israel found its deepest roots as Yahweh's Chosen People in these stories about their founders.

Abraham: Father of Faith

Abram was the first of the patriarchs to know Yahweh. As his story develops, his name will later be changed by God to Abraham. Like the other patriarchs, Abraham lived a *semi-nomadic* life, moving with his flocks and herds when the seasonal supply of pasture land and water demanded it, yet never venturing too far from the settled society.

Abraham's family originally came from Ur, which was south of Babylon along the Euphrates River (look again at the map on pg.58). The clan later moved to Haran along the northern part of the Euphrates.

Abraham's Call   The story of Abraham begins in Haran with a call from Yahweh:

> Go forth from the land of your kinsfolk and from your father's house to a land that I will show you.
>
> (Genesis 12:1)

Yahweh then promises Abraham that his descendants shall become the Chosen People. Yahweh says:

> "Look up at the sky and count the stars, if you can. Just so . . . shall your descendants be."
>
> (Genesis 15:5)

In a later story, Yahweh gives Abraham the sign of circumcision as a reminder of this covenant. In two separate accounts, God obliges Abraham to keep his promise to remain faithful. Abraham's role is to trust God and follow God's command.

God's Promises Fulfilled   For many years, Abraham had no idea at all about how God would fulfill the promises of "many descendants" made to him and Sarah since they had no children. He said:

> What good will your gifts be, if I keep on being childless?
>
> (Genesis 15:2)

In fact, Abraham and Sarah's frustration grew to the point that Sarah approved of Abraham having a child with her servant, Hagar. For a while, they thought Hagar's child, Ishmael, would be the child of the promise.

Golden Bull. Eighteenth Century B.C.E.

This Golden Bull, found in the city of Ur—Abraham's original city—represents the god of creation.

People of Note

Sarah

Sarah is remembered as a wife to Abraham and a mother of Isaac. She is considered as the matriarch, or founding mother, of Israel.

Sarah probably came from an important family. Her original name, *Sarai,* means "princess," so she may have been from a noble family.

Researchers also suggest that Sarah was a priestess, with a religious authority of her own. Evidence of this includes when she is admitted to the harem in Egypt *(Genesis 12)* and when she is taken into custody by King Abimelech *(Genesis 26).* In both stories, the rulers suffer serious difficulties because of her presence. If she had been a powerful priestess, such a reaction would have been expected.

Sarah also acted as a guardian of God's promise when she insisted that Hagar and Ishmael be sent away. Even God, though unhappy about it, tells Abraham to do as Sarah says *(Genesis 21:9–12).* Although the verses make Sarah sound like a shrew, the tradition of Yahweh's approval suggests that Sarah was acting under divine authority more than out of simple jealousy.

Noticing Sarah's important role in the early days of God's people helps correct the mistaken, but too often assumed, idea that God works only through men. Women also have an important role in God's plan.

Then, God spoke to Abraham again, this time through three visitors. They predicted again that Sarah would have a child. Overhearing them, Sarah, who was at that time over ninety years old according to Genesis, laughed aloud. When God's promise was fulfilled and Sarah did have a son, they named him Isaac, a Hebrew word meaning "she laughed."

When Isaac was young, Sarah worried that he would have to share God's promise with Hagar's son, Ishmael. Because Ishmael was born first, he had the first claim to inherit the promise from Abraham. Sarah argued that Ishmael should be run off, which upset Abraham because he loved Ishmael. God intervened and said that Hagar and her son should leave; God promised Hagar that Ishmael, too, would have many descendants. The religion of Islam traces its roots back to Abraham through Ishmael.

The Test   Isaac would be the son of God's promise. But God was not through testing Abraham's faith. In an "E" story in Genesis 22, God commands that Abraham sacrifice Isaac as a burnt offering.

What a blow! After finally receiving the son that he had been promised so many years in the past, Abraham is once again asked to surrender his desires to God's wishes.

As difficult as it may have been for Abraham to honor God's request, his struggle is not mentioned in Genesis. His response to God is, "Ready" *(Genesis 22:1).* Early the next morning he saddles up a donkey and heads off to Mount Moriah prepared to follow God's order. When Isaac is spared (an angel of God appears and tells Abraham to sacrifice a ram instead) God's promise is reinforced.

Test question

The stories of Abraham establish the model of faith for Israel; the faithful person is one who hears God's call and obeys. Yahweh was revealed as the master of history.

Isaac

Compared to the stories of the other patriarchs, there is relatively little information about the life of Isaac. The most famous of the Isaac traditions are his place in the near child sacrifice (*Genesis* 22), and as an elderly victim of his son Jacob's deception (*Genesis* 27).

However, the Priestly source considered Isaac's story an important one. He serves as the link in the family tree between Abraham and Jacob, and his story helps to give a better historical sense to the rest of Genesis. In fact, the entire grouping of Jacob stories is placed under the heading "This is the family history of Isaac, son of Abraham" (*Genesis* 25:19).

Part of the reason more of Isaac's life is not detailed may be for lack of drama concerning his acceptance of God's promise. His father, Abraham, uprooted and moved an entire people at God's command; his son, Jacob, outwitted an older brother to gain God's blessing. Isaac simply accepted God's promises. That he did so is an essential, though undramatic, link in the story of the patriarchs and the Israelites.

Jacob Who Became Israel

If Isaac was a man strong of character, Jacob was another sort altogether. At the least, Jacob can be described as clever. At the worst, he might be called a common thief. Nevertheless, his story shows the power of God to accomplish great things with less-than-perfect material. The story of Jacob reminded Israel that their election as God's People rests on God's free choice solely, and not on any individual's goodness or behavior.

The Inheritance   Jacob was the second son of Isaac; his brother, Esau, was the older twin. In what was the tradition of the time (in fact, still so in many countries of the world today), the first-born son would inherit the majority of the material goods or blessings from the father. This tradition meant that Esau was in line for the inheritance of Isaac. Jacob, meanwhile, looked for an opportunity to take it away from him.

Genesis 25:27–34 reports what happened. After a day of hunting, a famished Esau returned home. He asked Jacob for some of the lentil stew he was cooking. Jacob replied: "First give me your birthright in exchange for it."

"Look, I'm on the point of dying. What good will any birthright do me?" Esau said. The deal was quickly made; Jacob gave a starving Esau a bowl of stew, but only in exchange for his birthright.

The Final Blessing   Genesis leaves little doubt as to Jacob's true nature: he was a scoundrel. In Genesis 27:1–45, Jacob resorts to an outright lie to win his father's final and most powerful blessing.

- When Isaac is so old that he can no longer see, his wife, Rebekah, calls her son Jacob and advises him to trick his father.
- Jacob puts on Esau's clothes and enters Isaac's tent.
- Isaac is fooled, and grants Jacob his blessing.

In the ancient world, a father's final blessing was considered to be extremely valuable. Such attempts to steal a father's blessing (and, thus, a brother's inheritance) are condemned in other places in the Hebrew Scripture (see especially Hosea 12:4 and Jeremiah 9:3). Genesis, itself, leads the reader to sympathize with the innocent Esau. However, Jacob's behavior does serve a purpose. Through Jacob, Genesis shows how God uses even the weak and sinful to further the divine plan.

Jacob Marries   As you might expect, this last deception ends the relationship between the brothers. Jacob flees the area, and goes back to Haran (where Abraham had lived). There, he meets the shepherd, Laban. Jacob wishes to marry Laban's younger daughter Rachel, and agrees to work for seven years to win her hand.

Finally, the wedding night arrives, but Laban had planned a secret trick of his own. Older daughters were traditionally married before younger ones, so Laban substituted Rachel's older sister, Leah, for Jacob's beloved. Because brides were veiled and tents were dark, Jacob did not notice the deception until morning.

The victim of a devious scheme himself, Jacob now has to accept Leah as his wife and must labor another seven years to marry Rachel. Jacob does so. Later, he plans a return to Canaan where he will inevitably meet his brother again.

Jacob Wrestles with God   On the way home, Jacob encounters a messenger of God in a cave. The two wrestle until daybreak. Before the messenger departs, he asks: "What is your name?" After Jacob tells him, the man replies,

> *You shall no longer be spoken of as Jacob, but as Israel, because you have contended with divine and human beings and have prevailed.*
>
> (Genesis 32:29)

From that point on, the Genesis narrative no longer shows Jacob as the deceiver and thief, but rather as *Israel*, the important ancestor of Abraham and Isaac, and the father of the twelve tribes.

Notice how in both the Ishmael/Isaac story and the Esau/Jacob story, Genesis says that the divine promise passed to the younger brother. At this time, the standard practice among nations was that the oldest son inherited his father's place (for example, the oldest son of the king becomes king when the father dies). By showing that the promise passed to Isaac and Jacob, the authors of Genesis reinforced the idea that God's ways are often different from human expectations, and that God especially liked to use the weaker or lesser to accomplish splendid divine purposes.

Twelve Tribes

According to tradition, Jacob had twelve sons and one daughter.

- Six of the sons were born to Leah, his "unloved" wife (see Genesis 29:31–35). The names of those sons were Reuben, Simeon, Levi, Judah, Issachar, and Zebulun. Leah also had a daughter, Dinah.

- Through Leah's servant Zilpah, Jacob had the son, Gad.
- Like Sarah, Rachel was infertile, so she sent her servant Bilhah to Jacob. Bilhah had the sons Dan and Naphtali.
- Also like Sarah, Rachel had sons in her old age. They were named Joseph and Benjamin.

Over the centuries, as the final list of twelve tribes developed, the Israelites looked back to Jacob and credited him with fathering the first twelve tribes. The two sons of Joseph, Manasseh and Ephraim, split up his tribe, bringing the total to 12. (The tribe of Levi was not counted since they served as priests for all other tribes.) By tying all 12 tribes into a common family story, the authors of Genesis showed Israel that all her members shared a common bond. Despite the eventual split-up of Israel into northern and southern kingdoms, this family tree helped preserve an awareness of the unity of all Israelites.

Joseph

Jacob loved his sons by Rachel, especially Joseph. The story of Joseph in Genesis 37–50 is written as if it were a short novel, and shows evidence of both the "J" and "E" sources.

The story begins by establishing that Joseph is disliked by his older brothers because he is Jacob's favorite. Consider how you would feel toward a brother or sister whom you feel is your parents' favorite. Joseph is also disliked because he has the ability to interpret dreams. Unfortunately, every dream seems to elevate Joseph's stature, while downgrading that of his brothers. Joseph's brothers get even by selling him into slavery in Egypt.

In Egypt, however, Joseph's special abilities are soon noticed and he become a trusted assistant to the Pharaoh. Later there is a famine in the whole area of Canaan and Egypt. But Joseph, interpreting dreams, predicted the famine and organized a food

The saga of Joseph is preserved in the records of Egypt.

Egyptian, Fourteenth Century B.C.E.

conservation program in Egypt. When Jacob's sons come to Egypt to buy food, they once again meet Joseph. Because of Joseph's success, the whole family moves to Egypt. Thus Joseph, by remaining true to God in spite of adversities, was able to save the family of Jacob/Israel, the traditional ancestor of the people of Israel.

This story forms a bridge between the patriarchs in Canaan and the nearly 500 years of history before the time when Moses would mold the people of Israel into God's Chosen People. Once again, it also shows us that God sometimes picks unlikely people to bear the promises of the covenant, as Joseph is the next to youngest of his brothers, and is sold into slavery as a youth.

It's possible that the story of Joseph was written by someone other than the "J," "P" or "E" sources. Joseph is the perfect example of the "wise man" whose life is totally successful because he behaves in a wise and good manner. This type of literature is typical of the "Wisdom school" which you will study in Chapter 9. In later times, beginning with Solomon, wisdom was a valued type of education. Some scholars think that Wisdom writers crafted the story of Joseph.

Have You Considered?

1. Genesis stresses again and again that God's promises are always kept, even if they are not immediately accomplished. Since the book was finalized during the Babylonian Exile, why would God's faithfulness be an important theme for the Israelites?
2. Why do you suppose that the authors of Genesis told negative stories such as those told about Jacob? What might they have been trying to say?
3. America is a place where many different cultures live side-by-side. How important do you think it is that we all share some common family story such as the one in Genesis? Would such a common story help us deal with the tensions that always exist between different groups?

Spiritual Reflection

Praying for our Ancestors

God said to Jacob/Israel:
"I am God Almighty;
be fruitful and multiply.
A nation, indeed an assembly of nations,
shall stem from you,
and kings shall issue from your loins.
The land I once gave to Abraham and Isaac
I now give you;
And to your descendants after you
will I give this land"

(Genesis 35:11–12)

As members of the Church, we pray for our ancestors in faith as they pray for us. Recite this prayer of blessing (from the final commendation and farewell of the Funeral rite), in memory of a friend or relative who has died:

Leader: Saints of God, come to their aid! Come to meet them, angels of the Lord!

Response: Receive their soul and present them to God the Most High.

Leader: May Christ, who called them, take them to Himself; may angels lead them to Abraham's side.

Response: Receive their soul and present them to God the Most High.

Leader: Give them eternal rest, O Lord, and may your light shine on them forever.

Response: Receive their soul and present them to God the Most High.

Q/A

Section One

1. Why do all people and cultures cherish their family stories?
2. Define the term "source" as it is used in connection to the Bible.
3. Why are the three sources of Genesis known by the names Yahwist, Elohist, and Priestly? When did each of the three authors of Genesis ("J", "E", and "P") write?
4. What is a "myth"?
5. List and define the four functions of myth.
6. Define the "oral tradition."
7. What is a "legend"?
8. What is a "saga"?

Section Two

1. Name two differences and two similarities in comparing the "J" and "P" creation myths.
2. According to the Priestly author, what was the climax of creation?
3. How does the pattern of awareness, choice, conse-quences, and mercy repeat itself in the stories of Cain and Abel, the Flood, and the Tower of Babel?
4. Why were the stories of the patriarchs important to Israel?
5. What was the promise that Yahweh made to Abraham?
6. How is Isaac important to the story of the patriarchs?
7. What is learned from Yahweh's use of Jacob to further the divine plan?
8. How does the Joseph story show us that God some-times works through unlikely people?

BIBLE ACTIVITY

1. Psalm 104 is a hymn of praise to God the Creator. Select the verses that remind you of the Priestly story of creation.
2. Compare the waters of the Flood and the waters of Baptism. What are both waters intended to do?
3. Read Deuteronomy 26:5–10 and answer these questions: (a) Who is the "wandering Aramean"? (b) Who is "my father"? (3) What happened to the people in Egypt?
4. Write a story explaining how the patriarchs are your religious ancestors. If you don't feel that way about the patriarchs, pick people who you think are your religious ancestors, and write about them.
5. Divide a piece of paper into two columns. On the left side, list things that God asked Abraham to give up; on the right side list the blessings Abraham received from God. Use Genesis 12, 13, and 15 for reference.

Legend has it that Noah's ark landed safely on Mount Ararat in modern Turkey. No physical evidence of the ark has ever been found.

GLOSSARY

- **Abraham:** The original patriarch and the first to receive God's promise.
- **Cosmic Function:** The function of myth which tells us what the world is like and what its purpose is.
- **Elohist:** The writer of some parts of Genesis and other books in the Pentateuch. The Elohist (or "E") is so named for calling God "Elohim."
- **Ethical Function:** The function of myth which tells us what values humans should have and how they should behave.
- **Legends:** Unverifiable stories about heroic people and significant events of the past; they include both fact and fiction.
- **Matriarch:** A woman who is the ancestor of a people, the "mother" of generations.
- **Myths:** Symbolic stories which express religious truths that cannot be proved by historical or scientific means.
- **Oral traditions:** Stories about events and people which are preserved by retelling; they are usually quite consistent. Oral traditions form the basis of much of the biblical writing.
- **Patriarch:** A man who is the "father" of many descendants, the ancestor of a people.
- **Priestly writers:** People during the Exile and post-Exile period who collected the sacred traditions of ancient Israel, preserved them, and interpreted them for future generations.
- **Saga:** A form of legend which concerns some important person of the past.
- **Scribe:** A professional writer and copyist who has responsibility for taking care of a culture's literature. Scribes often felt free to add to and/or rearrange the books they were given.
- **Social Function:** The function of myth which tells us how society should be organized and who should be in charge.
- **Theological Function:** The function of myth which tells people what the gods are like and how they relate with humans.
- **Yahwist:** Also known as the "J" author; the writer of some parts of Genesis, the rest of the Pentateuch, and other books; uses *Yahweh* as the name for God.

UNDERSTANDING MORE ABOUT:

Holy Places

You have already heard of the "Ark of the Covenant" in Chapter 3, when King David brought it to Jerusalem. The Ark was a symbol for the Israelites of their days as wanderers, as in the time of Abraham and the other patriarchs.

The Ark of the Covenant was a special container made of wood and covered with gold that housed the tablets with the written words of the Law and other sacred items. The word "ark" means "chest." When the Israelites traveled through the desert, the Ark led the way.

When the Israelites camped, the Ark was placed in the center of the *Meeting Tent,* also known as the *Dwelling* or *Tabernacle.* The priestly writers described the Dwelling as a tent with a long wooden frame which fit together and made a rectangular building 30 x 10 x 10 cubits (a cubit, remember, is a measure equivalent to about 1 1/2 feet).

The Dwelling was the center of the political and religious life of the Israelites. The Priestly writers acknowledged that God lived in heaven and not on earth. Thus, they did not say that God lived in the sanctuary, but rather that God "pitched His tent" there. The authors did not say that the Tent contained God, rather that God's name dwelt there.

Elijah and the Divided Kingdom

Legend

● General History
● Biblical History
● Jewish History
● Books written

I n the early 1960s, General Motors (GM), one of the largest corporations in the world, built a very popular, inexpensive sports car called the "Corvair." Over the course of a few years, however, evidence began to mount that the Corvair was more than an enjoyable car; because of design flaws, it was also a dangerous one. While many people knew about the Corvair's problems, few were willing to take on powerful GM to get the problems corrected.

Ralph Nader was not frightened away by GM's political or financial power. In his book, *Unsafe at Any Speed*, (1965), Nader argued that the American auto industry made cars that were dangerous to drive. Because of Nader's outspokenness and dedication to the truth, GM eventually decided to stop building the Corvair.

Then, in 1966, the United States Congress passed legislation that set auto safety standards. Millions of people who have survived or even avoided auto accidents since 1966 owe their lives, in some degree, to the willingness of Ralph Nader to speak the truth without fear.

In 1940, Germany's war machine was wreaking havoc throughout the Western world. Its armies controlled all of Europe (except Great Britain and a few other countries) and Northern Africa, and was racing to Moscow in the Soviet Union.They seemed unbeatable. At home in Germany and in the territories they controlled, Adolph Hitler and his government were completing a plan that would be known as the "Final Solution:" the extermination of every Jew from the face of the earth.

While other citizens stood back and watched, the German police and groups of young thugs confiscated Jewish-owned properties, beat the Jewish people without mercy, and then stuffed them into cattle cars and shipped them by rail to concentration camps. Over 6 million Jews and a million others were murdered in these camps in what we now call the Holocaust.

Not all Germans stood quietly in the face of this evil. Some spoke out against the German government. Some, like Oskar Schindler—who rescued hundreds of Jewish prisoners from the death camps—did something quietly. Franz Jägerstätter simply told the truth. When drafted into the German Army, Franz refused to serve. He could have taken a status that would have allowed him to serve as a medical corpsman so that he personally would not have to fight, but he refused that as well.

Franz chose to denounce the evil that was all around him. He could not, as a person of integrity, ignore or be part of it. He was jailed for his statements and threatened with death. All that he would have to do was join the army and he would be saved. But Franz knew better, for he was a man of great faith. He was sure that God's teaching was against this war. Frans refused to join and was put to death for his stand.

Franz' death did not stop the war; it went on for several more years. But his death was not in vain either. Since the end of the war, Franz' story has spread throughout the world. He is honored as a hero in his country and serves as a solitary witness of strength for all people who take a stand against injustice. The book, In *Solitary Witness* by Gordon Zahn recounts Franz Jägerstätter's act of courage.

Have you ever met an inspiring person who was unafraid to speak the truth, even if it might embarrass someone very important? The Bible records the behavior and activities of a group of people who behaved in just this way. Today, these people might be called "loud mouths" or "troublemakers" for their seemingly rude or inconsiderate comments. The Bible, however, calls these people *"prophets."* In this chapter, you'll learn about these people who were unafraid to speak the truth.

From David to the Divided Kingdom

Prophets were deeply involved with the political and social concerns of their society. They weren't just politicians, however; they viewed politics and society from the perspective of God's word and Israel's obligation under the Covenant. In fact, if their prophetic work had not been focused on God, it would have lost all meaning and the prophets would have been forgotten long ago. The messages of the prophets that we will consider in this chapter and Chapter 6 developed over a period of about 400 years.

Learning Objectives for Section One

By the end of this section, you will be able to:

- Explain how the policies of Solomon led to the split between North and South and violated the Covenant.
- Define "syncretism" and explain why it was a problem for the Israelites.
- Identify the nations of "Israel" and "Judah" after the Civil War.

◆ Politics

It is not unusual for countries to dissolve because of internal political disputes. Consider what happened when the former nation of Yugoslavia divided into the countries of Serbia, Croatia, Bosnia-Hercegovina, Montenegro, and Macedonia in the early 1990s.

Yugoslavia had been formed from many smaller ethnic territories in 1918. As long as strong political leadership existed, these unlikely partners stayed together as a nation. But with the fall of the Soviet Union, Yugoslavia quickly came apart. Feuds dating back to the Middle Ages, anger over supposed ethnic favoritism, and nationalistic desires erupted into brutal warfare, resulting in Hitler-like "ethnic cleansing" and the destruction of a once prosperous nation.

The nation of Israel experienced a similar division. You remember from Chapter 3 that when the tribal groups became the people of Israel, it was because of the Covenant with Yahweh, not because

they agreed on any particular political system. The Covenant was the reason the nation of Israel existed, and even then it took the genius of King David to form these vastly different tribes into what is called the *United Monarchy*. Although the Bible talks about the 12 Tribes of Israel as if they were a close-knit family, historical evidence—in the Bible and elsewhere—reveals an uneasy union.

Throughout Israel's history, both before and during the monarchy, ancient rivalries and disputes simmered, needing only a slight breeze from an inept leader to ignite the people into full-fledged rebellion. While it's true that Israel was also held together through the power of the Covenant, that power was limited. Ultimately, the people's commitment to the Covenant could not overcome problems of state.

Disunity Under Solomon

Solomon, the son of David and Bathsheba, inherited a strong empire. Israel's borders were broad and secure, its influence was widespread, and it had been at peace with its neighbors for several decades. Yet, while the economy prospered, old hostilities festered like open wounds beneath the surface of outward tranquillity. As a result, the cracks of disunity widened in the kingdom during Solomon's reign.

Solomon's greatest strength, according to the Bible and Hebrew tradition, was a deep wisdom given to him by God. Solomon is said to have made excellent judgments and to have written thousands of proverbs. At the beginning of his reign, Solomon worshipped Yahweh and was humble before God.

Solomon may have been wise in important respects, but his policies contributed to the eventual division of Israel.

1. Even though the country was wealthy, the wealth was not equally distributed; the poor suffered while others became wealthy.
2. Solomon spent lavishly to build the Temple of the Lord, for which the Deuteronomic historian and all later biblical traditions honor him.
3. Solomon also built a large palace, including plenty of rooms for his huge harem.

Solomon spent Israel's wealth with little regard to stewardship for all his subjects.

Solomon Abuses His Power

Solomon's wealth was based on two factors: advantageous trade with other nations and the common use of forced labor. Both of these policies were disruptive to the life of Israel.

Scripture Workshop

Solomon's Wealth

- Read 1 Kings 10:14–29. If each shekel of gold was worth $10 in American money, and if each talent was worth fifteen hundred shekels, how much money did Solomon receive in gold every year? How much did he pay for horses and chariots? How much were each of his shields worth?
- Read 1 Kings 11:1–8. How many wives of princely rank did Solomon have? How did he show favor to them? (A "high place" is an altar or shrine to a foreign god, usually located on a hilltop.)
- Solomon built a large commercial shipping system. Read 1 Kings 9: 26–28. How much money in gold did these ships return from Ophir? In 1 Kings 10: 22–25, what did the ships bring Solomon?

Forced Labor   Forced labor meant that every able-bodied man was required to work directly for the king for a certain period every year. While he worked

Building the Temple is remembered as Solomon's greatest accomplishment.

for the king, his own job was neglected, he left his family behind, and he was not paid. It was his legal obligation to the king; he had no choice.

Many years before Solomon, when the people had begged for a king, Samuel had warned them that a king would use forced labor to generate wealth (1 Samuel 8:10–18).

Forced labor created discontent throughout Israel among the people and the leaders of the various tribes. This resentment was especially strong in the North, because most of the forced labor came from there, while most of the building took place in the South. The best example of a building project in the South is the famous Temple of Solomon.

Prosperous Trade Israel also enjoyed prosperous trade relations made possible by Solomon's many alliances with other countries. Solomon secured Israel's alliances with these countries through the use of *"summit marriages."* Such a marriage occurs when a member of one royal family marries a member of another royal family. Once married, the two royal families (and therefore the nations) were considered allies for the duration of the marriage.

Kings were expected to have many wives for the benefit of the country. However, when Solomon's foreign wives also brought with them their own gods, religious practices, and priests, it was too much for the people of the Covenant to bear.

Note that neither forced labor nor summit marriages were considered wrong at this time. Solomon was doing only what all other kings had done for centuries. Today, in the democracy of the United States, we recognize that forced labor is an injustice. But in the ninth century B.C.E., in an economy not totally based on money, forced labor was simply a form of taxation. It was, as 1 Samuel 8:9,11 clearly says, the right of kings.

Have You Considered?

1. In what sense did forced labor help cause the Civil War in the United States? How similar was this situation to the one in the time of King Solomon?
2. Why would it bother the people of Israel for Solomon's wives to introduce the worship of their own gods? What part of the Law did this act violate?
3. Summit marriages were used to link countries together as allies. How are agreements sealed today?

The Bible in Context

Solomon's Mines

Solomon built a temple which was one of the wonders of the ancient world. The Temple was built with cedar and stone, but most of it was plated with gold, so that it reflected the sun and could be seen even at a great distance. Inside the Temple, the stonework was plated with gold and ivory. It must have been an awesome sight.

Solomon used so much gold in building the Temple that some people have speculated that he must have had a secret gold mine. 1 Kings 10:11 says that Solomon's fleet brought gold from a place called "Ophir." People have debated the location of Ophir for centuries, with some saying it was in Arabia, others in India, and still others in Africa.

A famous adventure story by H. Rider Haggard, *King Solomon's Mines*, placed Ophir in a fictional Central African country. In the nineteenth century, many people thought that the lost city of Zimbabwe in Africa contained the secret mine (a Roman coin was even found at the site).

Archaeologists have established, however, that Zimbabwe could not have been built before 500 C.E. Today, the most likely site for Ophir is thought to be a spot on the Red Sea in Saudi Arabia. This theory, however, has not stopped adventurers from seeking the "lost mine" in obscure places across the globe.

◆ Violations of Covenant Law

Israel was different from other countries because of the Covenant with Yahweh, which was the basic reason for the existence of the nation. Solomon's policies were seen by many Israelites, especially those in the northern part of the kingdom, as a violation of Covenant law.

The justice issue of forced labor was a major problem. The unequal distribution of the country's wealth was not only a source of individual discontent, but it was also a violation of the Covenant principle that all people were of equal worth before Yahweh, and therefore equal before the Law.

Solomon's foreign wives violated the Covenant. They brought with them into Israel religious allegiance to gods other than Yahweh. In order for the wives to practice their religion, shrines were built to idols. Furthermore, as Solomon grew older, he joined his wives in the worship of these foreign gods (1 *Kings* 11:1–13). In doing so, Solomon was acting like any other king in the ancient world, who was expected to honor his wife's gods. What Solomon forgot, however, was the Covenant's demand that Israel be different than other nations.

The Importance of Religion

While living by their religious values is important for some Americans, for others today religion is largely separate from public life. Society is "secular," meaning non-religious. Our society does not assume that God is involved with politics, foreign policy, or military action. Many people who consider themselves religious think of religion only on Sunday or when tragedy occurs.

Even though we assume that this separation between religion and the rest of life is normal, it's not. Religion of some kind has influenced all previous cultures. Religion is the foundation of societies—their life-blood; the essence of their view of the world.

In the ancient Middle East, all of life was religious. A truly secular viewpoint was unimaginable. People believed that every event occurred because God wanted it to, so every event had religious importance. Religion included not only the individual, but the community and state as well. Government power was believed to come from their god, so foreign alliances were also religious alliances.

No doubt, an individual king might keep his private allegiance to his own god, as ordinary folks also did. In the Middle East, variety in religion was tolerated. Most people did not think it was a problem to mix religions, except for the Yahwists, whose God was known as the "Jealous One."

Why Worship Only One God?

Many people in Israel must have asked, "Why does Israel worship only Yahweh? If a lot of gods exist, why not respect and worship whichever ones can help us most?" This question was very practical, since ancient people assumed that different gods had different responsibilities: one god controlled the crops, another childbirth, another commerce, and so on. If this division of labor was true, didn't it simply make sense to honor all of those gods rather than just one?

People wanted very practical knowledge about the gods and wanted to know who was in charge. They wanted to know:

- Who can save us? Who can keep us from trouble and evil?
- Who is in charge of rain, storms and earthquakes?
- Who makes animals and plants reproduce? Who keeps the ground fertile? Who has power over this vast world?
- How does one get justice? Who is the real judge who keeps humans in line with justice? Who condemns and who sets free? What is the last court of appeal for people and for nations?
- Who answers prayer? Even if more than one god is "out there," who responds to my cry? How can I reach that one?
- Who determines which nation prospers and which languishes?
- Do human beings, especially the Israelites, have any control over their own lives? How?

These were living questions. The answers to them made a big difference in people's choices and behavior; the answers determined how people lived. Those answers also determined people's attitudes about how Israel should relate to other nations and their gods.

For strict Yahwists, the Covenant provided all the answers. Yahweh, the only God of the Israelites, was the force behind everything that happened to them. It took the Israelites centuries, however, to understand that Yahweh was the one real power in the universe.

Popular Religious Practice

Religions, in 850 B.C.E., were fully *syncretistic*. *Syncretism* means the attempt to blend differing religious systems into one belief, without distinguishing one from another.

Despite the demands of the Covenant, syncretism took place in Israel. Belief and worship of gods other than Yahweh gradually became part of Hebrew religious practices. This blending of beliefs came about quite gradually, so that most people would never have noticed the change. People could have mistakenly worshipped a foreign god when they thought that they were worshipping Yahweh as the Covenant demanded.

Ordinary people would probably have trouble explaining why they shouldn't mix religious practices. When the Israelites settled in Canaan among people who had been farmers for centuries, they had to learn how to be successful farmers themselves.

Gold figurine of Astarte. Tenth Century B.C.E.

The Canaanite people prayed to the goddess Astarte. The prophets complained that the Israelites also prayed to her.

in the Spotlight

Syncretism

Syncretism happens whenever different cultures come into contact and exchange religious ideas. As a result, almost all religions, past and present, have been affected by syncretism to some extent. Let's take two examples, one historical and one from the present, which illustrate how syncretism works.

Isis and Sarapis

Six centuries after Solomon, Alexander the Great conquered much of the world. He brought with him the culture of Greece, including Greek religious ideas. These ideas interacted with the religious concepts of the people Alexander conquered, often resulting in syncretism. An example of this are the Egyptian gods Isis and Sarapis.

Traditionally, the Egyptians thought of their gods in the form of animals. They worshipped the god Apis in the form of a bull, and Isis as a cow. Under the impact of Greek ideas, however, Apis was combined with the Greek god Zeus, and was pictured as a powerful male with a flowing beard. He was called Sarapis. Isis became the beautiful young female goddess Demeter. In this form, Isis and Sarapis became popular all over Europe and the Middle East. Like the Egyptian gods, they had power over immortality, but like the Greek gods, they had human forms and behaviors.

Santería

A contemporary example of syncretism is the religion called "Santería." Santeria has its roots in West African tribal religions focused on spirits and souls. When these religions were brought to islands such as Cuba and Haiti by African slaves, they interacted with the Roman Catholic faith of the European settlers. Santería, which blends elements of voodoo, tribal religion, and Catholicism, is a result of this interaction.

Santeros and Santeras (people who practice Santería) believe in many spirits (called orishas) who can bring good luck in business and love, and who can protect them from evil. Often, these spirits are depicted as Catholic saints, especially the Virgin Mary. Santeros sacrifice goats, chickens, pigs, roosters, and other animals to these spirits to win their favor. The U.S. Supreme Court ruled such sacrifices legal in 1993.

- They needed to be sure of nature's cooperation: the right amount of rain and sun, and the natural reproductive cycles of their animals.
- They needed protection from natural disasters—drought, violent storm, earthquakes.

The Israelites saw the successful Canaanite farmers worshipping the gods of nature—the fertility god, *Baal*, and the fertility goddess, *Astarte*—whose sexual activity was believed to keep the earth and its inhabitants fertile.

Since it was the fertility gods' sexual activity that kept everything going in nature, worship of these gods involved sexual intercourse with "sacred prostitutes," women who dedicated themselves to the fertility god and gave their bodies to male worshippers for religious rites. Male "sacred prostitutes" performed similar homosexual rites. These rituals seemed logical to many Israelites, who thought they kept the earth fertile and the crops growing.

Even when fidelity to the Covenant was strong, many Israelites practiced fertility religion in addition to their worship of Yahweh. Isn't it logical that a farmer would want to worship the god that he believed had power over farming? And isn't it logical that a newcomer in a culture would learn from the natives in the area what it took to live successfully there?

The Yahwists knew, however, that this logic was false. The people of the Covenant were committed to serve and worship one god only: Yahweh. Yahweh required total loyalty from Israel, and worship of other gods was a violation of the Covenant. Because of this violation of the Covenant, Yahweh sent prophets to call Israel back to faithfulness.

Have You Considered?

1. How do people today separate their religious life from their public or common life? What are the consequences of this behavior?
2. Israel was, for most of its history, a tiny nation against great empires. How do you think the prohibition against syncretism helped it maintain its identity in such a situation?
3. Exodus refers to Yahweh as "the Jealous One." Why would this understanding of the Covenant lead to inevitable conflict between those who strictly followed the Covenant and those who were willing to worship other gods?

Civil War is always brutal, whether in ninth century B.C.E. Israel or in twentieth century C.E. Bosnia.

◆ The Collapse of the Nation

The worship of foreign gods, the unequal distribution of wealth, and the injustice of forced labor were like small flames, waiting only for a wind to catch them and blow them into raging firestorms. This wind was to be Solomon's successor, his son, Rehoboam.

The elders of the northern tribes came to Rehoboam to find out what his policies were to be. Rehoboam, an egotistical brat, said to them, "If you think my father was difficult, wait until you see me." With that, the northern tribes rebelled. They expelled Rehoboam from the Covenant and seceded from the United Monarchy (1 *Kings* 12:1–16). It was civil war. The 12 tribes would never be united again.

The kingdom put together by David and Solomon now split into two separate nations at war with each other: Israel to the north and Judah to the south. After this time, only the Northern kingdom is called "Israel."

Israel and Judah accused each other of violating the Covenant. The North objected to Solomon's policies. The South thought that rebellion against the House of David violated the Covenant. Further, because the northern king, Jeroboam, set up national shrines in Dan and Bethel so that his citizens would not be tempted to look to Jerusalem as their center of worship and government, Judah accused Israel of false worship.

By 850 B.C.E., sixty or seventy years of civil war had left the two nations greatly weakened. The borders of David's kingdom were now much smaller. Conditions in the countries were bad because so much of their resources went into the fight. Even when Israel and Judah were not actively at war, they were spying, intriguing and plotting against one another.

Fortunately for Israel's and Judah's continued existence, neither Egypt nor any of the Mesopotamian nations were aggressive during this time. Israel and Judah did struggle with the smaller countries around them—Moab, Edom, Syria, and Phoenicia. Since all of these countries were fairly evenly matched, none could really dominate. Power would ebb and flow between them.

The poverty that most people lived in compared to the king's extravagance was a cause of Israel's civil war.

Conflicts between Rich and Poor

By 850, social conditions had also worsened. The poor were getting poorer, the rich richer. The weak had less and less power while the strong became more powerful. Royalty and the higher classes were now legally able to extort what they wanted from the lower class.

The two Israelite kingdoms were equally guilty of this behavior, although injustice seems to have been worse in the Northern kingdom than in the South. Such injustice was clearly a violation of the Covenant.

In the Covenant, Yahweh had established principles for people's relationship with each other based on *justice*. Yahweh's *Covenant law* was designed to ensure social harmony. The Covenant law treated all people equally: Just is just and crime is crime, no matter whether one is rich or poor, powerful or weak. Since the Covenant belonged to Yahweh, Yahweh was in charge of justice. But this aspect of Covenant Law was widely ignored by 850 B.C.E. Chief among those who were still loyal to the Covenant were the prophets.

Have You Considered?

1. What were the primary reasons the North broke away from the South? What were the secondary reasons?
2. Read 1 Kings 12:1–16. What major mistake did Rehoboam make with the people of Israel? What might he have done differently to preserve the nation?
3. Compare what you know about the American civil war with the fight between Israel and Judah. What do you think are the major similarities and differences?

LEARN FROM THE MAP

Ancient Israel

Although Saul was king of Israel, the country was surrounded by hostile neighbors. As king, David established Israel as a nation with borders respected by its neighbors. Under David's rule, Israel was able to expand its borders. Many of the small nations surrounding Israel were forced to pay tribute and to accept some degree of subordination to it.

After the death of Solomon, the ten northern tribes became the nation of Israel with its capitol and religious center in Samaria. The two southern tribes, Judah and Benjamin became the nation of Judah with its political and religious capitol in Jerusalem.

The two separate nations were never as strong as David's kingdom had been. They could not hold all of the territory that had been gained. The smaller nations that had paid David tribute reclaimed their independence and became military adversaries of Israel and Judah.

Compare David's empire with the kingdoms of Israel and Judah in 850 B.C.E. How do they differ? Explain the reasons for the differences.

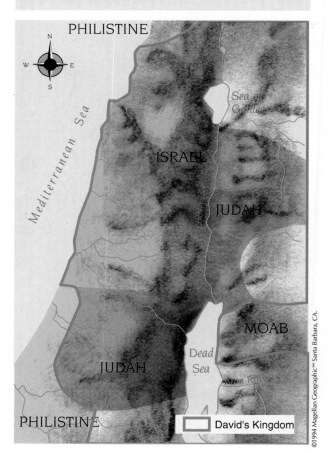

The Role of the Prophets

Michelangelo, *Sibyl, The Prophetess of Cuma. Sixteenth Century*

The Hebrew word translated as "prophet" is nabi (<u>*pronounced nah-bee*</u>). Nabi can mean either "one who calls out, announces" or "one who is called."

The essential point about all the great prophets is that they were "possessed" by the spirit of Yahweh. Yahweh's spirit filled the personality of the individual, somewhat as it had changed the personalities of the judges years earlier and impelled the prophet to speak Yahweh's word and act out Yahweh's message. God used the prophets to affect the lives of people in both kingdoms.

Learning Objectives for Section Two

By the end of this section, you will be able to:

- Identify the different kinds of prophets.
- Understand the three elements of the prophetic word.
- Explain the significance of the prophets Elijah and Elisha to the history of Israel.
- Recognize the parallels between the prophets' situation and our own.

◆ Who Were the Prophets?

Different types of prophets are mentioned in the Old Testament. Some of them had official positions in society while others did not. Among the people who made their living as prophets were seers and official court prophets. "Unofficial" prophets served only when moved by the spirit of Yahweh and for them, prophecy was not a means of livelihood. Let's look at each of these types of prophets in turn.

Seers

From the time that Israel crossed the Jordan following the Exodus, there had been prophets loosely connected with shrines and places of worship around the country. There they offered answers to people who came to worship, to seek advice, or to ask a divine favor. These prophets were called "ecstatics" or "seers."

Seers seem to have depended on altered states of consciousness to receive their messages from Yahweh. They might listen to music to help them into these states, and sometimes they danced or sang as well. These ecstatic prophets saw visions, heard messages in dreams, and predicted the future. Their behavior suggested that they were not their usual selves, but were "possessed" by the spirit of Yahweh, and they acted accordingly.

Most prophets lived in groups. Today, we might call these groups *prophetic guilds*. Participation in a group often enhanced ecstatic states, for the condition seemed to be quite contagious when a person was susceptible (like Saul in 1 *Samuel* 10:10–13). Group life also helped, no doubt, with such necessities as food and shelter. Prophetic guilds lived on the edge of society and were sometimes summoned by the king or other officials to answer a question by the spirit of Yahweh (1 *Kings* 22, for example).

Samuel (mentioned in Chapter 3) is an example of a seer. He became a great leader of the Israelites, who revered his closeness to Yahweh.

People of Note

Women Who Were Prophets

The Old Testament makes no distinction between male and female prophets. Even so, only a few women are called by that title. Female prophets include Miriam, Deborah, and Huldah.

- **Miriam** is the sister of Moses and Aaron and is often mentioned as one of the trio of leaders during the Exodus. The Lord spoke through her as well as Aaron and Moses, though Moses was clearly the greatest—as Miriam found out to her pain when she challenged him (Numbers 12:1–15). Miriam's death is recorded in Numbers 20:1, something the Old Testament does only for important people. Miriam is called a prophet in the Book of Exodus 15: 20–21.

- The prophet **Deborah** was a judge and a warrior in the period before Samuel. She held court under a palm tree, and people came to her to settle their disputes. She led Israel into battle and predicted its victory. The story of this battle is in Judges 4; it reads like a modern newspaper story. Judges 5 records a hymn of triumph attributed to Deborah herself.

- **Huldah** was also consulted by a king during a time of crisis. When he discovered a book in the Temple and wondered what to do, King Josiah (640–609 B.C.E.) ordered his priest and servants to "Go, consult the Lord for me." They went to Huldah, a prophet and the wife of the wardrobe keeper in the Jerusalem court. She gave them the word of the Lord. See 2 Kings 22:1–20.

Court Prophets

Other prophets, usually not of the ecstatic type, held official positions in the royal court. These prophets received messages from Yahweh through rolling dice or sometimes through a dream. They, too, were impelled by the spirit to speak and act out the words of Yahweh, no matter what the risk was to themselves.

Some court prophets had a function similar to public relations people today. Their job was to always predict great success and prosperity for the king, no matter what was going on. The king would usually keep a staff of such prophets to calm the public when things went wrong, and to dispute other prophets when they criticized the king. Nathan and later court prophets true to Yahweh were constantly arguing with these "P.R. prophets."

Although prophets were often treated with greater respect in Israel because the life of a prophet was considered sacred to Yahweh, their lives and income depended on the king. At this time, messengers who brought bad news to the king were often killed on the spot. A prophet who spoke the word of the Lord directly, no matter whom that word challenged—even the king—had to be courageous.

One such courageous prophet was Nathan. Nathan was the official court prophet for King David. He had personal access to the king and kept a history of events, which has been lost (see 1 Chronicles 29:29). David often sought Nathan's advice, such as when David wanted to build a temple for the Lord. Through Nathan, the Lord gave David information about his work and his dynasty (2 Samuel 7:1–17). We know little about Nathan except for his official prophetic work.

The word of Yahweh through Nathan was not always pleasant. As you recall from Chapter 3, God sent Nathan to challenge King David face to face, condemning David for taking Bathsheba and having her husband murdered. Review that story now by reading again 2 Samuel 12:1–25. Instead of concentrating on David, though, notice Nathan.

- What did Nathan do?
- Why did he do it?
- What does this story tell you about the role of a court prophet in Israel?

Nathan didn't always act solely on the word of Yahweh. He was also a shrewd political manipulator. Consider how he conspired with Bathsheba and the head of David's army to ensure Solomon's succession to the throne over his older brothers who had a better claim by birth (1 Kings 1:1–53).

Unofficial Prophets

Other prophets did not belong to a guild or hold a position at court or in the Temple. Most of the great prophets whose works appear in the Old Testament were unofficial prophets. Lack of a professional position, however, by no means kept the prophets from answering the spirit of Yahweh or from doing what that spirit requested of them. For them, prophecy was not a job—it was their whole life.

The Bible describes a prophet in Deuteronomy 18:15–22. This description, probably written after the year 600 B.C.E., tells us what ancient Israel believed about Yahweh's prophets. It is a perfect description of the prophetic message.

1. **Clear and Direct.** The prophetic message did not come in the form of philosophical or theoretical explanations. Its words and acts were always about concrete situations and real-life issues. The prophets spoke and acted with power and persistence, sometimes with bitterness, sometimes with tenderness. Whatever the tone, their message was always directed to people's actual life situations, never to abstract principles.

2. **Addressed to Specific Audience.** The message might be directed to individuals, if they were socially important like the king or queen. Other messages were addressed to all the people of Israel or Judah.

3. **Immediate Action.** The message corresponded to issues happening right then in the society or the government. It was most often political—including Yahweh's word on foreign, military, or social policy. Yahweh sometimes inspired revolution and chose kings through the prophets, as he did through Elijah and Elisha (compare 1 *Kings* 19:15 with 2 *Kings* 8:7–15).

The prophetic word was never just information or advice. Yahweh's word was always a demand for action. People expected Yahweh to act in Israel's life; after all, that was how they had become a people under Moses.

Have You Considered?

1. Describe in your own words the difference between a court prophet, a seer, and an unofficial prophet.
2. Why would it take a great deal of courage to tell the king the truth, especially if the truth would be considered bad news? What might a less-than-brave prophet do in difficult situations?
3. If a prophet is someone who speaks the truth about politics and society on the basis of God's word, who are modern day prophets? What criteria would you use today to determine a modern prophet?

◆ Elijah

Elijah was an unofficial prophet. While he knew the prophetic guilds and sometimes associated with them, he generally acted alone. He was a faithful servant of Yahweh (1 *Kings* 18:36, 19:10), who followed the direction of the Lord. He was certainly not an ecstatic prophet. The description of the ecstatic Canaanite priests is in total contrast to the calm Elijah in 1 Kings 18.

Yet, Elijah was thoroughly possessed by Yahweh's powerful spirit. Through the Spirit, Elijah was a persistent and forceful advocate of Yahweh's Covenant with Israel.

The Challenge from King Ahab

By 850 B.C.E., the affairs of the Northern kingdom had reached a crisis stage. Ahab, the king of Israel, had married Jezebel, the daughter of the king of Tyre and Sidon (also called Phoenicia). The wedding of Ahab and Jezebel was a summit marriage designed to ratify an alliance between Israel and Phoenicia.

Jezebel brought with her to Israel a huge staff, including hundreds of priests of Baal-Melkart, a god of nature. She supported her staff from the public treasury. Ahab had a temple built for her to use. Although he himself probably was a Yahwist, he clearly saw no reason to be exclusive about his worship. Syncretism posed no problems for Ahab.

Ahab's father, Omri, had been a powerful ruler who built the city of Samaria for his capital. Samaria was so splendid that it remained the symbol of the Northern kingdom for centuries after its destruction. The "House of Omri" is mentioned in written records from surrounding countries, always with respect. The writer of the Book of Kings, however, did not approve of Omri's religious activities, so very little is said about him there (1 *Kings* 16:23–28).

Ahab continued to build in Samaria and in Jezreel, both important military and economic sites, because they were easy to defend and near trade routes. Ahab had a rich kingdom indeed, but it was based on the same policies that Solomon had used—and he was also dominated by his wife, who was aggressive in her worship of the foreign god, Baal.

An Unconventional Powerhouse of a Man

Under Ahab and Jezebel, the existing conflict in the kingdom of Israel worsened.

A. Giovani, *Elijah and the Angel*, Fifteenth Century.

Elijah is considered the greatest prophet by the Jewish people.

- Violations of the Covenant were common.
- People worshipped whichever god seemed to have the most power for the matter at hand.
- Social conditions became more unequal.
- The king abused his royal power.
- The burdens of forced labor and taxation became far worse than they had been even under Solomon.
- International politics were more complicated and much more threatening than at any previous time in Israel's history.

The Northern kingdom may have looked reasonably prosperous to outsiders, but it was not at all a peaceful kingdom dedicated to the Covenant.

Into this chaos burst Elijah, perhaps the greatest of all the prophets. Even the gospels, nine centuries later, recognize him, telling us that Jesus' friends expected Elijah's return in their time (*Matthew* 17:9–13). Still today, Jewish tradition expects Elijah to return. At the Passover table, a place is set and wine is poured for Elijah—just in case he should return.

To have had such a powerful impact on people for more than twenty-five hundred years, Elijah must have been an extremely powerful person. The Bible suggests that he was ferocious and unpredictable. He wore animal skins, not cloth like other people. He lived alone in the desert, in caves and on mountains. He had a habit of appearing unexpectedly to challenge those in authority.

Elijah lived free of social restriction, coming and going as he wished, saying what he had to say. Elijah cared little about anything but Yahweh, to whom he was totally and fiercely devoted. At times, Yahweh's spirit and knowledge filled Elijah and drove him to action.

The Bible captures Elijah as a man of astounding power. He correctly predicted a long drought—some said he caused it! While other people suffered from thirst and hunger, Elijah ate and drank—first fed by ravens and then by a widow in Phoenicia. Elijah repaid her help by bringing her son back to life. Elijah is certainly best remembered, however, for his battles with Queen Jezebel.

Elijah and Queen Jezebel

Queen Jezebel worshipped Baal and Astarte, Canaanite gods. For unknown reasons, Jezebel set out to destroy the worship of Yahweh. Followers of fertility and nature gods usually were unconcerned with the worship of other gods, so Jezebel's hatred for the worshippers of Yahweh is unusual. Perhaps her dislike of Yahweh was politically motivated, since Jezebel was from Phoenicia.

Although prophets were considered sacred in Israel, this respect did not stop Jezebel from murdering the "prophets of the Lord" (1 *Kings* 18:3–4). When they opposed her plans to make Baal the god of Israel, she got rid of them. Jezebel was not an Israelite, and so was unconcerned about Yahweh's wrath. She

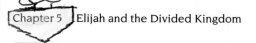

did not hesitate even to threaten Elijah's life when it suited her purposes.

Elijah Escapes   After Elijah's confrontation with the priests of Baal, Queen Jezebel was dishonored and bitterly angry. She put out a warrant for Elijah's death, forcing him to flee into the desert, frightened, near despair, and wanting to die. Yahweh, however, wasn't through with Elijah just yet; there was still work to be done.

An angel of the Lord fed Elijah and gave him orders: march to Mount Horeb (or Sinai), the mountain where Moses had received the Covenant for Israel. When Elijah arrived there, he was cared for by another angel, and reassured by a visit from the Lord (this part of the story is found in 1 *Kings* 19:1–18.) Back into the fray he went, even more faithful to Yahweh than before.

Elijah's Power   Elijah then entered politics. He stood up to Ahab when the king stole the vineyard

Scripture Workshop
Elijah and the Priests of Baal

One of the most dramatic scenes in the Bible is Elijah's public challenge to Jezebel's Baalist priests, the staff of her shrine. Read 1 Kings 18:16–46. What was Elijah's main purpose in this contest?

In your own words, explain what happens at the following points:

1. The situation on Mount Carmel (*18:18–20*)
2. The challenge (*18:21–24*)
3. The test (*18:22–24*)
4. The Baalist efforts (*18:25–29*)
5. Elijah's efforts (*18:30–37*)
6. The result (*18:38–39*)

At the end of this confrontation, Elijah announced the end of the drought—and the rains came. Then Elijah, certainly no longer a young man, but filled with the spirit of Yahweh, ran ahead of the king's chariot from Mount Carmel to near Jezreel, a distance of 80 miles!

Elijah and Moses are seen with Jesus at the Transfiguration in Luke 9: 28–36.

that had belonged to Naboth, an ordinary citizen, whom Jezebel had arranged to murder. This theft was an act particularly repulsive to Yahweh.

Later, Elijah condemned Ahab's son, Ahaziah, for seeking help from another god. Elijah also invoked the power of Yahweh to kill messengers sent by Ahaziah to request Elijah's help. Finally, Elijah climbed into a flaming chariot and was visibly lifted by a whirlwind into the skies. Elijah was seen no more, but hope for his return remained alive in the hearts of the Israelites.

Elijah's Successor, Elisha

Elijah, shortly before his death, was commanded by Yahweh to make Elisha his successor—the only time in the Scriptures that a prophet appoints a successor. Elijah's response to God's request is seen in 1 Kings 19:19–21.

In 2 Kings 2:1–18, we see Elijah passing on his spirit to Elisha, his disciple. Elisha picks up Elijah's fallen mantle or cloak and uses it with the same power with which Elijah had used it. In this way, the people of Israel learn that Elisha was a true disciple of Elijah and should be followed.

Elisha is remembered as a wonder-worker and a political activist, doing much that Elijah had done, including bringing a dead boy back to life (compare 1 *Kings* 17:1–24 with 2 *Kings* 4:1–37). He healed people (2 *Kings* 5), and found lost items (2 *Kings* 6). One of his miracles may remind you of an event in Jesus' life: compare 2 Kings 4:42–44 with John 6:1–13. Elisha also did a peculiar thing; read about Elisha and the children in 2 Kings 2:23–24. What do you think about Elisha's behavior?

Elisha was a central player in an important political drama. He inspired Jehu to revolt against Joram, Ahab's successor as king. Jehu's rebellion was successful, and Elijah's prophecy about the downfall of the house of Ahab came true.

When the king of Aram in Damascus, Ben-hadad, laid siege to Israel's capital, Samaria, Elisha was a key to Israel's survival:

> When told that the man of God had come there, the king said to Hazael, "Take a gift with you and go call on the man of God. Have him consult the Lord as to whether I shall recover from this sickness." On his arrival, he stood before the prophet and said, "Your son Ben-hadad, king of Aram, has sent me to ask you whether he will recover from his sickness." "Go and tell him," Elisha answered, "that he will surely recover. However, the Lord has showed me that he will in fact die.". . ."The Lord has showed you to me as king over Aram," replied Elisha. . . . And Hazael reigned in his stead.
>
> (2 Kings 8:8–10, 13, 15).

Elisha was a worthy successor to Elijah, and his countrymen remembered him.

Have You Considered?

1. What do you think of Elijah's behavior after he defeated the prophets of Baal? Why do you suppose he put them to death?
2. Ahab called Elijah the "troubler of Israel," accusing him of causing problems by speaking the truth. Describe another situation inwhich someone was accused of being a troublemaker for trying to do the right thing. Do you think they were acting as a prophet? Why or why not?
3. Read 2 Kings 2: 6–8. What other biblical story does this episode remind you of? Why do you think the author included this story about Elijah?

◆ Importance for Today

In Elijah's time, just as today, people had divided opinions about the major questions of life. Elijah had only one answer to all the people's questions: Yahweh. Yahweh is the power over everything, Yahweh is the source of justice, and Yahweh directs national policies.

Elijah matters to us because he spoke the word of the Lord. That is the important thing about all the prophets. We have little personal information on most of them. Even Elijah is not well known to us. But in the Old Testament, a prophet is only as important as the message he carried from Yahweh to Israel.

Today, we know more about nature and the world than Elijah's people did. What difference, then, does it make to us what Elijah thought about Baal, Astarte, and Yahweh? Aren't our lives and problems so incredibly different from theirs that they just don't have anything to say to us?

We may not believe in Baal and Astarte, but are we really sure how God relates to our world? Are we sure of our place in it? Consider these questions:

1. **What do we know today about the environment and its importance to our lives?** If Elijah were alive now, what do you think he might say about ecology? What do you think God's word might be to us today from Elijah about how we treat the environment?
2. **Do you personally believe that God is in charge of nature?** What does God have to do with fire, storms, earthquakes, rain, sunrise and sunset, the orbits of planets, and the twirling of galaxies?
3. **Are our modern questions so different from ancient Israel's?** Don't we want to know about controlling nature? Our technology has given us a lot—but volcanoes and earthquakes and tidal waves and tornadoes still happen. How are they ordered? Why do they happen?
4. **How does reproduction happen at the cellular or atomic level in plants and animals?** Science describes it to a point, but the essence of life still eludes us. Who is in charge of life?

These are only modern versions of the same fundamental questions that Elijah's people asked. In response, Elijah insisted on seeing God's power behind all that happened, and demanded that people respond to God with faithfulness and courage.

How do you respond to the prophet's answers? Do you know people today like the Israelites of Elijah's time, who cannot make a decision about God, who sit on the fence and try to have the advantages of life with God, as well as the indulgences of life without God? What do you think about people who can't decide? Elijah demanded decision. Have you decided for yourself? Are you thinking about it?

Raising Questions

If there had been newspapers in Elijah's time, someone might have written a letter to the editor like this:

> Dear Editor,
>
> Prophets like Elijah are a menace to the nation! The task of the prophet is to educate the people and to tell the word of the Lord. They are not supposed to interfere in the affairs of government and spoil the carefully laid plans of experienced leaders.
>
> Prophets like Elijah, who go beyond religion and play politics, are a serious threat to the country, and the only way to remove this danger is to remove its source, as Queen Jezebel has tried to do.

Do you agree or disagree with the letter writer?

What about justice? Why is justice often so difficult to achieve in the courts of our land or in our relationships with other people? Look again at the story of Naboth's vineyard (1 Kings 21). How does Naboth's story remind you of what you see on TV or in a newspaper today? What do you think the word of God might say through a modern Elijah concerning justice? If asked who is ultimately in charge of justice, how would you answer? Can the oppressed ever find justice?

What about history? Whose decision is it that one nation is strongest, and how long its dominance lasts? What happens to superpowers? Just as these were Israel's questions, so, too, are they ours. How are Elijah's answers good for us today as well? Even if you can't totally accept his answers, how do they help you look at these issues in a new way?

Have You Considered?

1. Imagine the prophet Elijah appearing on a television talk show today. What questions might he be asked? How do you think he would respond?
2. Do you see a plan, a design, in the things that happen to you? Do you think what happens is just a product of chance? Why or why not? Could you ever prove or disprove an answer to this question?
3. Do you think religious people should keep their opinions out of politics? Or is religious belief a legitimate point of view in political debate?

Spiritual Reflection

In the Whisper of the Wind

One of Elijah's experiences may suggest how you can experience God for yourself. Read what happened on Mount Horeb (1 Kings 19:9–13).

Have you ever tried to be quiet enough to feel God's presence? Here is one way to seek God inside your heart.

- Go to a quiet place, where you can be alone, as you have before. Remember to take only your Bible and no other entertainment. Make yourself comfortable.
- When you're comfortably settled, wait a few moments. Relax. Allow yourself to become quiet. Take a few deep breaths.
- Open your Bible to 1 Kings 19:9, and read again the story of Elijah in the cave. Read very slowly. Use your imagination. Imagine that you are beside Elijah, watching and listening with him. Take your time with this exercise. You too are waiting to experience the Lord. See if, with Elijah, you can be still enough to hear the "tiny whispering sound," inside yourself.
- Say something to the Lord in your heart. You may say anything, so long as it is honest. Prayer does not need to be special words or thoughts; it needs only to come from an honest heart.

When you are finished, thank God, get up, and go your way.

Q/A

Section One

1. Explain Solomon's policy of forced labor.
2. Why was forced labor a violation of the Covenant?
3. Explain what a "summit marriage" is.
4. Why were Solomon's summit marriages a violation of the Covenant?
5. Define "syncretism" and provide an example. How was syncretism a violation of the Covenant?
6. Identify: Rehoboam.
7. After Israel split into the Northern and Southern kingdoms, what do the terms "Israel" and "Judah" mean?
8. Why did fertility worship seem logical to the ancient Israelites?

Section Two

1. Define: seer, court prophet, unofficial prophet.
2. Identify: Samuel, Nathan.
3. Why did court prophets often say what the king wanted to hear?
4. What are the three elements of the prophetic message as described in Deuteronomy?
5. Describe the importance of Elijah in Jewish tradition.
6. What is Elisha best remembered for?
7. How do the questions Elijah raised relate to our own times?
8. How do Elijah's struggles for justice and the understanding of history relate to our own day?

BIBLE ACTIVITY

1. Read Sirach 47:23–25 and 48:1–12. These passages were written hundreds of years after the death of Elijah. (The unnamed person in Sirach 47:23 is probably Jeroboam, the first king of the Northern kingdom.) Answer the following: (a) What evils are meant in 47:24b–25? (b) What events are the basis for 48:1–3? (c) What future expectations are expressed in 48:10–12?

2. The stories of the battles between Elijah and Jezebel are detailed in 1 Kings 17–19, 21, and 2 Kings 1 and 2:1–12. Re-read them now. Imagine that you are making a video of these events. Let the scenes parade through your mind just as they are written. See the action, the colors. Imagine yourself in the middle of each event. Choose one of these stories and describe how you would make it come alive today if you were a video director.

Syro-Phoenician, *Woman's Head in a Window*. Eighth Century B.C.E.

GLOSSARY

- **Ahab:** King of Israel, the northern kingdom, during the mid-800's B.C.E.
- **Astarte and Baal:** Canaanite gods of nature, especially storms and fertility. Sometimes used to refer to someone other than the Canaanite god.
- **Court prophets:** Prophets who spoke Yahweh's word as officials of the royal court.
- **Deborah:** A prophet in the time of the Judges.
- **Elijah:** The great prophet who, by Yahweh's word, commanded nature to demonstrate Yahweh's power.
- **Elisha:** Elijah's successor as prophet.
- **Forced labor:** A policy pursued by Solomon and later kings, which required men to perform physical labor for the king during a certain portion of the year (or of their lifetimes) as a form of taxation.
- **Huldah:** A Jerusalem prophet of the Lord in the late 600s B.C.E. in the reign of King Josiah.
- **Jezebel:** The Phoenician princess who married Ahab, she brought foreign gods, especially Baal, with her to Israel.
- **Miriam:** The sister of Moses who is sometimes referred to as a prophet in the Biblical tradition.
- **Nabi:** The Hebrew word usually translated as "prophet."
- **Nathan:** A court prophet under King David who criticized the king for his affair with Bathsheba.
- **Prophet:** One who is filled by the spirit of Yahweh and is given a message to declare.
- **Rehoboam:** Solomon's son and successor.
- **Seer:** A type of prophet. They lived in groups and their messages appear to have been received through altered states of consciousness.
- **Summit marriage:** A marriage between one royal family and another, contracted in order to form an alliance between two nations.
- **Syncretism:** The attempt to blend differing religious ideas into one belief, without distinguishing one from the other.
- **Temple:** The structure built by Solomon for worship of Yahweh in Jerusalem.
- **Unofficial prophet:** A prophet who did not belong to a guild or hold a position at court.

UNDERSTANDING MORE ABOUT:

Caring for the Widow

A *widow* in the ancient Near East faced life-threatening circumstances. Because her husband was dead, she had no right to an inheritance and no other legal rights either. Women had very few opportunities to earn money on their own. While sometimes a second marriage took place with the dead husband's brother, this arrangement was rare. An adult son would take care of his widowed mother, but if she had no son, she could starve. What do you suppose might have happened to Naboth's widow after Jezebel killed him and Ahab took his property?

A widow was dependent on the good will of other people, including government officials, even for food. That is why Israel's laws include definite ways that widows are to be treated. Compare 1 Kings 17:7–24 with 2 Kings 4:1–7. If the prophet acts according to God's word, what do these stories tell us about God's attitude toward widows?

Widows still had the same problems in the time of Jesus and afterward. See Luke 7–11 for a story about Jesus and a widow. Notice especially the people's reactions.

Isaiah and Jeremiah

Legend

● General History
● Biblical History
● Jewish History
● Books written

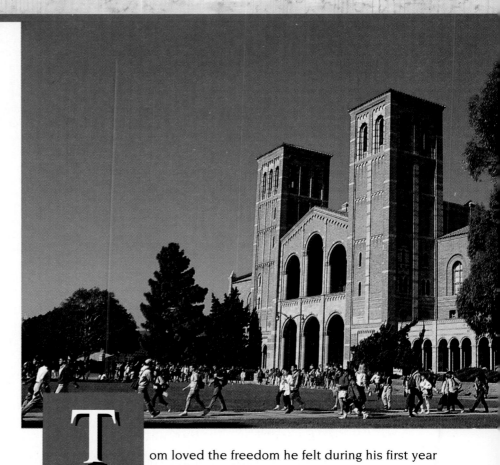

Tom loved the freedom he felt during his first year of college. He decided which classes he would take and what time he would take them. Especially, Tom liked living away from home in his own apartment; he cleaned his room when he felt like it, often kept late hours, and chose friends without worrying about whether or not his parents would approve of them.

When the second semester ended, Tom went home for the summer. He figured, "I am an adult now. There is no need for me to obey my parents' rules any longer."

Tom's parents had other ideas. They told him: "When you live in our home, you **will** follow our rules. That means keeping your room neat, letting us know when you won't be here for meals, and keeping a curfew at night." Tom listened to his parents' statement and agreed to abide by the rules. Then he ignored them and did what he pleased.

Late one night, about three hours after his parents' curfew, Tom came home and found the front light on and some of his clothes packed in a duffel bag on the porch. The note read simply,

> You know the consequences of not obeying our family's rules. Please find another place to stay for as long as you continue to disregard them. We love you very much, Mom and Dad.

Shocked and surprised, Tom picked up his things and headed off to a friend's apartment. "How unfair," he mumbled to himself.

Responsibility

Were Tom's parents unfair? They were only holding Tom accountable for his actions. If you make a deal with someone and then that person doesn't hold up his or her end of the bargain, what would you do? We know what happens in the "real" world. If you borrow money for a car and then don't make the payments, the lender will take away the car. If you try out for a sport but don't go to practice, the coach will cut you from the team. Why should one's parents, or God for that matter, treat you any differently?

After Elisha, the prophets recognized that God would hold Israel accountable for its sins, and tried to warn the people of both the Northern and Southern kingdoms that they were headed for trouble. They had accepted the Covenant with Yahweh and expected God to protect them. But the Israelites ignored the rules of the Covenant. The worship of other gods, civil strife, and individual greed became increasingly prevalent.

In this chapter, you will read of the collapse of first the Northern, and then the Southern kingdom. You will learn how the prophets Isaiah and Jeremiah worked to save Judah during the last days. During this period of 160 years—from Isaiah's call to Jeremiah's death—the two nations would descend from the heights of prosperity to the depths of despair.

As Tom learned the hard way, every choice has a consequence, be it pleasant or unpleasant. The consequences for Israel were the result of many decades of ignoring the Covenant. Yet, the prophets' warnings did not end with the nation's destruction: Yahweh stood ready to welcome Israel back to the Covenant. The prophets preached a message of hope for those who could amend their lives and return to God's ways.

Israel and Judah Are Destroyed

Assyrian, *Tiglath-pileser III.* Sixth Century B.C.E.

For almost two hundred years, the prophets warned the people of Israel and Judah of what would happen if they didn't obey the demands of the Covenant. From time to time the people would listen and repent, but they soon went back to living a lifestyle built on the worship of foreign gods and injustice. Israel, and then Judah, fell to their enemies. Yahweh allowed them to fall because of their disobedience. In this section, you'll follow the story of their destruction.

Learning Objectives for Section One

By the end of this section, you will be able to:

- Explain how the people violated the Covenant through the worship of foreign gods and injustice.
- Understand the warnings of the prophets.
- Explain the fall of the Northern kingdom.
- Explain the fall of the Southern kingdom.

◆ False Affluence

During the first fifty years of the eighth century B.C.E., both Israel and Judah were at the height of their material prosperity.

- They were strong, at peace with each other, and had considerable influence among their neighbors.
- Their populations increased and their industries flourished.
- Lucrative trade routes once again passed through Israel's territory as in the days of David and Solomon.
- More wealth was flowing into Israel and Judah than ever before—even Solomon's kingdom probably had not been as rich.

During this time of enormous confidence, it was easy for the people of Judah and Israel to believe that their prosperity would never end.

Growing Injustice

Wealth, however, was not a sign that Israel or Judah had found favor with God. Although they had become materially affluent, both societies had also become spiritually corrupt. Small farmers, for example, were constantly in debt to moneylenders. If one year's crop were to fail, the farmer could lose everything. The rich were getting richer and the poor were becoming poorer. Because the wealthy controlled the political system, the poor had little chance of justice.

Israel and Judah probably were no more unjust than any other country in either the ancient world or our own. But the People of God were supposed to be different—justice was one of the demands of the Covenant. When Israel and Judah put justice up for sale, they were not just acting like any other nation—they were violating the terms of their agreement with God.

Israel was a very rich country prior to its destruction in 721 B.C.E. Archaeological finds indicate thriving industries in the production of cosmetics and fine cloth.

Worship of Foreign Gods

As discussed in Chapter 5, the Israelites' worship of Yahweh was influenced by the religious practices of other nations. After the death of Elisha,

- Shrines to fertility and nature gods once again flourished throughout the land.
- The sexual rites in honor of Baal and Asherah increased.

Evidence of these abuses is found throughout the writings of the prophets, whose constant references to the worship of Baal suggests that this was a dominant threat to the life of Israel.

Although not in keeping with what God had demanded at Sinai, the Israelites were unable to resist the temptation to honor the gods of nature and commerce popular among their neighbors. Despite the occasional attempt at religious reform, this problem simply got worse over time.

The Prophets Forecast Destruction

False perception can create real problems.

- The water in the pool may *seem* deep enough, but if you don't check before you dive in, you could end up with a broken neck.
- The meat may look cooked because it's brown on the outside, but, if eaten, it can cause sickness or death.

- The car may look in good condition, but if you don't have it checked out by an able mechanic you could end up buying a piece of junk.

During the period of the prophets, Israel and Judah were confronted with their misperceptions. While the affluence and success of both kingdoms made them unable (or unwilling) to see the problems that God saw, the prophets tried every means within their power to bring the people to see things as they really were. The prophets warned that destruction was coming if the people didn't obey the Covenant.

Unfortunately, the prophets' dire warnings were ignored. People chose to listen to the seduction of prosperity instead. In other words, they preferred their false perception to reality. This view of things, however, could only last so long.

Have You Considered?

1. Do you think today's American Christians have to be concerned with mixed religious observances? Why or why not?
2. What similarities do you see between the injustices in ancient Israel and Judah, and in our society today? What message do you suppose the prophets would have for us?
3. Describe a time when your perception of a situation was challenged by someone. How did you respond to that challenge? Why?

Assyrian, Assyrian Warriors. Eighth Century B.C.E.

Assyrian warriors, like those shown in this relief from the Iraq Museum in Baghdad, captured Israel and scattered the Israelite people.

◆ Israel Is Destroyed

In time, neither Israel nor Judah could escape the consequences of their disobedience. Israel was the first to suffer, defeated by the Assyrians in 721 B.C.E. We have two records of the fall of the Northern kingdom. One is a historical interpretation of events put together by modern scholars. The other is the prophetic interpretation. According to the prophets, Israel's disobedient lifestyle was its most serious problem. To Israel's leaders, however, the threat of foreign invasion was the greater danger.

The Historical Interpretation

Historically, Assyria had been the major military threat to Israel's survival for over a century. But early in the eighth century Assyria declined, allowing Israel and Judah approximately 50 years to prosper without fear of war. Also, at this time both Israel and Judah

in the Spotlight

The Northern Tribes

Not everyone agrees that the ten tribes of the Northern kingdom were lost forever. Some people believe that they left Israel to look for a new home, and that their descendants still exist. One such group is the Church of Jesus Christ of Latter-Day Saints, popularly known in America as the "Mormons."

According to the *Book of Mormon,* a text they consider a third book of scripture, the ten tribes immigrated to America, where they built great civilizations. Ultimately, they all but destroyed themselves in a series of major wars. This is how they lost their historical memory and became the "Indians" encountered by European settlers. Mormons also believe that Jesus appeared in the New World to preach to the ten tribes after he disappeared from Palestine (when Christians believe he ascended into heaven).

The Bible in Context

Uncovering Other Records

Archaeologists have found many records left by the kings of other nations, including Assyria. Some of these records depict Israelite kings bringing tribute to Assyria's rulers. Others record the Assyrian takeover of Judah's cities, most notably, Lachish. One written record, called "The Annals of Sennacherib," was written in cuneiform on clay. It describes the result of Sennacherib's Palestinian campaign of 701:

> As for Hezekiah of Judah, he did not submit to my yoke and I laid siege to forty-six of his strong cities. . . . I made Hezekiah a prisoner in Jerusalem, like a bird in a cage. . . . Hezekiah was forced to send me 30 talents of gold, eight hundred talents of silver, precious stones, couches and chairs inlaid with ivory, elephant hides, ebony wood, box wood, and all kinds of valuable treasures.
>
> (Old Testament Parallels, by Victor H. Matthew and Don Benjamin. Paulist Press, 1991.)

had strong kings: Jeroboam in the North and Uzziah in the South. By 745 B.C.E., however, the situation was changing again.

After the deaths of Jeroboam and Uzziah, various kings ruled, many for only one to six months. These kings were murdered and then quickly replaced by others who wanted power. The civil battles in Israel provoked horrible atrocities. Because society was torn apart by the political chaos, the country was illprepared to face the renewed power of Assyria.

Israel's end was quick in coming:

- By the mid-700s, a new emperor, Tiglath-pileser, had Assyria prepared for conquest.
- Syria and Palestine with their natural resources and strategic locations were obvious targets for the Assyrians.
- Israel joined an alliance to resist the Assyrians.
- Tiglath-pileser invaded and demanded tribute from Israel.
- King Hoshea of Israel agreed to pay, but then held some of the tribute back.
- Sargon II became emperor of Assyria.
- In 721, Emperor Sargon II laid siege to Israel's capital, Samaria, which quickly fell.
- Israel became a province of the Assyrian Empire. Colonists from Babylonia and Hamath intermarried with the remaining Israelites.

In keeping with Assyrian policy, the defeated population of Israel was deported to discourage future rebellions. The ten northern tribes were removed, and resettled throughout the Assyrian Empire and Assyrian settlers entered Israelite territory. With that, the northern tribes depart from the pages of history.

How the Prophets Saw It

The prophets would not deny the historical facts covered above. They would say, however, that Assyria was not really the cause of Israel's problems: Israel was itself the cause. Without Israel's disobedience and neglect of the Covenant, the prophets would say, Yahweh would never have allowed Assyria to harm the Chosen People.

The prophets charged, among other things, that the unequal class structures and disregard for the poor by the rich caused the people of the North to be punished for their offenses. Consider:

- Merchants who tampered with scales to cheat customers out of their rightful purchase of food (Amos 8:5).
- Sexual abuses (Amos 2:7).
- Judges who accepted bribes to rule against the poor (Amos 5:12).
- A general mistreatment of the poor by those who were in power (Amos 2:6–13).

The prophets left no doubt that these atrocities, along with the mixing of religious practices, were the causes of Israel's destruction. As Amos said:

> I will turn your feasts into mourning and all your songs into lamentations. . . . Those who swear by the shameful idol of Samaria. . . . those shall fall, never to rise again.
>
> (Amos 8:10, 14)

Have You Considered?

1. Can the historical interpretation of the fall of Israel and the prophetic interpretation both be true? Why or why not?
2. Do you think it was fair of God to allow the destruction of Israel? Should God always allow people to suffer the consequences of their choices? Why or why not?
3. After the Assyrians deported them from Israel, the members of the ten northern tribes became refugees. Based on what you know about refugees today, what do you suppose life was like for them? What might this do to their faith in Yahweh?

◆ Judah Is Destroyed

When Israel had joined the rebellious coalition to try to resist Assyria, they had wanted to include King Ahaz of Judah. Ahaz refused, so the coalition threatened Judah with destruction. Ahaz, against the advice of the prophet Isaiah, then appealed to Assyria to save him. Ahaz apparently did not fully understand what could happen to him when he shared a border with Assyria.

When Israel then fell to Assyria in 721, Judah was little more than a province of the massive, aggressive empire. Now, Ahaz truly had reason to fear Assyria. To avoid trouble there, he repeatedly violated the Covenant by:

- Changing the altar in the Temple to conform to Assyrian patterns.
- Sacrificing his sons to a foreign god (according to 2 Chronicles 28) hoping for its protection.

In other words, Ahaz went against God in his attempt to save his kingdom. Needless to say, the consequences would come, but not in Ahaz's lifetime.

Ahaz's Successors

After Ahaz made his fateful appeal to Assyria, the end of Judah was assured. While the kings who followed him to the throne of Judah worked valiantly to undo the damage caused by Ahaz's folly, they were without success. Two kings in particular are singled out by the Bible for special attention: Hezekiah and Josiah.

Hezekiah   Ahaz's son, Hezekiah, tried to turn things around. He attempted to reform the religion of Judah by ending the worship of foreign gods. He also strengthened Judah militarily, and stopped paying tribute to Assyria. When the Assyrians invaded, they surrounded Hezekiah in Jerusalem and forced him to pay tribute, but stopped short of destroying the city. According to 2 Kings, God sent a plague upon the Assyrians, destroying the attacking army. Emperor Sennacherib was now forced to withdraw and end the siege.

Josiah   Like Hezekiah, King Josiah (641–610 B.C.E.) attempted religious reform in Judah. According to 2 Kings 22:8–23:7, the high priest Hilkiah found an ancient book of the Law in the Temple. When Josiah was given the book he was horrified by it because Judah had not been obeying these laws. He ordered that its rules should be immediately put in place.

This clay tablet records the military campaigns of the Assyrian King, Sennacherib (705–681 B.C.E.). Judah was threatened by the Assyrians (and paid tribute to them) but would not be destroyed by them. Judah remained independent until 587 B.C.E.

Most scholars agree that the book located by Hilkiah was the book of Deuteronomy, and for his devotion to it, the Deuteronomic historian honors Josiah as Judah's greatest king after David.

Judah Falls

Judah remained independent and at peace for some years after the fall of Israel. To some, it looked as if Judah might escape the verdict that had fallen upon Israel a hundred years earlier. This was not to be:

- Under Emperor Nebuchadnezzar, the Babylonians replaced the Assyrians as the major power in the Middle East.

LEARN FROM THE MAP

Assyrian Domination

The map illustrates Assyria's borders in 750 B.C.E. Nineveh was the capital of Assyria. Note that the areas of Judah and Israel are highlighted in green. While in a different color, both nations must be considered under Assyria's control and domination. The coalition of Israel and Damascus fought the Assyrians in Syria. Why, then, was Judah's position important to both sides?

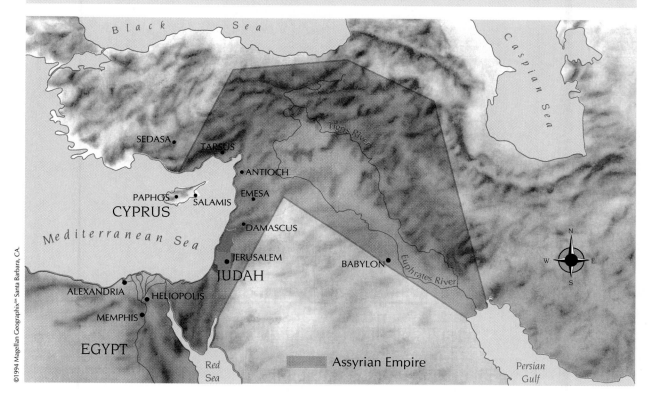

©1994 Magellan Geographix℠ Santa Barbara, CA.

- Judah turned to Egypt for protection, and refused to pay tribute to Nebuchadnezzar.
- In 598, the Babylonians invaded Judah, took everything of value in the Temple, and sent the royal family into exile.
- After a brief uprising in Judah, the Babylonians again invaded in 587, and this time sent most of Judah's population into exile.
- The kingdom of Judah was now history, and the Israelites would not be independent again for another 400 years. Their darkest days were ahead, as they were forced out of the land of promise and into exile in Babylon.

The Prophetic Point of View

The prophets Isaiah and Jeremiah were active during the decline and fall of Judah. Like their coun-terparts in the Northern kingdom, they denounced religious corruption and injustice, predicting that such behavior would not go unpunished for long.

Isaiah and Jeremiah also denounced what we might call the "foreign policy" of the kings of Judah. Both argued that faith in Yahweh, not alliances with foreign powers, was what would save the nation.

Isaiah denounced Ahaz for making a sacrifice to the Assyrians:

Unless your faith is firm, you will not be firm!

(Isaiah 7:9)

Isaiah also told Hezekiah to trust in God to save Judah and not fight back against the Assyrians. Hezekiah did what he was told and Judah survived. Jeremiah insisted that Judah not resist the Babylonians, and his warning also proved correct.

An altar to Baal was built in the Valley of Ben Hinom, near Jerusalem. According to Jeremiah 32:35, kings of Judah sacrificed their children here to the god, Molech, bringing destruction upon the nation.

In times of crisis, the advice of the prophets may often seem unrealistic or naive. The policies of the kings were surely more hardheaded and practical. But each was driven by different motives. The kings sought political survival while the prophets sought faithfulness to God.

Cold, rational decisions failed; Judah was conquered. The prophets, however, never abandoned their faith in God, and in the fall of Judah the people began to see that perhaps the prophets had been right all along.

Scripture Workshop

Josiah's Reforms

According to the Deuteronomic historian, Josiah was a great king because "He pleased the Lord and conducted himself unswervingly just as his ancestor David had done" *(2 Kings 22:2)*. Josiah's greatest accomplishment was his religious reforms. Read about his reign in 2 Kings 22:1–23:30, and answer the following questions:

1. What did Josiah do and say when the book found in the Temple was read to him?
2. Who was Huldah? What message did she have for Josiah?
3. What promises did Josiah make to God? What did he do to carry out these promises?
4. How does Josiah rank among the kings of Judah, according to the Deuteronomic historian?

Have You Considered?

1. Assuming that Ahaz's motive was good—to save Judah—what was the mistake he made in trying to accomplish it?
2. There are some people who believe that anyone who criticizes his or her country is unpatriotic. Are there circumstances in which criticizing one's country can be a form of patriotism?
3. The kings of Judah felt that they had to set aside God's law to defend the nation. Do you think it's unrealistic to believe that a country can always behave morally? Why or why not?

The Conscience of the People

You have already seen that during the period of the Northern and Southern kingdoms, prophets were powerful voices for God. They argued that the true threat to national security was neither Assyria nor Babylon, but disobedience to Yahweh. In their role as prophets they spoke with Yahweh's voice; they provided guidance and suggestions for moral living, and pronounced judgment on evil and unjust behavior. The prophets were the conscience of Israel and Judah.

In this section, you'll become more familiar with the lives and messages of these prophets.

Learning Objectives for Section Two

By the end of this section, you will be able to:

- Identify Amos' views on religious ritual.
- Explain Hosea's use of marriage as a metaphor.
- Describe the characteristics of Yahweh as revealed by Isaiah.
- Outline Jeremiah's career and message.

◆ The Prophets of the North: Amos and Hosea

Both Elijah and Elisha, studied in Chapter 5, were prophets who fought against the greed and foreign worship of the Northern kings. The same issues were later taken up by Amos and Hosea.

Amos

Amos was a herdsman, not a professional prophet. Although he addressed Israel, he was not from the North; he came from Tekoa in Judah around 750 B.C.E. After Yahweh commanded him to speak, Amos appeared one day at Israel's main shrine at Bethel and denounced the false worship taking place there. In uncompromising words, he proclaimed that their worship was useless because they lived unjustly.

Amos demanded to know why Israel seemed to have forgotten that Yahweh gave them the blessings of peace and prosperity. Why did Israel oppress the poor, trample the weak, and prostitute herself to fertility gods? Did they think that their religious rites were a substitute for just behavior?

Amos completely rejected the message of the court prophets, who said that God would smile on Israel as long as the correct religious rituals were observed by the priests. In rejecting this idea, Amos introduced a new emphasis in Covenant religion:

The person favored by God is not the one who performs the correct rituals, but the one who acts justly.

Amos says that public worship does no good for the person who "goes through the motions," but does not act in fairness to the disadvantaged and forgotten. These rituals, *by themselves*, mean nothing to God.

I hate, I spurn your feasts. I take no pleasure in your solemnities; Your cereal offerings I will not accept, nor consider your stall-fed offerings.

*Away with your noisy songs! I will not listen to the
melodies of your harps. But if you would offer me
holocausts, then let justice surge like water, and righteousness like an ever-flowing stream.*

(5:21–24)

Hosea

Shortly after Amos' ministry, Yahweh spoke
through another prophet, Hosea. His work encom-
passed at least two decades, from 740 B.C.E. into the
720s. Hosea had a troubled marriage, and he turned
this difficult personal experience into a powerful
metaphor for the relationship between Yahweh
and Israel.

Hosea's wife apparently deserted him and committed adultery, perhaps even in a fertility god's
shrine. Hosea's agony stands as a symbol for
Yahweh's suffering because of Israel's infidelity:

*When Israel was a child I loved him, … The more I
called them, the farther they went from me, sacrificing to the baals and burning incense to idols … I
drew them with human cords, with bands of love; I
fostered them like one who raised an infant to his
cheeks; Yet, though I stooped to feed my child, they
did not know that I was their healer.*

(Hosea 11:1–2, 4)

Yahweh commanded Hosea to buy back his wife
for the price of a slave, to discipline her, and reinstate
her fully as his beloved wife. Just so, the prophet
taught, will Yahweh do with Israel. Hosea named
Assyria as the destroyer whom Yahweh would use to
discipline Israel. As you already know, the Northern
kingdom fell to Assyria in 721 B.C.E.

Have You Considered?

1. Do you know people who participate in religious rituals
   (such as going to church) but don't do anything to help
   others? What do you think of their behavior?
2. Amos said acting justly, not public worship, is the basis
   of religion. Does this mean someone can be "religious"
   without participating in ritual? Which is more important
   for a good relationship with God? Explain.
3. Describe a difficult personal experience you've had.
   How could you use this experience as a metaphor for
   our relationship with God? What can you learn from it?
4. Read the first chapter of Hosea. What is the significance
   of the names Hosea gives his children?

◆ Isaiah of Jerusalem

Isaiah of Jerusalem was the most influential
prophet during the reigns of the Southern kings
Jotham, Ahaz, and Hezekiah; a period of more than
forty years.

The extent of Isaiah's influence is found in the
Second Book of Kings, the Second Book of Chronicles, and from the book that bears his name. In
actuality, not everything in the Book of Isaiah was
written by the original prophet.

- Chapters 1–39 of the Book of Isaiah are the
  words of the prophet himself.
- Chapters 40–55, sometimes called "Second
  Isaiah," were written in Babylon after the fall
  of Judah. These chapters speak of a liberator
  who will free Israel.
- Chapters 56–66 are hopeful oracles written after
  the Babylonian Exile and are often known as
  "Third Isaiah."

You will study Second and Third Isaiah in a later
chapter. The original prophet is called "Isaiah of
Jerusalem" to distinguish him from these other two
authors.

Isaiah's prophetic work extended far beyond his
advice to the kings of Judah. Modern theologians
credit Isaiah with understanding God and God's ways
in a new light. Some of the major themes which appear in Isaiah's prophecy include:

- The holiness of Yahweh.
- The faithfulness of Yahweh.
- The justice of Yahweh.
- God's justice extends to all nations.

Let's look at each one of these in turn.

The Holiness of Yahweh

The story of Isaiah's call in Isaiah 6 reflects the
holiness and reverence that Yahweh commanded.
Isaiah encounters Yahweh at the Temple. Gazing
through the Holy Place toward the Holy of Holies,
Isaiah hears God's angels utter, "Holy, holy, holy is
the Lord of hosts" (Isaiah 6:3).

Isaiah is frightened at the prospect of seeing God
and responds:

*Woe is me, I am doomed! For I am a man of unclean
lips, living among a people of unclean lips, yet my
eyes have seen the King, the Lord of hosts!*

(Isaiah 6:5)

Tiepolo, *Prophet Isaiah,* Eighteenth Century.

The prophet Isaiah, portrayed in this eighteenth century C.E. fresco receiving divine inspiration, called the nation of Judah to act justly and to trust in Yahweh.

In his vision, Isaiah saw Yahweh seated on a high and lofty throne. Isaiah also saw Seraphim stationed around Yahweh. The origin of the word *seraphim* suggests the "fiery one" or "burning one." In this passage, the Seraphim are Yahweh's heavenly servants.

Isaiah also referred to smoke surrounding the Holy One. While the smoke was physical smoke produced by the burning of incense in the Temple, it also symbolized the mysterious presence of Yahweh—just as the column of smoke had done during the Exodus. All of these elements of Isaiah's vision emphasize the supreme holiness of the God of Israel.

While Yahweh's holiness is seen here in the Temple, it is found even more clearly in God's action in the world beyond Israel. To understand more of Isaiah's vision of Yahweh's all-encompassing holiness, read the following passages:

- Isaiah 1:4
- Isaiah 10:17, 20
- Isaiah 12:2–6
- Isaiah 29:18–19

How would you describe Isaiah's understanding of Yahweh's holiness?

Because of Yahweh's holiness, any kind of pride—whether national or personal—was, for Isaiah, an insult. The holiness of God even ruled out pride in the nation of Judah. This idea is reflected in Isaiah's vision, in which the prophet says the Temple contained only the "train of God's robe." Yahweh is bigger, more holy, than even the great Temple. Isaiah, therefore, warns Judah not to rely on the Temple for protection, but rather, to do the will of God.

The Faithfulness of Yahweh

If it was false pride that brought destruction, then it was faith, according to Isaiah, that brought life. The prophet describes his own faith in Isaiah 8:17:

> For I will trust in the Lord, who is hiding His face from the house of Jacob; yes, I will wait for him.

Here are two other passages that help to define the meaning of faith for Isaiah: Isaiah 7:4, 5, 9a and Isaiah 30:15. What do these passages urge about waiting quietly for the Lord to act in God's way and in God's time?

According to Isaiah, everyone—whether king or commoner—is called to become quiet, renounce all fear, and wait in patience for God to act. According to Isaiah, Yahweh's salvation depends on the king's and the people's total trust.

The Justice of Yahweh

Faith is never self-satisfied, however. Even as faith expresses itself through waiting for God to act, it also expresses itself in personal acts of justice. Justice demands that every element in society be judged according to how it contributes to a harmonious and sufficient life for all. Justice is a key element in the Covenant.

Isaiah preached against injustice ferociously. According to Isaiah, only when people live justly in all facets of society will the blessings of Yahweh be completely fulfilled.

- **Read Isaiah 1:15–16, 23–26 and Isaiah 3:13–15.** What is the main context of Isaiah's warnings to the people?

In Isaiah 5:1–7, Yahweh tells Isaiah how the beloved vineyard will be destroyed because the people disregarded the message to live justly:

> Yes, I will make it a ruin: it shall not be pruned or hoed, but overgrown with thorns and briers.
>
> (5:6)

In this passage, Judah is the vineyard, and the ruin refers to its coming destruction because of its disobedience.

- **Read Isaiah 5:8–25.** List the things in this passage that the people have done which the Lord so utterly rejects.

As Yahweh demands justice from the people, so will God act with justice in judgment. Isaiah says that Yahweh will see that Judah receives justice—and, unless its disobedient ways change, that's not good news. Although God's love for the people never changes, God's justice requires that the people suffer the consequences for their rejection of their Covenant promises.

Justice to All Nations

All of the prophets criticized the lack of justice within Israel and Judah, but Isaiah is the first to announce that Yahweh's justice extends to *all*

Vanni, Heavenly Choirs, Fourteenth Century?

Isaiah experienced the holiness of God in a vision of fiery Seraphim gathered around the throne of Yahweh.

nations, and that Covenant commands apply to all people. For Isaiah, Yahweh commands all of the nations, not only Israel.

- **Read Isaiah 5:26–29.** What is the role of the "far-off" nation in this passage?
- **Read Isaiah 7:18–20.** How does this passage show that it is Yahweh who wields the real power?

According to Isaiah, nations are unknowingly used to accomplish God's purpose, but sometimes they go beyond God's wishes. When it destroyed much of Judah under Hezekiah, Assyria did not know that it was an instrument in the hands of Yahweh. When Assyria overstepped the task God had given it, Isaiah pronounced a message of doom on Assyria for its pride:

> *Therefore the Lord, the Lord of hosts, will send among His fat ones leanness, and instead of His glory there will be kindling like the kindling of fire.*
>
> (Isaiah 5:16)

The prophet foretold that after Assyria's destruction, Judah would be saved by Yahweh, but only through a small remnant of people. Read about the remnant in the following passages:

- Isaiah 8:3,16–20
- Isaiah 10:20–22
- Isaiah 14:32
- Isaiah 30:17

Hope in a Faithful One

Isaiah is not without hope for Israel in regard to its continuing relationship with Yahweh. Isaiah looks to the future and proclaims that a new king will arise, a king faithful to Yahweh and one specially appointed to do Yahweh's will. Isaiah tells us that this king is to be named "Immanuel," meaning "God is with us." He describes this new king and his kingdom in Isaiah 11:1–9. Read this passage and identify some of the qualities the expected king will have.

Even though this new king did not appear in Judah before the exile, Isaiah's prophecy kept hope alive for a king who would lead the people back to God.

Have You Considered?

1. Think about Isaiah's message concerning faith, destruction, social injustice, and hope for the future. What message would Isaiah give to our world and nation today? What should people do in response to that message?
2. Some people say that God's justice is too strict, that it was unfair of God to let Judah be destroyed. Do you agree? Why or why not? Could God allow people to have free choice, and yet not have to accept the consequences of their actions?
3. Isaiah said that Yahweh's holiness ruled out any false personal or national pride. How do you distinguish between pride that's legitimate, and pride that's false?

These seals from the thirteenth and twelfth centuries B.C.E. are marks of authenticity. Scribes, such as Baruch, would use these seals to guarantee that a document was genuine.

Michelangelo, *Prophet Jeremiah*, Sixteenth Century.

Michelangelo's painting of the prophet Jeremiah (from the Sistine Chapel in Saint Peter's Basilica in Rome) shows a troubled and brooding man. From your reading of the Book of Jeremiah, how would you describe the prophet?

◆ Jeremiah

Jeremiah was from a priestly family who lived two miles outside of Jerusalem in the small village of Anathoth. He never married or raised a family because he believed in the imminent destruction of Jerusalem. There is more information about the life of Jeremiah than about any other prophet. Jeremiah's prophecies were recorded by a secretary, Baruch. Jeremiah's career extended from the thirtieth year of King Josiah (627 B.C.E.) through the destruction of Jerusalem (587 B.C.E.).

As with all prophets, Jeremiah's message was addressed particularly to the times and conditions in which it was spoken. But its central themes have endured to warn, teach, and console many future generations as well. Many of Jeremiah's teachings are especially appropriate today.

Judah's Doom

According to Jeremiah, the kingdom of Israel had become as "a frenzied she-camel, coursing near and far" (*Jeremiah* 2:23). But Judah refused to learn from the experience of Israel:

Then, even though her traitor sister Judah saw that for all the adulteries rebellious Israel had committed, I put her away and gave her a bill of divorce, nevertheless her traitor sister Judah was not frightened; she too went off and played the harlot.

(Jeremiah 3:7–8)

The reforms instituted by King Josiah may have changed people's behavior somewhat, but to Jeremiah, they were simply a worthless, external show of devotion meaningless apart from any true internal conversion and repentance.

For the sake of the Lord, be circumcised, remove the foreskins of your hearts, O men of Judah and citizens of Jerusalem.

(Jeremiah 4:4)

Scripture Workshop

Jeremiah's Call

Jeremiah's personal agony began from the day he was called as a young man to be Yahweh's servant. Read Jeremiah 1:4–19. Answer the following questions:

- When did Jeremiah's call take place?
- How did Jeremiah respond? Who else in the Old Testament responded to God's call by worrying that he wouldn't know what to say?
- What was Yahweh's answer?
- What would be the purpose and character of Jeremiah's work?
- What was the main part of Jeremiah's message to be?
- What effect would the Lord's call have on Jeremiah's personality?

Read the following passages. Identify the reasons listed by Jeremiah for Judah's destruction:

- Jeremiah 2:1–13
- Jeremiah 5:26–31
- Jeremiah 9:1–5
- Jeremiah 23:13–17

What is a common thread in Jeremiah's warnings against Judah?

Jeremiah's Intense Views

Jeremiah preached of the coming disaster that would befall Judah. He was not, however, optimistic that Judah would listen to him and change its behavior. He felt that the hearts of the people were so hardened that their conversion was as unlikely as a leopard changing its spots (Jeremiah 13:23). According to Jeremiah, the day of reckoning was fast approaching:

The Lord said to me: "Do not intercede for this people. If they fast, I will not listen to their supplication. If they offer holocausts or cereal offerings, I will not accept them. Rather, I will destroy them with the sword, famine, and pestilence."

(Jeremiah 14:11)

How could the people of Judah be renewed? Read the following passages to find out.

- Jeremiah 4:1–4
- Jeremiah 5:1–9
- Jeremiah 13:20–25

Jeremiah's view of Judah is expressed in the story of the potter's flask in Jeremiah 18:1–12.

I went down to the potter's house and there he was, working at the wheel. Whenever the object of clay which he was making turned out badly in his hand, he tried again, making of the clay another object of whatever sort he pleased. Then the word of the Lord came to me: "Can I not do to you, house of Israel, as this potter has done?" says the Lord. "Indeed, like clay in the hand of the potter, so are you in my hand, house of Israel."

(Jeremiah 18:3–6)

The people of Judah refused to be shaped by the Covenant, just as the clay had not formed correctly in the potter's hands. If Judah could not be molded as God wished, then God would start over. To dramatize Judah's coming doom, Jeremiah smashed a clay pot to the ground and said:

Thus says the Lord of hosts: I will smash this people and this city, as one smashes a clay pot so that it cannot be repaired.

(Jeremiah 19:11)

Jeremiah's dramatic display of smashing the pot to illustrate God's unhappiness is called a "prophetic action." In the ancient world, prophetic action was a public gesture performed by a prophet for purposes of illustrating his or her message.

When Jeremiah smashed the clay pot in public, the priest, Pashur, had Jeremiah arrested and put in stocks for speaking out against the king's policies (Jeremiah 20:1–6).

Threats and Condemnations

To understand why Jeremiah's prophecies were so violently received, you need to remember a point made earlier: in the ancient world, there was no separation between religion and politics. Moreover, in Israel the spoken word was a vehicle of actual power, a real thing that could and did cause other things to happen. Therefore, when Jeremiah spoke against the king or the national policy, it amounted to an act of rebellion or near treason. Jeremiah's words were seen not only as predictions of the future, but also as causes of the results.

People of Note

Baruch

Although Jeremiah comments on how he sometimes felt alone, we know that he had at least one companion: his friend, secretary, and assistant, Baruch.

In chapter 36, Jeremiah says that he is prevented from going to the Temple to announce the word of God. Therefore, he dictates a scroll which Baruch copies. Jeremiah then asks him to go to the Temple and to read it aloud to all who are there. Baruch follows his instructions, and afterwards he is called before the scribes of the king to repeat what he had said. He did so fearlessly, imitating the example of Jeremiah.

We also know that Baruch imitated Jeremiah in one other way: he, too, sometimes felt forgotten and depressed. In chapter 45, God speaks to Baruch through Jeremiah, warning him not to seek personal happiness while Judah is being destroyed. Nevertheless, Yahweh says that Baruch's life will be spared because of his services to Jeremiah.

Baruch was remembered by later generations of Jews, who used his name for the "Book of Baruch." This book was written two centuries after the Exile, to encourage Jews to remain faithful to the Law in the middle of Greek culture. Even then, Baruch was remembered as someone who had remained loyal to Yahweh despite the hardship it caused.

Baruch also offered a promise of hope:

"Fear not, Jerusalem! He who gave you your name is your encouragement."

(Baruch 4:30)

Because his predictions did not come true for many years, Jeremiah was long accused of false prophecy. But in the end, Judah was destroyed and Jerusalem was demolished. The people of Jerusalem then hated Jeremiah for his words even more!

Read the following passages. Try to determine what it was about these political messages that upset the people so much.

- Jeremiah 26:1–19. How did Jeremiah's supporters rescue him?
- Jeremiah 21:1–10. What statements sound like treason? Why do you think Jeremiah's fellow citizens would hate him for these words?
- Jeremiah 37–38. These chapters describe the same incident as in 21:1–10. Describe King Zedekiah's actions. What do you think about his decision in this case?

Even though punished, Jeremiah's voice was never stilled. He continued to offer counsel to all who would hear, especially to the king, Zedekiah, who kept seeking a way out of his nation's troubles and a deliverance from Yahweh that would never come.

The Confessions of Jeremiah

Despite Jeremiah's persistence, he experienced periods of self-doubt and depression. In several places, he expresses a sense of failure, bitterness towards his enemies, and resentment over how God has allowed him to be laughed at and persecuted.

Read what he has to say in these passages:

- Jeremiah 11:18–12:6. What does Jeremiah want God to do to the unrighteous?
- Jeremiah 15:10–21. Why does Jeremiah say he wishes he hadn't been born?
- Jeremiah 17:14–18. What line does Jeremiah say that his enemies use against him? What does he want God to do?
- Jeremiah 18:18–23. What does Jeremiah remind God of in this passage? Why?
- Jeremiah 20:7–18. Why does Jeremiah fear that he will end his days in shame?

Jeremiah is remarkably open about his feelings in these passages. Nowhere else do we get the opportunity to look so freely into the soul of a prophet.

These "confessions" help us get a sense of Jeremiah as a human being, a person who experienced sadness, hatred, and doubt, just as we all do. Despite his loneliness and frustration, however, Jeremiah experienced the continuing word of God so powerfully that he could not stop announcing it. Jeremiah pondered:

I say to myself, I will not mention him, I will speak in his name no more. But then it becomes like fire burning in my heart, imprisoned in my bones. I grow weary holding it in, I cannot endure it.

(Jeremiah 20:9)

So he continued to prophesy, in spite of trouble, rejection, suspicion, and oppression. And Yahweh sustained Jeremiah, as he had promised in the beginning, "Have no fear ... because I am with you to deliver you" (Jeremiah 1:8).

Hope for the Future

Jeremiah offers hopeful words in chapters 30 to 33, sometimes called the "Book of Consolation." Many of Jeremiah's words of salvation recorded in these chapters were originally intended for the people of Israel after it fell to Assyria. Then, when Judah headed down the same path of destruction, the messages were extended to include it, too. Most of these writings were probably completed in the early part of Jeremiah's ministry.

Write on Their Hearts   Unlike Isaiah's hopeful prophecies of a future king who would be the deliverer of the people, Jeremiah centers his message on why the people had not been able to keep the Covenant promises. He finally centers on the stubbornness and hardness of their hearts. Judah could only pray that Yahweh would form new hearts in them and bring about a total conversion of Judah.

> *The days are coming, says the Lord, when I will make a new Covenant with the house of Israel and the house of Judah. . . . I will place my law within them, and write it upon their hearts; I will be their God, and they shall be My people.*
>
> (Jeremiah 31:31, 33)

Jeremiah's Purchase   Jeremiah's hope for Israel's restoration is real, so much so that he fulfills his family duty and purchases land from his cousin, even though the army of Babylon had already captured Jerusalem. This purchase symbolized the hope that someday he would be able to return and to farm the land. Jeremiah's purchase of the property was a sign that Judah would be restored and that the life of the people would continue:

> *Thus says the Lord of hosts, the God of Israel: Take these deeds, both the sealed and the open deed of purchase, and put them in an earthen jar, so that they can be kept there a long time. For thus says the Lord of hosts, the God of Israel: Houses and fields and vineyards shall again be bought in this land.*
>
> (Jeremiah 32:13–15)

While Jeremiah's words seemed to have few positive results at the time, they became a source of great comfort and hope during the time of exile. Through Jeremiah's guidance, the Israelites had reason to believe in God's goodness and looked for ways to revitalize the Covenant.

Have You Considered?

1. If Jeremiah was sure that Judah would not respond to his message, how do you think it made him feel to deliver that message anyway? Would you have delivered the message, if you were sure it wouldn't work?
2. Describe a modern example of a prophetic action.
3. Do you think that Jeremiah was right in believing that people's attitudes, rather than their leadership, would have to change if they were to follow God's law? Why or why not?

Spiritual Reflection

A New Covenant

Pray and reflect on Jeremiah's vision of a New Covenant between Yahweh and humankind, reading about it in Jeremiah 31:31–33. Do one of the following to express your images of the New Covenant in prayer:

- Reflect on the lyrics of a favorite song that includes a message of hope for the future. How can this song help inspire you to dedicate yourself to the vision of a New Covenant?

- Imagine a world where the New Covenant has taken effect. What would it look like? Draw this new world.
- Offer a sacrifice (a day of fast, a visit to someone who is lonely, etc.) in the name of the New Covenant.
- Compose a plan (either on your own or in a small group) of something you can undertake to help express the New Covenant.

CHAPTER 6 REVIEW

Q/A

Section One

1. Give an example of the injustice common in the Northern and Southern kingdoms.
2. What was Assyria's policy on what to do with conquered populations? Because of this, what happened to the ten northern tribes?
3. How did the prophets explain the destruction of Israel?
4. How did Ahaz disobey Yahweh?
5. Identify: Hezekiah.
6. Why does the Deuteronomic historian honor King Josiah?
7. Identify: Nebuchadnezzar.
8. How did the prophets explain the destruction of Judah?

Section Two

1. What were Amos' views concerning public worship and justice?
2. What metaphor did Hosea use to describe the relationship between Yahweh and Israel?
3. Why is the prophet Isaiah called "Isaiah of Jerusalem"?
4. What is unique in what Isaiah says about God's attitude towards other nations?
5. To what did the story of the potter's flask refer?
6. Define: prophetic action.
7. Identify: Baruch.
8. What is the nature of the "New Covenant" that Jeremiah predicted?

BIBLE ACTIVITY

1. Read Sirach 48:15–25 and 49:1–6. These verses show how one of the later writers remembered the main characters at the time of the fall of the Northern and Southern kingdoms. Make a list of the information that is similar to what you learned in this chapter. Also, list any new information you discover and any information that Sirach left out.
2. Read Hosea 2:15–22 and 11:1–4. How do these passages express God's love for the people of Israel?
3. King Josiah's story is told in 2 Kings 22. Read the chapter to find out information on (1) the important object which was found, (2) the person to whom Josiah went for advice (3) the prophecy, and (4) the reward Josiah received for his sorrow.
4. Read 2 Kings 18–19 and 21. What was life like in Judah during a time of brief independence from around 630 B.C.E.?
5. Read Jeremiah 24:1–10. What was Jeremiah's message in this story of the two baskets of figs? Read 2 Kings 18–19 and 21.
6. Read Jeremiah 29:4–15 to find out (1) Yahweh's plan for the Judah and (2) the length of their captivity in Babylon.

GLOSSARY

- **Assyrians:** The powerful nation that overthrew the coalition of Israel and Damascus, and eventually destroyed the Northern kingdom.
- **Babylon:** The nation that conquered Judah and pillaged Jerusalem and its people.
- **Confessions of Jeremiah:** Passages in Jeremiah where the prophet reveals his inner feelings of anger, fear, and doubt.
- **False Pride:** An attitude denounced by Isaiah as inconsistent with the holiness of Yahweh, false pride values the self or nation too highly in comparison with God.
- **Holiness:** Yahweh's main characteristic according to Isaiah; it means separateness, majesty, and power.
- **Justice:** The harmonious order in society which requires all people to be treated fairly; in the Old Testament it is based on Covenant.
- **Lost Tribes:** A term for the ten northern tribes after they were deported by the Assyrians.
- **New Covenant:** The future situation predicted by Jeremiah when God will give humanity "new hearts" so people will be able to love and obey Yahweh completely.
- **Prophetic Action:** A dramatic public act performed by a prophet to illustrate his or her message.
- **Seraphim:** A fiery angel seen by Isaiah of Jerusalem during his vision of God, described in Chapter 6 of Isaiah.
- **Writing Prophets:** Prophets with books in the Old Testament that bear their names.

UNDERSTANDING MORE ABOUT:

Micah

Micah was active in Judah at the same time as Isaiah, and the two form an interesting pair: where Isaiah's words are polished, Micah's are blunt. Both men, however, attacked the greed and injustice which infected the nation. Micah's prophecies are recorded in the Old Testament book that bears his name.

Both Isaiah and Micah predict the future coming of a king who will save Israel and return it to faithfulness to Yahweh. Micah said that the future king would be born in Bethlehem, a small village a few miles south of Jerusalem where King David was born.

The most obvious similarity between Micah and Isaiah is that they share a vision of a future world governed by Yahweh. In this world, peace shall be the rule among nations. Isaiah 2:4 and Micah 4:3 use the identical words to describe this new world:

They shall beat their swords into plowshares, and their spears into pruning hooks; One nation shall not raise the sword against another, nor shall they train for war again.

Today, their message is inscribed on a statue outside the United Nations, reminding the nations of the world of our common longing for peace.

CHAPTER 7

Exile: An Ending and a Beginning

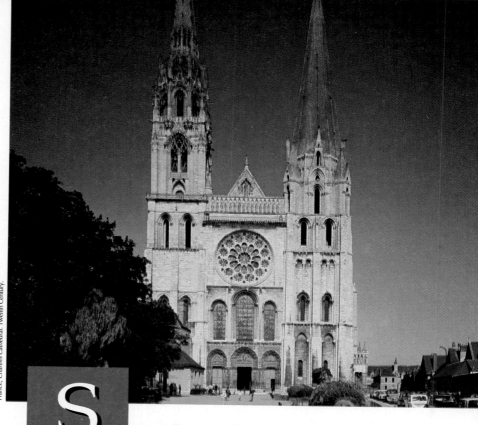

France, Chartres Cathedral. Twelfth Century.

Saint Fulbert was the Bishop of Chartres in France. Fulbert was a great scholar, a talented poet, and an inspired songwriter. He was also a gifted politician who knew most of the kings and diplomats in Europe. In 1020 C.E., he began a project that demanded the very best he could give in all of these areas: the building of the Chartres Cathedral.

Over the next 100 years, Christians from all over Europe donated time and money for the building of the finest cathedral ever raised in honor of the Virgin Mary. Fulbert began with the lowest part—the crypt. He then rapidly constructed the various chapels and the upper church. Finally, workers erected the towers, including the southern tower with its magnificent spire. In 1160, after Fulbert himself had died, "Fulbert's cathedral" was finished. It evoked awe in all who saw it. The people of

Chartres, exhausted from over 100 years of labor, thanked God for their success and rested.

Then, on July 10, 1194, the unthinkable happened: fire raged through the cathedral, destroying everything but the crypt and the towers. Fulbert's cathedral lay in ruins, and the people of Chartres were dazed. "How could God allow this to happen?" they wondered. Despite their sorrow and confusion, the people began the long process of rebuilding. Within only 25 years, the repairs were finished, and the people of Chartres could once again take pride in their beautiful cathedral.

How did they do it? A story told about the repairs gives us part of the answer. A European architect said that he had worked at construction sites for cathedrals all over Europe. At other places, he said, if you were to ask masons what they were doing, they would answer, "We're laying bricks," or if you asked the same question of carpenters, they would say, "We're cutting wood." But at Chartres, he said, even if you asked the most humble rock-hauler what he was doing, he would answer, "Why, I'm building a cathedral!"

The Importance of Attitude

This answer illustrates the importance of attitude in overcoming hardship. While the workers in other places knew their jobs, the people of Chartres had a sense of purpose—they were building a cathedral! Responding to the misfortune of the fire, the people showed courage and a positive attitude. These qualities enabled them to rebuild the cathedral that, even today, is acknowledged as one of the finest in the world.

When war destroys a country, and places its people under a new and unwelcome government, living with that, too, requires courage. After the fall of Jerusalem, the people of Judah faced the task of rediscovering what their faith and life meant during difficult times. What would be the attitude of the people? This chapter is about how they met their challenge.

A Conquered People

Babylon, Ishtar Gate. Sixth Century B.C.E.

When Babylon conquered Judah in 587 B.C.E. and took most of its citizens into the Exile, it caused a great crisis of confidence among the people. For centuries, the people of Judah had believed that as God's chosen ones, they were protected against this sort of humiliation. "How could God abandon us like this?" they asked. "Has God forgotten about us?" These and other questions were asked by the people of Judah as they walked under guard to Babylon.

Learning Objectives for Section One

By the end of this section, you will be able to:

- Identify the conditions of life for Jews during the Exile.
- Discuss why Jews questioned the promises of Yahweh.
- Explain why the Exile was a threat to the existence of the Jewish community.

◆ Life During the Exile

Like Assyria, Babylon deported the population of territories it conquered. There were two reasons for this policy:

- The chances for rebellion in the conquered territory were greatly reduced if much of the population—especially anyone with leadership ability—was removed.
- The conquered people would be more likely to think of themselves as Babylonians if they were living in Babylon.

In keeping with these two goals, many Judahites were forced to move to Babylon after the defeat of Judah in 587 B.C.E.

Of course, it was impossible to move everyone.

1. If people wanted to hide in the wilderness, the Babylonians had neither the time nor the resources to track them down.

2. Somebody had to stay behind to raise the crops and care for the herds. Babylon wanted the lands of Judah to be productive and the Babylonian governors did not want to perform these tasks themselves.

Babylon, Judah in Exile. Sixth Century B.C.E.

This relief from a palace in Nineveh shows the people of Judah being driven into exile in 587 B.C.E.

LEARN FROM THE MAP

The Babylonian Empire

The Babylonian Empire lay at the head of the Persian Gulf in what is now Iraq. Often called "Mesopotamia," Greek for "the land between the rivers." Babylonia began in the fertile valley between the Tigris and Euphrates Rivers. Examine the Babylonian Empire in 586 B.C.E. Compare it with the Assyrian Empire. Notice especially what has happened to Judah. Note the location of Babylon, the capital city. How far is it from Jerusalem to Babylon? Please note that while Judah is colored differently, it was definitely part of the Babylonian Empire.

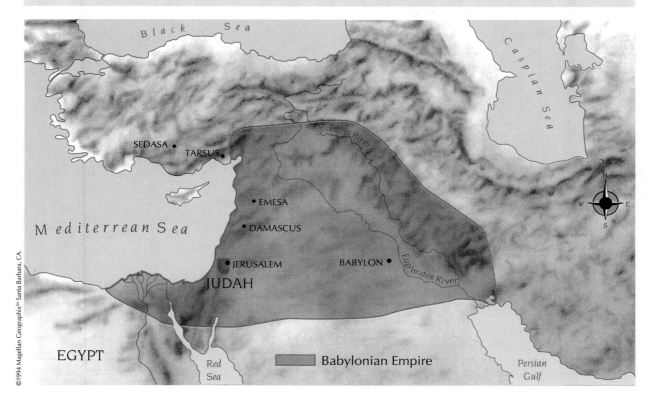

©1994 Magellan Geographix℠ Santa Barbara, CA.

Babylonian Empire

3. Preventing rebellion did not require that everybody be removed, just the scholars, priests, politicians, and community leaders. Many people stayed in Judah while their leaders went into Exile.

The Bible tends to focus only on those people who went to Babylon, because it is those people who produced the great literature of this period. The story of the Exile, however, also includes the fate of those who were left behind.

Unstable Government

After the Babylonian victory in 587, the immediate administration of Judah was left in the hands of a local governor, Gedaliah, a Judahite. He governed from the town of Mizpah, and supervised the Judahite farmers and herdsmen who had stayed.

Gedaliah's term in office was brief—only two years—before he was murdered by Ishmael, who wanted to be the governor himself. At a feast, Ishmael slaughtered Gedaliah and all of his followers, including some Babylonian soldiers. Two days later, he butchered seventy Judahites who had brought offerings to the site where the Temple lay in ruins.

Angered by this attack on its servant, Babylon deported all of the remaining Judahite leaders in 582 B.C.E. and divided the country into two parts. The northern half became part of an existing Babylonian province, while the southern part was annexed to Edom—a deep insult to the Judahites. Meanwhile,

The Bible in Context

What Is a Jew?

Up to now, we have used the term "Hebrews," and then "Israelites," to refer to the people of the original Covenant. Now, it's time to introduce the last such term: "Jew." After the split between the two kingdoms, people living in Judah thought of themselves as "Judahites" rather than "Israelites" (remember that the Northern kingdom was called "Israel"). In Babylon, people from Judah were called "Yehudi" or Judeans. It was not long before "Judeans" was shortened to "Jews."

Today, the term "Jew" is used to refer to people who, either through birth or conversion, identify themselves with the religious and cultural traditions of ancient Israel. "Judaism" is the religion centered on obedience to the Law of Yahweh, kept alive by the Jews during the Exile.

---

the remaining associates of Gedaliah fled to Egypt for protection, taking Jeremiah with them. As a result, the people who were left in Judah felt even more abandoned.

The Ones Left Behind

The Second Book of Kings 24:14,16 says that more than 17,000 people were taken into exile in Babylon, while Jeremiah 52:28 gives the number of 4,600. Obviously, these numbers are not in agreement. In any case, they probably reflect only the number of free men sent into exile.

Whichever number is correct, historians estimate that after the first deportation in 597, perhaps as many as 125,000 people remained in Judah. Even after the murder of Gedaliah and the second deportation, over 100,000 Judahites were left. But by 530, barely 20,000 Judahites were to be found there.

Why did the population of Judah drop so dramatically in such a short time? Archaeological evidence shows that most of the cities in Judah had been destroyed in the war with Babylon prior to the Exile. With houses, trades, and crops destroyed, the land lay in ruin. The leaders were gone, and the promise of Judah as the "people of God" seemed forgotten. Those left behind after the second deportation were faced with the near-impossible task of surviving in a country without leadership or natural resources. As a result, many of them fled to places such as Egypt and Arabia. Over time, the number of those remaining in Judah dwindled to a handful.

From this time in history, the majority of Judahites would live outside the land of Judah. Even today, the majority of Jews live outside the nation of Israel. There are more Jews living in the United States, for example, than there are Jews living in Israel. This situation, in which the majority of the members of a nation live outside their traditional homeland, is called a "diaspora."

One spark of life remained in the land of Judah. People still made pilgrimages to the site of the Temple, although only shattered ruins remained. As the center of faith for over four hundred years, Jerusalem remained the focus of hope for many Jews. Even in exile, Jews would sometimes journey to the Temple ruins to pray and (perhaps) to offer sacrifice. Many certainly dreamed of a day when the Temple would be rebuilt. The base of Jewish life, however, was now firmly in Babylon.

Babylon, *Babylonian Lion. Sixth Century B.C.E.?*

The growling lion was a symbol of Babylon's dominance. This wall painting was taken from Babylon and is now preserved in the Louvre Museum in Paris, France.

in the *Spotlight*
Other Forms of Worship

According to the Law, there could be no Temple or official worshipping cult outside of Jerusalem. For the Diaspora (Jews who did not live in Judah), however, visits to the Temple were impossible. Therefore, they had to find new ways to worship God.

- Jews living in upper Egypt, in a place called Elephantine, constructed and maintained their own temple. The worship there was an example of syncretism (the blending of various religious traditions). Influenced by Egyptian ideas, the Jews honored a female goddess as Yahweh's counterpart. The temple at Elephantine was destroyed by a rival religious group in 410 B.C.E.
- In Babylon, the exiles met in private homes for worship. These meeting places are the forerunners of the synagogue ("place of assembly"). Without altars for sacrifice, other modes of worship were used: prayers, the singing of psalms, oral readings, and the study of the Law. In these settings, Jewish children were trained in the faith and the community gathered. These meeting places were built facing the direction of the Temple in Jerusalem, and the worshippers faced Jerusalem when they prayed.

Conditions in Exile

For most Jews, what was happening in Judah no longer affected them directly. They now lived in Babylon, and it was the conditions in Babylon, not Judah, that determined the quality of their lives.

Actually, living conditions in Babylon for the Jews were not as horrible as one might think. The evidence we have shows that the Jews lived in communities of their own and that they enjoyed quite a bit of freedom. They could:

- meet together and listen to their leaders
- build houses
- farm
- engage in business
- work in the royal service

Work in Babylon   Archaeologists have found that banking was invented in Babylon a few decades before the Exile, and that soon after the deportations,

some Jews became involved in that occupation. Others found positions in the court or worked for tradesmen who needed their particular skills. The Jews were allowed to keep their earnings, and some prospered. In fact, the material standard of living was so high for many Jews that they chose to remain in Babylon even after it was possible to return to Jerusalem.

Physically, then, conditions could have been much worse. Nevertheless, things were far from perfect.

- While not imprisoned, the Jews were forced to remain in Babylon.
- Though not tortured, they were watched and could not act with total freedom.
- Although allowed to participate in regular city life, the Jews were treated as lower class citizens.
- Most importantly, they were forbidden to live on their own land, the land promised to them long ago by Yahweh.

Guidance from Jeremiah   Between the first (597 B.C.E.) and second (587 B.C.E.) deportations, Jeremiah wrote a letter to those already in Babylon. In it, he proclaimed God's message, and advised the Jews to make a full life in the unwelcome country—to make homes and families for themselves and to do well. They are to "promote the welfare" of Babylon, because it was God's hand which had banished them there and because their welfare depended on the well-being of Babylon itself (*Jeremiah* 29:4–7). Despite the frustrations and imperfections of life in Babylon, in many ways the Jews followed Jeremiah's advice. They made a life for themselves in exile.

Have You Considered?

1. Describe a situation in your life in which you faced some difficulty. How did your attitude help or hurt you in dealing with this situation?
2. What do you think would be the hardest part of being forced to live in another culture: learning a new language? new customs? different religion? missing old friends? something else?
3. In Babylon, the Jews were offered the chance to prosper and lead a secure life, but they were forbidden to return to the land of Judah. Do you think people are sometimes willing to give up freedom for security? Describe the different attitudes towards Babylon you might find among the Jewish exiles living there.

◆ Finding Meaning in Exile

Although conditions in Judah itself may have been bleak, for the Jews living in Babylon the physical consequences of exile were not all that bad. There was a deeper disaster, however, which no amount of prosperity or material comfort could erase. This disaster was an inner one, because the Exile had shattered the Jews' understanding of Yahweh, of themselves, and of life. Questions and doubts were everywhere:

- Why had God permitted Judah to be destroyed?
- Did Yahweh no longer care about the Covenant with the Jews?
- Should Jews still obey the Law?
- What did all this change and suffering mean?

What the Jews faced, in other words, was a crisis of meaning.

The "Western Wall" is all that remains of Herod's Temple, destroyed by the Romans in 70 C.E. It is a source of comfort for Jews even today. The ruins of the original Temple were also honored and served as a gathering place for prayer.

As you read now about this crisis, try to put yourself in the place of the Jewish exiles, for only by so doing can you understand what happened during this critical time.

The Promises of Yahweh

Recall that the faith of the ancient Israelites was founded on Yahweh's Covenant promises. The founding Covenant at Sinai promised the Hebrews land, prosperity, and a special relationship with the Lord. These promises had conditions. The conditions were listed in what we call "the Law." If the people obeyed these conditions, God's promises would also be kept.

When David was king, additional promises were made. Yahweh assured David that his descendants would always be on the throne in Jerusalem. As long as there was a king in Jerusalem, he had indeed descended from David. But the Jews believed that David's kingdom would last forever.

Over the years, the Jews forgot that the Covenant promises also included obligations. The people had come to believe that if they kept the required ritual of the Temple according to priestly interpretation, then Yahweh would always protect them and bring them prosperity. In spite of all the prophecies to the contrary, the Israelites were complacent.

With the destruction of Judah, Jerusalem, and the Temple, all such certainty was swept away. What were they now to believe about Yahweh?

God or Not? Their God or Not?

In one bitter decade, the people of Judah lost everything of value: families, friends, homes, and faith. Doubts about Yahweh were everywhere. Yahweh wasn't God at all, or if a god, Yahweh was at best only a very weak one. After all, the god of Babylon, Marduk, had defeated Yahweh's forces in battle. Even if Yahweh had been powerful once, now the conquering god must be stronger.

All the Jews needed to do to see which god was most powerful was look at the magnificence of Babylon. It was far more splendid than anything in Jerusalem, especially after the Temple had been stripped of its richest ornamentation to pay bribes to stronger nations. Even many Jews were materially better off in Babylon than they had been in Judah. It certainly looked as if Marduk was better able to provide for his people than Yahweh had been to provide for the Jews. Why should the Jews continue to worship Yahweh?

Scripture Workshop

Reactions to Exile

How did the Jews feel about their life in Babylon? Some poets of the Exile have left behind their reactions. Read Psalm 137 and Lamentations 5. To understand these two poems, you need to know that the word "Zion" means the same thing as Judah. Mount Zion was the hill in Jerusalem upon which the Temple was built, and, over time, came to refer to the entire country.

After you've read these two poems, answer the following questions:

1. What were the conditions in Jerusalem and Judah as described here?
2. What were the feelings of the people in Babylon?
3. How would you describe the tone of these passages?
4. In your own words, explain what these poems are about.

Who could blame the Jews if they started to wonder if Yahweh had come to hate them? Hadn't God abandoned them in their time of greatest need? Where was Yahweh when Babylon burned Jerusalem, or when they defiled and demolished the Temple, the house built especially for God? Perhaps God had not only abandoned the Jews, but had actually turned against them!

If these things were true, how could the Jews dare approach a god who either hated them, or couldn't do anything to help them? Why would one depend any longer on a god who had no power to protect or to save? Maybe they had deserved punishment for their national sins, but what good would punishment do if it destroyed the people forever?

For the Jews, Yahweh and their relationship with Yahweh were firmly connected to the land. It was centered in the Temple in Jerusalem, where Yahweh's glory dwelled. Even if Yahweh was still there, the Jews were not. Even if they repented of their sins, how could they reach God from Babylon to beg for mercy? However they interpreted the destruction of Judah, Jews found only despair.

The Threat to the Community

There were other problems facing the Jewish community as well. Since the Covenant was so closely connected to the land of Judah, faith in the Covenant was challenged when the people were scattered in the Diaspora. Think of the forces which threatened to pull their community apart:

- There was no central location where the people could gather for pilgrimage or festival.
- They were living far from the land and prevented even from visiting Jerusalem.
- They were dispersed over the vast ancient Middle East, far from other Jews.

How could such a non-community have any identity before the Lord? How could they be Yahweh's people if they were no people at all?

Furthermore, the wealth and power of Babylon and other Middle Eastern empires were a threat to the Jewish community. Many Jews were more comfortable in Babylon and Egypt than they had ever been in Judah. Their lives were secure, and they felt safe from danger. If the only reason to identify oneself as Jewish was because of the Covenant with Yahweh, and if Yahweh had failed to help the Jews, what was the point? Wouldn't it just be better to become Babylonians, or Egyptians, or members of another successful nation? Some Jews did exactly that; they stopped following the traditions of Judaism and *assimilated*.

These were the issues that faced the people of Judah during the Exile. In 721 B.C.E., the ten northern tribes had been scattered by the Assyrians, never to be heard from again. They were lost to Yahweh's community forever. Would history now repeat itself with the people of Judah? Would all of Israel disappear from the face of the earth?

Have You Considered?

1. What are living conditions like for refugees today? How does being a refugee affect a person's ability to earn a living? religious faith? family life? ways of thinking?
2. Describe a time when your self-image was challenged by a crisis. How did you respond?
3. Put yourself in the position of the exiled Jews. What reason would you have to continue to worship Yahweh? What would attract you to the gods of Babylon? Explain your answer.

Responding to the Crisis

Iran, *Torah Case. Twentieth Century.*

Despite appearances, Yahweh had neither abandoned Judah, nor was power-less. Yahweh's response was to act as God had always acted in times of national emergency: prophets were sent who spoke God's word. These prophets addressed the crisis of meaning experienced by the people and responded to their fears and doubts one by one. They brought the message that the relationship between Yahweh and the people was still intact. They helped the Jews maintain their community in the face of all the forces threatening to tear it apart. In this sec-tion, you'll hear the words that brought hope and consolation to the Jews in Exile.

Learning Objectives for Section Two

By the end of this section, you will be able to:

- Explain the important insights of Ezekiel.
- Describe the use of symbolism in Ezekiel.
- Discuss the importance of Law for the Priestly Writers.
- Explain Second Isaiah's message of hope.

◆ Ezekiel

Ezekiel was a priest and the first prophet of the Exile. He was respected by the people, and had been exiled with them in the first deportation in 597 B.C.E. His message helped the Jews respond to the various challenges facing them.

Ezekiel's Inner Experience

By modern standards, Ezekiel was quite strange. Even by Israel's standards—whose prophets had often behaved in an unusual manner—Ezekiel must have seemed weird. His personality was prone to pro-found spiritual experiences, dreams, and visions. These experiences were dramatic and unusual, even for prophets. Today they would perhaps be regarded as psychic, or even beyond that.

For example, Ezekiel described in detail his inte-rior "trips" to Jerusalem, carried there in spirit by the power of the Lord. He had wild visions. He acted out

his prophecies through symbolic gestures, like lying on his side for three months or digging his way under a wall. His emotions were tightly controlled by the Lord, so that he did not even mourn at the death of his wife, who was the "delight of his eyes."

So overpowering was Ezekiel's initial experience of Yahweh that for a week he sat among his people, overwhelmed, unable to tell them what he had seen. More experiences and visions followed, including ex-plicit instructions for speech and symbolic actions. Throughout the Book of Ezekiel, one gets the sense that this was a man whose prayer life was alive with a powerful awareness of God's presence. These ex-periences helped make Ezekiel's message captivat-ing for his audiences.

Symbolism in Ezekiel

Like Isaiah, Ezekiel was called through a vision. Ezekiel saw Yahweh's throne chariot approaching from a northern cloud, and surrounded by animals, birds, and human-like creatures supported on a moving wheel that was covered with eyes. Ezekiel describes his vision in great detail: strange forms and living winged creatures, brilliant colors and sheens, fire and more fire, interlocking wheels, and sound that was like the "din of an army." The splendor of his experience (like that of any true vision) was quite indescribable, so Ezekiel said, "such was the vision of the likeness of the glory of the Lord" (*Ezekiel* 1:28).

Through figures and symbols such as these, Ezekiel expressed that:

- The Lord is majestic and holy beyond imagination.
- Yahweh is totally mobile and can be anywhere in an instant.
- Yahweh can see everything at once, having eyes in every direction.
- Yahweh's power is awesome, and although it's held in check, it's ready at any instant to be unleashed.

Raphael, *Ezekiel's Vision*. Sixteenth Century.

The artist Raphael attempted to capture Ezekiel's vision on canvas. Read Chapter 1 of Ezekiel and compare Ezekiel's words to Raphael's depiction.

These were important realizations for Ezekiel and for the whole people. Ezekiel's visions responded to the concerns that the Exile raised about the nature of Yahweh. Throughout Ezekiel's career, he often communicated his understanding of God through such striking symbols and symbolic actions.

Before the Fall: Warnings of Destruction

Between the first deportation in 597 and the destruction of Jerusalem in 587, Ezekiel's responsibility to his people was just the same as Jeremiah's or Isaiah's had been: to call them to repentance before it was too late and Jerusalem destroyed. Like Jeremiah, Ezekiel sensed that his warning would be for nothing. Nevertheless, the Lord insisted that Ezekial give the people God's message.

Ezekiel told the Jews about the total devastation that was yet to come, even as some of the leaders were forced into Exile. Justice had to be fulfilled and, in Ezekiel's view, his people had much for which to suffer. According to Ezekiel, Israel had been untrue to the Lord from its first days in the desert, worshipping other gods and ignoring the Covenant. Yahweh's holiness, majesty, and justice demanded that now—finally, after centuries of disobedience and warning—discipline must be complete. The Lord would no longer hold back. These messages are found in the following verses of Ezekiel: 4; 5; 7:1–28; 20:1–17; 22:29–31.

Individual Responsibility

Among the crucial questions of the Exile, as you have read, was how the community could stay together now that the people were so scattered. This dispersion was a special problem for the Jews, who had always thought of themselves only as members of the group.

The Jews had a proverb to express this communal idea: "Fathers have eaten green grapes, thus their children's teeth are on edge." This proverb (which is also quoted in *Jeremiah* 31:29, so it must have been very common in ancient Israel) suggests that even though the parent disobeys the law, the children experience the bad results. That is, everyone is affected by the behavior of those who came before in community.

The proverb implied that the consequences of the sins of one generation were experienced by the next, or that the sins of a few in the nation would cause the whole nation to experience woes. This cultural assumption might be called "group solidarity." Yet in the sixth century B.C.E., with Jews scattered so widely, such cohesion could not be maintained.

Ezekiel 18:1–32 announces the beginning of a new era, in which a person is responsible only for his or her own choices. With this new understanding, Jews were free to form community without the unrealistic expectation of total group solidarity. People could think of themselves as "Jews," even if there were no local Jewish community.

After the Fall: Ezekiel's Message of Hope

After the destruction of Jerusalem in 586, Ezekiel's message changed. The consequences of Israel's behavior had been terrible, but now that they were completed, it was time to begin again. Remember, the Lord always spoke to the immediate situation. For them, the Word of the Lord was always applicable to their moment in time. They did not speculate about philosophical principles that should last forever. The truths they proclaimed often turned out to be lasting, but the immediate intention of God's message was foremost. Now, in this time of tragedy and bitter agony, the people needed hope.

Dry Bones Will Rise   Ezekiel's teaching includes the famous Valley of Dry Bones. In a vision, the prophet looked out over a valley filled with skeletons, and God tells him these bones will rise again. This vision means that God will restore the people of Judah to life. Further, Yahweh told Ezekiel that from this time on, the Lord would shepherd the people, since

the kings had so badly botched their responsibility. Read Ezekiel 34:7–16.

Yahweh's power, so evident to Ezekiel from his original vision, was about to be demonstrated again; this time not in terror, but in salvation and restoration. The actions of the Lord would begin in the heart, as Jeremiah, too, had understood. The land would be Israel's once again, but the center for God's people would be in their hearts (*Ezekiel* 36:23–28).

Vivid Visions   Ezekiel's vision was vivid. The people themselves would become truly holy: a holy people for a holy God. Because of this expectation of holiness, the land too would become holy. At the center of the land would be a restored Temple, now with pure rites and true worship. Ezekiel predicts that all of this will come to pass so that people (the Jews and others, too) will know what Yahweh means by saying "I am the Lord." Yahweh wants people to understand who God is, and that all power lies in God. By both devastation and then by promise of a re-creation, Yahweh communicates this reality, this power. Israel will understand Yahweh as Lord of all.

Ezekiel's prophecy of a new nation directed by God wouldn't come true quickly. Until it did, many of the exiles rejected Ezekiel's word. Their tragedy was too deep for a rapid healing. Ezekiel's message was heard by some, but there is little evidence that it was believed. After all, Israel had long been in the habit of ignoring its prophets!

Still a few among the Exiles did heed Ezekiel. It is clear that Ezekiel influenced various priests and the elders who responded to his message of hope.

When Hurricane Andrew devastated South Florida in 1992, many people were left homeless. Some moved on rather than rebuilding. The same was true for the Jews after the destruction of Jerusalem.

Have You Considered?

1. Ezekiel's inner experience of the Lord was dramatic and powerful. Have you ever had an experience like his? Do you think such experiences are necessary for communicating with God?
2. Remember that the Deuteronomic historian and others said that the Jews had gone into exile because of the sins of their kings and other leaders. In this context, how would Ezekiel's message of individual responsibility be good news?
3. Ezekiel's message was filled with symbolism. Where do you find symbolism in your religious life? Do you think symbolism sometimes works better than normal speech for getting people's attention and putting them in touch with God? Why or why not?

◆ The Priestly Writers

Ezekiel was not the only person who tried to understand God in the face of ruin. The Lord also inspired the Jewish priests to re-examine the history of Yahweh, the people, and the Covenant. They had to understand better what God intended and what God was really like. Then they had to reinterpret their sacred traditions so that they and their children could understand them as well.

To this end, the priests collected the traditions that the Jews had brought with them into Exile, wrote them down, and then edited them. Now in Exile, the Priestly Writers looked back through the written and oral traditions of their people, searching for deeper understanding than they had known previously.

The Torah

The Priestly Writers came to understand that Yahweh always acted for a purpose. Looking over their past, the priests saw patterns of Yahweh's involvement in Israel's history. By studying these patterns, they found an explanation for the Exile. They then organized the Jewish traditions so that they resembled the order clearly seen in God's actions.

The Priestly Writers began with the act of creation—Genesis 1:1–2:3 is their composition. Creation was followed by the "fall" of humanity from God's grace, and then by the story of how civilization began. You traced all of these traditions in Chapter 4—remember the "P" source? These are the same writers.

Their creation story in Genesis was followed by the legends of the patriarchs and the Covenant with Abraham. Then came the story of Yahweh's deliverance of Israel from slavery in Egypt, and the Exodus. Finally, the Covenant of Sinai was recorded, and the Book of Deuteronomy was included. To these, the Priestly Writers added lists of peoples and nations, as well as genealogies, to emphasize that everything proceeded in an orderly fashion, according to the divine plan. The result of their labors is the Torah, the first five books of the Bible as we now have them.

This emphasis on the divine plan was the priests' answer to the question of whether Yahweh had abandoned them. The priests invited the Jews to look back over their history. Hadn't Yahweh always shaped events to achieve God's purposes? Hadn't Yahweh always brought order out of chaos? In the Exodus story, hadn't God brought the order of the Covenant out of the chaos of the wilderness? Surely, the priests suggested, Yahweh will also bring meaning out of the Exile. They suggested that this chaos, too, was part of the order of God.

In arguing that the Exile was part of the divine order, the priests constructed what is known as a *theodicy*, a "defense of God's goodness in the face of evil." The existence of evil is a problem that theologians and philosophers have wrestled with over the ages, but few have improved on the answer given by the Priestly Writers. They concluded that however difficult it might be to understand, God will bring meaning out of suffering.

Chasidic Jews, like these children who live in an Orthodox community in Galilee, base their entire lives on faithfully living the Law. The Law gives meaning to everything that they do.

A Community Shaped by the Law

The Priestly Writers also considered the nature of the Jewish community. They recognized that as a scattered people, Jews could not rely on a nation to bind them with God. They would need to keep this bond alive in their own hearts and lives. But how?

They answered the question this way: people carry with them their traditional beliefs, customs and codes of behavior. From now on, these would be centered in the Law that unites the Jewish community with God. From this tradition, the Priestly Writers drew up the regulations governing thought and action that would hold the community together and keep it close to the Lord. The regulations they agreed upon emphasized

- Male circumcision as a sign of belonging to the Covenant.
- Keeping the Sabbath day holy.

These two acts, which could be done anywhere and under any circumstances, now became the chief expression of Jewish identity. In addition, the priests added many social and individual laws designed to promote justice and ritual purity. These laws are found in the Book of Leviticus. By keeping the Law, Jews would express their faith in God and their solidarity with one another.

The priests' answer to the Exiles' problem about community life would define for centuries what it meant to be Jewish: a Jew was one who kept the Law. This idea became the foundation of Judaism. The Law rooted the people in a community not bound by political borders.

Have You Considered?

1. In the middle of a tragedy, it is often difficult to see any purpose or order. Yet, people say they often learn most about themselves from difficult times. Describe a difficult time in your life. Looking back, can you see any purpose or order to the experience? Did you learn anything about yourself?
2. Describe a community to which you belong. How do your customs and traditions help unite the members of that community?
3. What is the importance of the rule of law in modern society? What are reasons people give for obeying or disregarding the law?

◆ "Second" Isaiah

When the Exile did finally approach its end, Yahweh sent a prophet to help the Jews understand what was happening. As Ezekiel had emphasized destruction and then hope and the Priestly Writers had collected the Law, this new prophet, known as Second Isaiah, proclaimed that Israel's time of punishment was at an end, and her future would hold unimagined glory.

In announcing this message, Second Isaiah expressed an understanding of God so profound and so moving, that many people feel that it has no equal anywhere. This writer (we don't even know his or her name) responded to the fears and despairs of the people living in Exile. This message was supported by events that the people themselves knew; Second Isaiah read the signs of the times and saw God's hands at work.

Why "Second" Isaiah?

This prophet of the Exile is called "Second" Isaiah because his or her words of comfort and expected greatness are found in chapters 40–55 of the Book of Isaiah. Second Isaiah was probably a later follower of Isaiah of Jerusalem, and the words of Second Isaiah were added to the works of the master after the Exile. There are many similarities in themes between the two, especially the common theme that God's kingdom would continue through a remnant of a people who have lived their lives in righteousness.

Nevertheless, there are easily recognizable differences of historical information, literary style, and theological interpretation that distinguish Isaiah of Jerusalem from Second Isaiah, who prophesied as the Exile was drawing to a close. Isaiah of Jerusalem's warnings of destruction are replaced by Second Isaiah's comforting promises of new life and restoration. Second Isaiah uses the words "comfort," "way," "servant," and "chosen" to call forth the hope of this new time.

Political Changes: Cyrus the Great

To understand Second Isaiah's message and the circumstances to which he or she spoke, we have to consider the changing players on the international scene. As Isaiah of Jerusalem had been the first to recognize, Yahweh's actions were not confined just to the people of Israel; foreign powers were used to accomplish God's purposes, too.

• Following the death of the emperor, Nebuchadnezzar, in 562 B.C.E., Babylon was thrown into turmoil. Meanwhile, change was brewing in the East.

• The chief, or king, of the Persian tribes was a man named Cambyses, who was married to a daughter of the king of Media. Their son was named *Cyrus.*

• By 559, Cyrus had succeeded his father as king.

• Although Cyrus was greatly ambitious, he was not cruel, as most Assyrian and Babylonian kings before him had been.

• He was an exceptional leader of warriors, and equally talented at persuasion. If he could accomplish his goals by negotiation, he did so. His combined talents made him, by 550, king of all the Medes and the Persians.

Turning his attention to the west, Cyrus quickly captured Assyria, Asia Minor, and parts of Greece. Moving rapidly, he found little effective resistance anywhere. Without pause, Cyrus next turned his armies east of Media and conquered present-day Pakistan and Afghanistan.

Just before Cyrus turned his attention to Babylon, the prophet we call Second Isaiah began his work. Popular opinion of the day probably expected Cyrus to capture Babylon. Cyrus indeed took Babylon, and he then issued an edict which allowed the Jews to return to Judah and rebuild their lives there. For Second Isaiah to see this event happening is not remarkable. The beauty and power of this prophet is in the significance he or she sees in these events.

No Other God

Second Isaiah begins with an announcement of the core of the Lord's message. Isaiah 40:1 says, "Give comfort to my people, says your God," which Second Isaiah did. The ideas expressed were not totally new, yet were expressed with great power and beauty. Second Isaiah responded with words powerful enough to calm the terror people still felt about their separation from Yahweh.

Second Isaiah answered their fears about the power of Yahweh by recognizing that:

• Yahweh was all-powerful—Yahweh was the creator of everything.
• Yahweh was the *only* God.

For Second Isaiah it was clear that Yahweh could not have been conquered by other gods, because there were no other gods. The statues of other gods were just that, statues, and nothing more.

Scripture Workshop

Second Isaiah's Promise of Glory

As you know, the basic message of Second Isaiah is to show that God was only correcting Judah because of its sin, just as a parent must correct a wayward child. However, God has never stopped loving Judah and is now preparing a new stage of Covenant living for the Jews.

Read the following passages from Second Isaiah and answer the corresponding questions about God's plan.

• **Read Isaiah 48:6b-8a and Isaiah 43:18–21.** What are the elements of Yahweh's new act so far?
• **Read Isaiah 48:14–21.** What must the people do (especially in verse 20) to receive the new action of God?
• **Read Isaiah 44:1–5.** What will the quality of their life be in the future?
• **Read Isaiah 49:8–32.** What will their trip homeward be like?

In saying this, Second Isaiah brought the growing monotheism of the Jews to completion. Previously, they had usually declared that Yahweh was the only god for them, but they had not denied the existence of other gods. Now, however, Second Isaiah tells the people that there are no other gods. Yahweh's power is unrivaled in the universe, because God is all-powerful, all-holy, and one. Faced with terrible alternatives, the Jews finally understood this to be the truth.

Just knowing that Yahweh was the Creator and God of all was not enough, however. The people in exile also felt abandoned by God. Second Isaiah responded to this fear as well. He asserted that Yahweh continued to care for Israel, just as God had cared for them from the beginning, and that God had brought about everything that had happened. Their present punishment was required by their sins, but their future glory would truly show the greatness of God.

A Glorious Future

One of the unique elements of Second Isaiah's message is the idea that God has great things in store for the nation of Israel. According to Second Isaiah,

People of Note

Cyrus the Great

Part of King Cyrus's character was a remarkable tolerance for people of other nations and cultures, certainly a rare characteristic for rulers of his day. Cyrus learned that he was able to govern conquered peoples better if he honored, rather than insulted, their religious beliefs.

He was also a brilliant general, whose military success put him in command of the largest empire the world had ever known. By 540 B.C.E., it was obvious to Second Isaiah that Cyrus would defeat the Babylonians. This prediction came true in 539 when the city of Babylon welcomed Cyrus as conqueror.

One way in which Cyrus respected the beliefs of his subject was by allowing all of the exiles to return to their homelands and rebuild their fallen shrines. In fact, according to Ezra 6:4, Cyrus even donated funds for rebuilding the Temple. No wonder, then, that Second Isaiah and other Jews saw the hand of God in Cyrus' victories.

Mount Zion will be the seat of God's rule over all the universe, and other nations will come streaming to Jerusalem to humble themselves before the throne of Yahweh.

You have seen that Second Isaiah stresses how all nations are part of God's saving plan. The consequence of this observation is that Yahweh is the real king of the world, and Second Isaiah announces that God's rule will now be made known to all. Second Isaiah does not speak of the return of a Davidic king to Judah. Rather, God will establish a covenant directly with the whole people, and will rule over them and all nations from Zion. All the peoples of the earth will come to Jerusalem to pay tribute, and to learn from Israel the power and goodness of the Lord.

These images of future glory brought tremendous excitement and comfort to the exiles. Perhaps, they began to sense that their suffering had not been in vain.

Why Had They Suffered? Even if the people began to comprehend that destruction was over and a wonderful future lay ahead of them, many must have still wondered why they had suffered. Yes, the nation had been sinful, that was clear enough. But now Yahweh was going to change it all around. Why? What was God's purpose in all this?

Second Isaiah said there were three reasons for God's action:

- It was necessary that Israel feel the consequences of its wrongs. That was merely justice.
- The destruction was to purify them.
- Yahweh did it for the sake of the holy name.

This last point was one that Ezekiel also had made: Yahweh doesn't act out of any particular desire to benefit people, but for the sake of the divine name.

The Holy Name What did it mean that Yahweh acted for the sake of the holy name? To help you understand, remember what "name" meant in Israel. One's name is one's essence, one's true being, one's own nature and source of one's power. So Yahweh's action here is not for the sake of a reputation, but because it is in God's nature to act in these ways.

When the nation was prosperous but rebellious and forgetful of the Covenant, it was Yahweh's nature and justice to discipline and purify Israel. When they were living in devastation, but willing finally to hear God's word to them, it was Yahweh's justice and holiness to act on their behalf.

In all actions, then, no matter how they may appear to human beings, Second Isaiah announces that it is the nature of God to act in majesty and holiness. That profound quality is often beyond human understanding, but holiness and integrity are Yahweh's essential nature. So of course they are expressed in all of God's actions.

The Suffering Servant

Second Isaiah includes a few passages of a special character. These passages have been called the "Servant Songs," because they speak of a particular servant of Yahweh who has a special calling from the Lord.

It's not exactly clear, however, who this servant is. Sometimes the songs seem to speak of an individual, and sometimes they seem to mean the whole people of Israel. At least once, Israel is mentioned by name, but most scholars think that this verse may have been added by a later editor. Even if we can't name the servant, however, it is still quite possible to see the servant's purpose.

• This servant fulfills a prophet's role. The servant is sent by Yahweh to speak God's message in word and in action to the people. That word will bring justice and mercy. The outstanding quality of the Servant's work is seen in its gentleness and patience. By fulfilling his purpose, the Servant will actually make people righteous before the Lord.

• The servant will be an intercessor between the people and the Lord, as Moses and other prophets were. In this role, the prophet prayed and argued with the Lord, trying to call forth divine mercy and forgiveness. This servant will do more than that: he will suffer the penalties of the people's sins, so that justice is satisfied and the people can enjoy a new relationship with God. The suffering of the servant will restore the people of Israel to God.

• The servant will be victorious over suffering through confidence in God. The servant will actually be glorified by God, not only in the sight of Israel, but in the sight of the whole world. Consistently, the servant's mission is not only to Israel, but is universal. People from all over the world will benefit from his suffering and will acknowledge him.

Thus the "Servant Songs" of Second Isaiah expand the meaning of Israel's Exile far beyond the exiled people themselves. They know now that other nations are being used as agents of Yahweh, for Yahweh is God of the whole world and creator of all. There is only one God. Although some of the prophets believed that, none before Second Isaiah announced it with such unmistakable power and clarity. The "Servant Songs" reveal that God plans to act to restore and redeem the whole world, not only the people of Israel.

Have You Considered?

1. Second Isaiah saw the hand of God in the political events of the time. Do you believe God is involved in political events today? Why or why not?
2. Second Isaiah said that God would make Israel glorious in the sight of all other nations. How would this promise help reassure the Jews that they were still a chosen people?
3. In the "Servant Songs," Second Isaiah said that Israel would be glorified through her suffering. Why is it that sometimes the greatest victories are won not through force, but through accepting suffering? Consider the examples of Gandhi and Martin Luther King Jr. in your answer.

Spiritual Reflection

Second Isaiah

Probably no experience in American history comes as close to the exile in Babylon as the enslavement of Africans before the Civil War. Like the Judahites, these people were forced into exile and made to labor for a foreign master. When they arrived in America, many of these Africans were baptized as Christians and became familiar with the Bible. They found comfort in the Bible and hope in the words of Second Isaiah. Of all the passages in the Bible, the most popular for sermons in slave churches may have been this one from Isaiah 40:

Comfort, comfort my people;—it is the voice of your God; speak tenderly to Jerusalem and tell her this, that she has fulfilled her term of bondage, that her penalty is paid.

(40:1–2)

These words remind us of the suffering of oppressed people, as well as the power of God to liberate them. For your prayer experience, do the following:

• Reread the passage above from Second Isaiah.
• Meditate upon the words.
• Think of someone you know who is suffering. This might be a group of people, or a personal friend or relative.
• Pray that God may see their suffering, and send consolation to them, as Second Isaiah brought comfort to Israel.
• Thank God for hearing you, and go your way!

Q/A

Section One

1. List two reasons why the Babylonians deported conquered people.
2. List two reasons why some people stayed behind in Judah.
3. Define: diaspora, Gedaliah, Jew.
4. What freedoms did the people enjoy in the Exile?
5. Were all Jews in the Exile poor?
6. Describe the crisis of meaning experienced by the people during the Exile.
7. List three threats to the Jewish community in the Exile.

Section Two

1. What was the first message of Ezekiel?
2. What did the symbolism of his visions teach Ezekiel about God?
3. What did Ezekiel's "Valley of Dry Bones" vision mean?
4. What did the Priestly Writers do with the traditions brought by the Jews into exile?
5. How did the Priestly Writers answer the question of whether God had abandoned the people of Judah?
6. How did the priests decide to unify the Jewish community?
7. What two actions were the center of the priestly Law?
8. Why is the last prophet of the Exile called "Second" Isaiah?

BIBLE ACTIVITY

1. Read the following passages from the Book of Psalms: Psalm 74:1–11, Psalm 79, Psalm 126 and Psalm 147. What relationships can you describe between these psalms and the events described in this chapter? When do you think these psalms might have been written?
2. Read Ezekiel 1:10–28 and 3:1–15, and then answer the following: (a) Where was Ezekiel when he received his call? (b) Describe the four living creatures he saw. (c) What did God command Ezekiel to eat? (d) Name the place where Ezekiel stayed for seven days.
3. Ezekiel and Second Isaiah both describe the restoration of Israel using the imagery of a shepherd and a flock. Read Ezekiel 34 and Isaiah 40:10–11. Write a comparison of the two passages.

GLOSSARY

- **Assimilation:** The process through which Jews abandoned their traditions and became members of other cultures.
- **Circumcision:** Jewish rite performed on male infants as a sign of membership in the community; made a central aspect of the Law by the Priestly Writers.
- **Cyrus:** King of the Medes and the Persians; conqueror of Babylon; freed Jews from Exile.
- **Diaspora:** Scattering of the Jews into many lands and nations after the Babylonian Exile.
- **Exile:** The period of time from 587 B.C.E. to 538 B.C.E. when the people of Judah were forced to live in Babylon.
- **Ezekiel:** Prophet of hope during the Exile.
- **Holy Name:** Phrase used by Second Isaiah to refer to the "essence" or "nature" of God.
- **Jew:** Short for "Yehudi" ("Judean"). Used for the Judahites beginning with the Exile.
- **Marduk:** The god of Babylon when Judah was exiled and when Cyrus took over the Babylonian Empire.
- **Nebuchadnezzar:** Babylon's most powerful king, responsible for the Exile.
- **Sabbath:** Rule that Jews must not work from sundown Friday to sundown Saturday; made a central observance by the Priestly writers.
- **Second Isaiah:** The author of Isaiah 40–55; prophet of the Exile who announced the end of suffering and the promise of future glory.
- **Suffering Servant:** Figure in "Servant Songs" in Second Isaiah who will announce God's words, intercede between God and the people, and glorify Israel through suffering.
- **Synagogue:** Term meaning "gathering place," referring to houses of worship built for Jews who could no longer go to the Temple.
- **Theodicy:** A defense of God's goodness in the face of evil.
- **Zion:** The hill in Jerusalem upon which Solomon's temple was constructed; usually refers to Judah.

UNDERSTANDING MORE ABOUT:

Isaiah 40–55

These chapters were written, as you know, by a much later disciple of Isaiah of Jerusalem. Nothing personal is known about the author, so this anonymous prophet is called simply, Second (or "Deutero," which means second), Isaiah. The reasons for separating chapters 40–55 from the earlier part of the book are historical as well as literary and content-oriented:

- **Historical,** because it is obvious that a different period in history is known and discussed.
- **Literary,** because the styles of the two sections are widely different in form and in vocabulary.
- **Contextually,** because chapters 1–39 speak primarily of future doom, while Second Isaiah speaks only of the restoration in the near future and the destruction in the recent past.

This work can be dated fairly precisely (540 or 539 B.C.E.) because of the prophet's knowledge of King Cyrus. The chapters of Second Isaiah are as complete a unit as there is in the Bible. Few scholars see much evidence of editorial work in these chapters.

CHAPTER 8

Return and Rebuilding

Legend

- General History
- Biblical History
- Jewish History
- Books written

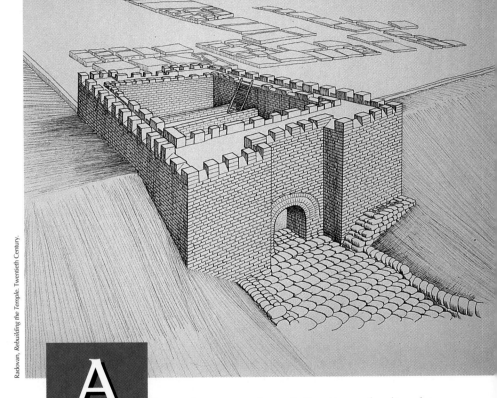

Radovan, *Rebuilding the Temple.* Twentieth Century.

Alexandra remembered the time she lived in California as the best of her life. Her family lived in a small town near the ocean. Their house sat on a quiet street, and Alex had the front bedroom with a big bay window. In the backyard, her grandfather had built her a wooden clubhouse with a swing and a slide.

Alex's favorite memory of California was of her best friend, Maria. As little girls, Alex and Maria would drag their doll collections up to the clubhouse. Then, Alex's mom would bring them lunch, which they would pretend to share with their dolls.

When she was in third grade, Alex's father was transferred to a new job in Ohio. Life wasn't all bad there for Alex, as she enjoyed her new school and made new friends. Still, she missed her old house, old school, and especially Maria. For a while, the two girls wrote letters to each other.

Then, the letters stopped. Things had changed since Alex and Maria were little girls; in the fall, both would be entering high school.

Just after junior high graduation, Alex's dad had another surprise: the family was moving back to California! They had never sold their old house. As their tenant's lease was expiring, they could move back right away. Alex was the most excited of all. She couldn't wait to see her old bedroom again, the clubhouse, and, of course, Maria.

The move back was difficult for Alex. Nothing was as she remembered it; her old room was decorated with football players, and the clubhouse was tiny and falling apart. Alex looked forward to seeing Maria and getting back to the way things used to be.

As she approached Maria's house, Alex was relieved to see Maria's father working in the yard. "Maria is inside with her boyfriend," he said. "Go right in, she'll be surprised to see you." The girls hugged and laughed. After a few minutes, Maria said that they were heading for the beach. Alex listened for an invitation to join them, but it never came.

Alex walked back home, feeling depressed. "This place isn't the way I remember it at all," she told her father angrily.

Unrealistic Expectations

Like Alex, the people of Judah went home expecting to pick up where they had left off. They remembered the promises of Second Isaiah:

- All of the people of Israel would return to their own land.
- The Temple would be rebuilt and Yahweh would once again dwell in Jerusalem.
- Judah would be the center of God's rule over the world.

They, too, were disappointed when life turned out different from what they had expected. Those who accepted King Cyrus's offer to return to Jerusalem found that fulfilling the prophet's predictions would not be easy. Building a city and reestablishing themselves as a people would be a major challenge.

Judah after the Exile

When the first group of Jews returned to Judah, they faced many challenges. Living conditions were terrible, and to survive they had to defend themselves from other groups. They also had to renew themselves as a community. All this had to be done while living under foreign rule, a special challenge for the people commanded to be "unlike other nations." What must it have been like to be one of the first returnees to Judah? Where would one start in rebuilding the nation? What unexpected surprises lay in store for the weary returnee?

Learning Objectives for Section One

By the end of this section, you will be able to:

- List several problems experienced by the Jews on their return to Judah.
- Discuss the importance of the work of Haggai, Zechariah, and Nehemiah.
- Explain the religious reforms of Ezra.
- Define "Hellenization" and describe its impact on Judah.

◆ Going Home: Promises and Perils

Second Isaiah had promised that greatness and glory would await the people when they returned to Judah. Those Jews who made the trip back went with high hopes. However, making Second Isaiah's promise come true would be a very difficult task.

Why Go Back?

King Cyrus had made it possible for the Jews to return to Judah, but many people simply did not want to go. Why should they? By 538 B.C.E., the date of Cyrus' edict, only a few of the oldest Judahites would have had any personal memory of their homeland. Everyone else would have been born and raised in exile, where they had become established. Babylon was now their home. For them to return to Jerusalem, would be a major uprooting.

There were other issues to consider about a possible move back to Judah:

- Since Jerusalem had been pillaged, it would have to be rebuilt.
- The journey from Babylon to Jerusalem was at least a 1,000 mile trip through a desolate desert, and most of the travelers would have to walk.
- Other people had settled in and around Judah, replacing the Jews. Tensions between those who were already there and those who would come could lead to conflict.

Second Isaiah had said to the people,

Go forth from Babylon, flee from Chaldea! I, the Lord, your God, teach you what is for your good, and lead you on the way you should go.

(Isaiah 48:20, 17)

Given all the obstacles listed above, it would take a special kind of person to take up Second Isaiah's challenge and make the trip.

The First Group

Only a tiny group, at first, returned to Judah. From the start, they experienced difficulty. The harvest was meager, so food supplies were short. Much of the economic aid that had been promised by King Cyrus never arrived. Survival itself became a challenge. It was painfully obvious that the resettlement demanded great vision and endurance. To make matters worse, the Jews experienced hostility from the people who had claimed their land during the Exile.

Imagine that your parents had bought an abandoned house 50 years ago. They had worked hard over the years, fixing the place up and making it their home. You were born there, and that's where your parents lived until they died. When they died, you inherited the house. One day, a stranger knocks on your door and says that her grandfather had owned the house many years before and had been forced to leave it by the government.

- How would you feel if she claimed that this house—the one that your parents had worked so hard for and that you thought was yours—really belonged to her?
- How would you react to her statement? What would you do?

You now have some idea of a problem the Jews faced when they returned from Babylon. After the Jews were forcibly removed, other people claimed their land. These people were not very happy 50 years later when the Jews returned, wanting their property back and claiming a slice of the already-scarce economic pie. Among the many groups who resisted the Jews' return, the biggest challenge probably came from the Samaritans.

The Samaritans   Over time, the citizens of the Northern kingdom who had been left behind by the Assyrians intermarried with members of the Canaanite, Assyrian, and other local nations. They became a new cultural group called "Samaritans" after the capital city of the area, Samaria. Tensions between these Samaritans and the returning Jews flared up when the Samaritans realized that the Jews intended to rebuild the Temple in Jerusalem. This project would make Judah a strong political and economic rival to Samaria.

The rivalry between the Samaritans and the Jews was further complicated by religion. The Samaritans—descendants of the nation of Israel who worshipped Yahweh—practiced their own form of religion, which was centered in the temple they had built on Mount Gerizim. The Samaritans believed that they were living faithful to the Covenant. Relations between the Jews and the Samaritans worsened, until, eventually, their hatred for one another became legendary.

Foreign Religions   The final peril faced by those who returned to Judah was spiritual. Jewish beliefs continued to be influenced by foreign religious ideas. Some of the returnees brought with them spouses from other religions and cultures whom they had married while in Babylon. These marriages resulted in a mixing of religion and worship—actions prohibited by Jewish law. Keeping the worship of Yahweh pure was the chief goal of the next generation of Jewish leaders.

Purity of worship was important to the Jews, because the memory of the Exile was fresh in their minds. They believed that this disaster had resulted from the nation's infidelity to the Covenant.

A Samaritan community continues to live in the Middle East and to worship Yahweh as they have for nearly 2700 years. This picture shows the slaughter of the lamb in preparation for Passover

Have You Considered?

1. Do you think the rivalry between the returnees and the Samaritans would have been as intense if the Samaritans had not also claimed God's Covenant? Why or why not?
2. Have you ever been part of a situation in which a person from one religion wanted to marry a person from another? Why do you think families often don't want their children to marry outside of their religion?

◆ A New Generation of Jewish Leaders

In the face of these obstacles, the people remained busy rebuilding their own homes and workshops. Judah began to take shape once more as a result of their efforts. Rivalries with neighbors and frequent economic problems seemed to be the biggest challenges facing the people. Yet, as these external troubles continued, Yahweh sent two prophets to remind them that their spiritual obligation came first.

Haggai and Zechariah: Rebuilding the Temple

Faced with the difficulty of physical survival, the people felt that they just didn't have the resources to rebuild the Temple right away. The prophet, Haggai, felt differently. He announced that the problems people were having were caused by their neglect of God. They had rebuilt their own homes first while neglecting God's house, the Temple. Haggai's message to them was,

> Now has the time come to rebuild the house of the Lord. Is it time for you to dwell in your own paneled houses, while this house lies in ruin?
>
> (Haggai 1:3)

Shamed by Haggai's message, the people began to rebuild the Temple.

The prophet, Zechariah, told of the "new prince" who was to rule Judah: Zerubbabel, a descendant of King David. In about 520 B.C.E., Zerubbabel did come to Judah, bringing with him the promised money from the imperial treasury. With the influx of additional workers and money, the new Temple was completed by 515 B.C.E. Although the new Temple was much smaller and less elaborate than Solomon's had been, it nevertheless represented a spiritual victory for the Jewish people. Their life as the People of God could begin anew.

Nehemiah: Rebuilding the City

Over the next 70 years, two other important leaders emerged. The first, Nehemiah, who was himself a Jew, served as an official in the Persian court. Nehemiah convinced King Artaxerxes to make Judah an independent province and to make him its first governor.

Scripture Workshop

The Chronicler

Working at the same time as Ezra, another Jewish leader put together a work which reviewed the history of the nation. We call this person "the Chronicler" because the two books he or she produced are 1 and 2 Chronicles. Like Ezra, this author emphasized the importance of the Temple and personal piety.

By comparing Chronicles to the Deuteronomic history, we can get a sense of the special interests of the Chronicler. Try it for yourself—read 1 Chronicles 29:1–20 and 16:8–36, both of which are episodes not in the Deuteronomic history. Then read 2 Samuel 11:2–29, a part not in Chronicles. Now answer these questions:

- How is the Chronicler's interest in the Temple evident in the passages added to the history?
- How is the Chronicler's interest in personal piety obvious in the passages left out of the history?

During this time, as new returnees continued to arrive, the population of Judah doubled. While their new energy and money helped to improve civic life, the increased numbers of residents also intensified the conflicts with the neighboring peoples who felt threatened by Judah's growth. Faced with these new threats of attack, Nehemiah's first task was to rebuild the city walls of Jerusalem. According to the Book of Nehemiah, the people's reply to Nehemiah's request was, "Let us be up and building!" (Nehemiah 2:18). The walls were rebuilt in only 52 days, a task that normally would have taken many months. Nehemiah must have been a great motivator and a super organizer!

Now that the walls had been rebuilt and Jerusalem could be defended, Nehemiah arranged for volunteers to move from their outlying farmland and villages into the ruined capital. Jerusalem needed a population to care for it and to gradually rebuild it, surrounding the new Temple with the beginnings of a city. Rebuilding the city, however, was still only a first step: the Jews also had to rebuild themselves as a people.

Ezra: Renewing the Law

The second important leader after the Exile was Ezra, a priest and a "scribe well-versed in the law of Moses" (Ezra 7:6). Ezra was sent by the king to check on the religious conditions in Judah, to organize its funding, and to install judges to rule using the Jewish law. Since he was appointed by the king, he had legal as well as religious authority. Because of this combination, he was able to do more than Nehemiah in regard to the regulation and reform of Jewish life.

Reading the Law   At the time of the ancient Feast of Booths, Ezra called the Jewish community together in Jerusalem. Then he stood on a platform and read to them the scroll of the Law which he had brought from Babylon. Some scholars think this was the Torah, the first five books of the Bible, recently compiled by the priests. Ezra read for hours in Hebrew as the Levite priests stood nearby to translate the words into Aramaic, the language of the common people.

Unknown, *Ezra*. Seventh Century?

When the Jews returned to Jerulsalem from Exile they survived because of the leadership of Nehemiah and Ezra (shown here).

The Bible in Context

The Feast of the Booths

The Feast of the Booths, also known as the Festival of Tabernacles, was originally a Canaanite celebration of the end of the harvest. The people would live in booths to symbolize the small huts that farmers stayed in during the harvesting season. Later, the Jews applied a new religious meaning to the festival, viewing it as a reminder of their wanderings in the wilderness.

Recalling Ezra's reading of the Law, the Festival of Booths requires that the Torah be read to the entire community. Throughout the year, the reading of the Torah is arranged so that it is completed during this festival. As soon as it is finished, however, the cycle of readings begins again. This shows that the Torah has no beginning or end. This part of the festival is called Simhat Torah, which means "Rejoicing of the Torah."

When Ezra finished, the people began to weep. They had no idea their lives were so far from God's Law! Ezra urged them not to be sad, but to rejoice because it was a holy day to the Lord. Yahweh was offering a gift to the people—the gift of a renewed awareness of the Law.

> *"And, now, but a short time ago, mercy came to us from the Lord our God, who left us a remnant and gave us a stake in his holy place; thus our God has brightened our eyes and given us relief in our servitude. . . . O Lord, God of Israel, you are just; yet we have been spared, the remnant we are today. Here we are before you in our sins. Because of all this, we can no longer stand in your presence."*
>
> (Ezra 9:8,15)

Sacrificing for the Law   Two months after the reading of the Torah, the people assembled again before the Temple, this time in a driving rainstorm. Ezra said that God required them to separate from their non-Jewish wives. As a result of Ezra's words, Jews divorced their spouses who were not Jewish and forced them to leave the land.

What else did the Law require? The Jewish community agreed that they would:

- Keep holy the Sabbath and the holy days of the year.
- Support one another in the form of tithes and offerings.
- Help to maintain the Temple with an annual tax.

LEARN FROM THE MAP

Alexander's Conquests

The map outlines the course of Alexander the Great's conquests. Note that Alexander's route of conquest did not travel through Jerusalem. According to legend, Alexander was so impressed by a procession of priests from the Temple that he did not destroy the city.

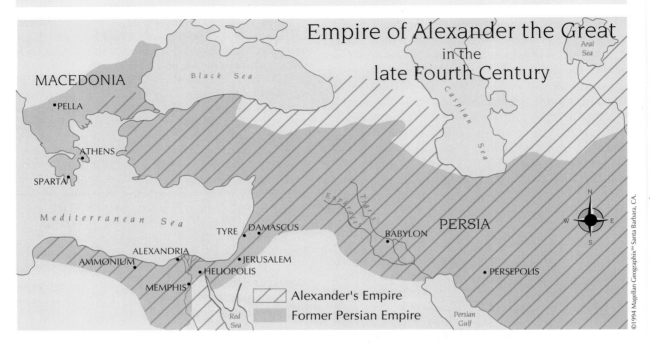

Empire of Alexander the Great in the late Fourth Century

Alexander's Empire
Former Persian Empire

©1994 Magellan Geographix™ Santa Barbara, CA.

Ezra's return marked a turning point for the Jews. In the first stages of the return to Judah, their struggle was to make the new nation survive. Ezra reminded them, however, that their first loyalty was to the Covenant, not the nation, and therefore their chief goal must be to keep the Law. Ever after, Judaism would be centered on the Law.

Have You Considered?

1. Why do you suppose Haggai insisted that rebuilding the Temple should be such a priority for the Jews? What did the Temple symbolize that would help them meet the challenges they faced?
2. Why is it often difficult for people of different religious and cultural backgrounds to live together in peace? Apply your answer to the conflicts faced by those who returned to Judah.
3. Are you part of a group that's scattered in more than one location? How does your group stay together despite the distance?

◆ Living Under Foreign Rule

Although the Jews were able to return to Judah from Babylon, they were not to have political freedom. They were continually under the control of foreign powers, a situation their Israelite ancestors had never tolerated, and one that the Jews also considered unacceptable. The Jews' desire to be ruled by God and through God's Law made them different from other cultures. This lack of political freedom was to be an ongoing source of conflict for Judah and its neighbors.

The Persians

Very little is known of Jewish history during the final century of Persian rule after the reforms of Nehemiah and Ezra. Judah was an isolated nation during this time and still a part of the larger Persian empire. One result of Persian rule was the widespread use of the Aramaic language among Jews. Aramaic was the official language for the Persians, and Jews had to learn it to do business in the empire.

Alexander the Great: The Rise of Greek Influence

In 336 B.C.E., Alexander the Great defeated the Persians. For the next 272 years the Middle East, including Judah, would be dominated by the Greeks. Under their rule, Greek political, social, and religious customs became common practice, even for many Jews. Greek became the language of educated people everywhere.

Hellenization

Contact between Greek and Jewish cultures produced incredible changes within Jewish life.

• Because Greek commercial life often required sacrifices to gods of commerce such as Hermes, Jewish businessmen were often forced to participate in Greek religious rituals.
• Greek education emphasized physical fitness, Greek philosophy, and respect for the gods. All citizens who wished to prosper under Greek rule had to participate in this educational system.
• The Old Testament was translated into Greek, a translation called the "Septuagint" (Greek for "seventy"). According to legend, 70 translators, working independently, each achieved exactly the same translation from the Hebrew text.

All of these changes added up to a process known as "Hellenization," which means "becoming like the Greeks." Conservative Jews saw this behavior as a betrayal of the Law and were opposed to it.

The Maccabees' Revolt

After Alexander's death, his empire was split into several kingdoms, including the *Ptolemies* in Egypt and the *Seleucids* in Syria. It was the Ptolemies that originally ruled Judah after Alexander's death. There was to be no peace, however. The Ptolemies and Seleucids were to fight for control of the Middle East—including Judah—for close to 150 years, before the Seleucids emerged victorious.

Like the Ptolemies before them, the Seleucids originally chose to leave the Jews to their own internal affairs. This policy was to change radically under King Antiochus IV. When Antiochus needed money, he raided the Temple. Antiochus's greater crime, though, was the desecration of the Temple.

As an emphatic proponent of Greek religion, Antiochus decreed that a statue of Zeus was to be worshipped in the Temple. He also ordered that pigs be sacrificed there. These decrees were meant to humiliate the Jews. Putting a statue of Zeus in the Temple not only violated the Commandment against false God, but placing the statue in the Temple was terribly offensive. The sacrifice of pigs violated the Jewish prohibition against unclean animals and called into question all Jewish sacrifices. By this decree, Antiochus mocked the Jews and, in effect, slapped them in the face.

Outraged by what had happened, the Jewish people rebelled. In 167 B.C.E., Mattathias, the leader of a strong Jewish family, did not remain quiet.

When he [Mattathias] saw the sacrileges that were being committed in Judah and in Jerusalem, he said: "Woe is me! Why was I born to see the ruin of my people and the ruin of the holy city, and to sit idle while it is given into the hands of enemies, and the sanctuary into the hands of strangers?"

(1 Maccabees 2:6–7)

He refused to offer the repulsive sacrifice and took a group of soldiers into the Judean hills. After Mattathias' death, his son Judas—nicknamed Maccabeus ("the Hammer")—took over as the leader of some 3,000 troops.

Using guerrilla style warfare, Judas and his men were successful in battle against Antiochus IV's army. They also waged war on any Jew who sided with the Greeks. The Maccabee fighters were zealots determined to defend the faith of their ancestors and cleanse Judah of its oppressors.

After three years of bloody struggle, the revolt succeeded. The Temple was cleansed and the Jews gathered in joy to celebrate its rededication. The Feast of Hanukkah ("dedication") commemorates that event, when the lamps of dedication miraculously burned for eight days, even though the Maccabees had only enough oil to last one day.

The rebellion of the Maccabees continued in an effort to gain full political independence for the Jewish nation. And, for a brief period of time, the Jews gained independence. But this freedom did not last. In 63 B.C.E., the Roman general Pompey came to Jerusalem, imprisoned the Jewish high priest, and appointed his own puppet high priest, Hyrcanus. Once again, the Jews served a foreign master, this time the mighty Republic of Rome.

Have You Considered?

1. No nation enjoys being ruled by another, but given their identity as the Chosen People and their law against worshipping false gods, why do you think it was especially hard for Jews to be ruled by other nations?

2. Read through the list above of the ways in which Greek culture influenced Judaism. Which of these acts do you think would be most offensive to traditional Jews? Explain your answer.

3. The Maccabees killed many Jews who supported Hellenization to insure the existence of the Jewish community. Explain why this behavior can or cannot be justified.

in the Spotlight

The Book of Esther

The Book of Esther was written near the close of the fourth century B.C.E. to explain the winter feast of *Purim*. Purim celebrates the Jews' deliverance from Persian oppression during the reign of King Xerxes (485–465 B.C.E.). In the Book of Esther, Xerxes is known as Ahaseurus.

Esther is a fictional account of how a Jewish princess, Esther, and her cousin, Mordecai, were successful in stopping a Persian plot led by the evil official, Haman, to massacre the Jews. Being fictional doesn't make the story any less important, however. Today in Jewish synagogues, the scroll of the Book of Esther, called the Megillah, is read in its entirety twice on the Feast of Purim. This story is a remarkable sign of God's love for the Jews.

The Jewish feast of Hanukkah celebrates the rededication of the Temple after the Maccabean revolt.

God's People in Changing Times

You have already learned that the term "salvation history," means that God directs the events of history to bring us to salvation. God's plan unfolds over time, and throughout history Yahweh has shaped our traditions and beliefs to help us better understand God's will. In this section, you'll see how God used changing historical circumstances after the Exile to reshape Judaism and to bring the people to a new level of spiritual awareness.

Learning Objectives for Section Two

By the end of this section, you will be able to:

- Discuss the purpose of Ezra's rule on intermarriage.
- Describe the roles of the synagogue and the priesthood in Judah.
- Explain God's use of foreign nations to broaden Israel's religious understanding.
- Explain the process of discernment.

◆ A New Identity for the Diaspora

You read in Chapter 7 how, because of the Diaspora, the Priestly Writers tried to unify the Jews through their common traditions rather than through a national government. Ezra confirmed that decision and put it into practice. God had scattered the Jews throughout the world, and Ezra recognized that the Law would have to be adapted so that it would hold the Jews together as a people wherever they might live. Ezra's first responsibility, however, was to boost the morale of the returnees in Judah and to make sure that they remained loyal to the Covenant.

Ezra and the People of Judah

The Jews had hoped that when the Temple was rebuilt, all their people would come streaming back to Judah, and they would live in perfect obedience to the demands of the Covenant. These hopes, however, were soon disappointed. The presence of the rebuilt Temple failed to attract many Jews to return to Jerusalem. In fact, as reported in Malachi, the general lack of support for the Temple resulted in unpaid taxes and unholy sacrifices:

> Oh, that one among you would shut the Temple gates
> to keep you from kindling fire on my altar in vain!
> I have no pleasure in you, says the Lord of hosts;
> neither will I accept any sacrifice from your hands.
> (Malachi 1:10)

Breaking the Law   The most basic commands of the Law were neglected. The law forbidding work on the Sabbath was broken as peasants cut grain and merchants set up tables at the Temple on the Sabbath as if it were just another day. Levites, members of the priestly family who were supposed to be cared for by the community, now had to take jobs in the fields. The increasing number of marriages between Jews and *Gentiles* (non-Jews) also proved a most serious problem.

People of Note

"Malachi"

The Book of Malachi was written during the period between the prophecy of Haggai and the arrival of Nehemiah in Judah (approximately in 445 B.C.E.). It is the last book of the Old Testament in the Christian arrangement of the Bible.

Early translators thought that the word, "malachi"—an unusual Hebrew word—was the name of the prophet who wrote this book. The word is, in fact, merely a title meaning, "My Messenger." It is used twice, in Malachi 1:1 and 3:1, to refer to the book's author, indicating the author's desire to remain anonymous. The title is a good choice for a name, though, because in a sense all of the prophets were "malachi:" messengers from God.

The Book of Malachi is the source of the Jewish belief that the prophet Elijah will return to earth (*Malachi* 3:23–24). Barely three chapters in length, the Book of Malachi can be read quickly.

Ezra's Motives Ezra's motives in forbidding marriages between Jews and Gentiles were not based on hatred of a particular race of people. Rather, Ezra understood that the very survival of the Jewish people depended on their preserving their religious culture. Marriages between Jews and Gentiles had always meant a mixing of the two religious cultures. Ezra's demand served to purify the Jewish religion from the influences of other religions to insure its survival.

Given this motive, Ezra's command can be viewed as a necessary measure taken to save Jewish culture. Still, it may seem to have been a harsh reaction, especially unfair to those non-Jews whom Ezra forced out of Judah.

The Center of Jewish Life

Ezra's rule against intermarriage helped the new nation of Judah survive. The future of Judaism, however, would no longer depend on the nation of Judah. Following the Exile, the majority of the Jewish people would now live elsewhere than Judah. Although many Jews dreamed of a ruler (a *messiah*) who would be anointed by God to restore the people to Israel, for now the focus would be on religious and cultural solidarity rather than on political unity.

Ezra responded to this new situation by making the Law the center of Jewish life, and for this achievement he is know as the "Father of Judaism." From his time onward, the Jewish people would be known as the people of the Law, or the "people of the book." Ezra looked to the Torah, or Pentateuch, as the unifying basis for all of Jewish life.

There was a danger in Ezra's method, however. Many have accused him of being a legalist who placed a far greater emphasis on the letter of the law than he should have. By raising the importance of law to

Orthodox Jews continue to follow Ezra's law concerning intermarriage. The ceremony binds the couple together as part of the Covenant.

such a high standard, a false emphasis could be placed on obeying laws simply for the sake of obedience. All law is designed to protect and enhance people's lives, but no law is complete, and there are times when the purpose of a law conflicts with its literal meaning.

Ezra's positive influence cannot be overestimated. Without his efforts, there would have been no focal point for Jewish identity—especially among the people living in the Diaspora. Without the focus on the Law, it is doubtful that Judaism could have survived the influence of Greek culture.

Ezra and the Canon of the Bible

The *Talmud*—the Jewish book that interprets the Law and Tradition—calls Ezra the "second Moses," and says that the Torah would have been given to Israel through Ezra, had not Moses lived first. The Talmud also recognizes Ezra as the person who established the canon of the Tanakh. It was Ezra's Hebrew canon, or list of accepted books, that would later be adopted by the rabbis, and, much later, by the Protestant churches. You will remember that the Catholic Church accepts the Greek canon of the Septuagint. Several books and parts of books included in the Septuagint are not found in Ezra's collection. These books, which are part of the Bible for Catholics but not for Jews and Protestants, are often called *apocrypha*. They include Judith, Tobit, Baruch, 1 and 2 Maccabees, Sirach, and Wisdom, along with parts of Esther and Daniel.

The Synagogue

The Exile in Babylon, through God's guidance, gave Ezra a model for reorganizing Jewish worship, the synagogue, based on Jewish community gatherings in Babylon. Ezra began this reform during his first meeting with the people.

> Now when the seventh month came, the whole people gathered as one man before the Water Gate, and they called upon Ezra the scribe to bring forth the book of the Law of Moses which the Lord prescribed for Israel.
> (Nehemiah 8:2–3)

Synagogue Origins   The origins of the synagogue came from the need to have a meeting area where the Torah could be studied and taught. Jews living in the Diaspora needed a place to worship. Over the next several centuries, synagogues were built in villages in Judah and throughout the Roman empire.

Synagogue Architecture   The architecture of the synagogue was based on the Jerusalem Temple. There was a gathering place open to men, women, and children and a central chamber for prayer and the reading of the Law. The Torah and other scriptural scrolls were contained in a special area. There was no table for sacrifices, because the Temple was the only place where sacrifices could be made. For the same reason, there were no priests in the synagogue. A rabbi, or "teacher," was elected to supervise the worship, teaching, and maintenance of the synagogue.

Synagogue Worship   The Sabbath prayer was the main worship service. The Sabbath started at sundown on Friday. The worship service was quite simple. As it began, everyone would turn toward Jerusalem and then recite a prayer. The prayer was followed by a reading from the Torah according to the particular season of the year. The reader would then offer a comment on what was read. This change enabled Judaism to survive the final destruction of the Temple in 70 C.E., and continues even today.

Scripture Workshop

Hanukkah

A mark of modern Jewish identity is the Jewish celebration of the Feast of Light, or *Hanukkah,* which lasts for eight days in December. The feast commemorates the Maccabees' victory over the Seleucid king, Antiochus IV, the purification of the Temple, and the people's rededication to God and the Law.

The story of this ceremony is found in 1 Maccabees 4:26–59. Read it and then answer these questions:

1. Describe the Temple as the Maccabees found it after their victory.
2. What do you suppose the "Abomination" mentioned was?
3. What did the Maccabees do with the altar that had been desecrated?
4. How long is the festival?
5. When is the festival supposed to occur?

Functions of the Priestly Office

The end of the exile gave Ezra an opportunity to restore the the priests to their proper function in Temple ritual. Prior to the Exile, the king would commonly offer the sacrifice. After the Exile, Nehemiah and Ezra told the people that this practice was wrong, and that only the priests were to offer sacrifice.

After the Exile, the head of the clergy became designated as the high priest. When Joshua, the high priest, assumed the position of leadership in 537 B.C.E., the office took on a new dual role. The high priest became the political leader as well as the religious leader. Following the Maccabee's revolt in the second century B.C.E., the high priest also adopted the title of "king." Although it sounds as if making the priest and the king the same person might be a good idea it didn't actually work out well. The holders of the office quickly became corrupt, using it for their own personal power.

On the positive side, the restored priestly office was of great religious benefit to the Jews. The high priests encouraged the study of the Law and Jewish traditions. Through their efforts, people in all walks of life became familiar with the Torah.

The reformation efforts of Nehemiah and Ezra helped the people not only to recall their past, but to look with hope to the future as well—a future in which their identity would be based on allegiance to God's Law, as found in the written word. The Jewish identity of this period was one of restored spirit and hope that Yahweh was still their God and that they were still God's people.

Have You Considered?

1. What do you think of Ezra's rule against intermarriage? Do you think it was justified by the need for survival, or was it unfair to the foreign wives? Could it be both? Explain your answer.
2. Describe a situation in which someone followed the letter of the law rather than its spirit. How would you have handled the situation differently?
3. What do you think the dangers would be in having religious leaders serve as political leaders as well? Do you think it would be more difficult for people to challenge their decisions? Why or why not? Are there situations today where the political and religious leader of a country are the same person?

◆ New Religious Ideas

The prophets recognized that Yahweh sometimes used foreign nations to teach Israel lessons. For example, Isaiah said that Assyria had been Yahweh's "rod in anger" and "staff in wrath," with which the Northern kingdom was punished for its disobedience (Isaiah 10:5). After the Exile, the people also realized that foreign nations could also be God's instruments for positive change.

Following the return to Judah, the Jews were dominated by a series of foreign powers. As was mentioned earlier, the Jews did not willingly submit to the influences of these nations. There were, though, ideas and beliefs expressed by these other religious traditions that expanded Judah's understanding of God. Because of the demands of the Covenant, however, the Jews never merely "borrowed" these new ideas and beliefs. Instead, they used them as gifts from God. They studied them deeply and eventually made them a part of their religion, faithful to their unique tradition.

The Persian Influence: Angels and Demons

While Cyrus allowed the Jews to return to Judah and rebuild the Temple, Judah was not given its political freedom. It remained a Persian province. During their 200 year rule, Persian beliefs gradually found their way into Jewish beliefs and practices.

The Persian religion was founded by Zoroaster, who lived around 600 B.C.E. He was a monotheist, who gave the name Ahura Mazda ("God of Heaven") to the one God he worshipped. In the Book of Ezra, this same title is used for Yahweh nine times, showing just how much Jewish religious practice was influenced by Persian religious thought.

Zoroaster taught that God created everything in existence, and was ultimately just and totally powerful. According to Zoroaster, the universe was also filled with other spirits.

- The two most powerful of these lesser spirits or "angels," were a chief good spirit and a chief evil spirit.
- Each one had its own creation within the creation of the one God, and there was a constant battle between the forces of good and the forces of evil.
- Below these two chief spirits, there were numerous lesser good and evil spirits.

Signorelli, Angels at the Last Judgement. Sixteenth Century.

The Persian beliefs of angels and devils influenced Jewish thought. The Jews did not simply adopt these teachings, however. Angels were seen solely as messengers of God and never as gods themselves.

We know from Acts 23:8 in the New Testament that some Jewish groups, especially the Pharisees, accepted the existence of angels and demons as fact. Although the Jews adopted the idea of angels from the Persians, they developed it in light of their own experience of Yahweh.

- Where Zoroaster had thought that the good and evil spirits had separate creations, Jewish tradition emphasized that there is only one created world, and it is good.
- Where the Persians saw angels and spirits as separate powers, apart from God, the Jews recognized God's supreme power over all that existed.

In this way, the Jews acknowledged the role of spiritual beings, without forgetting that all real power flowed from Yahweh.

The Qualities of God

After the Persians, the Jews were ruled over by a series of Hellenistic kingdoms. The Greeks had very definite ideas about God. Although Greek mythology was full of bloodthirsty, petty behavior among their gods, these images were not taken literally by most educated people. Their understanding of God came from philosophy, which thought of God as eternal, unchanging, all-powerful, and completely perfect in every respect.

Although Jews had always known of Yahweh's power, they were also accustomed to thinking of Yahweh as capable of love and hate, anger and compassion, and as someone who acted in human history. From the Greeks, the Jews learned to express God's complete perfection in precise philosophical terms. However, they never lost their sense of Yahweh as active and passionate for them. Again, therefore, they adapted these ideas to their tradition, and in so doing arrived at a deeper understanding of God.

The Second Book of Maccabees shows the influence of this process, in which the Jewish and Greek understandings of God are fused. In it, God's power is described by the qualities of justice, kindness, and providence. God is active in the lives of the people and has chosen them specially. The Jewish priest Jonathan prayed:

> *Lord God, creator of all things, awesome and strong, just and merciful, the only king and benefactor, who alone are gracious, just, almighty, and eternal, Israel's savior from all evil, who chose our forefathers and sanctified them.*

(2 Maccabees 1:24–25)

Afterlife and Judgment

The ideas of an "afterlife" and of "eternal judgment" did not appear in the Old Testament prior to the Exile. The Jewish people, on the whole, had not believed in an afterlife. When you died, you were simply dead, period. Their name for the place where the spirits of the dead went is *sheol*. The spirits in sheol, however, lost their individual personality, and simply existed in a vague "holding pattern."

Persian religion preached the reality of an afterlife; it was viewed as a time when the dead would be resurrected and judged, and then sent to heaven or hell according to their earthly deeds. After the time of Alexander, the Greeks also developed the idea of an afterlife. They stressed that some gods loved human beings enough to make sure that they had a happy fate after death, and these gods could be approached through secret rituals called "mystery cults." On the other hand, the unrighteous would be punished in the afterlife by physical torment.

The vivid imagery of the afterlife, which came from the Persian and Greek traditions, definitely influenced Jewish authors. As Jews grew in their understanding of the afterlife, they came to believe in a final judgment and the resurrection of the dead.

As had happened with other foreign religious ideas, however, these concepts were enhanced as they passed into Jewish tradition. The Jews did not understand resurrection simply as a return to life as it had been; they believed that Yahweh would create new lives for them in a new world. In this way they associated their belief in judgment and resurrection with the prophets' prediction of a coming "Day of the Lord" which would mark the end of the present order of existence.

The story found in 2 Maccabees 7:1–42 presents the themes of afterlife and judgment. This is the story of a woman and her seven sons who are *martyred* (when someone is killed for his or her faith) because they will not give up the Jewish Law. This story expresses the belief that the just are rewarded for their goodness and the wicked are punished for their crimes. The story also expresses the belief in the resurrection of the dead:

- God will raise the just to new life with their bodies fully restored.
- The sins of the wicked, however, merit punishment; they will suffer and not share in the resurrection.

As the first brother pointed out to Antiochus:

You are depriving us of this life, but the King of the world will raise us up to live again forever. It is for His laws that we are dying.

(2 Maccabees 7:8)

Intercession

Both the Greeks and the Romans believed it was possible to call upon their dead ancestors to intercede for them with the gods. This idea is called "intercession," and it is first expressed in the Second Book of Maccabees.

From 2 Maccabees we learn of the value of intercessory prayer in which both the living and dead can help their brothers and sisters attain full salvation. Second Maccabees 15:12–16 tells how, prior to battle, Judas Maccabeus related a vision to his soldiers in which he saw Onias, a former high priest, praying with outstretched arms for the entire Jewish community. This revelation introduced the belief that the dead pray for us before God; a whole new concept in bibilical faith.

From the Greeks and the Romans the Jews learned to call upon their ancestors for support in prayer. Unlike the Greeks and Romans, however, the Jews never developed a "cult of the dead" in which they worshipped their ancestors. The Jews realized that only Yahweh deserved worship. Instead, they came to understand that the dead, preserved through the love of God, could still help the living through prayer.

Apocalyptic Literature

The term "apocalyptic" refers to the visions and warnings given by the prophets, such as those made by Isaiah and Jeremiah, announcing what will happen at the end of the present age. In the Persian and Greek periods, apocalyptic warnings became more frequent, and they developed into a style of literature all their own.

Daniel   The best example of apocalyptic literature in the Old Testament is the Book of Daniel.

Pinturicchio, *Resurrection*. Fifteenth Century.

The idea of an afterlife and resurrection entered Jewish thought through Persian influences.

Daniel 2:32–35 illustrates this well. This book is set during the Babylonian Exile, but it was clearly written during the reign of Antiochus IV, most likely between 167 and 164 B.C.E. after the Temple had been desecrated but before the Maccabees' revolt.

Chapters 7–12 are the main apocalyptic section of the book. They recount visions and symbols which purport to predict the future. They tell of the end of captivity for those Jews living in Babylon during the Exile, and of the end of persecution for those Jews oppressed by the Greeks centuries later. The effect on the hearers of these visions was to assure them that God had known all along about the modern persecutions, and that God was very much in control of their history.

Symbolic Language   Apocalyptic literature is filled with symbolic language. It tries to communicate what the experience of seeing God is like.

You probably use symbolic language regularly. Symbolic language helps us to express our feelings and experiences most vividly. If the day is very hot you might say, "It's as hot as a furnace outside." Is that statement literally true? Of course not. Furnaces reach temperatures well over 300°F. The temperature outside is merely 98° in the shade. But, 98° does not communicate the idea of oppressive heat nearly as well as the word "furnace."

Symbolism, then, evokes feelings as well as facts, enriching the ideas. As you remember, the prophets Isaiah and Jeremiah used symbolic images to express their visions of God.

Symbolic language also very easy to misunderstand or misinterpret. Unfortunately, symbolic language is sometimes taken literally by those who misunderstand its purpose. In Daniel 7:1–14, Daniel has a vision in which he sees a beast devouring the entire earth. He says that this beast will have its way for "a year, two years, and a half-year" before it is destroyed by God. On this basis, various groups have tried to calculate when God will end the present age.

Apocalyptic literature is not designed to be read literally. Its purpose is, through the use of symbols and warnings, to assure people that God knows their struggles, and that God's help is on the way. Again, the events of history are used to bring people to a new understanding of God's design.

Have You Considered?

1. Describe your own understanding of angels and demons. How do you picture their appearance? What do you think their functions are?
2. Apocalyptic literature is usually popular among groups who feel that they are oppressed. Why do you suppose this is? How does apocalyptic literature offer them hope?

Spiritual Reflection

Rededication Ceremony

During part of the modern Hanukkah ceremony, Jews place lighted wicks in dishes of olive oil and read a prayer of dedication. You can rededicate yourself to God through a similar ceremony.

What would you like to change in your life? How can you live more in touch with God's love? Decide what you need to do and how you need to change your life in order to rededicate it to God. Then, light a candle and speak this psalm prayer aloud.

Let my cry come before you, O Lord; in keeping with your word, give me discernment. My lips pour forth your praise, because you teach me your statutes. May my tongue sing of your promise, for all your commands are just. Let your hand be ready to help me, for I have chosen your precepts. I long for your salvation, O Lord, and your law is my delight. Let my soul live to praise you.

(Psalm 119:169, 171–175a)

Q/A

Section One

1. Why would Jews living in Babylon not want to return to Judah?
2. Why were relations between the Samaritans and the returning Jews tense?
3. What did Haggai tell the people?
4. What was Nehemiah's major accomplishment?
5. Provide two examples of the process called "Hellenization."
6. Why did many Jews oppose Hellenization?
7. Identify: Ptolemies, Seleucids
8. Who were the Maccabees?

Section Two

1. How did God use foreign nations for the betterment of Judah?
2. Why is Ezra called "the father of Judaism"?
3. What was the danger in Ezra's emphasis on the Law?
4. What is a synagogue?
5. Define: rabbi, high priest
6. Cite two differences between the Persian and the Israelite views of angels and demons.
7. How did the Jews adapt Greek ideas about God?
8. What is the purpose of symbolism in apocalyptic literature?

BIBLE ACTIVITY

1. Nehemiah 11:1–2 describes the willingness of some of the Jews to make a sacrifice for God by moving into Jerusalem's ruins for the benefit of the whole community. What is one sacrifice that you have made? How did your sacrifice benefit another?
2. Read the selection of the hymn of the three young men in Daniel 3:52–90. Illustrate your favorite verses.
3. Read Nehemiah 8:1–12. Imagine that you were in the crowd listening to Ezra. Write your reactions to Ezra's words.
4. Read Ezra 4:1–5. Write additional details explaining to the crowd of Samaritans why they should not be permitted to help with the rebuilding of the Temple.
5. Read the entire Book of Jonah. Retell the incident of the vine (chapter four) and explain its symbolism.

Athens, Greece, Acropolis. Fifth Century B.C.E.

GLOSSARY

- **Ahura Mazda:** The chief Persian god, referred to as "God of Heaven"; this phrase is used of Yahweh in Ezra.
- **Apocalyptic literature:** A stylized and symbolic literature that spoke about immediate problems and their solutions as if they had happened in the past.
- **Apocrypha:** Term for the books and parts of books included in the Septuagint, but not in Ezra's canon of the Old Testament.
- **Feast of Booths:** Originally an agricultural festival during which the people would live in outdoor huts, this festival also became a celebration of the Torah in the time of Ezra.
- **Hanukkah:** Eight-day celebration which commemorates the victory of the Maccabees over the Seleucids.
- **Hellenization:** To "hellenize" means to imitate Greek culture.
- **High Priest:** Title invented under Ezra; the term referring to the chief priest.
- **Intercessory prayer:** Prayers of the living or dead that have benefit for the salvation of all in the human race.
- **Maccabees:** Family of conservative Jews, led by Judas Maccabeus, who revolted against the Seleucids.
- **Martyr:** From the Greek word for "witness;" a person who dies for his or her faith.
- **Rabbi:** The "teacher" of the Law.
- **Samaritans:** Cultural group made up of descendants of the northern tribes who intermarried with Canaanites and Assyrians.
- **Seleucids:** Kings after Alexander the Great who ruled Syria.
- **Septuagint:** The Greek translation of the Hebrew Scriptures.
- **Sheol:** Place where Jews believed the "shades" of the dead were kept.
- **Synagogue:** The meeting place of the Jews for study and worship.

UNDERSTANDING MORE ABOUT:

Apocalyptic Literature

Between the Maccabees and the time of Jesus (usually called the "Intertestamental Period"), apocalyptic literature was abundant. Several apocalyptic books were written during this period, among them 1 and 2 Enoch, Jubilees, and the Testaments of the Patriarchs.

These books typically are even more mystical and symbolic than the apocalyptic parts of the Bible. The chief difference between these books and those in the Bible, however, is that intertestamental texts are much more pronounced in their opposition to the Romans. Jews resented the presence of Roman troops as occupiers, and they hated the taxes and forced labor that Rome demanded. Jews dreamed of a day when God would send a messiah, an anointed king, to overthrow the Romans and reestablish the throne of David. Apocalyptic authors used symbols and visions to describe the coming of the messiah and the punishment that he would inflict on the unrighteous, especially the Romans.

These books were not included in the Bible, but they show us the hopes and fears of many Jews at an important time. Their popularity is reflected in the fact that the New Testament Book of Jude quotes the apocalyptic Book of Enoch.

CHAPTER 9

Wisdom

I t was 6 am and Daniel was not in the mood to read the note he found posted on Mr. Miyagi's door: "Gone fishing. Paint the house. Remember: up-down, up-down."

Daniel ripped the note. He kicked the paint cans. He threw the paint brush. What was going on here? Miyagi had promised to teach him karate, and all Daniel had done so far was polish Miyagi's cars, sand his deck, and paint his fence.

"I haven't learned a thing," Daniel yelled on Miyagi's return. "Things are not as they seem," Miyagi reminded Daniel.

If you've seen the movie *The Karate Kid*, you know the story. Daniel, a new student in high school, is threatened by a group of bullies. He finds comfort in the workroom of the building's manager, an older man from Japan who shapes bonsai trees. Daniel appreciates the man's kindness, and listens carefully to his words. As Daniel begins to trim his own tree, Miyagi tells him: "Close your eyes and trust. Make a picture. Nothing else exists in the whole world except the tree. Trust the picture."

Eventually Miyagi agrees to be Daniel's karate master. "I promise to teach you karate. I say, you do. That's your part." What follows is a series of unusual orders given by Miyagi.

"Wash my cars, then wax them. Wax on with right hand. Wax off with left hand."

Daniel obeys, but resents being treated like a servant. After he blows up over Miyagi's note, the karate master shows Daniel how each of the movements he has perfected by waxing, sanding, and painting are used in karate.

Daniel learned more than karate from Mr. Miyagi; he was given a new view of life. He was able to understand more about how all the pieces of his life fit into the whole. He really was able to see things in a new way, much as Miyagi had promised him: "Things are not as they seem."

For centuries, the people of Israel sought out masters for answers to life's big questions in much the same way that Daniel attached himself to Miyagi. These wise teachers, called *sages*, searched for the best quality of life. They wanted to be in tune with universal wisdom. They sought it by observation and practice, then passed it along to their students.

The oral teachings of the sages were eventually developed into the Wisdom literature of the Bible. Wisdom literature was designed to teach people how to live well and wisely. In this chapter, you will explore Wisdom literature. You'll look at some of the questions these books pose and the answers they provide about the real meaning of life.

The movie "The Karate Kid" offers an example of how students learn a skill through a master's teaching. Students of biblical wisdom also learn through the patient teaching found in the Wisdom literature.

The Development of Israelite Wisdom

Egypt, V Dynasty, Scribe Accroupi.

Israel searched for wisdom from the very beginning. Several wisdom books in the Bible have teachings that have been passed down for thousands of years from Israel's sages, from the time before Israel became a nation after the Exodus from Egypt. The Wisdom tradition developed gradually over many centuries. Growth came as new ideas were developed in response to Israel's neighbors, and as Israel came to new understandings of its tradition in light of changing historical circumstances.

Learning Objectives for Section One

By the end of this section, you will be able to:

- Define wisdom.
- Demonstrate an understanding of the relationship between Israelite wisdom and other ancient Middle Eastern wisdom traditions.
- List and discuss several of the Wisdom books.

◆ The Wisdom Tradition: Beginnings

Every ancient Middle Eastern culture, including Israel, was involved in the search for wisdom. Israel's own Wisdom tradition grew up in the context of this wider Middle Eastern interest. For the Israelites, the search for wisdom was especially important, because it helped them to better live out their relationship with Yahweh. The Israelites studied the Wisdom teachings of other Middle Eastern cultures for any insights they could offer. Before we can focus on this tradition, however, we first have to define the concept of wisdom.

What Is Wisdom?

If you look up the word "wisdom" in a dictionary, you will find a definition that speaks of knowledge or intelligence. Although these words can sometimes be used interchangeably, the Wisdom tradition used them quite differently. To the sage, someone can be wise but have very little knowledge, or someone can be extremely intelligent and yet not be wise. What, then, does the Wisdom tradition mean by wisdom?

"To have wisdom" means to have an understanding of what life is all about and how to live well. The Wisdom tradition is concerned with difficult questions:

- "What is the purpose of life?"
- "What can I do to gain lifelong happiness?"
- "How should I treat other people?"
- "How can I know right from wrong?"

Wisdom also includes the ability to make responsible moral decisions.

You can see from the following example how wisdom differs from knowledge or intelligence. During the Second World War, medical doctors in Nazi concentration camps performed cruel experiments on prisoners, such as plunging them into ice-cold water and observing their reactions. These doctors were not insane. They were well-trained scientists who made careful notes and observations. However, they treated people in a heartless way. Despite their scientific intelligence, these doctors could not see that what they were doing was wrong.

For the ancient Israelites, a wise man was one who knew how to live a moral life of self-discipline, moderation, and justice. Such wisdom depended upon a long period of study and thought, and nowhere was the devotion to wisdom pursued with more dedication than in the ancient Middle East.

Wisdom in the Ancient Middle East

One form of Middle Eastern Wisdom teaching originated in the courts of kings. In Egypt, sages working in the court of the pharaoh developed sayings and stories with which they instructed their young students. They stressed self-control and eloquence as trademarks of the wise person, two qualities someone living at court surely needed. In ancient Egypt, this ideal was called *ma'at*. Other cultures developed similar ideals.

Other sages were not attached to the king's court. These teachers were interested in discovering what a wise life meant for ordinary people. Their instruction emphasized obedience and respect for elders. Later, after the development of cities and trade, wisdom sayings stressed the qualities of honesty and hard work important to merchants.

Israel's Wisdom teachings reflect these common Middle Eastern concerns. Because Wisdom teaching

Raphael, *School of Athens*. Sixteenth Century.

The study of wisdom has been important throughout human history. This painting by Raphael attempts to capture the great Greek philosophers and scientists at work.

addressed questions about the nature of life and how to live it, it was international. This universality encouraged the sharing of traditions, which is evident in the Wisdom literature of the Old Testament.

- Psalms 29 and 68, for example, seem related to Canaanite wisdom texts.
- Much of the Book of Proverbs is similar, either in form or content, to wisdom sayings drawn from Egyptian culture.

The Israelites were open to these new ideas, but they were always adapted to Israel's unique religious beliefs, especially their faith in Yahweh as the Creator and source of all wisdom.

Faith in Yahweh made the Wisdom tradition of Israel different from those of her Middle Eastern neighbors. In other countries, the search for "wisdom" was not an especially religious act. Most ancient peoples believed that wise living could be learned by observation of nature and society. In Egypt and Babylon, for example, sages did not refer to the gods, nor did they say that a wise person should pray or make sacrifice. Because Israel regarded Yahweh as the creator of both nature and society, however, Israelite wisdom from the beginning emphasized respect for God. This concept was often expressed as "fear" of Yahweh, a word which meant respect and admiration rather than actual fright. This idea is expressed in Proverbs 9:10, "The beginning of wisdom is the fear of the Lord."

Wisdom Schools

In Israel, as well as elsewhere in the Middle East, sages often banded into groups we call "Wisdom schools." Generally, these were groups of students who studied the wisdom of a master, and developed it into new sayings and stories. In Israel the various Wisdom schools kept alive the sayings, poems, and essays which make up the Wisdom literature of the Bible.

These Wisdom schools developed alongside the historical and prophetic books. Some of the Wisdom literature (many of the Proverbs, for example) are very old, perhaps the oldest material to be found in the Bible. Much of the Wisdom literature was not written until after the Exile, and some books are among the Bible's most recent writings. As the search for the good life continued throughout Israel's history, so did the search for wisdom.

The problems Wisdom literature deals with are universal human themes:

- love
- honor
- honesty
- justice
- the goodness of God

Such themes make the Wisdom literature "timeless." Works such as the Psalms and Book of Job are extremely popular today because people continue to find meaning in their words.

The Personification of Wisdom

In Israel, where goodness was directly connected to the Jewish people's special relationship with Yahweh, wisdom was especially important. This search for wisdom became so intense that Israelite authors began to depict it as an entity who called to people, asked for their obedience, and offered them comfort.

This personification of wisdom comes across most clearly in the Book of Proverbs. There, Wisdom speaks in the same manner as one of the prophets.

She demands obedience to her instructions, and says that her enemies are doomed to destruction. Those who listen to her and follow her voice, however, will find rest and peace. The author contrasts Wisdom to a woman named Folly. Wisdom invites her guests to a great banquet. Folly, a word meaning "error," invites people to a meal of stolen bread and water, which leads to Sheol (something like a land of ghosts). The point of the contrast is that wisdom leads to life, while ignorance brings death.

Wisdom says that she has always existed, and that she assisted God in the act of creation. Wisdom is depicted as measuring the heavens and laying plans for the earth. These images express the Israelite belief that the world exhibits the wisdom of God, and that creation is one way God is revealed to humanity. Studying nature can put us in touch with God's plans and intentions for our lives.

As time went on, a new facet was added to the traditional characterization of Wisdom: not only did she come to reveal truth, but it was her fate to be rejected by her people, to suffer under them, and to return to God. In the period between the Old and New Testaments, Wisdom schools in Israel were very interested in the idea of a "suffering revealer."

The personification of wisdom in the Bible shows that the Wisdom tradition was alive and growing throughout Israel's history. This is because Wisdom teaching answers a very basic human need, the need to know how to live correctly and happily.

Have You Considered?

1. Describe a person, such as a historical figure or a TV character, who was intelligent without being wise, or wise without being intelligent.
2. Ancient Israel's Wisdom tradition differed from those of her neighbors by concentrating on God. Do you think it's possible for a person to be wise without considering God? Why or why not?
3. Do you agree that we can learn about God from studying nature? Provide an example with your answer.

The Bible's Wisdom Books

Wisdom writings in the Bible offer an incredible degree of diversity in style, content, and point of view. These books reveal the thoughts of authors who struggled to understand God, the meaning of life, and the moral dimension of human behavior.

Job

The Book of Job is one of the most challenging portions of the Old Testament. Its main subject is the problem of righteous suffering, but it also studies the questions of goodness, evil, justice, and how they relate to human life.

The Book of Job is divided into two major sections. The first, written as prose sometime during the Exile (after 587 B.C.E.), frames the book (chapters 1–2 and chapter 42:7–17). The second (written as poetry),

Bartolomeo, *The Prophet Job*, Sixteenth Century.

The Book of Job is one of the most unusual stories found in the Bible. A work of fiction, the book considers why evil things happen to good people.

includes everything in between. The poetic section, believed to have been written during the eighth century B.C.E., contains the complaints of Job, a man who was faithful to Yahweh and yet experienced all sorts of troubles. This section of the book begins by asking the question, "Why do innocent people suffer?" and ends with the admission that only God knows the answer to that question, and God's not telling! Although the prose section reveals that God was only testing Job's faith, scholars believe that this explanation for Job's suffering were not part of the original. They were added to take some of the sting from Job's suffering.

The poetic section of the Book of Job challenges a common opinion found in Wisdom literature, that suffering results from sin. People commonly believed that those who suffered were being punished for evil they had done. The Book of Job rejects this view. Job suffers in spite of his righteous life. When Job is visited by three "friends" who try to convince him that he must have done something wrong, Job strongly disagrees with them. Job knows the truth—he has not sinned—and so continues to affirm his innocence.

Job endures losses, physical pain, and obnoxious visitors. Eventually, after a long period of suffering, Job takes his appeal directly to God and demands a response. When God finally responds to Job (see Chapter 38)—it is not with words, but with an experience deep within Job's heart. Job is satisfied by his experience of God. Job says, "I had heard of You by word of mouth, but now my eye has seen You" (42:5). Now Job's heart understands what his mind cannot comprehend or explain.

The Book of Sirach

Sirach was written in the late second century or early first century B.C.E. when conflicts between the Jewish tradition and the Hellenistic way of life were at their height. The writer, Ben Sira, was a scribe and a teacher. He had his own academy where he instructed Jewish youth in the true values of life as set forth in the ancient holy writings of Israel. Also, he was an expert in the Prophets, the Law, and the Writings: the entire Tanakh.

The Book of Sirach (also called *Liber Ecclesiasticus* or "Church book") was used by the early Christians to teach the basic principles of good living. The book is written mostly in the form of proverbs. Beginning with Chapter 44, it praises the heroes of Israel and the traditions of the Jewish people, saying that wisdom comes through the Law. Sirach therefore underlines the unique Israelite perspective: Wisdom comes from one's relationship with Yahweh. There is no wisdom without that relationship.

The Book of Wisdom

Bible scholars offer many differing opinions about the Book of Wisdom—especially concerning its authorship and original language. The Book of Wisdom is assumed to have been written around the time of 100 B.C.E. when many Greek ideas were being adapted to Jewish thought. Written in the name of King Solomon, its author is, nevertheless, anonymous.

Besides considering the age-old question about why good people suffer, the Book of Wisdom also examines the belief in life after death. The Book of Wisdom recounts the story of the Exodus to help strengthen the faith of the people. The author exhorts the Jews to seek wisdom, for even though there are many things people do not understand, if they have wisdom they can see their way through difficult situations.

The Bible in Context

Parallelism in the Psalms

Psalms is the best example we have of religious poetry from ancient Israel. Developing from song and dance, Israel's poetry appealed to the ear through rhythm rather than rhyme. Rhythm was created by a structure called "parallelism," in which the second line expresses the basic idea of the first in slightly different words.

There are three different kinds of parallelism, that differ by the way the second line expands the thought of the first. The three kinds are:

- **Similar.** The idea in the first line is repeated in the second, with only minor word changes. Psalm 19:1 is an example: "The heavens declare the glory of God, and the firmament proclaims his handiwork."
- **Opposite.** The first line expresses an idea, and the second line states its opposite. Psalm 27:10 illustrates this type: "Though my mother and father forsake me, yet the Lord will receive me."
- **Completed.** The second line adds to the thought expressed in the first, bringing it to completion. Psalm 28: 7 provides an example: "In him my heart trust, and I find help; then my heart exults, and with my song I give him thanks."

in the Spotlight

Conflict in the Wisdom Tradition

The early Israelite sages said that God would reward the wise with happiness. Of course, they recognized that this wasn't always so, but they were passing on "tried and true" advice that usually worked. Some people misunderstood the advice, and came to believe that God's justice would ensure that the good always prosper and the bad always suffer.

After the Exile, the Wisdom literature shows a dissatisfaction with such neat, logical positions. Instead, Wisdom writing points out that, indeed, evil people **did** sometimes prosper, and the good **did** sometimes suffer. Disasters could happen without any obvious reason or purpose. The Book of Job considers this final point of view.

Job criticizes those sages who claimed to be able to see the logic of God behind certain events. "How agreeable are honest words; yet how unconvincing is your argument!" *(Job 6:25).* The Book of Job argues forcefully that the workings of the universe are often beyond human understanding. The Book of Job's author knew nothing about black holes, quarks, or any of the modern discoveries of physics, yet his or her conclusions remain true. Even in our scientific world, much about the universe continues to be beyond human understanding. Although we trust in faith that there are reasons for everything, Job's story reminds us that we cannot fully understand God's plan.

The Book of Psalms

The Book of Psalms is a collection of 150 songs that were written at various times by the people of Israel. Although not generally considered one of the books of wisdom, the poetry of Psalms responds to many of the themes considered in Wisdom literature. Most of the psalms were written to be used in public worship, although some are designed for individual, ritual use in the Temple.

There are a number of types of psalms. Some were composed for specific occasions or needs, while others are quite general. Among these are:

- **Laments,** or prayers of deliverance from a terrible need or danger. Examples: Psalms 9, 30, 118, and 124.

LEARN FROM THE MAP

Greece and Israel

Find Greece and Israel on this map. Notice how close they are to one another. Because Alexander the Great opened new possibilities for trade, increased boat travel across the Mediterranean contributed to the spread of Greek ideas to Israel.

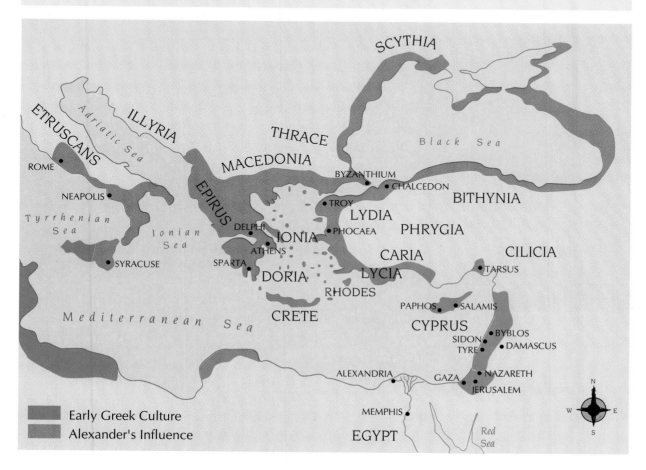

Early Greek Culture
Alexander's Influence

- **Hymns of praise** set as accolades to God. Usually the reasons for praise are given in the psalm itself. Examples: Psalms 29, 103, and 148.
- **Royal psalms** related to the king in some way. They may have been written for his personal worship or enthronement ceremonies. Examples: Psalms 2, 18, 45, and 132.
- **Wisdom psalms** including proverbs, a teacher's address to a student, or general advice about living. The writing style of the wisdom psalms is similar to other Wisdom literature. Examples: Psalms 1, 37, and 112.

Have You Considered?

1. The Book of Job was probably finished during the Exile. Why do you suppose Job's point of view would have been popular to people living then?
2. Summarize in a few sentences the explanation given by the Deuteronomic historian for why the Exile happened. Would Job agree or disagree with this explanation? Explain your answer.
3. Sirach was written at a time when the Jewish community was worried about losing its identity to foreign beliefs. How would Sirach's claim that wisdom was contained in the Law help the community maintain its identity?

Learning from the Wisdom Tradition

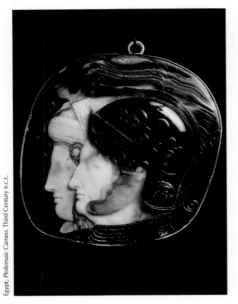

Egypt, *Ptolemaic Cameo, Third Century* B.C.E.

You have seen how the sages, or wisdom teachers, devoted themselves to the "big questions" of human life. Looking for answers to these questions, the sages developed a method of finding clues to the big picture in nature and daily events. In the end, they identified the qualities which a wise person should possess. In this section, you'll investigate these qualities. First, however, you'll study the insight contained in the three most famous wisdom texts of all.

Learning Objectives for Section Two

By the end of this section, you will be able to:

- Explain the methods taught by the sages for seeking wisdom.
- List and explain the qualities of the wise person.
- List several ways wisdom helps people to live well.
- Identify the qualities of a wise person and explain how those qualities can be recognized in daily living.

◆ Wisdom and the Spiritual Life

Saint Gregory of Nyssa (332–395 C.E.) was a theologian and biblical scholar who was especially interested in the Wisdom literature. Saint Gregory commented that the Book of Proverbs was the best book for beginners to use in order to develop a spiritual life; that Ecclesiastes was better suited to those a bit more advanced in wisdom; and that the Song of Songs was a book for those who had mastered the spiritual experience.

In a sense, Gregory suggested that these three books provided a school for the spiritual life. Much as a person learning the martial arts moves up by a belt color each time he or she has mastered the earlier level, or a scout moves up in rank after completing a particular challenge, so to, according to Gregory, should people progress through these books.

Proverbs

The Book of Proverbs is not a collection of works by one author. Israelite tradition credited Solomon with many of the proverbs as it credited the Torah to Moses and the Psalms to David, but Solomon is not the author of the book as it now stands. Perhaps some of the proverbs originated in Solomon's court. Scholars generally agree that the majority of the proverbs were written before the Exile. The introduction (chapters 1–9) was probably completed in the fourth century B.C.E.

The Book of Proverbs is divided into two parts:

1. Instructions about how to live.
2. Sayings, in couplet form, which are actual proverbs.

The Book of Proverbs also uses a literary style called the *mashal*—short sayings based on practical experience and application. The Hebrew proverb is a short, simple saying meant to be retained through the generations. They suggest that the way to true

People of Note

Gregory of Nyssa

Gregory wrote his own exposition of the Catholic faith, the Catechetical Discourse. In his studies, he concentrated on the spiritual and mystical meaning of the Bible. Throughout his life, Gregory had a special interest in how people could grow spiritually through appreciation of the Bible's symbolism and insight. Gregory died in 395 C.E., and his feast day is March 9.

On Perfection
"Therefore, let no one be grieved if he sees in his nature a penchant for change… For this is truly perfection: never to stop growing towards what is better and never placing any limit on perfection."

---

happiness is through the common virtues of hard work, careful speech, good manners, and discipline. Though the Book of Proverbs has a distinctly religious dimension too, these themes of universal wisdom provide an opportune starting place for the beginner, as Gregory of Nyssa suggested.

Gregory of Nyssa is a Father of the Church. Gregory's entire family, including his brother, Basil the Great, have been named saints by the Church.

Borgognone, *St. Gregory of Nyssa, Fifteenth Century.*

On the surface, the book offers little more than the wisdom of the world. In the introduction, chapters 1–9, the collection represents the earliest stage of Israel's understanding of wisdom. Men and women both are warned to avoid drunkenness, poor manners, and laziness. They are encouraged to seek out wisdom through study, training, instruction, and discipline. The purpose of the proverbs is described in the introduction:

> That men may appreciate wisdom and discipline, may understand words of intelligence; may receive training in wise conduct, in what is right, just, and honest; that resourcefulness may be imparted to the simple, to the young man knowledge and discretion. A wise man by hearing them will advance in learning, an intelligent man will gain sound guidance, that he may comprehend proverb and parable, the words of the wise and their riddles.
>
> (Proverbs 1:2–7)

In some places, the wisdom of Proverbs comes out of the actual experience of the sages themselves. Read the following passages and imagine the dialogue taking place between an instructor and a student concerning the content of these readings:

- Proverbs 1–9
- Proverbs 22:17–24:22
- Proverbs 31:1–9

Yet, from a wider view, the wisdom of Proverbs particularly emphasizes Israel's religion. Much of the moral code of Israel is found in the second part of the Book of Proverbs, especially that part of the code which speaks of the love and service of one person for another.

All of the principles of the Ten Commandments as well as the Sabbath regulations are included in the Book of Proverbs. Familiar themes covered by the prophets are mentioned as well. See if you can find the themes of injustice, mistreatment of the poor, compassion, and kindness in the following passages:

- Proverbs 15:27 and 17:15
- Proverbs 22:22ff
- Proverbs 11:17, 14:22, 16:6, and 24:10

Proverbs represents the traditional ideas about wisdom which were inherited by later writers such as the authors of Job and Ecclesiastes. As such, they set the tone for all of Israel's later seekers of wisdom.

Ecclesiastes

A man serving a life sentence in prison was asked if he had a favorite book in the Bible. "As a matter of fact I do," he said. "My favorite book is Ecclesiastes because it tells the truth about life." Similarly, a dying woman in a nursing home also named Ecclesiastes as her favorite book. Why? "It makes me feel part of the great stream of life. It keeps me from feeling all alone." What is it about Ecclesiastes that inspires people in such difficult conditions? What is the secret of its appeal to so many people, so different from each other?

Ecclesiastes challenges the reader to look more deeply at life and its issues than does Proverbs. The book takes the form of a series of personal reflections by the author, known as *Qoheleth*, from the Hebrew word for "one who assembles a congregation." The grammatical form of Qoheleth is feminine, so it is possible that this author/sage was a woman. The Book of Ecclesiastes is generally thought to have been written in the second century B.C.E.

In Ecclesiastes, Qoheleth shares new and unconventional views on a wide range of topics. The author's aim is to see life with total clarity, without bias caused by beliefs, desires, or culture. According to the author, such clarity is important if one is to develop a true relationship with God, because only a person who wants to know the truth can really know God.

Basically, the message of Ecclesiastes is a simple one: the pleasures of this world are not able to satisfy the desires of human beings. There is nothing secure about earthly happiness. Even if someone gained every imaginable pleasure and desire, he or she would not be perfectly happy. True happiness is the major theme of the Book of Ecclesiastes. It is also a natural "second course" in discovering the meaning of true wisdom.

The form of the book is a series of personal reflections, expressed through the popular sayings of the day and through longer poems. The book begins and ends with the same words: "Vanity of vanities! All things are vanity" (*Ecclesiastes* 1:2 *and* 12:8). To Qoheleth, finding true happiness and pleasure in the world is not possible because this ideal truth cannot be found there. For example:

- A just person is outlived by his wicked neighbor (see *Ecclesiastes* 7:15).
- Gaining material riches does not guarantee happiness (see *Ecclesiastes* 5:10–17).
- Ultimately, death claims all human beings just as it does any "beast." (see *Ecclesiastes* 3:19–21).

Ecclesiastes shows with total clarity that only God never changes. That is why reflection on the Book of Ecclesiastes is useful for the person who is moving forward in spiritual growth. It teaches and reminds the disciple of what must be fully realized in daily attitudes and daily choices. Only God is permanent; the person who clings to anything less than God will suffer much pain in life.

When everything has been completely considered, Qoheleth finally decides that the best thing to do—since nothing in life is guaranteed—is to enjoy what you have in the present moment and not to reach for what is too far beyond your grasp. For example, if you have a family, work, and food, enjoy them! Whatever comes your way, do it wholeheartedly, so that some joy might be yours in the doing. Nevertheless, do not expect too much from life.

Perhaps the greatest contribution of Ecclesiastes is its skepticism and its accompanying message that humankind would do well to reject all the simple solutions to the mysteries of life. This is a quality of the Book of Ecclesiastes that continues to attract people to its message.

Song of Songs

The Song of Songs is a poem about love. It describes ideal human love, as well as the great depth of love between God and people. The author of Song of Songs presents Israel as the intimate lover of the Lord, united to God in perfect love. Saint Gregory considered this book to be important for the "advanced" students of wisdom. Those who had reached this point are able to find true knowledge of God in love.

The Song of Songs translates from the Hebrew as "The Greatest Song." It was originally written as a long, intense, and beautiful poem about love. With this interpretation, the Song of Songs is often quoted in love notes and even in wedding ceremonies. The presence of such love poetry in the Scripture suggests that married love has a sacred dimension, merging at some mysterious point with divine love.

But as you know, biblical writings are not limited to one meaning only, and the celebration of love in Song of Songs can be understood on several levels. For example, Jewish tradition understands Song of Songs as a parable that describes the delights of the love between God and Israel.

On another level, Song of Songs conveys the ecstasies of love that flow between God and humanity. This power and wonder can never be simply described in words. Rather, images must be used to communicate what the experience is like. The author uses the beauty of mountains and sunsets as symbols of the beauty one experiences in union with God. Song of Songs sums up Israel's Wisdom tradition, helping the reader to understand the love of Yahweh.

Have You Considered?

1. Proverbs says that hard work and good moral behavior lead to success in life. Do you think this is true?
2. Describe a time when someone tried to give you a simplistic explanation. How did it make you feel? Do you agree with Ecclesiastes that it's important to reject simplistic answers?
3. Do you agree with Song of Songs that what two people feel for each other when they're in love is a symbol for the love between God and humanity? Why or why not?

◆ The Methods of the Sage

The task of the sage was to help people to reach their fullest potential. To do this, they corrected, approved, praised, and condemned their students. While their subject matter was concerned with the entirety of human behavior, the importance of God was never overshadowed in their message.

The sages taught their students two primary principles or methods of uncovering wisdom:

1. **Observation**
2. **Reflection**

Let's look at these two methods in more detail.

Observation

The sages were great observers. They noticed everything that happened around them. They observed nature, its cycles, the growth and decay of plants, the sky, the earth, and the sea. They paid special attention to human behavior. They taught their students how to observe the changes in human circumstances and their interconnections. Wisdom students learned how to observe human choices and their results. The examples used in Wisdom literature resulted from these precise observations.

Most people see well enough to get by in life, but very few people are actually careful observers who closely examine themselves, their lives, and the people around them. Few people truly consider circumstances before acting. People who observe carefully, learn to take a more detached attitude towards life, much as witnesses to a crime must do in court. They "step back" and pay attention to what happens, not just what they think is happening.

Skillful observation increases only through practice. As people master this skill of external observation, they can then begin to observe more internal things. For example, the sages were very skilled at observing their own emotions and how the body was affected by them. For example:

Anxiety in a man's heart depresses it, but a kindly word makes it glad!

(Proverbs 12:25)

A tranquil mind gives life to the body, but jealousy rots the bones.

(Proverbs 14:30)

Reflection

The second method for finding wisdom is reflection. Once you've made careful observations about nature and other people, you have to sort out what you've seen, and decide which behaviors and attitudes seem most wise. This is the act of reflection.

Reflecting on your observation of nature, which attitudes feel most appropriate? Does respect for the natural world seem like a better, more fitting response than carelessness? Watching other people, who seem the most content and at peace with themselves? What makes them that way? Thinking about such questions leads one to a wise, mature understanding of life.

The sages asked many of these same questions. They took the time to observe their own and other's experiences more closely. In reflecting on these observations, they came to a clearer understanding of the meaning of wisdom.

Have You Considered?

1. How do you think the study of nature can help teach us wisdom? Write down one lesson you think human beings should learn from the natural world.
2. Describe a time when an event changed your life in some way. Do you think it's true that everything that happens to you has some meaning or purpose? Why or why not?

The sages came to their wisdom often through the study of nature. What can you learn about how to live your life from studying the way the world is?

◆ The Advantages of Wisdom

Have you ever tried to juggle three or more balls in the air? Unless you are a rare exception, your first attempts at juggling left balls scattered everywhere. Juggling requires excellent hand/eye coordination. Until you develop that skill, you simply can't keep more than two balls in the air at the same time. Once you can juggle three balls, however, you can proceed to more difficult juggling skills.

Learning to be wise is very similar to learning how to juggle. There are skills that must be learned at the basic level before moving on to the more difficult ones. It takes time to develop new skills. The difficulty in becoming wise is not that the answers themselves are very difficult—concepts such as respect for others, honesty, love of God, and care of oneself are not exactly new. The hard part is developing a character based on these ideals. Doing so takes time, effort, and moral courage.

The Qualities of a Wise Person

There are four main characteristics of being wise, and they will benefit anyone who pursues them. They are **balance, certainty, integrity,** and a **listening heart**.

Balance   A balanced person is able to respond with true wisdom of heart and mind to anything that happens, just as an excellent tennis player is balanced and ready to return the ball no matter to what area of the court it is hit.

A balanced person knows how to enjoy life, but is not thrown around by extremes. For a balanced person, every setback is not a crisis, and every step forward is not a major triumph. He or she responds calmly, thoughtfully, and confidently to situations, feeling his or her emotions, but also controlling them.

Certainty   A person of certainty is one who has a strong sense of security and is able to live without anxiety in most situations. Inner certainty means knowing who you are and what your life is about; it means being strong enough that you can be yourself, without worrying about what everybody else will think.

Such certainty requires a willingness to accept responsibility for one's own choices and their consequences. Everyone makes many choices about actions and attitudes, but some mistakenly think that these choices are without consequence. The wise person knows that every choice brings with it a result or consequence, takes that information into account, and then accepts full responsibility for his or her personal choice. This requires conviction and security.

Integrity   A person of integrity is honest about his or her experiences, observations, and perceptions. The wise person does not buy into every new or faddish idea that comes along, especially when it conflicts with his or her own experience.

People of integrity are humble. They recognize that they do not know everything. People of integrity accept criticism and corrections willingly; it's just a part of the learning experience. Wise people are humble; they want to know and to improve themselves. Learning is more important than defending themselves or proving that they are right.

Sometimes people speak as if they are on automatic pilot. They gossip about others and their words

The four main characteristics of a wise person — balance, certainty, integrity, and a listening heart — take time to develop. This is why most wise people are older. However, not all older people are wise and not all younger people are foolish.

are thoughtless. The wise person speaks with care and speaks only what is well-said and true. Oftentimes, this means that the wise person speaks hardly at all. "As you hedge round your vineyard with thorns, set barred doors over your mouth" (*Sirach* 28:24).

Integrity also means that the wise person practices a virtuous life. Did you know that the word "virtue" means strength? What do you think it means to have virtue?

There are also inner virtues which wisdom says matter more than external actions: honesty, humility, kindliness, generosity, justice, love, and purity of intention.

A Listening Heart   Like the other qualities embraced by wisdom, a listening heart is the product of long practice.

In the Bible, the heart is the center of the person, from which all thoughts, feelings, and actions come. Listening with one's entire being is different from listening only with one's ears or mind. One "takes it to heart," contemplates what is heard, and seriously applies its lessons to life. A "listening heart" requires that we stop thinking of ourselves as having all the answers or that others have nothing to teach us. Everyone has a story to tell, and a person with a listening heart will learn from other's experiences.

Most of all, those with such wisdom realize that they are not the center of creation, but simply and deeply **belong to** creation. They acknowledge that they, along with all other people, are subject to the Creator as a participant in God's gifts. For them, every experience is an occasion for thanksgiving, even those

Chagall, Ahasver, The Wandering Jew. Twentieth Century.

The Bible's Wisdom tradition recognizes that wisdom was not something to be had, but a journey to be traveled. The wise person continues to grow wiser each day. The legendary Jewish figure, Ahasver, wanders eternally seeking true Wisdom.

that at first seem unpleasant. All that happens in creation happens in relationship to God—this is something that the sages never forgot.

How Wisdom Helps

The sages communicated to their audiences the numerous advantages of gaining wisdom. In no particular order of importance, here are some of the results of having wisdom. Find others as you read from the Wisdom literature.

- **Wisdom is a protector and guard.** It keeps a person away from dangerous situations. It gives one security and freedom from fear.
- **Wisdom helps a person to live a long time.**
- **Wisdom keeps life peaceful and pleasant.** Being happy and content helps a person to prosper.
- **Wisdom is like a light in the darkness.** It enables a person to live without confusion or ignorance.
- **Wisdom keeps you from making a fool of yourself in public.** The wise person knows when to act and when to do nothing.
- **Wisdom makes you thankful and keeps you from depression.**
- **Wisdom keeps you away from quarrels.**
- **The wise spread healing and joy.**
- **Wisdom draws the favor of authorities.**

- **The wise one does not have to hurry.** He or she understands the importance of good timing and knows how to use it.
- **Wisdom brings self-respect and the respect of others.**
- **Wisdom brings wonderful, loyal friends.**
- **Wisdom never fails, even when everything seems lost.**

How can wisdom benefit you? Wisdom allows you to interpret all of human experience and determine the most intelligent and practical way of living. As you uncover more of the depth of Wisdom literature, consider how it can be of service to your own life and the lives of those around you.

Have You Considered?

1. Pick one of the four characteristics of the wise person discussed above. Do you think you have this quality? If so, how did you get it? If not, how do you think having it would help you?
2. Describe a situation in which you learned a valuable lesson from an unexpected source. How does this help show you the value of a listening heart?
3. Pick one of the benefits of wisdom listed above. How could this help you? Be specific.

Spiritual Reflection

Psalm 29

Psalm 29 is an ancient hymn of praise to God. Scholars believe that it was composed for worship in the Temple. This hymn of praise to God has been used in prayer for nearly 3000 years.

The psalm uses symbolic language throughout.

Open your Bible to Psalm 29. Read each verse to yourself slowly. Picture the image that is being painted for you by the psalmist. See the mighty deeds of the Lord, feel the Lord's mighty words. See how many symbols you can find.

What do you think the following symbols might mean?

- The voice of the Lord breaks the cedars.

- He makes Lebanon leap like a calf and Sirion like a young bull.
- The voice of the Lord strikes fiery flames; the voice of the Lord shakes the desert, the Lord shakes the wilderness of Kadesh.
- The voice of the Lord twists the oaks and strips the forests.

When you finish reading the entire psalm, select one phrase that you like. Keep that phrase clearly in mind while you meditate on some problem you're facing, then ask God to see you through it. Pray quietly for a few moments, letting the phrase you picked run through your mind. Try to feel God's concern and love for you as you meditate on this phrase.

Q/A

Section One

1. Define what the term "wisdom" means in Wisdom literature.
2. Explain why wisdom is not the same thing as knowledge or intelligence.
3. What is one quality that distinguishes wisdom in ancient Israel from other Middle Eastern wisdom traditions?
4. What is a Wisdom school?
5. What aspect of Wisdom interested Wisdom schools in the period between the Old and New Testaments?
6. How does Job challenge the earlier Wisdom tradition?
7. What unique insight does Sirach have?
8. List and describe four kinds of Psalms.

Section Two

1. Who was Gregory of Nyssa?
2. Define "mashal."
3. Who is Qoheleth? What is unusual about this name?
4. What is the basic message of Ecclesiastes? How can it be interpreted positively?
5. What kind of love was originally described in the Song of Songs?
6. How does the Song of Songs sum up the Wisdom tradition?
7. Describe the two methods of learning wisdom developed by the sages.
8. List and define four qualities of a wise person.

BIBLE ACTIVITY

1. Go back to Section One and review the "The Bible in Context" feature on parallelism. Write three couplets in your own words, one for each of the types of parallelism.
2. Choose one of the following books: Proverbs, Ecclesiastes, Song of Songs, and Sirach 1–43. Look for verses that apply to you or to people you know. Copy them on index cards. Give them as gifts or keep them as personal, inspirational reminders.
3. Read Proverbs 12:19. Share a story about gossiping and about how you have found this proverb to be truthful.
4. Write a story detailing the importance of friends in your life. In your story, quote these passages from the Book of Sirach: 6:5–17, 13:5–7, and 22:19–22.

GLOSSARY

- **Balance:** One of the qualities of a wise person; a state of calmness and the ability to use good judgment.
- **Certainty:** One of the qualities of a wise person; refers to inner confidence in one's identity.
- **Fear of the Lord:** Respect and humility before God; not the same thing as actual fright.
- **Integrity:** One of the qualities of a wise person; means honesty about one's observations, perceptions and experiences.
- **Listening heart:** One of the qualities of a wise person; having a willingness to hear what others have to say and learn from what is heard.
- **Ma'at:** Egyptian concept of wisdom as self-control and eloquence.
- **Mashal:** A short saying based on practical experience that is universal in its application.
- **Parallelism:** Structure of Hebrew poetry in which rhythm is produced by pairs of lines, in which the second repeats the idea of the first in slightly different words; types include similar, opposite, and completed.
- **Proverb:** A saying which expresses something true in an artful and easy-to-remember way.
- **Qoheleth:** The Hebrew word for teacher or preacher, feminine in grammatical form. It is another name for Ecclesiastes.
- **Sages:** Wise people who are venerated and respected for their wisdom, experience, and judgment; the term is often used to describe the writers of Old Testament Wisdom literature.
- **Secular:** Relating to worldly things rather than things of religion.
- **Wisdom:** A sense of what life is all about and how to live it well; insight into God, human nature, and ethical behavior.
- **Wisdom School:** A group of students organized around the teaching of a certain sage.

UNDERSTANDING MORE ABOUT:

The Divine Office

Every day, at fixed times established by centuries-old tradition, Catholics around the world pray something called the "divine office." It is a liturgy for individual or small group use. It is also called "the Liturgy of the Hours," because different prayers are used at particular times of the day. The Church considers it her duty to say these daily prayers—indeed, the divine office is considered to contain some of the most important prayers of the Church.

The heart of the divine office consists of psalms. The Church believes that these psalms should be recited every day, because they so perfectly express God's glory and majesty and because they profoundly reflect every human heart. Since the psalms also formed part of the daily Temple liturgy in ancient Israel, this means that for nearly 3,000 years, these songs have been lifted up every day in praise of Yahweh.

Review

Looking Back

The Old Testament is the story of the people of Israel and the Covenant which unites them with God. The books of the Old Testament are an important part of the family story of the Christian faith community. These books teach us, inspire us, and fill us with a sense that God's loving concern for us never ends, despite all the changes that happen over the course of our lives.

Bible Literacy

1. Define the term "covenant."
2. Why is Moses such an important figure in Israel's history?
3. How did the Hebrews' time in the wilderness form them as a people of faith?
4. What is the decalogue?
5. What is meant by the phrase "the Deuteronomic history"?
6. Discuss the differences in approach between ancient and modern historians.
7. What is the main theological idea in the Book of Judges?
8. Describe God's covenant with David.
9. In biblical studies, what is meant by the word "source"?
10. In what sense are the creation stories in Genesis myths?
11. How are the "J" and "P" creation stories similar? How are they different?
12. What was Yahweh's promise to Abraham?
13. How did King Solomon violate the Covenant?
14. What is syncretism, and why is it a violation of the Covenant?
15. Summarize the important events in the career of Elijah.
16. In what ways was the social situation during Elijah's life similar to our own?
17. How were the Northern and Southern kingdoms unjust?
18. How did the prophets explain the fall of the Northern kingdom?
19. How are the messages of Isaiah and Jeremiah different? How are they similar?
20. Why did some Jews stay behind in Babylon after the Exile?
21. What is the diaspora?
22. List three important messages of the prophet Ezekiel.
23. How did Second Isaiah encourage the people of the Exile?
24. What was Nehemiah's major accomplishment?
25. How did Alexander the Great change life for the Jews?
26. How did God teach Israel with foreign nations after the Exile?
27. In what way is life a conversation with God?
28. Define Wisdom literature
29. How are the Israelite wisdom books similar to and different from non-Israelite wisdom?
30. Explain the qualities of a wise person.

Review

Bible Activities

The Laws of Exodus

Many of the laws given to Moses on Mount Sinai are found in Exodus 20-23. Imagine that you are an Israelite lawyer in 303 B.C.E., and people ask you the following legal questions. Look up the law that applies to their case, and then write a response.

1. "I have served my master as a slave for five years, and have never married. Now he says I have to work five more years for him before I can go free. Is he right?"
2. "My neighbor asked me to take care of his ox while he was away on business. While he was gone, the ox died, even though I took good care of it. No one witnessed what happened, and now my neighbor is demanding that I pay him for the ox. Do I have to?"
3. "My brother stole some money from a Hittite. I told him he'd better pay it back, but he said that since the Hittite is an alien, he doesn't have to pay him. What should I tell him?"

The Judges

Open your Bible to Judges. Find the stories of the following four judges: Deborah, Samson, Ehud, and Gideon, and then answer the following questions.

1. In what order do these stories appear?
2. Which tribe does each judge represent?
3. Check the map in Chapter 3 on page 42. What pattern do you notice when you compare the order of the stories to the judge's tribe? What importance do you find in this pattern?

Solomon's Temple

How big was Solomon's Temple (see 1 Kings 6)? Knowing that a cubit equals 18 inches, in yards:

1. What were the dimensions of the Temple?
2. How wide were the three stories of the annex?
3. What was the area of the sanctuary for the Ark of the Covenant?

Ezekiel's Symbols

Drawing on your knowledge of the circumstances surrounding the Exile, explain the meaning of the following symbols.

1. The Lord tells Ezekiel to take two sticks, labeled Judah and Israel, and to put them together in his hand. He is then to show the united stick to the people.
2. Another time, the Lord tells Ezekiel to pack his luggage as if he is about to move. He is to take his bags out in public and leave them there. Later, he's to move from where he lives to another place, covering his eyes so he can no longer see his home.

Now look up the description of these symbols in Ezekiel and see whether your interpretation agrees with his. The symbol of the sticks in Ezekiel 37:15-22; the symbolic trip is in 12:1-6.

Praying with the Bible

The most important concept in the Old Testament is the Covenant which binds Israel to God. In Chapter 2, you learned that the Covenant was accepted by the people through a special ritual, based on the elements of an ancient Middle Eastern vassal treaty. As a class, you can also pledge yourself to honoring the Covenant through your own ceremony.

Description of the Greatness of God Read aloud the description of God's majesty and special love for Israel in Deuteronomy 10:12-22.

Rules and Stipulations Take turns reading aloud the list of the Ten Commandments found in Deuteronomy 5:6-21. After each, pause a moment to let everyone think about what God is asking.

Witnesses Another reader announces the witnesses to the Covenant proclaimed by God in Deuteronomy 30:19-20.

Blessing and Curses As Moses and the ancient Israelites did, you will finish your ceremony by pronouncing the curses for breaking the Covenant and the blessings for keeping it as found in Deuteronomy 27-28. One person acts as the leader, and the rest of the class will be the community. After each curse or blessing is read, everyone should respond, "Amen."

The New Covenant

Chapter Listings

Chartres Cathedral, West portal, Twelfth Century

The New Covenant can never be viewed apart from the Original Covenant. The people, customs, religious practices, and beliefs about God found in the New Testament can only be understood by first understanding the Old Testament.

The term "New Covenant" originates from the life and actions of Jesus, who not only gave new meaning to the Original Covenant, but also established a new way for human beings to relate to God. For Christians, Jesus' actions—the giving of himself in Eucharist and through his death and resurrection—define the meaning of the New Covenant.

Christians do not abandon the lessons and discoveries of God found in the Old Testament. Rather, they expand their view in order to include the new understandings of God offered by Jesus through his teaching and by his example.

Books of the New Testament

The collection of writings that forms the New Covenant includes

- **Four Gospel Accounts.** *Mark, Matthew, Luke,* and *John.* These books provide us a look into Jesus' life. They tell us some of what Jesus said and did while he was alive. These four books were each written for different audiences and so emphasize different aspects of Jesus' life and teaching. Although similar in style to a biography, the gospel accounts are a new type of literature.
- **The Acts of the Apostles.** This book describes how Christianity grew in a world officially hostile to Jews and their descendants. The stories of the missionary work of the early followers, especially Peter and Paul, are preserved here. The "main character," however, is the Holy Spirit.
- **Letters.** There are 21 documents that take the form of letters. Paul is associated with thirteen of these letters.

   Captivity Letters—Philippians, Philemon, Colossians, and Ephesians are known as "captivity letters" because they were written by Paul to Christian communities while he was in prison.

   Pastoral Letters—Other letters attributed to Paul are known as "pastoral letters" because they pay special attention to the organization of Church structures and to the moral issues facing the early Christians.

   Catholic Letters—Seven letters are traditionally known as "catholic letters" because they were addressed to the entire universal Church. These letters are attributed to Paul, James, Peter, John, and Jude.

- **The Revelation to John,** or the *Apocalypse,* speaks in a symbolic way of the Church that is to come. It is written in an apocalyptic style.

These books of the New Testament were written by a number of authors over a period of fifty years or more. The earliest writing in the New Testament canon is a letter attributed to Paul written around 50 C.E. The latest may be the Second Letter of Peter, which reached its final form possibly as late as 125 C.E.

Living the Good News

Whereas there are four specific gospel accounts, there is only one Gospel, or "Good News," present in all of the Christian Scriptures. This Good News describes the great victory over death won by Jesus for all who believe. This use of the term "gospel" is the original one. Paul refers to his message about the death and resurrection of Jesus as his "gospel"—his "Good News."

In Unit 2, you will read of the Good News of the New Covenant as it was arranged in Christian Scriptures. The *synoptic* acounts ("seeing together with the same eye")—Mark, Matthew, and Luke—emphasize similar words and events from Jesus' life from different perspectives. John reflects the Christian community's growing understanding of Jesus as Lord and Savior.

These books of the New Covenant are important to Christians because they describe the life of Jesus and the faith of his early followers, the Church.

The Second Vatican Council taught that the gospel accounts

> faithfully hand on what Jesus, the Son of God, while he lived among men, really did and taught for their eternal Salvation, until the day when he was taken up. For, after the ascension of the Lord, the apostles handed on to their hearers what he had said and done, but with that fuller understanding which they, instructed by the glorious events of Christ and enlightened by the Spirit of truth, now enjoyed. The sacred authors, in writing the four Gospels, selected certain of the many elements which had been handed on, either orally or already in written form, others synthesized or explained with an eye to the situation of the churches, the while sustaining the form of preaching, but always in such a fashion that they have told us the honest truth about Jesus. Whether they relied on their own memory and recollections or on the testimony of those who "from the beginning were eyewitnesses and ministers of the Word," their purpose in writing was that we might know the "truth" concerning the things of which we have been informed.
>
> (Dei Verbum, V, 19).

Intimately tied with the Original Covenant, the New Covenant ushers in a new age in which all people are invited to share in God's kingdom. It is this invitation and this story that is told in the pages of the Christian Scriptures.

CHAPTER 10

Jesus' Life and Message

Legend

● General History
● Biblical History
● Jewish History
● Books written

Michael was the kind of guy nobody really liked. He was rude, and always saying mean things to people. His appearance and personal habits didn't win him many friends either. If people paid any attention to him at all, it was either to laugh at or to pity him. The only people at school who ever talked to him were the counselors, who constantly called him in to talk about his poor behavior.

One day a new student, Joshua, arrived at school. People liked him right away. Josh seemed to have a different take on life. He was self-confident, but he didn't need to put people down to make his point. He became popular enough that he could have his pick of friends.

Not long after Joshua arrived, he spotted Michael sitting by himself in the cafeteria. He went over and sat down. After a few minutes, Michael got up, screamed "Leave me alone!" and stomped away. The other students in the cafeteria laughed loudly at Michael's response. They were sure that Joshua would realize his mistake and forget about Michael. Joshua was not so easily discouraged. He sought out Michael each day, and gradually Michael let his guard down. As Michael accepted Joshua's persistent attention, he began to trust him. Within a few weeks, Michael looked forward to seeing Joshua and talked with him about many things. Eventually, Joshua and Michael became friends, and with such a good friend, Michael's outlook on life improved. The counselor called this change in Michael a "miracle."

The rest of the student body was very much aware of Joshua's affect on Michael. They asked a lot of questions: "Why did Joshua spend so much time with Michael? Why did he care so much?" "What was it about Joshua that enabled him to get through to Michael when everyone else had failed?" "How could one person have so much impact on another?" "Is it possible for other people to be like Joshua?"

An Amazing Man

Jesus had a similar impact on the people he met. People living in the first century of the common era asked many similiar questions after Jesus' life, death, and resurrection. Like Joshua, Jesus came on the scene unexpectedly and attracted large crowds of people. Yet, he didn't seek out the company of only the elite; he also spent a great amount of time with social outcasts and the poor. During his short life, he, too, accomplished what people called miracles. After he was gone, people wondered "Who was this man and what do his life and teachings mean?" In the New Testament, we read the answers to these questions as given by a variety of early Christian authors.

Who Was Jesus?

Ravenna, *Christ as Warrior. Second Century?*

Imagine that you are asked, "Who was Jesus?" What would you say? You might think of him as God, or as a great teacher, or as a healer. Depending on the teaching you have received, you might know some theological ideas about Jesus, like those in the Creed we say at Mass. You might call him savior or redeemer, too. But theology about Jesus is not everything we want to know about him.

In this section, you'll learn what we can know about the life and times of Jesus. You'll also discover the limits to a truly historical investigation of Jesus' life, and why our faith in Jesus goes beyond what can be proven about him.

Learning Objectives for Section One

By the end of this section, you will be able to:

- Define: "Christ of faith," "Jesus of history."
- Discuss the problem of knowing the historical Jesus.
- Understand the various Jewish sects at the time of Jesus.
- Explain the origins of the four gospel accounts.

◆ The Historical Jesus

Bible scholars often distinguish between the "Christ of faith," the Jesus who we believe is Lord and Savior through the tradition of the Church, and the "Jesus of History," the flesh-and-blood person, Jesus of Nazareth. You probably already know a lot about the Christ of faith. But what do you know about the historical Jesus? What was his life like, and what did he do and say that caused people to see him as special and even divine?

Gospel Accounts: Historical Sources?

The basic sources of evidence we have about the life of Jesus are the four gospel accounts in the New Testament. Each gospel account is full of information about the details of Jesus' life, and much of this information is accurate and reliable. The gospel accounts are not, however, historical works. Their primary purpose was to preach about the risen Jesus, and to convince others to recognize him as the Lord, **not** to record historically accurate information. Remember what you learned in Chapter 1: what is important is that the meaning is presented correctly.

Throughout the years, the gospel accounts have presented Jesus' life and teaching to millions of believers. As statements of faith they have been wildly successful. As statements of fact, however, they often frustrate our historical curiosity.

If you were to write a biography of Jesus, what material would you include?

- Where and when he was born?
- Did he have a happy childhood?
- Who were his best friends?
- Where did he go to school and who were his important teachers?

Wouldn't you want to include as much background on his childhood and adolescence as you could find?

Oddly enough, except for one story in Luke (see *Luke* 2:41–52), the writers of the gospel accounts show no interest in Jesus' childhood, adolescence, and young adulthood. They move directly from Jesus' infancy to his life at about the age of 30, when he began his public career.

Once again consider what you would include in your biography of Jesus, but this time concentrate on his years of ministry. You most definitely would want to know how he got started, when he made his first major speech, as well as the important people with whom he dealt. You would think that for a man of such importance, writers would want to follow his career carefully, documenting everything to make sure that nothing was left out.

The writers of the Gospel didn't think of history in these terms. They actually tell us very little about what physically happened during Jesus' ministry. Most of the events they record could have taken place over a period of a few weeks. How did Jesus spend the rest of his time? What else did he do? We don't learn about it from the gospel accounts. The Gospel writers are interested only in enough details from Jesus' life to show his significance; those that will help us see him as the Son of God and teacher about God's kingdom.

Layers within the Gospels

"Okay," you may be saying, "the gospel accounts are not historical records, but I can at least be sure about the details they do include, can't I?" Well, the gospels do include a wealth of historically accurate information, but sometimes details are confused or altered to bring them into line with the overall purpose of the particular gospel account.

The Catholic Church (see *The Catechism of the Catholic Church*, #126) recognizes three layers of information in the gospel accounts:

1. Sayings and events which go back to the historical Jesus.
2. Material which comes from the teaching of the apostles.
3. Material which comes from the teaching of the gospel writer.

The gospels do not distinguish these layers for us, so in some cases we're not sure if we're reading about the historical Jesus, or if it comes from the later teaching of the apostles, or if it was created by the writer directly. Therefore, even though the Gospel tells us a great deal about the historical Jesus, it leaves out information we would like to have.

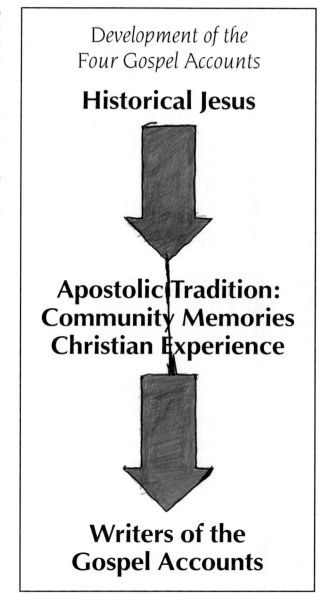

Development of the Four Gospel Accounts

Historical Jesus

Apostolic Tradition: Community Memories Christian Experience

Writers of the Gospel Accounts

Have You Considered?

1. How important do you think it is to know about the historical Jesus? What do you think we need to know?
2. Think about a favorite relative or friend. If you were to write a biography of this person, how might your memories be influenced by how you felt about this person?
3. Can a life-story of someone be wrong about some of the minor details, and yet still be "true" in its overall picture? Explain your answer.

◆ The Context of Jesus' Life: Roman Palestine

One way to know more about the historical Jesus is to investigate the time and place in which he lived. Jesus' work took place in Palestine in the first century C.E., during the time Palestine was part of the Roman empire. To understand Jesus, we need to know how Roman occupation changed life for his Jewish community.

Life under the Romans

In 63 B.C.E., the Roman General Pompey conquered Jerusalem and annexed Palestine. From then on, Palestine was under the control of Rome.

- The Roman territory of "Judea"—basically the same as that of ancient Judah—was ruled by a king, "Herod the Great" from 37 to 4 B.C.E.
- After Herod's death, Judea was ruled by his brother Archelaus. He was such an ineffective king that Caesar Augustus banished him and made Judea a province.
- Provinces were governed by Roman governors called prefects or procurators such as Pontius Pilate, whose rule in Judea began in 26 C.E.
- Pilate was hated in Judea, because he had no respect for the Jewish religion. In Jerusalem, he put up images of the emperor for the Roman soldiers to worship. Only the threat of widespread armed rebellion convinced Pilate to remove these idols. Even so, the adversarial relationship with the Jewish leadership was firmly established.

The Romans continued the process of Hellenization begun in the early fourth century B.C.E. Some Jews embraced Roman rule and adopted a Hellenized lifestyle, often becoming wealthy in the process. For most Jews, however, the Roman period was a time of increasing poverty and hardship.

- They lived under the heavy taxation of the Romans.
- Land was increasingly concentrated in the hands of a few wealthy property owners.
- Small farmers were forced off their farms and into the city, where they generally did not find work.
- Economic and social unrest was common. This was not a peaceful time.

Many people blamed these conditions on the Romans and their governors. For these reasons, the threat of outright rebellion was never far away. When Jesus preached the kingdom of God, therefore, many people wanted to hear in his words a promise of action against the Romans, leading to Jewish independence. As we will see, however, this was not Jesus' message.

Jewish Sects at the Time of Jesus

One of the important aspects of Jewish life in Jesus' lifetime was the existence of groups of Jews organized around certain ideas. We sometimes call these groups "sects," although they may have been only interest groups similar in some ways to political parties.

---

in the Spotlight

A Portrait of Jesus?

If you were asked to describe Jesus' physical appearance, what would you say? A man with long hair, a beard, and perhaps wearing a robe? That's certainly the way Jesus has been pictured in Western art for centuries. However, that's not the way the earliest artists depicted Jesus.

The oldest picture of Jesus is a wall painting in the Greek Chapel, found among the "catacombs," or early Christian burial chambers, in Rome. In this painting, dated to around 150 C.E., Jesus is shown as a beardless young adult with short hair. A third century house in Syria also shows Jesus as beardless. Other early pictures show Jesus with long, curly hair, but still no beard. The beard doesn't appear until the fourth century.

The picture of Jesus with long hair and a beard may be closer to the truth than the earlier examples. The earliest painting of Jesus is clearly idealized. They show him much as an upperclass, Roman Christian, with short hair and a clean face. This portrait would be very acceptable and non-threatening to Roman citizens. However, Jewish males in Palestine during Jesus' day were very likely to have long hair, both because of observance of the laws regulating shaving, and as a way of protesting Israel's occupation by the short-haired Romans.

The Bible tells us nothing about what Jesus looked like. But since Jesus was from the Middle East, he almost certainly would have had dark hair and skin.

The Sadducees   The *Sadducees* came from wealthy, aristocratic families who controlled the Temple and supported Roman rule. Some had priestly ancestors. A few seem to have been high priests in the Temple. They emphasized the Torah, and rejected religious ideas such as angels, demons, and resurrection. Opposed to Jesus, their leadership was too cozy with the Roman ruler to be popular.

The Pharisees   The *Pharisees* were closely associated with another group called the "scribes." The Pharisees stressed the Law, but they believed that it should be interpreted differently under different circumstances. They avoided contact with Gentiles and with Jews who did not keep the Law, whom they called "sinners." The Pharisees and the Sadducees often opposed each another. The Pharisees believed in the idea of a resurrection (an afterlife). They were highly regarded by the Jewish people. Rabbis (teachers) usually came from this group.

The Essenes   Originally the *Essenes* and the Pharisees were part of a larger group of Jews opposed to Hellenization. Unlike the Pharisees, however, the Essenes decided that to keep the Law it was necessary to flee the cities and live in the wilderness. They

The Dead Sea Scrolls were found in these and other similar caves in the hills surrounding the Dead Sea.

The Bible in Context

The Dead Sea Scrolls

In 1945, a shepherd boy discovered a few old jars in a cave near the Dead Sea. Inside these jars were pieces of leather covered with ancient writing. Soon many more documents were found in the desert caves. These documents, usually written on animals skins called "parchment," are known as the "Dead Sea Scrolls."

The scrolls were hidden in the caves sometime before the fall of Jerusalem in 70 C.E., but most of them were written more than a hundred years earlier by unknown writers. Some scrolls are copies of individual books from the Old Testament, and they represent the oldest Bible manuscripts in existence.

The rest of the manuscripts are original writings that show us the concerns and ideas which were current among Jews at this time. One such original writing is the "War Scroll," an apocalyptic book which predicts the overthrow of the Romans and the purification of the Temple.

Early Christian writers such as John may have been influenced by this or another such writing which contrasts "light" and "darkness." Another scroll uses the phrase "Son of God" to refer to the coming Messiah, showing that some Jews expected such a figure during this period.

built communities in the desert for their members. Despite this isolation, many of their religious ideas were well-known. Some early Christians were influenced by them, although they are not mentioned in the New Testament.

Have You Considered?

1. How does the culture and time period in which someone is raised affect his or her ideas and values? Provide an example with your answer.
2. Describe any parallels you see between Roman Palestine and the world today. Which area of the world today most resembles the conditions of Roman Palestine? Why?

◆ The Gospel Accounts

The four gospel accounts are the basic sources we have for the life and teaching of Jesus. The common message shared by these four writings is called the "Gospel," from a Greek word meaning "good news." Although all the gospel accounts feature Jesus as their central character, each tells the story in a unique way, based on the circumstances in which it was written and the viewpoint of its writer. Despite these differences, Mark, Luke, and Matthew have much in common. They're often called the "synoptic" gospels, meaning "seeing together." John offers a distinctive account of the Gospel. Let's take a look at these four different ways of telling the "good news" about Jesus.

Mark

Mark was written in the 60s C.E., and like all the gospel accounts, it was originally written in Greek. Mark repeatedly explains Aramaic words and Jewish customs, he seldom makes reference to the Old Testament, and he seems confused about the geography of Palestine, so it seems likely that Mark's readers were Gentiles who lived outside of Palestine, probably in Rome.

Mark's account is rather stark. For Mark, the suffering of Jesus is the main point of a *Passion Story*, a story about the suffering and crucifixion of Jesus. Mark also presents the least flattering pictures of Jesus' disciples—they are often afraid of Jesus, unable to understand his message, and they fail miserably at Jesus' death.

Luke

The Gospel according to Luke and the Acts of the Apostles were written by the same person, whom we call "Luke." Luke's Gospel account interprets the Greek Old Testament (Septuagint) from a Gentile viewpoint, for a Gentile community. Because Luke's account is aware of the destruction of the Temple in 70 C.E., but does not treat this as an immediate crisis, its writing is usually dated to 80–85 C.E.

Wm. Blake, *Christ Appearing to the Apostles after the Resurrection.* Eighteenth Century.

Each of the gospel accounts describe Jesus' appearing to the Apostles following the Resurrection, but each report is different. Read the last chapter of each account to see how they differ.

Scripture Workshop

Q

Bible scholars believe that Mark was the first gospel account to be written, and that Matthew and Luke copied much from Mark. There are passages that Matthew and Luke have in common, however, that did not come from Mark. Because it's clear that Matthew and Luke did not copy from each other, scholars believe they must have used another source, which is called "Q" (from the German word *Quelle*, meaning "source"). You can examine this theory for yourself. Look up the following pairs of verses from Matthew and Luke:

(1) Luke 7:6–9, Matthew 8:8–10
(2) Luke 10:13–15, Matthew 11:21–23
(3) Luke 11:24–26, Matthew 12:43–45
(4) Luke 13:34–35, Matthew 23:37–39

In your Bible, underline once all the words that are exactly the same in the two passages. Then underline twice the words that are basically the same as those in the other passage. Answer these questions:

1. Are these similarities strong enough to support the theory of a common source?
   Why or why not?
2. What do these four pairs of passages have in common?

Matthew found in Acts of the Apostles 1:13. Because this gospel account is aware of arguments between Christians and Jewish leaders, which became intense after the destruction of the Temple, the writing is usually dated to 85–90. Matthew's text is full of allusions to the Old Testament. Judging from the interests expressed in the book itself, Matthew wrote for a community that included mostly Christians who were Jewish in background, but also Christians who were Gentiles. Matthew is interested in the ongoing relationship between the Old Testament (Law and Prophets) and Jesus and his followers. This account relies heavily on the Old Testament, in order to show what is in the new Covenant and how the new "fulfills" the old.

John

John did not rely on the traditions used in the synoptic gospels. Instead, John formed the traditions of early Christianity into a unique vision. Because of John's view of Jesus, his nature and his mission, many scholars think John was written later than the other accounts, perhaps in the 90s C.E. It's possible that a community of students, founded by John, was involved in putting together the account that bears his name.

John's gospel account features speeches by Jesus. While Jesus usually begins the speech, the writer's reflections blend it into a consistent teaching. John uses symbols more than the other gospels do. John's irony is famous: he puts truth into the words of Jesus' opponents, for example, or has a person totally misunderstand what is happening so that Jesus can discuss the truth. Finally, John's story of the passion of Jesus portrays a Jesus quite different from the one seen in the Synoptic accounts.

Nowhere in the accounts are we given even a hint about where Luke lived. Some have thought he was from either Asia Minor or Syria, but no one can know for sure. Luke shows greater interest in women, in the poor, and in those who have no social status. He also develops the theory of salvation history, dividing time into the three periods of Israel, Jesus, and the Church.

Matthew

The author of the Gospel according to Matthew could not have been the same person as the apostle

Have You Considered?

1. As discussed, each gospel account has its own point of view. How is it that two people can write about exactly the same subject, and yet end up with very different stories?
2. None of the gospel accounts is likely to have been written by actual followers of Jesus. What does that mean, in terms of their value as historical sources about the life of Jesus?
3. All of the gospel accounts were written in Greek. What can we learn from this observation?

LEARN FROM THE MAP

Roman Palestine

To follow Jesus' story more closely, use this map and locate the following places: the district of Galilee, the Sea of Galilee, Judea, the Jordan River, the Dead Sea, Samaria, Nazareth, Bethlehem, Jerusalem, Cana, Capernaum, Bethany, and Jericho. Using the distances from the map legend, answer these questions:

1. Determine how far Jesus might have walked from Capernaum to Jerusalem. How many days might that have taken if he went directly?
2. The Gospel says that Jesus made at least one trip to Phoenicia, looking (unsuccessfully) for solitude. If he left from Capernaum, how far did he walk?
3. Apparently from Phoenicia Jesus went further north, then around to Decapolis, healing and teaching among the Gentile cities there. How long a trip might that have been?

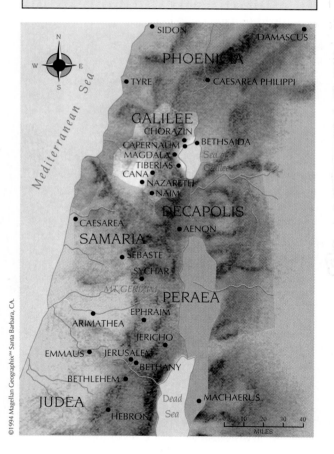

©1994 Magellan Geographix™ Santa Barbara, CA.

◆ The Quest for the Historical Jesus

On the cover of *Time* magazine on August 13, 1988, were the three words "Who Was Jesus?" The accompanying article covered the various theories scholars have proposed over the years in answer to this question, using the gospel accounts and information from Roman Palestine as their sources. This debate among scholars about who Jesus of Nazareth was, and what he stood for, is called the "quest for the historical Jesus."

Although each of the theories is interesting, none is provable because of the limits of the historical evidence. So what's the value of the historical approach, if it can't give us certainty about who Jesus was?

For one thing, what can be established about the historical Jesus is important. The historical evidence shows us a Jesus who valued all people equally, whether they were poor or rich. Jesus looked into the heart of each person with compassion and offered healing and goodness to all. The importance of the historical approach is that it emphasizes that Jesus was fully human, subject to the demands, temptations, and frustrations we all feel. By itself, this insight justifies the search for the Jesus of history.

Ultimately, however, our faith in Jesus does not rest on the historical evidence. As Catholic Christians, our faith includes the testimony of Church tradition, that Jesus is the Lord of humanity, the Son of God, who existed from the beginning of time, became human, died for our sins, and rose again. These points cannot be proved historically, but are verified in the experience of Christians who open their hearts to Jesus' healing presence.

Have You Considered?

1. Why can't our faith in Jesus be based only on historical evidence?
2. Can you believe something in faith if it can also be proven? Or does "faith" require the absence of proof? Explain your answer.
3. What does it mean to say that Jesus was subject to the same problems and concerns that you face?

The Kingdom of God

Unknown, St. John the Evangelist. Second Century?

One point on which historians do agree is that the center of Jesus' preaching and teaching was a reality he called the "kingdom of God" (some Bibles translate this as the "kingdom of Heaven" or as the "reign of God"). In fact, many Bible scholars have suggested that everything Jesus said and did illustrates the nature of the kingdom. Many people thought Jesus meant royalty, political authority, and military power. In this section, we'll explore the kingdom of God as Jesus understood it.

Learning Objectives for Section Two

By the end of the section, you will be able to:

- Explain the two dimensions of the kingdom of God.
- Demonstrate the special aspects of parables.
- Explain how Jesus' healing power paints a picture of what the kingdom is like.
- Describe how the kingdom applies to everyday life.

◆ The Nature of the Kingdom

We call the period in Jesus' life from approximately age 30 to 33, his *public ministry*. During this time, Jesus traveled from place to place, teaching people, healing the sick, and proclaiming the kingdom. Jesus built his ministry around the message he brought concerning this kingdom, and it was this message that changed peoples' lives and the course of history. Despite the tremendous importance Jesus attached to the phrase, "kingdom of God," it was often misunderstood. People formed many different expectations of what a "kingdom of God" could be.

Has this ever happened to you: a friend invites you to a party, but doesn't tell you what type of party it is? When you arrive, you find that you're dressed inappropriately because your idea of a party differs from that of the party's giver? That is exactly the experience of the people who heard Jesus' message.

They accepted Jesus' invitation to the kingdom but had the wrong idea as to what that kingdom was to be.

Misconceptions about the Kingdom

Jesus' message that the kingdom was at hand was frequently misunderstood by his first listeners, who doubtlessly understood this teaching through their own long-held expectations: they expected God to re-create an independent Jewish nation, ruled directly by a messiah (anointed king). As God had ruled the Israelites in their earliest days, so many Jews thought God would one day rule again. Included in this belief was the expected defeat of the oppressive Romans. It's not surprising, then, that many of the first people who heard Jesus, understood a political message about an earthly, Jewish kingdom.

After Jesus' death and resurrection, however, people came to understand that he had not been talking about an earthly kingdom at all. They remembered that he had said things like "the kingdom of God is

Balling, *Ulysses S. Grant, Nineteenth Century.*

Many people heard Jesus' message of the kingdom and expected a great military leader to come forward to defeat the Romans, much as General Grant was able to defeat General Lee in the American Civil War.

at hand" or "the kingdom of God is within you" or "the reign of God is in your midst," and he referred to the parables he told as "the mysteries of the kingdom." What, then, did Jesus have in mind?

Two Dimensions of the Kingdom

The early Christians gradually realized that the kingdom of God Jesus proclaimed had two dimensions:

1. Jesus would return at the end of time when everything that he had promised would be fulfilled.
2. Jesus was inviting his followers to adopt a new style and quality of life.

The Second Coming   Following Jesus' ascension into heaven, Christians expected him to return to earth during their lifetimes to establish the kingdom. This return is known as the *Second Coming,* or the *parousia.* The early Christians, in keeping with the traditional Jewish idea, expected Jesus to rule over the world and to destroy all the existing sources of power and authority when he returned. Saint Paul even had

to write a letter (Second Thessalonians) urging Christians not to quit their jobs and leave their families in expectation of the parousia!

The Kingdom Is Now!   As they studied Jesus' ministry, Christians discovered the second dimension of his teaching about the kingdom: a spiritual, interior quality of life in relation to God that is available now, here, in this life on earth. This kingdom of God occurs in an individual who recognizes God as a real king and experiences himself or herself as a child in that kingdom. In this kingdom, people experience God as their common ruler, and treat others as fellow subjects of their heavenly king.

Living in the kingdom means living a life centered on:

*   Love of God
*   Love of others.

This was what Jesus said when asked about the commandments:

> *"You shall love the Lord your God with all your heart, with all your soul, with all your mind, and with all your strength…You shall love your neighbor as yourself. There is no other commandment greater than these."*
>
> (Mark 12:30–31)

Living in the kingdom, therefore, means loving God and serving others in loving ways.

The Kingdom Gives Rest

This kingdom is good news for everyone, because the qualities of life in Jesus' kingdom are the qualities everybody wants: a life that is deeply serene and confident; a life that is full of joy and enthusiasm and energy; a life that is happy because it is lived in love. This kind of life takes effort, but it doesn't feel like a constant test of the will. Instead, living in the kingdom feels like a giant weight has been lifted from your shoulders:

> *"Come to me," Jesus said, "all you who labor and are burdened, and I will give you rest…. For my yoke is easy, and my burden light."*
>
> (Matthew 11:28–30)

Why does living in the kingdom feel so restful and satisfying? It's because life in the kingdom is the only true path to happiness. When we're focused on ourselves, happiness always seems to be just out of our reach. Just when we feel that we've found happiness, it quickly fades away. But when we focus on something larger than ourselves—on God and others, perhaps—and concentrate on service, we find that our own happiness results. Happiness comes from seeking the beauty of God and the good of other people, not from seeking personal satisfaction. This simple truth is the real secret of the kingdom of God.

Entering the Kingdom

While Jesus insisted that the life of the kingdom is waiting for all who wish to enter it, we can't become people of the kingdom all at once. Learning to live in the kingdom takes time and effort. The hardest part is simply getting started.

In reality, the only thing that must be given up is selfishness. Instead of putting ourselves at the center of the universe and measuring everything by how it affects us, we can put the kingdom of God at the center and measure everything else by its effect on our experience of God and other people. In fact, that's what Jesus said eventually would happen in the daily living of anyone who desires this kingdom.

Jesus said the kingdom begins for most people in small ways, then grows little by little until it embraces everything. Its growth is like the growth of a plant. Read Luke 13:18–19 and Matthew 13:31–32 to see how Jesus compares this small beginning to a mustard seed, which is very tiny, but grows into a large plant. In actuality, a mustard plant does not get big enough for birds to roost in it, but Jesus is exaggerating to show the tremendous fruitfulness—beyond all expectation—of the kingdom in a person's life.

Your tiny beginning might be anything—a single choice made with God in mind, or a small act of generosity for the sake of the Lord, or a change in your thinking. You only have to decide that you want kingdom-quality life and begin to cooperate with God's action to help it happen inside you.

New Attitudes

Jesus says the kingdom is always available to anyone who will accept it. But what does that mean? People who accept the kingdom also choose a new way of living and a new attitude about life.

One important area in which our attitudes need to change concerns material things. How much of your personal happiness is connected to items you may own: stereo system, designer clothes, $100 shoes? Western culture tends to judge happiness in terms of what we own, which promotes greed. When a person is greedy, who or what is the focus of attention? Is it God? Is it Jesus? Is it oneself? Is it the physical object that is desired?

Jesus taught people to have a new attitude toward God. The Sermon on the Mount taught people to be concerned for others as a way to fulfill the Law.

Angelico, The Sermon on the Mount. Fifteenth Century.

When a person is focused on himself or herself, the kingdom is treated as just another object to own, worth no more than anything else. Jesus said,

"No one can serve two masters. He will either hate one and love the other, or be devoted to one and despise the other. You cannot serve God and mammon [money]."

(Matthew 6:24)

Jesus urges people to forgive. In Matthew 18:21–22, Peter asks Jesus how often a person is to forgive wrongs. Jesus says, "seventy-seven times." In symbolic language this number means "every time." Think of it in mathematical terms as "infinity X infinity."

e You Considered?

1. What do you think the world would be like if everyone lived the kingdom of God as Jesus described it?
2. Give an example of a situation in which someone's desire to accumulate material things interfered with his or her happiness.
3. What do you suppose it means to "let go of anger"? How can we train ourselves to do this?

◆ Jesus Uses Parables to Illustrate the Kingdom

In Jesus' teaching about the kingdom, he employed many forms of speech, such as wisdom sayings and stories. The most distinctive kind of speech Jesus used, however, is called a *parable*. From two Greek words meaning "to throw alongside," a parable is a figure of speech in which two things are thrown together for purposes of comparison. Jesus used these comparisons to help people understand life in the kingdom.

What Is a Parable?

A parable is a specific type of comparison, in which something familiar is used to explain something unfamiliar. For example, someone might explain the concept of justice by telling a story about a little boy who stole an apple from a neighbor's tree, and got caught. The everyday, familiar example of the boy's behavior helps people understand the more abstract concept.

Parables were a common form of speech in the ancient world. Jesus, however, used them in a special way. His parables upset the familiar by featuring surprise endings and unexpected behavior. Through these "twists," Jesus shows us how the kingdom is different from the world. The key to Jesus' parables lies in the element of surprise.

The Good Samaritan

Probably the most famous of all Jesus' parables is about the Good Samaritan. It reads as follows:

> "A man fell victim to robbers as he went down from Jerusalem to Jericho. They stripped and beat him, and went off leaving him half-dead. A priest happened to be going down that road, but when he saw him, he passed by on the opposite side. Likewise a Levite came to the place, and when he saw him he passed by on the opposite side."
>
> (Luke 10:30–32)

So far, the parable is drawing on experiences and images which would have been extremely familiar to Jesus' audience. Travel in the ancient world was very dangerous, and there was a constant risk of being robbed. This danger was especially real in first-

century Palestine under Roman occupation. Further, the lack of concern shown by the priest and Levite would also have been familiar to the common people, who often accused their leaders of indifference to their suffering. The refusal of the priest and the Levite to help the injured man would also have made sense to Jesus' audience, who knew about the ritual purity laws in Leviticus—Jews who had touched blood could not offer sacrifice in the Temple without first being "purified."

Jesus' teaching about the kingdom does not lie in these familiar ideas, however; it's found in the element of surprise which comes next:

> "But a Samaritan traveler who came upon him was moved to compassion at the sight. He approached the victim, poured oil and wine over his wounds, and bandaged them. He then lifted him up on his own animal, took him to an inn, and cared for him. The next day he took out two silver coins and gave them to the innkeeper with the instruction: 'Take care of him. If you spend more than what I have given you, I shall repay you on the way back.'"
>
> (Luke 10:33–35)

Scripture Workshop

Interpreting the Parables

A key to understanding the parables of Jesus is to study the "surprise endings" which reverse traditional images and expectations. Read the following parables:

- The Wily Manager *(Luke 16:1–8)*
- The Laborers in the Vineyard *(Matthew 20:1–16)*
- The Invitation to the Banquet *(Matthew 22:1–14)*

After you have thought about these parables, answer the following questions:

1. What is the "surprise ending" in each parable?
2. Why would this surprise Jesus' audience?
3. What does the surprise ending in each parable tell you about the kingdom?
4. What lesson do you take away from reading these parables?

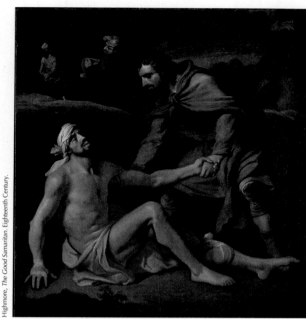

Highmore, *The Good Samaritan.* Eighteenth Century.

From what you know about the Good Samaritan story, why would Jesus' listeners have been troubled by it?

A Samaritan! This development would have struck Jesus' hearers as a major surprise. Remember what you read about relations between Jews and Samaritans in Chapter 8; the two groups were legendary for their hatred of each other. The dislike was so intense that Jews traveling from Galilee to Jerusalem would cross the Jordan River and go dozens of miles out of their way to avoid crossing Samaritan territory. By suggesting that the Samaritan did the right thing where Jewish leaders had failed, Jesus turns this traditional hatred upside down.

Jesus ends the parable by saying "Go and do likewise." A person living in the kingdom will, like the Samaritan, put the expression of love above law, custom, tradition, or individual preferences.

Have You Considered?

1. Explain why Jesus' understanding of the kingdom is best revealed in surprising, rather than in everyday, images.
2. One lesson of the parable of the good Samaritan is to see people as individuals, rather than as members of groups. Do you think this lesson is important for us today? Why or why not?

◆ Jesus' Healing Illustrates the Kingdom

Jesus didn't rely just on his parables or other sayings to share his vision. His actions also were designed to illustrate what life in the kingdom was like. Saint Augustine recognized this when he said that Jesus' actions are "for us, words, too." What Jesus *did* can teach us as much as what Jesus *said*. Probably the best example of how Jesus' actions reveal the kingdom is the healing stories. By healing people, Jesus showed the love for others, and the power to renew life that comes from living in the kingdom.

Types of Healing

Jesus performed several kinds of healing. In each case, the healing reflects the compassion that always moved Jesus to reach out to others. The healings can be broken down into four categories: physical healing, spiritual healing, resurrection, and moral healing.

Physical Healing   Jesus healed people who suffered from physical illnesses, such as blindness, uncontrollable bleeding, and leprosy. He made a special effort to reach out to lepers, people often neglected and scorned in his society. Two physical healings that you can read are the healing of a deaf person who could not speak well in Mark 7:31–35, and the healing of a leper in Luke 5:12–13. We call such healings *miracles,* exceptions to the normal course of ordinary events. Through these healings, Jesus demonstrated enormous power over nature and illness. The point of the healings was never, however, simply to display Jesus' power. Instead, they expressed the compassion and concern for others which is part of kingdom life. Later, Jesus' disciples also healed sick people in his name. Even today, some people have been given the capacity to heal in Jesus' name.

Spiritual Healing   At several points in the Gospel, Jesus heals people who are described as possessed by an "unclean spirit." Because the ancient world had no concept of psychology as we understand it, some behaviors which we would see as the result of mental illness were ascribed to demon possession.

Jesus showed amazing powers to heal such illnesses. One of the best known is the healing of the man from Gerasa. This man had been living naked

People of Note

The Blind Bartimaeus

Bible scholars have observed that the healing stories in the gospel accounts sometimes serve literary purposes as well. A good example of this is Mark 10:46–52, the healing of a blind man named Bartimaeus. Mark says that as Jesus left Jericho, Bartimaeus called out to him, referring to him as the "Son of David." Jesus approached him and asked him what he wanted. Bartimaeus, calling Jesus "Master," asked to see. Jesus told him, "Go your way; your faith has saved you." Immediately Bartimaeus recovered his sight.

This story comes at the end of a section in which Mark talks about how Jesus' message was misunderstood. The literary message of the story is that while a blind man could "see" the truth about Jesus because of his faith, those with good eyes who lacked faith could not.

The Bible tell us neither what happened to Bartimaeus after he recovered his sight nor how he felt about this remarkable gesture. Finish his story. Describe Bartimaeus's feelings once he could finally see. Would this gift turn out to be a blessing or a problem? How does Bartimaeus witness to the power of the kingdom?

---

out in the cemetery and was so strong that no chain could hold him. He sometimes attacked other people without cause. Today, he might be called psychotic. Was he possessed or was he mentally disturbed? All we know is that Jesus healed him. This frightening man calmly sat at Jesus' feet "clothed and in his right mind" (Luke 8:26–35). As with the physical healing, Jesus' use of power demonstrates a sign of the kingdom, where people are healed in mind and body.

Resurrection   Jesus, like the great prophet, Elijah, brought people who had died back to life. Consider the story of Lazarus in John 11:17–44.

Jesus was some distance away when he heard that his friend, Lazarus, was ill. When he finally arrived, Lazarus had already been in his tomb for four days. In fact, when Jesus said the tomb should be opened, Lazarus' sister Martha—a very practical woman—objected because the corpse would surely be corrupt. But Jesus insisted that the stone cover be removed. Then he prayed to his beloved Father and cried out, "Lazarus, come out!" Lazarus came, still wrapped in the burial clothes. This episode shows us that the kingdom has the ultimate power, the power of life.

Moral Healing   Finally, Jesus healed people in a way that did not involve their bodies directly. It might be called a healing of character or a moral healing. Luke tells the story of Zacchaeus, a tax collector who had gotten rich off his job—an achievement easily possible if the collector was a crook. Zacchaeus was also a very short man.

When Jesus came to his town, Zacchaeus tried to see him, but couldn't see over the crowd, so he climbed a sycamore tree alongside the road. Jesus spotted Zacchaeus in the tree and invited himself to Zacchaeus' house for dinner.

The story does not say exactly what happened, but at dinner Zacchaeus promised Jesus he would give half of his possessions to the poor and repay anyone he had injured four times over! Jesus rejoiced that "salvation has come to this house" (Luke 19:1–10). The story indicates that the kingdom has the power to change our lives, if we accept it.

Healings Reveal the Kingdom

The healings performed by Jesus illustrate the nature of the kingdom of God in several important ways:

- The kingdom has tremendous power to heal our bodies, minds, and souls.
- Living in the kingdom means having compassion for the suffering of others. We cannot ignore physical, mental or spiritual pain, wherever we find it.
- In the kingdom, the focus is always on God, and then on others. By living close to God, kingdom people *want* to respond to the needs of other people. In doing so, they find their own mental and spiritual peace.

When Jesus healed, he acted from a profound compassion for people. He also wanted people to wake up to the power of the kingdom in their midst. If Jesus is our example, we, too, are called to learn compassion—to feel deeply for all other living beings. Then, following Jesus, we are invited to act out our compassion.

What can you do in your daily living that will reveal God's kingdom to others?

- We can pray for others.
- We can take actions that relieve suffering.
- We can express understanding for the pain of others.

In doing so, we will discover a joy that belongs to the kingdom of God and cannot be taken away from us.

Have You Considered?

1. How does the behavior of people tell you more about them than what they say? Explain your answer.
2. Most of us do not have the power to heal physical illness immediately as Jesus did. What can you do to ease physical suffering?
3. Describe two or three examples from your own experience where you see people in mental or spiritual pain. What could you do to bring them relief? Be as specific as possible.

Spiritual Reflection

Praying the Parables

Read Jesus' parable of the Rich Fool in Luke 12:16–21. Quietly put yourself in God's presence. Now, think about these questions:

- What are my goals, as far as I know them right now? What long term or short term dreams or hopes do I have? Do they involve money or other material things?
- What do you think would be a good attitude to cultivate about goals and material things, judging from this parable?

- One of the best ways to handle material things well is to consider that they are "on loan" from God and that you are responsible for them. Try thinking about the "Rich Fool" in this way: if he had thought that the material possessions were on loan from God, what might he have done differently? Explain your answer.

Use your answers to these questions as an occasion for prayer. Ask God to guide you in forming goals that will bring you lasting happiness. Also ask God to help you encourage the hopes and dreams of others as well as your own. After you're finished, thank God for this time.

Q/A

Section One

1. Define: "Christ of Faith," "Jesus of History."
2. What is the primary purpose of the gospel accounts?
3. List three layers of material in the gospel accounts.
4. Why did Roman occupation mean economic hardship for most Jews?
5. Name and describe four important Jewish groups at the time of Jesus.
6. What is the significance of the Dead Sea Scrolls?
7. How do we know that Mark's community was outside Palestine?
8. What are Luke's special interests?
9. Define "Q"
10. What are two reasons why the historical approach is valuable?
11. Why does our faith not rest on the historical approach?

Section Two

1. Why did many Jews misunderstand Jesus' message about the kingdom?
2. What does living in the kingdom mean?
3. Why does life in the kingdom feel restful and satisfying?
4. Explain two areas in which the kingdom requires a new attitude.
5. Define: "parable"
6. What is the key to understanding Jesus' parables?
7. What is the surprise in the parable of the Good Samaritan?
8. Explain the four kinds of healing performed by Jesus.
9. Why did Jesus work miracles?
10. List three ways in which the healing revealed the kingdom.
11. In kingdom living, is it enough to feel compassion for others? Why or why not?

BIBLE ACTIVITY

1. Life in the kingdom means, above all else, a life centered on loving God. One of the most important ways this happens is through prayer. Read what Jesus had to say about prayer in two passages from Matthew: 6:5–8, and 7:7–11. Based on these two passages, describe what you think is the attitude towards prayer of someone living in the kingdom.

2. Read Jesus' parable of the hidden treasure in Matthew 13:44–46. What's the element of surprise in this parable? How does this parable illustrate the kingdom? Make a list of what you'd be willing to "sell" to acquire life in the kingdom.

3. Go back over the parable of the good Samaritan in Luke 10:29–37. Now rewrite the parable, bringing it up to date. Include characters and events that reflect modern times, but be sure that the message of the parable remains the same.

4. Read the healing story in Matthew 12:22–28. What do the Pharisees accuse Jesus of doing? How does Jesus respond? Why do you think Matthew includes this story?

The Good News of Jesus calls us to find our rest in him.

GLOSSARY

- **Christ of Faith:** Jesus as he is known through the faith tradition of the Church.
- **Dead Sea Scrolls:** Writings which reflect opinions within Judaism shortly before the time of Jesus.
- **Gospel:** The "good news" of Jesus contained in the four gospel accounts and other Christian literature.
- **Gospel Accounts:** The four New Testament books which provide evidence of Jesus' life and importance.
- **Jesus of History:** The flesh-and-blood person, Jesus of Nazareth.
- **Kingdom of God:** The main theme of Jesus' preaching and teaching; a life centered on love of God and love of others.
- **Miracle:** An exception to the normal flow of ordinary events.
- **Moral Healing:** Healing of someone's values and character.
- **Parables:** Comparison of something familiar to something unfamiliar, used by Jesus to teach about the kingdom.
- **Parousia:** When Jesus will return in power to establish the kingdom in its fullness; "Second Coming."
- **Pharisees:** Jewish group which stressed the Law, but interpreted it to fit new situations.
- **Physical Healing:** Healing a bodily illness, such as leprosy.
- **Procurator:** Head of Roman government in Judea.
- **Province:** An area of the empire under direct Roman control.
- **Public Ministry:** Jesus' career from age 30 to 33.
- **Q:** Hypothetical sayings source used by Matthew and Luke; the letter comes from the German word, "Quelle," meaning "source."
- **Sadducees:** Wealthy aristocrats who were religious conservatives, held the power in the Temple.
- **Second Coming:** The event at the end of time when Jesus will return in power to establish the kingdom in its fullness; also called "Parousia."
- **Spiritual healing:** Healing of a mental illness, often thought of by ancient people as casting out a demon.
- **Synoptics:** Matthew, Mark, and Luke.

UNDERSTANDING MORE ABOUT:

The Zealots

In Luke 6:15, we hear of a follower of Jesus known as "Simon the Zealot." Many people associate Simon with the Jewish political party called "the Zealots." This party was violently opposed to Roman rule of Israel, and its members were ready to rise up in armed revolt. The party is not mentioned in other historical sources until the 60s C.E., however, and so the word "zealot" in Simon's case may have its more normal meaning of someone who was determined to uphold Jewish traditions in any circumstances.

There is another disciple of Jesus, however, who may have been connected to armed opposition to Rome: Judas Iscariot. Before the Zealots came together as a party, individual Jews tried to undercut the Romans by assassinating their officials, as well as any Jews who went along with them. Because they used short daggers known as "sicae," they were called the "sicarii." Some Bible scholars think that "Iscariot" may be related to the term "sicarii."

Responding to Jesus

L uisa couldn't believe it. She'd always looked forward to Mass on Sunday mornings—she liked the singing, and the family breakfast afterwards was always fun. But she had *never* experienced anything like this.

This Sunday, Father Reuben announced to the parish that a visiting priest, Father Gabriel, from Zaire, Africa, would be giving the homily. Luisa hadn't even realized that there were Catholics in Africa. Father Gabriel looked to be about her parents' age, and walked with a slight limp. He was truly an African, too, which surprised Luisa even more. She had never considered that dark skinned people could be priests. All of the priests that she had ever seen had been white. As soon as Father Gabriel began to speak, however, Luisa forgot about everything else; she sat spellbound, listening carefully to what he said.

Father Gabriel started slowly, talking about his experience of bringing the Gospel to poor families in rural Africa. As he went on, he talked more loudly about God's love and kingdom. By the time he finished his talk, Father Gabriel was almost shouting, crying out about how the Holy Spirit fills us with love for God and one another. Some members of the parish were clapping and shouting in response, and Luisa found herself joining them. No homily had ever made her feel this way before.

For the rest of the Mass, Luisa felt a new enthusiasm. She joined in the singing, prayed deeply, and went to Communion eagerly. Father Gabriel was right; she could feel the Spirit filling her with love. As she looked around at the other members of her family, she could tell they felt the same way.

After Mass, Luisa hurried to get into the line to meet Father Gabriel. She wanted to thank him for making this Mass so memorable. Luisa knew that her faith was now more important to her than ever before.

As she neared Father Gabriel, she could tell something was wrong. "What was that all about?" she heard someone snap angrily. "Church is no place for shouting and carrying on!" Another parishioner yelled, "You're a disgrace!"

"I'm sorry you feel that way," Father Gabriel said. "But it's important for people to know that God's love is real, and that God is reaching out to them, right now." Not satisfied with his words, several people walked away, complaining that he behaved more like a rock star than a priest.

Luisa couldn't believe people were reacting like this. Couldn't they tell that Father Gabriel was special, someone who really made God's love come alive? What was it about him that bothered them? Why couldn't they hear what she had heard?

Hearing the Message

People also reacted in many different ways to Jesus' words and actions. Some were touched by him, and gave up everything to follow him. Others liked what they heard, but stayed at a distance. Some felt threatened by Jesus, violently opposed him, and eventually had him killed. The story did not end there, however, for Jesus rose from the grave, met with his followers, and then returned to God. In this chapter, you will study the different ways people reacted to Jesus during his lifetime. You'll also take a closer look at how the writers of the four gospel accounts found in the Bible responded to Jesus and his message. In so doing, you'll discover that Jesus called people to him, and that we also are invited to answer Jesus in our own way.

A Sign That Will Be Opposed

Schottenmeister, *The Presentation of Jesus in the Temple*. Fifteenth Century.

Luke's gospel account tells how Joseph and Mary brought the infant Jesus to the Temple for a blessing (Luke 2:25–35). Simeon, the old man who blessed the child, told Mary that Jesus would be "a sign that will be opposed." For some people, Jesus was a sign who pointed the way to the kingdom of God. For others, Jesus was a threat who had to be dealt with once and for all.

In this section, you will study about those who followed Jesus, those who opposed him, how Jesus died, and how he was glorified in the Resurrection.

Learning Objectives for Section One

By the end of this section, you will be able to:

- Identify the different kinds of disciples who followed Jesus.
- Identify the various groups which opposed Jesus and explain why they did so.
- Describe the events of Jesus' passion.
- Understand how the Resurrection affected Jesus' followers.

◆ The Disciples

The word "disciple" is Latin for "student." We use this word for followers of Jesus because they study and try to live out his teachings. Just as today there are many kinds of people who follow Jesus, there were different groups of followers in Jesus' lifetime. Some traveled with Jesus. Others were called to leadership roles. Still others supported him without leaving their homes or jobs. Christians continue to respond to Jesus in a variety of ways.

Literal Followers

One group of disciples literally followed Jesus. They moved about Judea with him wherever he went. Some of these disciples left their friends, their family, and their jobs to be close to Jesus. Members of this group studied Jesus' message, shared part of his ministry, and helped him meet his needs. For example, these disciples arranged for Jesus' important meals, such as the Passover supper (Mark 14:12–16).

In the ancient world, it wasn't unusual for a teacher to have disciples who followed him to receive his teaching. Two things, however, make the relationship between Jesus and his disciples noteworthy for us:

1. Jesus offered personal invitations. Jesus called these disciples by name, asking that they leave their past lives behind to follow him. In Mark's gospel account we read how Jesus saw Simon and Andrew fishing on the shores of the Sea of Galilee. He offered them this invitation, "Come after me, and I will make you fishers of men" (Mark 1:17). Simon and Andrew dropped everything and followed Jesus. This story illustrates an important point about discipleship. Following Jesus isn't only something we choose; it's also an answer to an invitation, another response in our on-going conversation with God.

2. Jesus called unlikely candidates. Jesus didn't always call the type of disciples that people expected. For one thing, Jesus invited many women to follow him. He was willing to teach them and treat them as partners. In a society that assumed women

should be "seen and not heard," this was quite radical. Jesus also called "sinners," people who were not considered pure according to a strict interpretation of Jewish law. The disciple, Levi, a tax collector who worked for the Romans, was scorned by many Jews. Jesus invited him to become one of his disciples, showing that all people can follow Jesus.

The Twelve

Within the larger number of his disciples, Jesus formed a special group called "the Twelve." To these twelve people Jesus entrusted leadership responsibilities. After the death of Jesus, "the Twelve" became the leaders of the early Church. Although each gospel account names the Twelve slightly differently, five stand out as important members: Peter, Andrew, James, John, and Judas Iscariot.

Remember that ancient Israel was organized into 12 tribes. By choosing twelve members to lead his disciples, Jesus showed symbolically that all Israel was called to live life in the kingdom. The Twelve also shared in Jesus' mission. In Mark 6:7–13, the disciples are sent out by Jesus to bring the message of the kingdom to Israel. The Twelve are usually called *apostles*, a Greek word which means "messengers."

A Wider Circle of Friends

Jesus touched many people with his words and deeds, but not all of them left their families and jobs to follow him. These people became supporters of Jesus. While they remained in their communities, doing their regular jobs, they experienced life differently because of their commitment to Jesus.

The most familiar members of this wider circle of followers were Martha and Mary, sisters who lived in

Jesus' first followers were fishermen from Gallilee. Growing up in Nazareth, Jesus would have felt very comfortable around fishermen.

The Bible in Context

Jesus and Women

Jesus stood out from other important teachers of his day in many ways. One was his attitude towards women. Many ancient cultures considered women "impure," meaning that they were unfit to offer proper worship. Women were often viewed as inferior to men, sometimes even as property. Despite these prejudices, Jesus respected women and treated them equally as individuals. He demonstrates this attitude in the story of the woman with a hemorrhage.

In Mark 5:25–34, a woman who is suffering from a hemorrhage (a flow of blood) approaches Jesus, hoping to be cured. As a woman, and especially one who is bleeding, she knows that under Jewish law she is considered impure. A man who touched her, even if only accidentally, would immediately become impure, and thus unable to worship God in the Temple. Thus women during menstruation and at other time when they bled vaginally (such as after childbirth) avoided all contact with men.

Nonetheless, this woman tries to touch Jesus without being noticed, hoping to be healed by his power. Jesus, realizing immediately that someone in need of healing has touched him, searches for the person. The woman, caught in her act of desperation, falls down before Jesus in fear. Instead of reprimanding her, however, Jesus commends her faith and sends her home in peace.

By such public gestures as this, Jesus showed that he was not controlled by public attitudes or tradition.

Bethany with their brother, Lazarus. Luke 10:38–42 describes the hospitality they extended to Jesus. He stopped at their home on the way to Jerusalem to rest and prepare for the remainder of his journey. Jesus had supporters like Martha and Mary located throughout Israel. Many such supporters lived in Jerusalem, which is one reason why the early Church developed there after Jesus' death.

Have You Considered?

1. Do you think Jesus still calls disciples today? If so, how? If not, why not?
2. Why do you suppose Jesus didn't ask all of his disciples to become literal followers?
3. As disciples of Jesus, what lesson do you think we should learn from his call of people who were looked down upon by the rest of society?

◆ Jesus' Opposition

Jesus attracted followers because he announced that the kingdom of God was here, and that Israel was being renewed. Many people greeted this as a hoped-for message of joy. Others, however, who benefited from the injustice of the way things were, or who had a different vision of Israel's future, were threatened by what Jesus said. Those groups responded to Jesus by opposing him, and eventually they killed him. Why would anyone oppose Jesus? Because what Jesus had to say challenged people not willing to accept the kingdom.

Conflicts over the Law

One source of tension between Jesus and other Jewish leaders was the Law. Since the time of Ezra, Jews had regarded the Law as the single most important way they expressed their relationship to God. Observance of the Law was the way they maintained their part of that relationship. God would give well-being according to the ancient Covenant. Over time, the Law became an end in itself, and obedience was a demand rather than an expression of love for God. Jesus challenged this view, arguing that the Law existed to serve people, and there were times when the Law had to be ignored to meet people's needs.

Mark 3:1–6 tells of a man with a withered hand. Jesus was in the synagogue in Capernaum on the Sabbath, a day on which no one was supposed to work (healing was considered work). When he spotted the man whose hand was shriveled, Jesus asked him to stand up. Jesus then asked the crowd whether it was better to do a good deed on the Sabbath by healing the man, or an evil one by allowing him to suffer. Jesus then healed the man in violation of the Sabbath law. This act angered those Pharisees and Sadducees who were present. Mark goes on to say that from this point forward, these groups plotted to kill Jesus.

Jesus was not alone in reminding people that the original purpose of the Law was to help others. In the first century B.C.E., Rabbi Hillel was asked to summarize his religion "standing on one foot" (meaning "briefly"). Hillel responded, "What is hateful to you, don't do to your neighbor. The rest is commentary—now go and study." Jesus says much the same thing in Matthew 7:12. It is important to remember that even when Jesus criticized the attitudes and practices of some of his fellow Jews, he did so as someone speaking from inside the Jewish tradition.

Scripture Workshop

Controversy Stories

The conflict between Jesus and other Jewish groups is often expressed through a literary form called a "controversy story." This type of story has three elements:

1. a specific place and time
2. an attempt by Jesus' enemies to trap him with a leading question (a question in which either way he answers, he says something that can be held against him)
3. a short, powerful statement by Jesus which avoids the trap

Matthew 22:23–33 contains a controversy story in which the Sadducees ridicule Jesus' belief in resurrection. Read this story, outlining it using the three story elements listed above.

Jesus Denounces Hypocrisy

Opposition to Jesus didn't arise only because he reminded people of the real purpose of the Law. He went further, criticizing the hypocrisy and self-interest which many leaders disguised as religion. He called on people to reject this kind of behavior. His words in Mark must have sounded like a direct challenge to those he addressed:

> "Beware of the scribes, who like to go around in long robes and accept greetings in the marketplaces, seats of honor in synagogues, and places of honor at banquets. They devour the houses of widows and, as a pretext, recite lengthy prayers. They will receive a very severe condemnation."
>
> (Mark 12:38–40)

In Jesus' day, some professional scribes used their positions selfishly. As Jesus said, they enriched themselves on the contributions of widows and other poor people. Of course, not all Jewish leaders behaved this way, but some gave in to the temptation that comes with positions of power. By publicly criticizing these wealthy and powerful men, Jesus knew he was inviting dangerous opposition. Despite the danger, Jesus had to denounce behavior that so obviously contradicted the message of the kingdom.

The Powerful Feel Threatened

As Jesus spread the message of the kingdom, he attracted a large number of followers. His popularity made the official leaders, the Jewish high priests and the Romans, nervous. Although the Romans ruled Israel, they allowed the native officials to run things, as long as there was no trouble. A popular figure such as Jesus, by denouncing injustice, threatened the control of the local leaders, and possibly, the Romans themselves, was a danger to everyone in authority.

Added to this general concern was a very specific issue: Jesus' teaching of the kingdom. Although Jesus did not present himself as an earthly king to rival the Romans, he did say that life in the kingdom was very different from the way things were. He criticized how

the Temple was used, saying that it was for fi[n]
gain rather than for honoring God. The Temple was th[e]
center of political as well as religious authority. When Jesus denounced its leaders, the priests and Romans heard this as a direct challenge to their authority.

Have You Considered?

1. Along with other Jewish teachers, Jesus said that it was wrong to obey the Law when it contradicted the goal of helping people. Give an example of how obeying rules might get in the way of helping people.
2. Jesus denounced powerful people who used religion to disguise their own greed. Do you think this still happens today? Why or why not?
3. Jesus had a lot to say to those in authority. What do you think the qualities of a good leader are, from Jesus' point of view?

The Temple in Jerusalem was the center of religious power in Judea. This model of the Temple can be found in modern Israel.

Jesus' Death and Resurrection

The opponents of Jesus wanted to publicly humiliate him. They wanted to show that Jesus was nothing special. By killing him, Jesus' opponents thought that they had solved their problems. Little did they know of the power of God!

When Jesus rose from the grave and appeared to his disciples on Easter Sunday, he wrecked the plans of his opponents. Instead of being silenced, Jesus was now able to spread his message to a much larger group than ever before. He commissioned his disciples to spread the word of what had happened to the whole world, making disciples as they went.

The Church recalls these events during Holy Week, the days leading up to Easter Sunday, and on Easter itself. These are the holiest days of the Church year, because they celebrate the central event in salvation history: Christians believe that all of Israel's past led up to this moment, and all of Church history

Every year on Palm Sunday, the Lord's joyous entrance into Jerusalem is celebrated with a procession and a blessing of palm branches.

flows out of it. Let's look at how the gospel accounts record this story.

The Entry into Jerusalem

In Jesus' day, Jews who could afford the trip traveled to Jerusalem for the spring festival of Passover. The final week in Jesus' life began with his arrival in Jerusalem to prepare for the holy day. All four gospel accounts agree that Jesus entered Jerusalem in a very public way. He rode into the city on the back of a donkey, in fulfillment of prophecy:

> Rejoice heartily, O daughter Zion, shout for joy, O daughter Jerusalem! See, your king shall come to you; a just savior is he, meek, and riding on an ass, on a colt, the foal of an ass.
>
> (Zechariah 9:9)

Bible scholars generally agree that Jesus focused on his message of the kingdom, rather than on himself as the messenger. This gesture, therefore, was probably not intended to proclaim himself as king or

Angelico, The Women at the Tomb, Fifteenth Century.

On Easter Sunday, Christians celebrate Jesus' Resurrection from the dead. Mark 16:1–8 tells of the women who came to the tomb to anoint Jesus.

MAK PARK

LEARN FROM THE MAP

Events of Holy Week

The four gospel accounts vary as to Jesus' actions during Holy Week. Tradition holds that Jesus entered Jerusalem on Sunday, celebrated the Passover meal on Thursday, and was convicted and crucified on Friday.

The locations of Jesus' activities during his last week are not known with great certainty, but even so, it will help you visualize them if you find them on the map. Locate the following places:

• Kidron Valley • Garden of Gethsemane • High priest's neighborhood • Golgotha • Herod Antipas' vacation palace

Trace on your map the route Jesus and his friends might have taken.

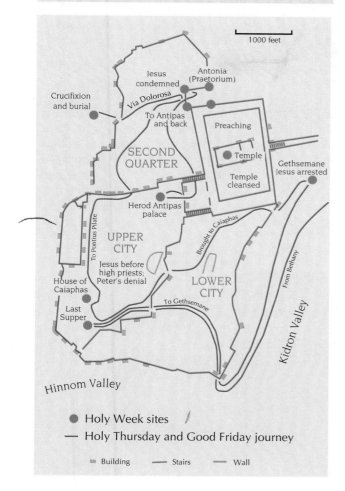

● Holy Week sites

— Holy Thursday and Good Friday journey

▪ Building — Stairs — Wall

messiah, although it would be seen this way by later Christians. Instead, the act was intended to announce to the Jews gathered in the city that the kingdom which Jesus preached had arrived.

This public act excited the crowds gathered for the festival. What Jesus did next also got people's attention: he marched onto the Temple grounds and threw out the merchants and money-changers doing business there! He shouted that they did not belong in the house of God. In taking this step, Jesus claimed the authority to decide what was appropriate in the Temple, a privilege claimed by the priestly families. Jesus' action directly challenged how the priests oversaw their office. This was the last straw; Jesus had to be stopped.

The Last Supper

Over the next few days, opposition to Jesus grew stronger. By Thursday of that week, it was clear to Jesus that they intended to arrest him. Jesus gathered his closest disciples together for what he knew might be their final meal together. This is the meal we know as the "Last Supper."

The synoptic accounts say that the Last Supper was the Passover meal itself, while John indicated that the meal took place the night before Passover. Many scholars today tend to follow John, and place the meal the night before the Passover. No one knows for sure when the Last Supper occurred.

However, we do know that during this meal, Jesus performed three actions of great importance:

1. **Jesus washed the feet of his disciples.** In the ancient world, when most travel was by foot, servants would wash the feet of their masters when they arrived home. It was the work required of the lowest household servants. Peter, knowing this, protested that Jesus should never wash *his* feet. But Jesus explains that acceptance of the master's service is part of the relationship between the disciple and the Lord. Moreover, Jesus tells them to follow his example and do this for one another. For the kingdom of God, service is more important than a desire for power or glory.

2. **Jesus asked his disciples to go out and continue his mission.** In John's gospel account, Jesus recites a long prayer for the disciples, asking God to guide them as they proclaim the kingdom to the world.

3. Jesus gave the gift of the Eucharist to his disciples. At the Last Supper, Jesus took bread and wine and pronounced the traditional Jewish blessing over them. He then added that in consuming the bread and wine, the disciples were eating his own flesh and blood. He said that the disciples were to repeat this ritual in memory of him. Every day, when Christians receive Communion, they are carrying out these instructions of Jesus. The word *Eucharist* means "thanksgiving," and when we repeat these actions of Jesus, we thank him for his gift of himself.

Trial and Execution

After the Last Supper, Jesus and a few of his disciples went to the garden of Gethsemane on the Mount of Olives. There, Jesus prayed intensely about God's will, for he knew what was coming.

Soon, a party of guards sent by the high priest arrived with Judas, the disciple who betrayed Jesus. When Judas identified Jesus, the guards arrested him and took him to the priests. Although the gospel accounts give slightly differing versions of what happened next, they generally agree that the Jewish officials charged Jesus with blasphemy—probably for his remarks about the Temple. The Jewish officials then took him to Pilate, the Roman procurator of Judea, seeking the death penalty.

Pilate didn't care much about the religious differences between Jesus and the Jewish leaders, but he

---

in the Spotlight
What Did the Last Supper Look Like?

Many people have a copy of Leonardo Da Vinci's famous painting "The Last Supper" somewhere in their homes. This masterpiece shows Jesus in the center of a long bench with disciples on either side. Jesus is seated behind the table.

Da Vinci visualized the Last Supper in the same way that Italian peasants of the sixteenth century ate their meals. Jesus and his disciples, however, lived in a Hellenistic world. They would have eaten the Last Supper laying on their sides on couches surrounding a small table called a *triorium*.

The most important suggestion for this idea comes in John 13:23, which says that the disciples "reclined" at the table. This verb generally means "to lie down." Da Vinci's painting shows us, therefore, that sometimes our imagination of Biblical events has been colored by influences far removed from the Bible itself.

---

was known as a ruthless governor who would execute anyone who might threaten his control of Judea. Jesus was not unknown to Pilate. Jesus' popular following, and his preaching about the kingdom, worried the governor. Brought to him as a criminal, Pilate had Jesus beaten, in an attempt to force Jesus to admit that Caesar was the only king. When this tactic failed, Pilate ordered Jesus put to death. Although the gospel

da Vinci, *The Last Supper.* Fifteenth Century.

Leonardo da Vinci's painting of the Last Supper portrays the Apostles as they are identified by the gospel accounts. From this painting, what would you say about the Apostles?

Johnson, Mount Calvary. Twentieth Century.

The Romans used crucifixion as a means of capital punishment, especially against those people found guilty of rebellion against the state. Which Gospel passages are illustrated in this painting?

accounts present Pilate sympathetically, it was the Roman government through Pilate, and not the Jewish leaders, who ultimately had Jesus put to death.

Jesus was forced to carry his own cross up Mount Golgotha, where he was crucified. The sign above him on the cross listed Jesus' offense: "Jesus of Nazareth, King of the Jews." Although death by crucifixion could sometimes take days, by that afternoon Jesus cried out—quoting Psalm 22—and then died.

He was surrounded at his death by only a handful of women, his male disciples apparently having deserted him in fear. The synoptic gospel accounts indicate that they either watched "from a distance" or make no mention of them. The exception is in John 19:26–27, where the "beloved disciple" remained at the cross. Later, Jesus' body was taken down and placed in a tomb. For a while, it appeared as if the opposition had succeeded in silencing Jesus' message.

Resurrection!

The story did not end there. Each gospel account tells what happened next differently, but they all agree on certain points.

- The women who followed Jesus went to the tomb on Sunday to anoint the body and prepare it for final burial.
- When they arrived, they found the tomb empty.
- A messenger (sometimes described as an angel) told them that Jesus was risen from the grave, and that they should tell the other disciples.

- Later, Jesus himself appeared, first to Mary Magdalene and then to his other disciples.

The risen Jesus was not some kind of ghost; John says that Jesus invited Thomas to feel his wounds in order to convince Thomas that Jesus was real (John 20:26–28). In Luke we learn that the risen Jesus ate with his disciples even though his body had been glorified.

> While they were still speaking about this, he stood in their midst and said to them, "Peace be with you." But they were startled and terrified and thought that they were seeing a ghost. Then he said to them, "Why are you troubled? And why do questions arise in your hearts? Look at my hands and my feet, that it is I myself. Touch me and see, because a ghost does not have flesh and bones as you can see I have." And as he said this, he showed them his hands and his feet. While they were still incredulous for joy and were amazed, he asked them, "Have you anything here to eat?" They gave a piece of baked fish; he took it and ate it in front of them.
>
> (Luke 24:36–43)

He had the ability to pass through locked doors (John 20:19). Through experiences such as these, the disciples became convinced that Jesus had risen from the dead.

Jesus commissioned his disciples to continue his work. They were to become "apostles," or messengers, carrying the news that Jesus had risen and the kingdom had begun. After a period described as lasting 40 days, Jesus gathered his disciples for a final time, promised that the Spirit would guide them, and then ascended into Heaven. He left behind the memory of his victory over death, and the promise of life in the kingdom for those who would hear his words. Preserving these memories and promises was the mission of the early Church.

Have You Considered?

1. Why do you think Jesus objected to finding merchants and money changers in the Temple?
2. By washing his disciples' feet, Jesus said that leadership must be built on serving others. Give an example of leadership built on service from your own experience.
3. Put yourself in the position of one of Jesus' disciples. What would it have taken to convince you that Jesus was risen from the grave? Do you think Thomas was wrong to want proof?

What Does It Mean to Be a Disciple?

The "good news" of Jesus' resurrection from the dead spread quickly. Many people who heard this message responded to Jesus in faith and became Christians. Joining the Church, however, was only the first step in a long journey. These early Christians then had to figure out what it meant to be a disciple of Jesus. The gospel accounts helped early Christians discover the meaning of discipleship. They can help us do the same. In this section, you'll look at the four gospel accounts, paying special attention to how each interprets discipleship. Then, you'll consider what being a disciple means today. In this way, you'll think about the consequences of responding to Jesus by becoming his follower.

Learning Objectives for Section Two:

By the end of this section, you will be able to:

- Discuss the unique perspectives of the gospel writers.
- Explain how each gospel writer understands the meaning of discipleship.
- Describe what it means to be a disciple.

◆ Discipleship in the Gospels

Jesus' disciples quickly took his message far and wide. While they weren't successful everywhere they went, Christian communities soon developed around the Mid-East. Before long, these newly formed communities were asking for guidance in how to "follow Jesus." The gospel accounts were written, in part, to answer the needs of these Christians.

The authors of the gospel accounts organized their stories and sayings about Jesus with several goals in mind. One key aim of each writer was to help Christians in the community grow in discipleship. Each writer shares a common faith in Jesus, but expresses the meaning of that faith differently. Taken together, these four accounts provide us with a well-rounded picture of what discipleship means.

Saint Irenaeus, an early Church Father of the third century, said that the four gospel accounts are like the four points of the compass: without each of the four, we wouldn't be able to find our way.

Mark

Mark is the shortest of the gospel accounts, and the first to be written (probably around 66–70 C.E.). In Mark, Jesus is presented as the Son of God who possessed great authority: in fact, all of his words and deeds reflect his divine power. Often, Mark presents demons as recognizing Jesus and bowing to his authority, suggesting that they knew him as the Son of God. For example, a demon cries out upon seeing Jesus: "I know who you are—the holy One of God!" (*Mark* 1:24,). Mark also points out that not everyone accepted Jesus' authority; Jesus was killed by those who rejected it. The Resurrection, however, showed that Jesus had the greater power.

Despite this emphasis on his authority, Mark shows Jesus as more than a powerful, divine figure. Mark also stresses that suffering was part of Jesus' mission. Throughout Mark, Jesus reminds his followers that he must suffer and die before his mission is complete. Mark presents the disciples as often misunderstanding this point. Peter, for example, argues that as the Messiah, Jesus should not allow himself to suffer. Jesus responds intensely:

"Get behind me, Satan! You are thinking not as God does but as human beings do."

(Mark 8:33)

In other words, Jesus tells Peter that his glory will come only by accepting suffering, not by avoiding it.

One of the unique themes in Mark's account is the "messianic secret." This modern term refers to the fact that in Mark, Jesus demands that his identity as the Messiah be kept secret until after his suffering and death. At one point Jesus asks his disciples who they think he is:

Now Jesus and his disciples set out for the villages around Caesarea Philippi. Along the way he asked his disciples: "Who do people say that I am?" They said, "John the Baptist, others, Elijah, still others, one of the prophets." And he asked them, "But who do you say that I am?" Peter said to him, "You are the Messiah!" Then he warned them not to tell anyone about him.

(Mark 8:27–30)

Here Mark shows Jesus accepting Peter's recognition of him as the Messiah. Why then would Jesus order them not to tell anyone what they believed? Probably because Mark wants to drive home the point mentioned above: that no one can understand Jesus' mission until they know that he had to suffer and die to do God's will. In other words, Mark says that what it means for Jesus to be the messiah can only be understood after his passion. One can understand Jesus only in light of the end of his life, especially his death on the cross.

For Mark, discipleship is revealed through emphasis on the suffering of Jesus. The true disciple, according to Mark, is one who suffers along with Jesus. Jesus says:

"Whoever wishes to come after me must deny himself, take up his cross, and follow me. For whoever will preserve his life would lose it, but whoever loses his life for my sake and that of the gospel will save it."

(Mark 8:34–35)

Mark's purpose here is very clear. Mark wrote for a community of Christians who faced the danger of persecution by the Romans, and he reminded them that this was part of the plan. "Don't worry," Mark seemed to say. "We must suffer just as Jesus suffered.

Mantegna, *Crucifixion*, Fifteenth Century.

While all four gospel accounts have the soldiers throwing dice for Jesus' garments, which ones mention: the disciple that Jesus loved? the faithful women? the thieves? the centurion?

But just as Jesus was glorified through his suffering, glory awaits us, too." For Mark, the true disciple is one who follows Jesus even if it leads to suffering or death.

Matthew

Matthew, like Mark, stresses the authority of Jesus. He uses the title "Son of God" to refer to Jesus. Matthew also shows Jesus speaking and healing with authority.

Jesus the Teacher   Matthew is most interested, however, in Jesus as a teacher. Matthew organizes the sayings of Jesus into five major speeches, the most famous being the Sermon on the Mount, which is found in Matthew 5–7. By collecting these sayings into five units, and giving each such promi-

nence, Matthew identifies them as the basic teachings of the Church. If you want to understand what Jesus stood for, Matthew suggests that you turn to these speeches.

Some Bible scholars think the Sermon on the Mount was structured as a parallel to the Torah, the first five books of the Old Testament, called "the books of Moses" by Jews. Matthew is clearly comparing Jesus, the new lawgiver and teacher, to Moses, the original lawgiver and teacher. In addition, Matthew also compares Jesus to Moses in the infancy story which opens the gospel account. Matthew's purpose in making the comparison between Jesus and Moses is to show that Jesus has also created a community centered around the Covenant, in this case, the early Church.

The Gospel according to Matthew presents Jesus as the great teacher. The challenge of discipleship is to follow the master and live out what he taught.

Matthew's special interest in the teaching of Jesus comes across in the two main themes that he finds in that teaching: justice and the Law. Matthew's Jesus stresses that obedience to the Father requires us to act in just ways toward others. Matthew shares with Luke the saying of Jesus known as the *golden rule*: "Do to others whatever you would have them do to you" (*Matthew* 7:12.)

As mentioned earlier, Jesus also shared this idea with other Jewish teachers such as Rabbi Hillel. When Matthew adds, "this sums up the Law and the prophets," it suggests that just behavior is required as an obligation to God. In Matthew, Jesus also points out that it was not his intention to overturn the Law. In fact, he came to confirm it:

> *"Do not think that I have come to abolish the Law or the prophets. I have come not to abolish but to fulfill. Amen, I say to you, until heaven and earth pass away, not the smallest letter or the smallest part of a letter will pass from the Law until all things have taken place."*
>
> (Matthew 5:17–18)

Matthew does not mean that Jesus viewed the Law as absolute; like Mark, Matthew points out that Jesus would sometimes disobey the Law in order to help people in need. Rather, Matthew says, Jesus came to "fulfill" the Law, to accomplish its purposes. The original purpose of the Law was to guide people in moral behavior towards God and each other, and Jesus says that the Law must continue to perform this function.

Jesus and the Old Testament   Matthew also stresses the connections between Jesus and the Old Testament. Matthew uses *formula citations*—quotes from the Old Testament—that show Jesus fulfilling prophecies. Consider one of Matthew's infancy stories: Jesus' family fled to Egypt to escape King Herod's order that all male infants should be killed.

> *He stayed there until the death of Herod, that what the Lord had said through the prophet might be fulfilled: "Out of Egypt I called my son."*
>
> (Matthew 2:15)

Taken from the prophet Hosea, this line referred to Israel's deliverance from Egypt. Matthew uses the quotation to show God's protection of Jesus.

By emphasizing the Law and the traditions of Israel, Matthew grounds his community firmly in the ancient ways. He shows that Jesus did not destroy those foundations, but built upon them. Note how Matthew's community resolved problems: They looked to the Jewish traditions and also to the teach-

Scripture Workshop

The Beatitudes

Read Matthew 5:1–12 and Luke 6:20–26, then do the following:

- List all the differences between the two versions.
- Describe how these differences illustrate Luke's concern for the poor.
- Tell what values are present in Matthew's Sermon on the Mount?
- Describe how Matthew challenges Christians to live as a community of faith.
- Explain from the differences, Matthew's special concern.

ings of Jesus as they remembered them for guidance. Some of these procedures are reflected in Chapter 18, the third in a series of chapters related to discipleship and community. There, Jesus establishes procedures for settling disputes among Church members and for making decisions affecting the whole community. Jesus also indicates that the community has the power to forgive sins. In Chapter 16, Jesus designates Peter to head the Church. These passages in Matthew reflect early applications of Jesus' teaching in the Christian community.

Jesus and the Community   As Matthew well knows, true discipleship does not take place in isolation. Sharing life and faith with others is important for keeping discipleship strong. The teachings of Jesus are not always easy to follow, though they always result in a much richer life.

Christians help each other by participating in a community of faith. Just as the very first disciples became a community of friends because of their shared love for Jesus, so today Christians can become a community because of the same shared love and faith. The community helps the individual disciple and the disciple in return nourishes the other members of the community. In this way, the church continues to grow in knowledge of the Lord and in Christian action in the community and the world.

For Matthew, discipleship means being part of a believing community. In that community, the Church applies Jesus' words about justice and the Law to daily life. Discipleship means studying the teachings of Jesus, especially those contained in the five speeches that detail the obligations of those who accept the Covenant with God established through Jesus. The role of the disciple is to study and live out these teachings as a member of the wider Church community. A disciple participates in the community and includes the community in decision making.

Luke

Luke addresses his gospel account to an audience that is primarily Gentile (non-Jewish). They are mostly Greek-speaking people who have converted to Christianity.

Life is very difficult for these Christians. They are trying to live out their faith in an empire hostile towards Judaism. The Romans originally considered Christianity as just another Jewish political party.

The Christians to whom Luke writes have recently experienced the destruction of Jerusalem. They are worried about their own fate. If God allowed Jerusalem to be wrecked and the Temple to be demolished, how can they believe that God will be faithful to them?

Luke's answer to this question is that God has been faithful to Israel, but in an unexpected way. Through Jesus, God has created a "new Israel" which includes Gentiles, people considered to be "sinners" such as tax collectors, and all those at the margins of society: the poor, the elderly, and the forgotten. Luke identifies this new Israel with the Christian Church, and says that it has inherited the promises made by God in the Old Testament.

In this new Israel, membership is no longer determined by birth, or by obedience to the Law. Everyone is eligible to share in God's promise of the eternal Covenant. The only requirement for sharing in God's gift is to have a heart open to love. The story of the penitent woman makes this point:

Now there was a sinful woman in the city who learned that he was at table in the house of the Pharisee. Bringing an alabaster flask of ointment, she stood behind him at his feet weeping and began to bathe his feet with her tears. Then she wiped them with her hair, kissed them, and anointed them with ointment.

When the Pharisee who had invited him saw this he said to himself, "If this man were a prophet, he would know who and what sort of woman this is who is touching him, that she is a sinner." . . . [Jesus said] "So I tell you, her many sins have been forgiven; hence, she has shown great love. But the one to whom little is forgiven, loves little."

(Luke 7:37–39,47)

Luke's gospel account is sometimes called the "social gospel" because it emphasizes a concern for the poor and those neglected by society. For example, in Luke 14:13, Jesus says that when we have a reception, we should invite beggars, the crippled, the lame, and the blind, rather than our relatives and wealthy neighbors. In this way, Jesus says, we will be rewarded in the resurrection.

Luke's concern for the poor also comes across in his version of the "Beatitudes" or the Sermon on the Plains. This list of blessings which Jesus offers is given in both Matthew and Luke. The lists are not the same, however. Whereas in Matthew Jesus says, "Blessed are the poor in spirit," (Matthew 5:3) Luke quotes Jesus as saying, "Blessed are the poor." (Luke 6:20) Like sinners and gentiles, the poor are welcome in the new Israel which Jesus has founded.

What, then, is required of the members of this new Israel? Luke emphasizes that being a disciple means spreading the good news about Jesus. He says that God will give his messengers special powers to accomplish this task. In both Matthew and Luke, Jesus sends out disciples to spread his teachings. Only in Luke, however, do they report the powers they were given:

The seventy-two returned in jubilation saying, "Master, even the demons are subject to us in your name." [Jesus] said in reply: "I watched Satan fall from the sky like lightning. See what I have done; I have given you the power to tread on snakes and scorpions and all the forces of the enemy, and nothing shall ever injure you. Nevertheless, do not rejoice so much in the fact that the devils are subject to you as that your names are inscribed in heaven."

(Luke 10:17–20)

Here, Jesus indicates that God will provide the abilities necessary to ensure that Jesus' messengers succeed. Luke stresses many times that God will respond when the disciples present their needs in prayer.

Such gifts from God, however, mean that the disciples have a special responsibility to do God's will. Luke quotes Jesus as saying,

When much has been given a man, much will be re-
quired of him. More will be asked of a man to whom
more has been entrusted.

(Luke 12:48)

A disciple, therefore, is under an obligation to
use God's gifts positively. In Chapter 17, Luke also reminds his readers not to expect tremendous honors
or riches for their efforts; spreading God's word is
simply their duty.

For Luke, therefore, a disciple is one who does
the work of God, especially spreading the good news
about Jesus, believing in faith that God will provide
the gifts needed to succeed. Luke reminds his readers that anyone, regardless of social status or past
mistakes, may be a disciple of Jesus. All that is needed
is a loving heart and confidence in God's protection.

John

John's account is very different from the other
three. Unlike the synoptics, which follow basically the
same story line, and include much of the same material, John's account uses very different stories and
sayings. Probably the most unusual feature in John
is his tendency to quote Jesus as giving long
speeches, called "discourses." In fact, the majority of
the gospel account consists not of stories about
Jesus, but of these discourses. In most cases, biblical scholars believe that these discourses are not
Jesus' own words. Instead, they represent ideas which
came from Jesus that were shaped by John to teach
his own Christian community.

Most Bible scholars think that John's account of
the Gospel was written later than the other three, and
that the members of his community were already
familiar with the accounts written by the synoptics.
John's account was then written to deepen their
faith and to guide them in becoming better disciples
of Jesus.

John's gospel account presents a very exalted
view of Jesus. Jesus is the "logos," or "Word," that has
existed with God from the beginning of time. It was by
the Word, in fact, that the universe was created. Later,
John says, the Word became flesh in Jesus. Although
the synoptic gospels referred to Jesus as the Son of
God, and thought of him as divine, John emphasizes
that in Jesus, God took on human form. We call this
theological point the *Incarnation*.

John recognizes Jesus as the divine Son of God.
In John, Jesus repeatedly makes "I am" statements.
You remember that for the Jews, the name of God is
"Yahweh," a word which means "I am." When Jesus
refers to himself as "I am," John's Jewish audience
would clearly understand Jesus to mean that he was
God. Such a saying is found in John 8:24.

This saying highlights another important aspect
of John's thought. John believes that faith in Jesus is
necessary for his readers to be saved. John defines
"faith" as believing in the special relationship which
connects Jesus and the Father and trusting totally in
Jesus for everything related to eternal life. Jesus
speaks of this relationship in many places within the
gospel:

"Whoever has seen me has seen the Father. How can
you say, 'Show us the Father?' Do you not believe
that I am in the Father and the Father is in me?"

(John 14:9b–10a)

John stresses that to know Jesus is to know the
Father (*John* 8:19). By reflecting on Jesus' words and
actions, therefore, John's readers come to a deeper
understanding of God.

More than with any other gospel account, John
is written with the specific needs of a particular community of believers in mind. Therefore, it is not surprising that John provides guidelines for discipleship.
In chapters 13–17, John presents Jesus as delivering
his last discourse before his arrest. In it, Jesus tells
his followers what being his disciple means.

1. Service. Jesus washes the feet of his disciples,
telling them that even though he is the master and
they are the servants, it is necessary for him to humble himself and serve them. In the same way, it is
necessary for disciples to humble themselves and
serve others.

2. Doing his works. This involves teaching, healing, and revealing the Father to other people. Jesus
promises his followers that whatever they ask, if they
ask in his name, the Father will provide it to them.
Like Luke, John stresses that God will provide the disciples with what they need to do Jesus' work. In John,
Jesus promises the disciples that he will send a
Paraclete to them. In Greek law, a "paraclete" was like
a defense attorney: someone who defends you and
speaks for you. Jesus refers here to the Holy Spirit,
who will come to the disciples and guide them in following Jesus.

3. Living out the commandments he has given. The most important of these commands, he says, is to love one another, even to the point of accepting death:

> "This is my commandment: love one another as I love you. No one has greater love than this, to lay down one's life for one's friends. You are my friends if you do what I command you.
>
> (John 15:12–14)

The true test of discipleship is love. If we love one another, then we are obeying Jesus' commands and living as his disciple.

4. Seeking unity with Jesus. The foundation and goal of everything else in John is the possibility of becoming one with Jesus. This glorious hope is the basis of John 14–17. There, Jesus speaks again and again of how he wants his disciples to be one with him and with the Father, just as he himself is one with the Father. He says he and the Father will dwell in the heart of the disciple who keeps his words and loves his commandments. Without this goal, the other actions are incomplete. With this hope, everything else is seen to be as full and rich as Christ himself.

John warns his readers that following Jesus will not be easy. "The world will not support you," he says, "in fact, people will persecute you." John tells his community to accept that they are not "of the world," and to endure in being disciples no matter what comes. If they do this, he says, God will not abandon them in need. "Your fruit must endure," Jesus says,

> "It was not you who chose me, but I who chose you and appointed you to go and bear fruit that will remain, so that whatever you ask the Father in my name he may give you"
>
> (John 15:16).

Have You Considered?

1. Mark says that one cannot understand Jesus without knowing about his suffering. Do you agree? Why or why not?
2. Matthew and Luke both contain Jesus' golden rule: "Treat others as you would have them treat you." Explain what this statement means.
3. Luke says that Christianity must reach out to the poor and neglected people in society. Do you think Christianity today does this? Why or why not?
4. In John, Jesus refers to himself as "I am." What can we learn from this about the religious background of John's audience? How might they have reacted to Jesus calling himself by this name?

◆ Being a Disciple

The four gospel accounts give us four complementary images of discipleship. Discipleship is:

1. For Mark, suffering with Jesus.
2. For Matthew, following Jesus' teaching in a believing community.
3. For Luke, proclaiming the kingdom to all.
4. For John, loving others and seeking unity with Jesus.

In thinking about what being a disciple might mean for you today, let's consider each image in turn.

Suffering with Jesus

In the early Church, when persecution by the Romans was a constant threat, Mark's theme of suffering with Jesus was understood very literally. Even today, there are places where Christians suffer and die for their faith. In 1980, Archbishop Oscar Romero was shot and killed while saying Mass in El Salvador. Romero was murdered because he demanded justice for the poor. A disciple of Jesus must be willing to suffer for Jesus.

Since most of us will, hopefully, never experience any suffering this dramatic, how can we "take up the cross" and suffer with Jesus? Although we may not always have to endure physical pain, all of us have our share of suffering. All of us have disappointments and frustrations with which we have to deal. Maybe it's a job we hoped for over the summer that fell through; maybe it's a relationship that grew apart. Whatever it is, we know what it feels like to be sad and hurt. Suffering with Jesus means accepting these trials as part of God's plan. Being a disciple means finding meaning and value in the disappointments that come our way.

What value can there possibly be in suffering? According to Mark, it can be found in at least three ways:

1. **Suffering can help us in our prayer lives.** Suffering can help us to understand and appreciate the sacrifice Jesus made on our behalf. We can offer up our own pain to Jesus, putting it in his hands and reminding ourselves of his suffering on the cross.
2. **Suffering can help us feel the pain of others.** It can make us more sympathetic and sensitive when we see others having trouble. We are better able to help others when we've dealt with pain ourselves.

People of Note

Saint Perpetua

In the first three centuries C.E., the Church often faced persecution. Hundreds of Christians shared the suffering of Jesus in the most literal way, by dying for the faith. Among the most famous of these early martyrs is Saint Perpetua. Although the story of her death has been exaggerated, as many legends about the saints have been, it served to convince its early hearers of the love of God and the holiness of martyrdom.

Perpetua was arrested in North Africa (in modern Tunisia). As part of their public festivals, Romans sometimes executed prisoners by putting them in a pit with wild beasts. Perpetua had to walk through two lines of men striking her with whips before she was thrown into the pit. The beasts attacked her, but she was not injured. Next, a Roman soldier was sent to kill her with a sword. He struck her, but again God preserved her from harm. Finally, Perpetua guided the soldier in putting the sword to her throat. She died from this wound, a model of a disciple who embraced suffering in faith.

3. **Suffering can help us appreciate God's blessings when they come.** We can put all the good things about our lives into better perspective when we've experienced a few disappointments.

   By finding value in our pain, and using our bad experiences to become better people, we grow in maturity and become close disciples of Jesus.

Belonging to the Community

As you have read, the Gospel according to Matthew has a special interest in community life. That's understandable, for Matthew was written, many scholars think, to provide direction to the early Christian communities. Remember, these communities did not have the gospel accounts, letters of Paul, or, for that matter, the church structure that we know.

Perugino, *Christ Delivering the Keys to St. Peter.* Fifteenth Century.

For Matthew, discipleship means being one with the community of faith. Read Matthew 16:13–20 for an explanation of this photo. What does this say about being a disciple?

They were pioneers, figuring out as they went how to bring Jesus' teaching to life.

In those early days, community life had its ups and downs, just like shared life anywhere always has. Even though Christians were focused on Jesus, they did not always agree or do the right thing. They were growing into their faith through participation in the community. It's understandable that tensions developed.

Matthew's approach to these tensions was to urge Christians to have a forgiving and loving heart out of love for Jesus. Today, these principles are just as true as they were then.

Matthew's emphasis on the disciple's life in community can be applied to your life. You can make any situation better by putting your Christian faith into action.

What does it mean for you to be a disciple? What can you do to live as a student of the Lord Jesus and proclaim the Gospel with your life?

Proclaiming the Kingdom

Luke's account emphasizes that a disciple spreads the Good News about Jesus regardless of the dangers or difficulties involved, confident that God will help. For the early Church, the danger of spreading the Gospel was much more immediate. Christians risked arrest, torture and death. Today, that risk still exists in some places. In the People's Republic of China, for instance, it is illegal to belong to the Roman Catholic Church. Anyone caught distributing its literature or speaking on its behalf risks persecution.

Most of us will never face this kind of organized opposition. In fact, we live in a country that, at least statistically, is overwhelmingly Christian. What does "proclaiming the kingdom" mean for us now?

First, it means being willing to talk openly about our faith. Many people find it difficult to talk about their spiritual lives with others. Often this reluctance comes from humility, which is, in itself, a good thing. Sometimes, however, people don't get the encouragement they need to grow in their relationship with God. People, especially teenagers, need support from their peers to feel good about what they're doing. Being a disciple means reaching out and sharing God's love when it is possible to do so in a quiet, supportive way.

Second, proclaiming the kingdom means living out its values as an example for others. Our challenge is to provide people with living examples of what the kingdom has to offer: peace, contentment, and moral conduct. As the saying goes, "Actions speak louder than words." The best way to proclaim the kingdom is to live lovingly. By doing so, we'll serve as role models for others and be effective disciples.

Loving One Another

Finally, John said that a disciple is one who follows the commandment of Jesus to love one another as the core of their unity with Jesus. This command, however, is very general. Practically, what does it mean to say a disciple is one who loves others?

The Greek word used here for love, "agape," is not primarily an emotional attitude. It has little to do with how you *feel*. Agape means "to value" or "to prize." In other words, "loving one another" means valuing other people, treating them with great respect and caring for them as people with dignity. The word concerns your attitudes and how you *act*. Agape has to do with the way you interact with the people in your life. "Loving one another" means valuing the well-being of others. We can express agape on two levels.

1. **"Large-scale agape"** refers to the value we attach to the well-being of groups of people. As disciples, Jesus calls us to be aware of the world in which we live. Where we see poverty and injustice, conditions in which people don't enjoy the dignity they deserve, it's our duty to act. This may mean volunteering to help the homeless, supporting a candidate for office, or giving money to a charitable organization. Whatever our contribution may be, as disciples, Jesus asks us to help make the world a place that values the worth of all people.

2. **"Small-scale agape"** is the way we treat the individuals in our own lives. It means taking the time to do something around the house without being asked. It means behaving with respect in the classroom. It means standing up for somebody in school who needs your help. Whatever

the situation, as disciples we have to show our love to the people we meet on a daily basis. Actually, practicing small-scale agape can be much more difficult than large-scale agape. It's easy to make a small gesture for someone you've never even met. It can be very difficult to act generously towards someone who irritates you. Nevertheless, Jesus calls us as disciples to show love towards all.

Have You Considered?

1. Describe a disappointment you've experienced. How can you find value in this experience?
2. Which communities do you belong to? How can you be a good member of these communities?
3. Do you think it's more effective to proclaim the kingdom by example rather than through words? Are both necessary? Explain your answer.

Spiritual Reflection

On Being a Disciple

The New Testament provides us with many examples of discipleship. Luke 10:25–37 offers one of the most intriguing parables in the Gospel. You've probably heard the story of the good Samaritan many times; now, take the time to pray with the story and see what it tells you about discipleship.

Read the parable slowly and carefully, making sure that you understand everything. When you're finished, take a moment to become quiet inside. Then, think about the various characters that are presented in the story:

- Why does the scholar come to Jesus? How should a disciple come to Jesus?
- Although you would expect the Levite and priest to be good neighbors, they would be violating the Law if they helped the wounded man. What does this tell you about being a disciple?
- What do you know about the relationship between Jews and Samaritans? Think about your worst enemy,

the person you dislike most in the whole world. That person is the Samaritan in this story. How can this person remain an enemy? What is the responsibility of discipleship?

- Try to picture the scene in which Jesus says to the scholar, "Which of these three, in your opinion, was neighbor to the robbers' victim?" Imagine that Jesus is talking to you. Hear Jesus' tell you to go and show mercy to those you meet. How do you respond?
- Pray that God may strengthen you to be a good disciple, and give you the ability to forgive those who have injured you and to show mercy to those most in need of it.
- Decide on one thing that you can do differently in your life, immediately, in order to be a better disciple of Jesus; then act on your decision.

When you've finished, take another moment to be quiet inside, and then thank God for this time.

Q/A

Section One

1. What does the word "disciple" mean?
2. What did it mean to literally follow Jesus?
3. List two things that made the literal followers of Jesus noteworthy.
4. What was unusual in Jesus' attitude towards women?
5. What was the purpose of the group known as "the Twelve?"
6. What did the Twelve symbolize?
7. To what attitude about the Law did Jesus object?
8. Why did Jesus criticize the hypocrisy of some religious leaders?
9. Why did Jesus' popularity among the common people of Judea threaten the Romans?
10. What two actions did Jesus perform when he arrived in Jerusalem for Passover?
11. What three important actions did Jesus perform at the Last Supper?
12. What was the charge against Jesus by the Jewish leaders?

Section Two

1. How is Jesus presented in Mark?
2. What do the disciples in Mark misunderstand about Jesus?
3. What is the "messianic secret?"
4. How does Mark understand discipleship?
5. How does Matthew compare Jesus to Moses?
6. In Matthew, what are the two most important themes of Jesus' teaching?
7. For Matthew, in what sense does Jesus fulfill the Law?
8. How does Matthew understand discipleship?
9. In what way is Luke the "social gospel?"
10. How does Luke understand discipleship?
11. What does the term "logos" mean in John?
12. What does the term "incarnation" mean?
13. What is significant about Jesus saying "I am?"
14. What is John's understanding of discipleship?
15. Define "agape."

BIBLE ACTIVITIES

1. Each of the four gospel accounts contains a different story about the resurrection of Jesus. Read these stories in Mark 16:9–20, Matthew 28, Luke 24, and John 20–21. For each story, answer the following questions:
   - To whom did Jesus appear?
   - Where did the appearances occur?
   - What did Jesus say?
     What do all four stories have in common? How do you explain the differences between them?
2. Both Matthew and Luke begin their accounts with stories of Jesus' infancy. These stories are very different from one another. Read both stories in Matthew 1–2 and Luke 1–2. List all the elements the two stories have in common. On what do both stories agree concerning Jesus' infancy?
3. Matthew's account shows a special interest in Church discipline. Read Chapter 18:1–14, 21–35 in Matthew, and then answer the following question: according to Matthew, what should I do if a fellow Christian wrongs me in some way?

GLOSSARY

- **Agape**: Greek word for "love"; it refers to valuing others for who they are.
- **Beatitude**: Important teachings of Jesus which begin "Blessed are."
- **Controversy Story**: Story in which Jesus' enemies try to trap him in a dilemma, but from which he escapes.
- **Disciple**: Term meaning "student"; one who learns from Jesus and follows him.
- **Discipleship**: The process of trying to live like Jesus.
- **Discourse**: Long speeches given by Jesus in John; Jesus' own words blended with the understanding of the gospel writer and his community.
- **Easter**: The day on which Jesus rose from the grave.
- **Eucharist**: The word means "thanksgiving"; the sacrament of receiving bread and wine as the body and blood of Christ.
- **Formula Citation**: A device used in Matthew to show that Jesus fulfilled Old Testament prophecy.
- **Incarnation**: The Christian belief that God took on human flesh in Jesus.
- **Last Supper**: The final meal shared by Jesus and his disciples.
- **Literal Followers**: People who gave up their families and jobs to travel with Jesus and receive his teaching.
- **Logos**: Greek term for "word"; in John, Jesus is identified as the Word of God which has existed from the beginning and assisted in creation.
- **Messianic Secret**: In Mark, the idea that Jesus kept secret his identity as the messiah until he had suffered and died.
- **Passion**: The suffering and death of Jesus.
- **Sinner**: Under a strict interpretation of Jewish law anyone who was "impure," such as people holding certain jobs (for example, tax collector).
- **The Twelve**: The inner group of Jesus' disciples entrusted with leadership responsibilities; the "apostles."

UNDERSTANDING MORE ABOUT:

The Twelve

You learned in this chapter that the Twelve were sometimes called apostles. The word "apostle" literally means "one who is sent." This word was later used for other disciples besides the Twelve, including Paul and Barnabas. You also learned that the various gospel accounts differ slightly in their lists of the Twelve. Compare the lists below. How do they differ?

Matthew 10:1–4

"Then he summoned his twelve disciples and gave them authority over unclean spirits to drive them out and to cure every disease and every illness. The names of the twelve apostles are these: first, Simon called Peter, and his brother Andrew; James, the son of Zebedee, and his brother John; Philip and Bartholomew, Thomas and Matthew the tax collector; James, the son of Alphaeus, and Thaddeus; Simon the Cananean, and Judas Iscariot who betrayed him."

Mark 3:13–19

"He went up the mountain and summoned those whom he wanted and they came to him. He appointed twelve [whom he named apostles] that they might be with him and he might send them forth to preach and to have authority to drive out demons: [he appointed the twelve:] Simon, whom he named Peter; James, son of Zebedee, and John the brother of James, who he named Boanerges, that is sons of thunder; Andrew, Philip, Bartholomew, Matthew, Thomas, James the son of Alphaeus; Thaddeus, Simon the Cananean, and Judas Iscariot who betrayed him."

Luke 6:12–16

"In those days he departed to the mountain to pray, and he spent the night in prayer to God. When day came, he called his disciples to himself, and from them he chose Twelve, whom he also named apostles: Simon, whom he named Peter, and his brother Andrew, James, John, Philip, Bartholomew, Matthew, Thomas, James the son of Alphaeus, Simon who was called a Zealot, and Judas the son of James, and Judas Iscariot, who became a traitor."

CHAPTER 12

Acts of the Apostles

Legend

● General History
● Biblical History
● Regional History
● Books written

LaTina hated summer camp. Every year, she went to the same hot, dusty place for two weeks. She had to go without TV, shopping with her friends, and all the other things that made summer great. Mostly, though, she had to put up with a roomful of other girls she'd never met and wouldn't like. All in all, LaTina thought camp was a miserable experience.

This year threatened to be the worst yet. Since she was starting high school next year, LaTina thought her parents might let her stay home this year. No such luck; not only was she going, but her parents had signed her up for the overnight canoe trip down the river as well. LaTina was horrified. At least this would be her last year there.

When her parents dropped LaTina off at camp, she headed for her assigned bunkhouse. Slowly, the other girls arrived. They didn't seem to be any happier to be there than LaTina. They unpacked their bags in relative silence, not saying much at all. Before long it was dinner time, and they went to the mess hall.

Over dinner, the girls began to talk, since there was nothing else to do. They started by making fun of the baked beans.

"Gross," Millie said. "Do they really expect us to eat this stuff?"

Then somebody dropped a roll on the table. "Thunk!" The roll didn't bounce or roll at all. It simply stopped where it had landed.

"I think these are the same rolls that we had at last year's closing dinner. They weren't any softer then either." Soon everyone was laughing and having a good time.

They talked about school, their friends back home, and even how much they hated coming to camp. Their laughter could be heard all over the mess hall. LaTina found herself actually enjoying their company. "This is amazing," she thought.

Over the next two weeks, the girls from LaTina's bunkhouse grew very close. Working as a team, they won most of their competitions: archery, tug-of-war, even arts and crafts. What worried LaTina was the canoe trip; she was the only one in the bunk house scheduled to go. She told one of the girls about her concern. Before she knew it, the entire group went to the counselor's office and added their names to the list. With her new friends along, the canoe trip was a great success, and LaTina had the best time of her life.

When her parents came to pick her up, her Mom hugged LaTina and said, "Well, you don't have to go through that again. How do you feel?" When LaTina said that she had a delightful time and wanted to come back next year as a counselor, her mother was shocked.

"Something different happened this time," LaTina explained. "It really felt good, like we were a family. I don't know what it was, but there was a different spirit with these girls."

The Guiding Spirit

LaTina's Mom smiled and said a silent prayer of thanks to the Holy Spirit. LaTina's mother, like generations of Christians, had faith that the Holy Spirit was active in her daughter's life. She believed that the Spirit shaped and guided the lives of every believer, just as the Spirit guided the members of the early Christian communities.

Much of what we know about the Spirit's role in the Christian community comes from the Acts of the Apostles. In Acts, we see how the Church grew under the Spirit's guidance and how Christians overcame hardship and persecution with the Spirit's protection.

Acts and Salvation History

The book known as the Acts of the Apostles was written by Luke, the author of the gospel account which bears the same name. Acts tells the story of the early Christian Church, and pays extra attention to the two apostles, Peter and Paul, who were its most important leaders. Originally, Luke's gospel account and Acts went together as a two-volume set. In them, Luke shows that all of the events in the salvation story—from the birth of Jesus to the spread of Christianity to Rome—were directed by the Holy Spirit in fulfillment of God's will. In this section, you'll look at the unfolding of salvation history in Acts.

Learning Objectives for Section One

By the end of this section, you will be able to:

- Explain Luke's idea of salvation history.
- Discuss how Luke understood the relationship between Christianity and the Greek and Roman religions.
- List important aspects of Peter's ministry.
- Describe the highlights of Paul's ministry.

◆ Acts: The Book of the Spirit

In Acts, we read about the growing number of people in the first century who changed their lives based on the Gospel of Jesus. At first, these people were simply called members of the "Way"; only later, first in Antioch, were they known as "Christians." Although Acts contains the stories of many memorable Christian leaders such as Peter, Paul, Stephen, Philip, and Barnabas, the most important character in the story is really the Holy Spirit.

From the very beginning, Luke tells us that the spread of the Christian faith was the work of the Spirit. Acts emphasized that the growth of Christianity was part of God's plan to bring salvation to the world. With the guidance of the Spirit, the early Christian apostles spread the good news about Jesus throughout the Roman Empire.

Why the Gentiles?

When the Gospel according to Luke and the Acts of the Apostles were written, the Church consisted of small communities found in cities throughout the Mediterranean Sea area. The missionaries who started these communities often were persecuted because of their message. In many places they were simply ignored or received with indifference. It took many years of witnessing to Jesus' message for even the smallest community of believers to start.

Most Jews rejected the message that Jesus was the promised messiah, and many were hostile to any claim that Jesus might be God's son. There was only one God, Yahweh. Any claim that Jesus was divine called that belief into question.

The missionaries had better luck converting Gentiles to the new faith, although the total number of believers was still very small. Luke wrote Acts, therefore, to point out the direction the Spirit was leading the Church.

Before Luke could convince his readers that Christianity was destined to reach the ends of the earth, he first had to deal with the doubts held by many people. Such doubts can be expressed in two basic questions:

- Why do so many Jews reject the Gospel?
- How can Gentiles claim salvation from the fulfillment of a promise made to Jews?

These were important questions. Remember, Jesus was a Jew, and Christianity was rooted in the traditions and beliefs of Judaism. Yet, while Gentiles were responding to Jesus' message, the Jews rejected it. Luke's answer to these questions was the same: God's plan for salvation had always included the Gentiles.

According to Luke, God's salvation is first made known through the people of Israel and then through the message and ministry of Jesus. Following Jesus' death and resurrection, salvation is offered to the

Scripture Workshop

Peter and Paul

In Acts, Peter and Paul are presented as heroes of the faith whose lives are modeled on the experiences of Jesus. Luke deliberately parallels Peter and Paul to show that the Spirit guided both of them in similar ways. Read the following pairs of passages from Acts and, for each, determine the similarity between Peter and Paul which appears in that pair:

1. 8:9–24 and 13:6–12
2. 10:25–26 and 14:13–15
3. 9:36–43 and 20:9–12
4. 12:6–11 and 16:24–26
5. 8:14–17 and 19:1–6

whole world through the Church. For Luke, each of these stages represents a particular part of God's plan. It is clear in Acts that after Jesus died, the teachings of the Old Testament, all the promises of the Covenant, and the hope of salvation were offered to Jews and non-Jews alike.

From Luke's time onwards, Christianity became less a group within Judaism and more a new religious movement of Gentiles. Luke shows that this change was neither an accident nor a clever strategy: it was the result of the Spirit working to fulfill God's plan for salvation history.

The Guidance of the Spirit

Throughout Acts, Luke sees the influence of the Spirit in the Church. He announces this theme at the very beginning of the book, when Jesus says to the disciples:

"But you will receive power when the Holy Spirit comes upon you, and you will be my witnesses in Jerusalem, throughout Judea and Samaria, and even to the ends of the earth."

(Acts 1:8)

Michelangelo, Conversion of St. Paul. Sixteenth Century.

Saul was a pious Jew before his conversion. He persecuted those Jews who became Christians. After his conversion, Paul became a missionary who spread the Good News of Jesus.

The Bible in Context

Greek and Roman Religion

The Greeks and Romans were "polytheists," meaning that they worshipped many gods. During the first century C.E., the Greeks and Romans adopted many new gods, sometimes borrowing them from Eastern religions. Afraid that they might miss an important god, the Romans built a temple in Rome called the "Pantheon," or "Temple of All the Gods." In this way every god would be worshipped, even if not directly by name.

Paul responds to this desire for true worship by pointing out that behind every image of divinity lies the one God who raised Jesus from the dead. This message appealed to many Gentiles, who became Christian and helped to spread the Gospel of Jesus.

The spread of Christianity throughout Palestine and into the rest of the Empire, therefore, happened through the guidance of the Spirit. The power Jesus had promised became real on the Jewish feast of Pentecost, when the Holy Spirit filled the gathered community members with its presence, and inspired them to preach the faith courageously (*see Acts 1:13–14, and 2:1ff*).

The first Christian mission started when Greek-speaking Jewish Christians were thrown out of Jerusalem because of their belief. They left Jerusalem and made converts in Samaria and the surrounding areas of Syria as they traveled.

The Heroes of the Faith

Besides the Holy Spirit, the leading characters in Acts are the apostles, Peter and Paul. Peter is seen as the leader of the early Christian Church who begins the mission to the Gentiles. Paul is the apostle called by Jesus to take over this mission and to bring it to completion. Luke sees Peter and Paul as the most important leaders of the Church, after Jesus himself.

Peter and Paul both begin to preach under the influence of the Spirit, both heal and teach, both have visions related to their missions, and both are imprisoned for their beliefs. Finally they both are put to death in Rome because of the message they proclaimed. These major parallels are supported by many smaller similarities.

The pattern Luke sees in the lives of Peter and Paul comes from the life of Jesus. In their experience of preaching, healing, suffering, rejection, and imprisonment, Peter and Paul follow the path walked by Jesus. In this way, Luke shows that the same Spirit of Jesus also guided Peter and Paul.

Hope of the Gentiles

Luke believes that just as Christianity fulfills the promises of the Old Testament, it also fulfills the religious hopes of the Gentiles. Consider the speech Paul makes in Athens:

> *"You Athenians, I see that in every respect you are very religious. For as I walked around looking carefully at your shrines, I even discovered an altar inscribed 'To an unknown God.' What therefore you unknowingly worship, I proclaim to you. The God who made the world and all that is in it, the Lord of heaven and earth, does not dwell in sanctuaries made by human hands, nor is he served by human hands because he needs anything. Rather, it is he who gives to everyone life and breath and everything."*
>
> (Acts 17:22–25,31)

Paul here says that the Greeks and Romans have been worshipping the Christian God, ignorant of God's true name. The Spirit has been at work in their religious longings, preparing them to recognize Jesus as Lord. Even though Paul did not make many converts in Athens, Luke considers the trip a success: the Gospel has been proclaimed to the Gentiles.

Have You Considered?

1. Why do you suppose it worried Christians that many Jews seemed to reject the Gospel of Jesus?
2. Luke says that the Holy Spirit can use misfortune to bring about God's plan. Can you think of a time in your life when a misfortune led to a positive outcome?
3. Luke says that the Greeks and Romans worshipped the God of Christians without knowing it. Do you think it is possible for people to worship God today without knowing it? Why or why not?

◆ Peter, the Leader of the Apostles

In the Acts of the Apostles we see Peter acting with authority as the leader of the early Church. We also see him beginning the mission to the Gentiles, and spreading this new era in salvation history.

Peter's Authority

Peter is the leader of the early Christian community according to Acts.

- When the apostles chose a replacement for Judas Iscariot, Peter is the one who decided how it would be done (*Acts* 1:15–26).
- The Holy Spirit filled Peter and inspired him to preach the Gospel without fear. (*Acts* 2:14–41).
- Peter was given the power to heal, and he used it to convince people of the truth of the Gospel. (*Acts* 3:1–10).
- Peter is arrested as the leader of Jesus' followers and is tried, but because of the power of his preaching, he is set free (*Acts* 3:11–4:22).
- People would carry their sick into the streets hoping that Peter's shadow would fall upon them and heal them (*Acts* 5:12–16).
- Peter welcomed the first Gentile believers in Jesus into the Christian community (*Acts* 10:1–48).
- Peter sides with Paul at the Council of Jerusalem on accepting Gentiles into the faith (*Acts* 15:1–12).

Ribera, *St. Peter.* Sixteenth Century.

Saint Peter is usually shown holding keys and a book. The keys stand for his authority in the Church (see Matthew 16:13–20) and the book, his proclamation of the Gospel of Jesus Christ.

in the Spotlight

God-Fearers

Luke calls Cornelius, the first Gentile convert, a "God-fearer." This term had a technical meaning during the first century C.E. It referred to Gentiles who attended the Jewish synagogue because they admired Judaism, but who were not willing to accept circumcision and the other demands of the Law of Moses. Many Gentiles were attracted to Judaism because of its monotheism and moral code. Because they weren't members of the people of Israel, however, they couldn't participate fully in the worship or practice of the faith. The Gospel appealed to these people very much. Paul often addressed this group in the synagogue, as he does in Acts 13:16.

Peter and the Gentiles

Luke shows that the mission to the Gentiles began with Peter, so that Christian missionaries who made Gentile converts could point to Peter's example as the authority for their work.

Peter's first Gentile convert was Cornelius, a Roman officer. At first, Peter did not want to convert him, but several visions inspired by the Holy Spirit led Peter to understand that this was God's will (*Acts* 10). Peter baptized Cornelius and made him a member of the Christian community. This act set the stage for Paul, the man who would become known as the "apostle to the Gentiles," to take Christianity to most of the Roman Empire.

Have You Considered?

1. What is the significance of Peter using his authority to open the Gospel up to the Gentiles? How did this decision change the life of the Church?
2. How are the signs of Peter's authority as presented in Acts similar to stories about Jesus?

◆ Paul, the Apostle to the Gentiles

Paul is an even more important character in Acts than Peter. While Peter figures in eleven chapters in Acts, Paul dominates 20. As you will see, Paul's most important gift to the early Church were the many letters he wrote. Luke, however, is not interested in Paul's letters, and he never mentions them. (Luke may not have even known of Paul's letters; remember, there were no printing presses or national bookstore chains in the first century C.E.) Paul is the ideal missionary, empowered by the Holy Spirit to spread the Gospel to all people.

Corinth was a major center of commerce in the first century C.E. Ships from all over the Roman Empire traded there. Christianity took root quickly in this city through Paul's preaching.

The Early Years

Luke tells us that Paul (earlier known as Saul) was from Tarsus, an important Hellenistic city (now part of modern Turkey). Paul was born a Roman citizen. Growing up, he was educated in Greek literature and culture, as well as in the traditions of his Jewish ancestors. Paul studied in Jerusalem with the highly influential rabbi, Gamaliel. Paul was a very strict Jew and considered himself a Pharisee. He took it upon himself to enforce the Law. As the apostles proclaimed Jesus' Resurrection, Paul took offense. He persecuted followers of the Way, whom he considered violators of the Law.

Paul's Missionary Career

While traveling to Damascus, in Syria, to persecute Christians, Paul experienced a vision of Jesus. Paul's life was radically changed by this vision. After several years of prayer and preparation, Paul became a missionary for the very Way which he had once opposed. Paul's home at this time was Antioch, whose Christian community supported his missionary efforts. Today, some scholars divide Paul's travels into three great "missionary journeys."

The First Journey (46–49 C.E.)   This journey saw Paul in the company of Barnabas and John-Mark. They traveled across many islands in the Mediterranean Sea, and then landed in South Galatia (modern Turkey). Each place they went, Paul preached in the synagogue, where he often met with resistance and even with violence. Rejected by the Jews, Paul began preaching to Gentiles.

The Second Journey (50–52 C.E.)   His second trip took Paul into Europe for the first time. Paul founded Christian communities (which he called churches) in Philippi, Thessalonica, and Corinth in Greece, and at Ephesus in Asia Minor. Paul practiced his trade while preaching the Gospel. (Luke calls Paul a "tent-maker.")

Because of his lengthy stay there, Paul's church in Corinth grew rapidly and became one of the most important communities in the early Church. Towards the end of his stay there, some Jews complained about Paul to the Roman governor, Gallio. Gallio investigated the complaint but found no cause to charge Paul with a crime. Paul left Corinth shortly thereafter, stopping in Jerusalem before returning to his home in Antioch.

The Third Journey (54–58 C.E.)   Paul stayed for three years in Ephesus. On leaving Ephesus, Paul

LEARN FROM THE MAP

Paul's Missionary Journeys

Using the scale of 1/4" = 60 miles, figure out how many miles Paul traveled on each of his three missionary journeys. Use the key to determine which arrow goes with which journey. Then, find each of the places below on the map. On which journey did Paul visit each city?

Antioch, Salamis, Lystra, Thessalonica, Corinth, Ephesus

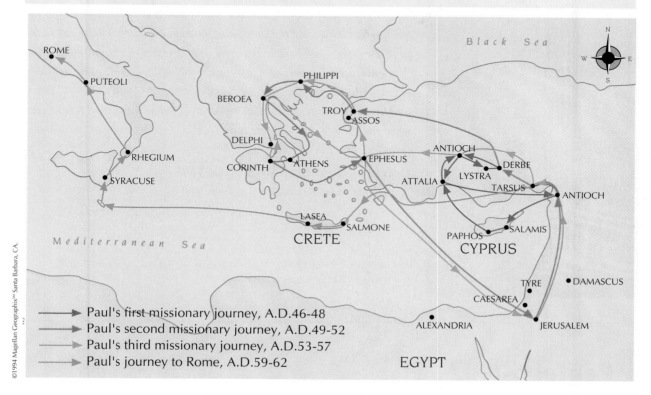

Key:
→ Paul's first missionary journey, A.D.46-48
→ Paul's second missionary journey, A.D.49-52
→ Paul's third missionary journey, A.D.53-57
→ Paul's journey to Rome, A.D.59-62

©1994 Magellan Geographix℠ Santa Barbara, CA.

traveled through Macedonia on his way to Corinth and then sailed for Jerusalem.

Paul's Arrest

Paul was a very successful apostle to the Gentiles, but some people resented the growing number of Gentiles who were becoming Christian. This resentment exploded on Paul's return to Jerusalem. Paul escaped death only because he asserted his Roman citizenship. He was taken into protective custody by the soldiers.

The Romans usually ignored local religious feuds as long as they did not cause public uprisings. As a citizen of Rome, however, Paul had a right to have the argument heard by the procurator, Felix. Although he was once again found innocent, Paul was kept in prison this time for two years. Felix, it seems, thought Paul an important person and expected a bribe for Paul's release.

Felix was replaced as procurator by Festus, who sent Paul to Rome with a guard. Despite experiencing many obstacles on the trip, Paul safely arrived in Rome, where he was kept under house arrest for two years. Acts ends there, with Paul in Rome receiving people who wanted to hear the Gospel of Jesus.

Have You Considered?

1. As a young man, Paul was such a loyal Jew that he persecuted others who didn't observe the Law. Why do you suppose people sometimes strike out at those who don't agree with them?
2. How do you suppose Christians would have reacted to seeing Paul, who had once persecuted them, now preaching the Gospel?

The Spirit Leads the Way

El Greco, Pentecost. Sixteenth Century.

You have seen how Luke believed that the growth of Christianity among the Gentiles was the work of the Holy Spirit, through the apostles Peter and Paul. In this section, you'll look more closely at four critical points in this growth: (1) **Pentecost**, *when the Spirit first came upon the disciples. (2)* **The baptism of Cornelius**, *when Peter began the Gentile mission. (3)* **Paul's vision of Jesus and his call** *to become a Christian missionary. (4)* **The Council of Jerusalem**, *when the Church approved the conversion of Gentiles without first making them Jews.*

Learning Objectives for Section Two

By the end of this section, you will be able to:

- Explain how the Spirit guided the apostles at Pentecost, the baptism of Cornelius, the call of Paul, and the Council of Jerusalem.

- Discuss the gifts the Holy Spirit offers to us today and how those gifts shape our lives.

◆ Pentecost

The Book of Acts opens with the ascension of Jesus to heaven. After Jesus' resurrection, the apostles had retreated to a locked room in Jerusalem, where they were joined by Mary, Jesus' mother, some members of his family, and some of the women who had followed Jesus. There, they prayed and waited for the Spirit that Jesus had promised.

On the festival of Pentecost, 50 days after Passover, the Holy Spirit came upon the gathered disciples and filled them with God's gifts, especially the ability and courage to preach the Good News boldly.

When the time for Pentecost was fulfilled, they were all in one place together. And suddenly there came from the sky a noise like a strong driving wind, and it filled the entire house in which they were. Then there appeared to them tongues as of fire, which parted and came to rest on each one of them. And they were all filled with the Holy Spirit and began to speak in different tongues, as the Spirit enabled them to proclaim.
(Acts 2:1–4)

Luke says that people from all of Israel were in Jerusalem for the festival. Just as Jesus came to announce the kingdom to all of Israel, the apostles preached to all. For Jews, Pentecost was a celebration of God's gifts of the land of Israel and the Law. To that celebration God has added the gifts of the Holy Spirit. With the Spirit, they will preach the Good News, heal in Jesus' name, and lead people to God's kingdom.

After being filled with the Spirit, Peter rose and delivered a sermon to the assembly of Jews. His words were *inspired*—filled with the Spirit. Quoting the prophet Joel, Peter said:

"It will come to pass in the last days, God says, that I will pour out a portion of my spirit on all flesh. Your sons and daughters shall prophesy, your young men shall see visions, your old men shall dream dreams."
(Acts 2:17; Joel 3:1)

Peter told the crowd about Jesus, who worked

signs among them, who had risen from the dead, and now was at the right hand of God. Jesus' spirit had filled the disciples.

Many in the crowd were amazed at the force of Peter's words. They asked, "What should we do?" Peter responded by telling them that they must reform their lives and be baptized. This passage is the first to identify baptism as the sacrament of initiation into the Christian community. As Luke tells us later in Acts, when a person is baptized, he or she receives the Holy Spirit. Acts says 3,000 people were moved by Peter's sermon and accepted baptism on Pentecost.

Here, Luke underlines the central point of the Book of Acts: Christianity originated in the inspiration of God, not in human activity. The spread of the Gospel is the work of the Spirit, Luke says. Today, Pentecost is the feast day on which Catholics celebrate the gift of the Holy Spirit.

The Conversion of Cornelius

Acts 10:1–11:18 describes Peter's conversion of Cornelius, a Roman officer and a Gentile. The story opens with a messenger from God speaking to Cornelius in a vision. The messenger tells Cornelius that God has seen his prayer and good works. He instructs Cornelius to send for Peter and to await his arrival. Cornelius agrees, and immediately sends two men to find Peter.

Before they arrive, Peter also has a vision.

- He sees all the animals of the earth on top of a large canvas.
- A voice tells him to slaughter and eat what he sees.
- Peter, being a good Jew, refuses, insisting that he has never eaten anything impure in his life. The voice, however, says, "What God has purified, you are not to call impure" (Acts 10:15).
- The Holy Spirit then speaks to Peter, telling him that he should receive Cornelius' messengers.

These two visions emphasize that Peter's encounter with Cornelius is not something that either man planned. Instead, God is bringing Peter to Cornelius, and what follows is God's will.

When Peter arrives at Cornelius' home, he goes inside and greets Cornelius' household. He says that as a Jew, he would never associate with impure Gentiles, but God has shown him that no one should call another person impure. Peter then delivers a sermon, saying that all who fear God are acceptable to Him. He relays the good news that Jesus is risen. As he is talking, the Holy Spirit descends on everyone present, and they begin to "speak in tongues."

This ability to "speak in tongues" is known as *glossolalia*. It enables a person to speak without intentionally doing so. Sometimes this means speaking in a foreign language (as with the disciples on

Lippi, St. Peter Visited in Prison by St. Paul, Fifteenth Century.

The Acts of the Apostles tells of the spread of Christianity. Peter and Paul, through the guidance of the Holy Spirit, are the central characters of the book. This painting shows Peter, imprisoned in Rome, being visited by Paul.

Pentecost), and sometimes it means uttering mysterious, unknown words. In this case, Luke tells us that the Gentiles "glorified God," so those around them were able to understand what they said. Peter, along with the other Jews who had traveled with him, is amazed that the Holy Spirit should come upon Gentiles in this way.

Peter declares that since the Gentiles have received the Holy Spirit, there is no reason they should not be baptized. He then baptizes them, making them part of the Christian community.

Afterwards, when he returns to Jerusalem, some Jewish-Christians object to Peter's conversion of Gentiles. Peter describes how God led him through signs and visions to take this step. Those present realize that what has happened is God's will:

> When they heard this, they stopped objecting and glorified God saying: "God has then granted life-giving repentance to the Gentiles too."
>
> (Acts 11:18)

The Conversion of Paul

Luke considers the story of Paul's conversion so important that he repeats it. The original form of the story is in Acts 9:1–19, and then Luke quotes Paul as giving two different versions of the story in 22:3–21 and 26:2–23. In each case, there are differences in minor details. Could those who were with Paul hear the voice which spoke to him? Were the others standing or kneeling when the voice spoke? Although the answers to these questions vary, the point of the story is always the same: Saul, who had persecuted Christians out of zeal for the Law, becomes a Christian.

You already know that Saul was a very religious and obedient Jew. He was willing to force Jews to follow the Law's commands. At the time of his conversion, Luke says that Saul was on his way to Damascus to arrest Christians. He had been given power to do so by the high priest. Although usually this power was reserved by the Roman procurator, this event probably occurred in the period between the administrations of Pilate and Marcellus (approximately 36 C.E.). If so, the local Jewish leaders may have temporarily assumed the authority that normally belonged to the Roman governor.

While Saul is on the road, a light from the sky flashes above him and knocks him to the ground. A voice calls out "Saul, Saul, why do you persecute me?" Saul asks who is speaking, and the voice replies that it is Jesus, the one whom Saul is persecuting. Notice

Scripture Workshop

Paul in Acts

Bible scholars generally agree that Luke had a source about Paul's conversion which he edited for use in the Book of Acts. Because the speeches in Acts show much evidence of Luke's editing, the version of Paul's conversion in Acts 9 is generally regarded as the closest to the original.

In the two retellings of the conversion contained in Paul's speeches, at 22:3–21 and 26:2–23, we see Luke's point of view. To understand Luke's point, do the following:

- Read each of the three versions of Paul's conversion.
- Make a list of the things Luke adds in the last two versions of the event.
- Based on these additions, tell what Luke believes is most important about Paul's conversion.
- Compare these versions with Paul's description in Galatians 1:11–18.

Luke's idea about discipleship in this passage: Jesus is with the disciples, and when Saul persecutes them, he persecutes Jesus himself.

After this event, Saul is referred to by a new name: Paul. (Remember similar stories from the Old Testament—Abram becomes Abraham, Jacob becomes Israel.) The name change symbolizes that Saul has been touched by God. Next, the voice tells Paul to go into the city and wait for God's call. Paul has been blinded by the flash of light, so his companions lead him to Damascus. There, Paul refuses food or water for three days, waiting to see what the Lord has in store.

As Paul waits, the Lord comes in a vision to Ananias, a disciple of Jesus. God instructs Ananias to go to Paul, to pray for him, and to cure his blindness. Ananias protests, reminding the Lord that Paul has persecuted Christians and presently has the power to arrest Christians on sight.

The Lord insists that Ananias carry out these instructions. God then announces that Paul has been chosen to be the person who brings the Gospel to the Gentiles:

"Go, for this man is a chosen instrument of mine to carry my name before the Gentiles, kings and Israelites, and I will show him what he will have to suffer for my name."

(Acts 9:15–16)

With a disciple's true courage, Ananias went to Paul, placed his hands on him, and prayed for him. Paul recovered his sight and was filled with the Holy Spirit at Ananias's touch. For the rest of his life, Paul preached the Gospel of the risen Jesus, beginning in Damascus.

As you already know, Paul is the hero of the rest of Acts. His success in converting Gentiles, however, was not celebrated by everyone. Some Christians saw

Ciuffagni, St. James. Sixteenth Century?

Saint James, one of the Apostles, was the leader of the church in Jerusalem. He headed the council there in 49 C.E. that validated Paul's preaching the Good News to Gentiles.

his mission as a betrayal of Judaism, and the result was a controversy that could only be settled by a meeting of all the leaders of the Church.

The Council of Jerusalem

In Acts 15, Luke tells the story of this meeting in Jerusalem in 49 C.E. Biblical scholars say that in this chapter, Luke has combined two separate events. One was a meeting of the apostles to discuss the question of the mission to the Gentiles. The other was a later controversy over whether Gentile converts should have to follow the Jewish dietary laws. Luke puts these two events together because they both involve the Spirit's guidance of the community towards accepting Gentiles as Christians.

James, described as a "brother of the Lord," heads this meeting in Jerusalem. Whatever his exact relationship to Jesus, James was a member of Jesus' family, and in the ancient world this meant that he had a claim to inherit his relative's authority. (This idea remained so strong that several decades later, the Emperor Vespasian arrested two distant cousins of Jesus, afraid that they might challenge his authority.) Because of James' relationship with Jesus, he became the head of the Christian community in Jerusalem.

Luke's story begins with Paul in Antioch, after the first missionary journey. Some Pharisees who had converted to Christianity traveled to Antioch, where they saw Gentiles worshipping with Jewish-Christians. The Pharisees demanded that the Gentiles should be circumcised in keeping with the Law of Moses. Paul refused, arguing that it was not necessary for the Gentiles to become Jews before entering the Christian community. They were members because of their faith in Jesus, not because they obeyed the Law. The Pharisees were not satisfied with Paul's response, so they demanded a hearing in Jerusalem.

When Paul and Barnabas arrived in Jerusalem, the apostles and other assembled leaders listened to their case. Next, some believing Pharisees stated their objections. The council considered the matter for a while, and then Peter rose to speak. He reminded them that the Spirit had called him to make the first Gentile convert. Then, he asked why the Gentiles should be required to obey the Law, since neither the apostles nor their ancestors had been able to do so:

"And God, who knows the heart, bore witness by granting them the Holy Spirit just as he did us. He made no distinction between us and them, for by faith he purified their hearts. Why, then, are you now

putting God to the test by placing on the shoulders of these disciples a yoke that neither our ancestors nor we have been able to bear? On the contrary, we believe that we are saved through the grace of the Lord Jesus, in the same way as they."

(Acts 15:8–11)

This speech was probably the original end of the discussion. As a result of Peter's words, the leaders of the community decided to accept Gentile converts without insisting that they first become Jews or obey Jewish laws. Because it was the Spirit which led Peter to convert Cornelius, they agreed that it was also the Spirit which led them to this decision.

Luke also includes here a speech given by James about the question of whether Gentile Christians need to obey the dietary rules in the Law of Moses. James says that they do not have to obey the entire law, but they should observe three basic rules:

- Do not eat the meat of animals sacrificed to idols.
- Do not eat the meat of strangled animals.
- Do not drink blood.

James also adds that Gentiles should also observe the basic rules of sexual morality and thus avoid scandal.

We have looked at four crucial events:

- Pentecost
- The conversion of Cornelius
- Paul's conversion
- The Council of Jerusalem

In describing these events, Luke expresses his belief that at every critical moment, the Holy Spirit led the early Christian community. Through the working of the Spirit, God's plan for salvation opened its third and final stage, the period of the Church.

Have You Considered?

1. Peter said that no one should call another person impure. Do you think some people still regard others as "impure"? Explain your answer.
2. Paul went from persecuting Christians to preaching Christ. Has your mind ever been changed completely like this? Describe your experience.
3. Why do you suppose James thought it would be a problem for Jewish-Christians and Gentile-Christians to live together if the Gentiles didn't follow the dietary rules?

◆ The Gifts of the Spirit

Catholics believe that the Holy Spirit continues to be with Christians today. In fact, Pope John XXIII, who called the Second Vatican Council (1962–65) because of a sudden prompting from the Spirit, called our age "a new Pentecost." He said that our times should be called "the age of the Holy Spirit," because the Spirit calls us today in a special way to reform and renewal.

The Holy Spirit is at work today in the life of every believer, helping us to become better, more holy people. In Catholic tradition, the help the Spirit can give to each of us has been described as seven "gifts." The original list is found in Isaiah 11:1–2, but we can also see the basis of these seven gifts in Acts.

Wisdom   The first gift of the Spirit is wisdom, a quality you've already studied in Chapter 9. The wisdom given by the Spirit is different, however, from the insights that can be achieved solely through human effort. The Spirit gives us the wisdom to "see through God's eyes," to evaluate things as God sees them. This is the challenge God gave to Ananias, when he was afraid to go to Paul. The Lord said that Ananias must see Paul in God's terms, not his own fear. This kind of wisdom is shaped by love, so that we judge everything from a loving perspective.

To see as God sees might mean looking past external appearance or behavior to see the good-hearted, loving person inside. It might mean judging a social situation not by the fun you might have, but by whether others are being excluded or hurt by it. The wisdom of the Spirit helps us to set aside our own self-interest and perceive a situation honestly, so that we can make decisions based on love.

Understanding   Understanding is the ability to grasp revealed truths easily and deeply. A "revealed" truth is one which has been given to us by God through Jesus and the teaching of the Church. For example, we believe that God the Father, God the Son, and God the Holy Spirit are three really distinct Persons relative to each other in the one and only God. This truth can't be "proven" by human reason, but we believe it still. Paul didn't come to the conclusion that Jesus was the Lord by reason. Through the Spirit, he simply "saw" that it was true. The Spirit gives us the ability to see the truth of revealed teachings without struggle or doubt.

Understanding is an important gift, because we all face doubts at different points in our lives. For example, when a close friend or family member is ill, it's difficult to understand how God can be loving and yet allow such things to happen. Sometimes we know Catholics who are mean-spirited or dishonest, and we have trouble believing in the Church. Understanding helps us overcome such doubts by seeing the truth of God's love and the inspiration of the Church, even when we can't prove them by facts or logic.

Knowledge   The knowledge given by the Spirit has been called the "science of the saints." It enables us to recognize the true value of created things. We appreciate them as gifts of God, but we recognize that they have no meaning in themselves. Only our salvation has true value; other things may bring us pleasure, but they can never be at the top of our priority list. Cornelius, the Roman centurion, had this gift. Although he was a powerful military leader, he saw that without salvation, all his worldly success meant nothing. This realization led him to call for Peter's help.

Knowledge helps us cope with the conflicts over material things that always come up in our lives.

Sometimes we want something so much that we're tempted to behave badly to get it. Knowledge helps us see that no created thing is worth sacrificing our morality or our relationship with God and other people. Knowledge helps us to see the true worth of things, and to see that only love has lasting value.

Counsel   Wisdom, understanding, and knowledge are gifts which help us understand things properly. Counsel helps us apply that understanding to the practical situations that we face every day. As Saint Augustine said, it is not external teachers who show us the truth, but the "Truth that presides within."

Through counsel, we are able to make wise moral judgments even in complicated circumstances. Counsel also helps us to give good advice to others, always guided by the principles of forgiveness and generosity.

When the other apostles turned to Peter on the question of whether or not to accept Gentiles, he spoke with counsel. He applied his own experience with Cornelius to the larger issue of Gentile

One of the gifts of the Holy Spirit is Counsel. This gift helps us to apply the Gospel to practical situations we face everyday.

People of Note

Barnabas

As you know, Barnabas traveled with Paul on his first missionary journey. In fact, Barnabas was a prominent leader in the early Church, and Paul was probably originally his assistant. Paul, however, quickly became a leader in his own right.

Barnabas and Paul separated at the beginning of the second journey, and like Paul, Barnabas continued to travel widely. He founded the Christian Church on the island of Cyprus, and the Church Father, Tertullian (along with some biblical scholars today) credited him with writing the *Letter to the Hebrews*. Barnabas' success as a missionary, and as the person who launched Paul's career, again shows the active role played by the Holy Spirit in the life of the early Church.

Christians, and steered the Church in the proper direction. We all have to deal with difficult moral decisions. Counsel helps us make the best possible one.

Piety   The gift of piety helps us worship God in the proper way. Piety means much more, however, than simply praying sincerely. Piety means that we show reverence for God and all of God's creatures. A pious person honors God with his or her work. A pious person also sees other people as brothers and sisters rather than competitors or enemies. This kind of piety led Paul to defend the right of Gentiles to become full members of the Christian Church.

A cliché says that we should love people and use things, not the other way around. When we are pious, we treat other people with dignity and respect, because they are images of God. They are members of our family, with God as our Father. With the gift of piety, we also honor God by thinking and acting in ways of which we can be proud. Piety helps us regard ourselves, other people, and the whole world as deserving of our love and care.

Fortitude   The word fortitude means "courage." This gift helps us to be brave. There are two different kinds of fortitude which the Spirit gives:

Hagueneau, *Sts. James the minor, Philip, and Barnabas. Fourteenth Century?*

Although Paul is the best known missionary of the early Church, Saint Barnabas also played an important role in spreading the Gospel. Barnabas is shown in this woodcut with Saint James the minor and Saint Philip.

1. The courage to undertake difficult tasks.
2. The courage to persist in our commitments.

The first kind of courage helps us not to be afraid when something seems impossible. We can face the challenge bravely, knowing the Spirit will provide the strength we need. The second kind of courage helps us to keep going, even when we're tired and the road ahead seems long. The Spirit is there to help us on the way.

Both kinds of courage are necessary. On Pentecost, the apostles faced a large, hostile crowd and still preached the Gospel. Later, Paul's mission took many years and required thousands of miles of traveling. In overcoming such hardships, he showed great courage. Both kinds of courage are necessary to live the Gospel, and the Spirit offers both through the gift of fortitude.

Fear of the Lord   Fear of the Lord was also discussed in Chapter 9. In the Israelite wisdom tradition, fear of the Lord meant awe and respect for God and commitment to the Covenant. These ideas are included in this gift, but the Spirit moves us beyond them to also feel an intense love for God. This kind of love is similar to what you feel for a parent, or for your favorite teacher or priest. You don't want to let them down in anything that you do. The "fear" you feel is not the fear of punishment, but the fear of causing disappointment.

Sin sometimes involves an injury to someone else, but it always injures our relationship with God. When we are motivated by fear of the Lord, we feel shame for sin most of all because we've strayed from the love and trust God offers us. We want forgiveness not because we fear God's anger, but because we want to repair our relationship. The Spirit gives us this intense love, and helps us to keep our love for God central to every decision we make.

Have You Considered?

1. Give an example of how "seeing things through God's eyes" is different from the way the world normally looks at things.
2. Have you ever had an experience where you simply "saw" that something had to be true? If so, describe it. If not, describe what you think such an experience might be like.
3. Describe an example you have personally witnessed of each of the two different kinds of fortitude.

Spiritual Reflection

Prayer to the Holy Spirit

Many great poets have expressed their love for the Holy Spirit. One of the most famous hymns to the Spirit is that of Brother Adam, who lived in the Abbey of Saint Victor near Paris in the twelfth century C.E. Adam was famous for his knowledge of Scripture and his use of it in his poems.

Use his "Hymn for the Feast of Pentecost" below as the basis for your prayer. Become quiet and ask the Spirit to enter you. Reflect on the gifts of the Spirit, thinking about how each could help you face the challenges in your life. When you feel ready, quietly pray the words of Brother Adam's poem:

You who come from the Father and the Son,
Equally from both, the Paraclete!
Give us eloquent speech,

And make our souls on fire for you
Through the flames you send.
The loved one of the Father and the Son,
Equal of both, companion and exact likeness of each:
Inspiring all, loving all,
Guiding the stars and moving the heavens,
Always the same.
Clear light, dear light,
Chase away the mists of my inner darkness.
The world and everything in it comes from you.
May you do away with sin,
And the stain sin leaves behind.

When you're finished, silently ask the Spirit's blessing.

Q/A

Section One
1. Who wrote the Book of Acts?
2. Who is the most important character in the Book of Acts?
3. What two doubts about early Christianity does Luke address?
4. Why was the conversion of Gentiles controversial?
5. List three ways in which the stories about Peter and Paul parallel each other.
6. Define: "god-fearer"
7. Describe Paul's early education and religious formation.
8. Describe Paul's three missionary journeys.

Section Two
1. When was the feast of Pentecost held?
2. What did Peter say in his sermon on Pentecost?
3. What is the central message of Acts?
4. What does Peter's vision in the Cornelius story mean?
5. What leads Peter to baptize the Gentiles?
6. Explain why it is historically possible for Paul to have had authority to arrest Christians as Luke says.
7. How does Paul's conversion show Luke's idea of discipleship?
8. What was the issue addressed by the Council of Jerusalem? What position does Peter take in this controversy?
9. Who is James? What does James say regarding Gentiles and the dietary laws?
10. List and describe the seven gifts of the Holy Spirit.

BIBLE ACTIVITIES

1. In Acts 8:26–40, Luke tells the story of the encounter between Philip and the Ethiopian. Read this story. Use the footnotes in your Bible to figure out where the scripture passage Philip quotes originated. Then, write an essay on how you would explain this passage to the Ethiopian.

2. Luke says that Paul always began in a new city by preaching to the Jews, but in almost every case they opposed him. Read the story of what happened to Paul in Thessalonica *(Acts 17:1–9)*. Then answer these questions: (a) What charge do the Jews bring against Paul? (b) Why would this charge be likely to get the attention of the Roman governor? (c) Is this charge true? Why or why not?

3. Paul gives several speeches in his own defense in the Book of Acts. Read the speech he gives to the Miletus elders in 20:17–35. Based on this speech, make a list of the charges against Paul which were known to Luke. Write an essay taking the position of a Jewish-Christian opposed to Paul, and include these charges.

GLOSSARY

- **Cornelius**: The first Gentile convert to Christianity, baptized by Peter.
- **Council of Jerusalem**: Meeting of the early Church in 49 C.E.; approval of the mission to the Gentiles.
- **Counsel**: Gift of the Holy Spirit; the ability to apply other gifts to practical situations.
- **Fear of the Lord**: Gift of the Holy Spirit; a love of God so intense that we are motivated to please God.
- **Fortitude**: Gift of the Holy Spirit; the courage to undertake difficult tasks and to persist in our commitments.
- **Glossolalia**: Ability, given by the Holy Spirit, to speak (or understand) in foreign languages or in mysterious tongues.
- **God-fearer**: A Gentile who respected the religious ideas and traditions of Judaism but who did not accept circumcision or other Jewish laws.
- **Inspire**: Literally means to fill with the Spirit.
- **Knowledge**: Gift of the Holy Spirit; helps us realize the true value of created things.
- **Pentecost**: The day on which the Spirit descended on the disciples and they began their mission of spreading the Gospel.
- **Piety**: Gift of the Holy Spirit; reverence for God and for one another.
- **Understanding**: Gift of the Holy Spirit; helps us accept revealed truths easily and deeply.
- **Wisdom**: Gift of the Holy Spirit; the ability to "see through God's eyes," to evaluate things as God sees them.

UNDERSTANDING MORE ABOUT:

Simon Magus

Chapter 8 of Acts describes a magician named Simon, whose abilities to perform tricks impressed the Samaritans. Although he had been baptized by Philip, Simon's desire was to acquire more power, not to reform his life.

When Peter and John blessed people after their baptism, they received the Holy Spirit. Simon, who had not received the Spirit following his baptism, offered the apostles money if they would give him this amazing power as well. Peter refused, saying that the Spirit was not for sale.

The word "simony" comes from this passage in Acts. Simony is the sin of buying or selling an office in the Church. According to tradition, Simon Magus, angered by the apostles' rejection, became a most difficult opponent for them. The *Acts of Peter,* a non-canonical Christian book, tells of a clash of powers between Simon and Peter at the Roman Forum, in which Peter triumphed.

The Teaching of Paul

Legend

● General History
● Regional History
● Christian History
● Books written

J avier was devastated when his father died. He remembered things they had done together: the fishing trips, baseball games, going for doughnuts on Saturday morning. When he first heard that his father had cancer, he didn't believe it. As things got worse, Javier slowly realized that his father wasn't going to get better. Nothing could prepare him for the shock he felt at the news of his father's death. Javier didn't know that it was possible to feel so much pain.

As time passed, Javier learned to live with the fact that his father was gone, but he didn't miss him any less. To live with his loss, Javier drove himself to make his father proud. A freshman in high school when his father died, Javier threw himself into his studies. He went on to excel in college and then in business school. After graduation, Javier quickly found an exciting job. Before long, he had a family of his own. He loved taking his children to visit their grandmother, who still lived in the house where Javier grew up.

On one such trip, after the children had gone to bed, Javier sat down to talk to his mother.

The other day, Helena asked why she had three grandparents and other kids in second grade had four. So I sat down with her and Enrique and started telling them about Papa.

Then, Helena wanted to know where he was born, and I didn't know, except in Mexico somewhere. I realized that after all these years of missing Papa, I still really don't know that much about him. What was he like as a young man? How did he build his business? Who were his friends? There are so many things I wonder.

His mother smiled, took him by the hand, and led him into the old study. "After your father died," she said, "I collected copies of everything I could find. It's all here in this storage box. These records will tell you much about him." With that, she handed Javier a stack of correspondence, and left the room.

Javier sat down at his father's desk and began to read. Some of the letter were written to his mother, some were for business, and others were to friends. There were even several "Letters to the Editor."

Javier learned that his father arrived in America from Jalisco, Mexico, where he had been born. His father didn't speak any English when he arrived in America, and went to night school to learn it. His father got a job working at a garage sweeping floors, working his way up to Head Mechanic, then built a thriving auto-parts business.

Javier also discovered that his father loved poetry, and had written several poems home to his wife during the Vietnam War. Javier had had no idea! His father also had strong political convictions, and had written to the local newspaper to protest city regulations frequently.

From these letters, Javier discovered much about who his father was. They confirmed the impression he had formed as a child of his father as being a strong, caring man. Now, it was Javier's turn to be proud. The next morning, Javier thanked his mother for showing him the letters. "Now I know who Papa was," he said, "and I feel closer to him than ever."

A Lasting Impression

Just as his father left a strong impression on Javier, the apostle Paul left a lasting impression on the early Church. To get to know Paul, we have to turn to his letters. In them, the personality and the ideas of the apostle are revealed in passionate, forceful language. In this chapter, you'll learn about the letters of Paul.

Letter-Writing and Paul's Mission

Monreale, St. Paul Preaches in the Synagogue. Twelfth Century.

You already know from Chapter 12 that Paul was a great missionary. As the "apostle to the Gentiles," Paul founded Christian churches throughout the Roman Empire. In this section, you'll study the external circumstances and Paul's own inner qualities that accounted for his success. This section also introduces you to the format used in these letters, and how Paul used letters as part of his mission.

Learning Objectives for Section One:

By the end of this section, you will be able to:

- Explain how the organization of the Roman Empire contributed to Paul's success.
- Describe Paul's gifts as a missionary.
- Discuss the format of Paul's letters.
- Understand the character of Paul's letters as part of his mission.

◆ Paul's Success as a Missionary

In the Acts of the Apostles, Luke tells us of Paul's success as a missionary. Luke emphasizes that the Holy Spirit was the driving force behind Paul's progress. An important factor in Paul's success, however, was Paul's willingness to carry out the Spirit's task.

Throughout the empire, Paul founded Christian communities who responded to the gospel message he carried. Through his letters, Paul continued to guide and inspire these communities even after he had moved on to another city. These communities prospered under Paul's leadership. Paul's letters continue to give direction to the Church even today.

The Roman World

When Paul began his missionary career, the Roman Empire was in many ways the ideal place for him to work. Paul's travels took him to locations in what are now the modern countries of Syria, Turkey, Macedonia, and Greece. On his second trip, he traveled approximately 1,800 miles, a distance more than one-half the width of North America. Paul made this journey several times in almost 20 years.

Paul was able to speak to people in a language they would understand. Wherever he traveled, he was initially accepted as a friend because he was Jewish. All of these factors contributed to Paul's success.

A Common Language   In Paul's day, almost everyone spoke Greek. The form spoken by most people was called *koine*, or "common" Greek. In cities, Greek was always used on the job and in politics. When Paul entered a city, he could preach in Greek and assume that he would be understood; this was an enormous advantage for a missionary who didn't have time to learn local languages.

Safe Travel   Conditions were perfect for Paul's mission. Before the Roman Empire, anyone who ventured onto the sea was in danger of being kidnapped by pirates, and travelers over the roads had to worry about thieves. The Roman army and navy did away

LEARN FROM THE MAP

The Roman Empire

Transportation around and across the Mediterranean Sea was generally easy and safe under Roman administration. The Romans called the Mediterranean "mare nostrum," or "our lake." Using the route marked on the map, trace the course Paul probably followed from Philippi to Thessalonica.

- What was the name of the route he used?
- Approximately how far would the trip have been? (scale: 1/3" = 100 miles)

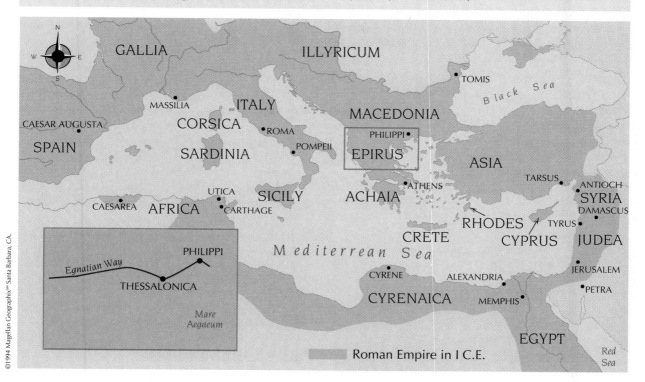

with most of these problems, making travel safe. This period of peace is known as the *Pax Romana*, or "Roman peace."

Under the Emperor Augustus, travelers did not need special papers to pass from one area to another. Certain tolls might be charged, but they had been significantly lowered under Augustus. A regular schedule of boat travel had been established across the Mediterranean. Paul also did not have to worry about encountering different laws as he moved about, since Roman law applied everywhere.

The Jewish Community   A third factor which contributed to Paul's success was the presence of Jewish communities in every large city. Paul knew that he could find lodging and work through them. He would also be allowed to preach in the synagogue. Even though most of the Jews would reject his message, he always made a handful of converts. These people, then, helped him reach out to the Gentiles in that city.

All of these conditions helped Paul's ministry succeed. However, it was Paul's unique personality that allowed him to use these conditions to spread the gospel "to the ends of the earth."

Paul's Character

Sometimes people think that when God calls someone to do a job, he or she has to change completely to carry it out. Although this may sometimes be true, it was not the case with Paul. Rarely has anyone been more perfectly suited to a vocation than Paul was to his missionary calling.

- Paul was raised a Jew and spoke Hebrew. He had instant access to Jewish communities.

- Paul knew Greek literature and spoke Greek fluently, so he was equally at home with Gentiles.
- Paul tailored his preaching specifically to each audience, guiding them in their growth.
- He was able to make his complex message understandable. He looked for practical solutions to immediate problems.
- Paul was a driven, energetic man. After his vision of Jesus, he devoted his life to helping people believe and live the Gospel.

Paul could speak with authority about the risen Christ, because Jesus had personally made him an apostle.

Paul's prayer life, might today be called mystical. He describes a few of his prayer experiences in 2 Corinthians 12:2–7. This profound spiritual experience gave him energy and a never-ending commitment to his mission. Paul's dedication—he never quit no matter what he encountered—can be attrib-

Unknown, Augustus Caesar, First Century B.C.E.

During the reign of Augustus Caesar, trade and travel flourished in the Roman Empire. This time of prosperity, the Pax Romana, made Paul's missionary journeys possible.

The Bible in Context

Roman Roads

One of the longest lasting physical remnants of the Roman Empire are its durable roads. In Paul's day, travel along these roads was safe, and, in some places, much more efficient than it is today. Some people, usually wealthy citizens or high government officials, traveled in carriages pulled by oxen, horses, or mules. Other travelers would ride on horseback. To travel by foot was a sign of poverty, or a commitment to a simple life. Paul may have made longer trips on horseback and shorter ones on foot. On the road, he would encounter travelers of all types: politicians, soldiers, traders, lawyers, and even tourists.

uted to his strong commitment to prayer, the heart of his relationship with Jesus.

Although his supporters often helped him, Paul did not take advantage of others. Because he had learned his family's leather goods trade (remember Luke calls Paul a tent-maker) as a young man, Paul earned a living while he did his missionary work.

Though other apostles traveled and founded Christian communities, none could match Paul's intellectual abilities or his success with the Gentiles. In Paul, God found the perfect tool to ensure the spread of the Christian faith.

Paul's Communities

When Paul arrived in a new city:

1. **He would head for the local synagogue.** There, Jewish tradition held that a visiting male should be invited to address the assembly. Paul used this opportunity to announce the Good News about Jesus. Reactions to Paul's message were usually mixed. Some immediately rejected it, while others wanted to hear more. A few even accepted faith in Jesus.
2. **The Jewish leadership would drive Paul out of the synagogue.**
3. **Paul would then take his message to the Gentiles.** He would preach outside the Gentile temples, in the marketplace, even in private homes.
4. **Paul would begin a local church.** Usually, this group of believers met in a private home. To have a house big enough to accommodate everyone, that person had to be fairly wealthy. This person generally became one of the leaders of the local church.

5. Paul would stay with the local group for a while before moving on. He stayed for varying amounts of time; he was in Corinth for over two years, but in other places he stayed only a few days.

When Paul was ready to go, he left "elders" in charge of the local community. These new leaders inherited a challenging situation. For one thing, their community was made up of Jews and Gentiles, who often did not get along. Also, if the community was located in a major city, new ideas and philosophies were common. These new ideas were often made part of the communities' belief in Jesus whether they were compatible with that faith or not. Finally, problems would occur that Paul had never discussed. Because Paul was no longer around to immediately resolve these matters, arguments developed that threatened to split the community apart.

When such problems arose, the elders appealed to Paul for directions. Paul responded to these requests by letter. His letters reveal his missionary and leadership abilities.

Have You Considered?

1. How similar were the conditions in the Roman Empire in Paul's time to conditions in America today? What are some important differences?
2. Which part of Paul's character do you think helped him most as a missionary? Why?
3. Why do you suppose the local Jewish leaders usually drove Paul out of the synagogue?

◆ Paul's Letters

Paul's success in making converts didn't mean that things always went smoothly in his new churches. To deal with problems as they came up, and to remind these Christians of the practical side of their faith, Paul wrote letters. Several of these letters were passed from church to church, and they eventually became part of the New Testament.

Generations of people have studied Paul's letters because of their rich personal advice to Christians, as well as their importance in Church history. In their studies, scholars have made important observations about their structure and content. These observations can help us better understand Paul's message.

The Letter Formula

Paul's education shows in his letters. He wrote in the proper Greek letter form, but adjusted this format to his own unique purpose. Paul's letters usually follow the following format:

1. Opening
- Paul identifies himself as the author, and indicates to whom the letter is addressed.
- Co-senders, usually fellow missionaries with Paul, are mentioned.
- Paul greets people, usually wishing them "grace and peace." This element is a combination of the customary Greek greeting ("grace") and the Jewish one ("peace").

2. Thanksgiving Here, Paul expresses his gratitude for the goodness shown to him in the past by the people to whom he is writing. He may also talk about how the community has made him proud by their growth in Christian living. When Paul is angry, he skips this stage entirely.

3. Message The bulk of the letter comes in this section. Usually, Paul divides what he has to say in two sections. The first is the doctrinal section, containing his ideas about the Father, Jesus, and the Church. The second section is instructional; Paul tells this community how it should live.

4. Conclusion At the end of his letter, Paul sometimes passes on personal news or advice for specific people. Sometimes he indicates that he has signed the letter in his own hand, to guarantee its legitimacy.

5. Final blessing Usually, Paul ends his letters with the blessing "May the grace of our Lord Jesus Christ be with you." Grace is one of the most important themes in Paul's thought.

The Genuine Letters of Paul

Paul's letters were so well received by the churches that they were shared between cities. Other authors imitated Paul's style or attributed letters to Paul so that their letters would be accepted by the churches as well. Although these letters were not written by Paul, they did represent his ideas. Over the course of time, however, some of these letters became identified as Paul's. Today, there is some confusion as to which of the "letters of Paul" in the New Testament were actually written by the apostle.

Catholic Bible scholars usually divide the letters into three categories:

- **Definitely written by Paul**: 1–2 Thessalonians, Galatians, Philemon, Philippians, 1–2 Corinthians, and Romans.

What do you say when you answer the telephone? Do you use a standard greeting? Paul, in his letters to the various communities he founded, usually began by wishing them grace and peace.

Scripture Workshop

The Letter Formula

Using the letter formula given in this section, outline Paul's letter to the Philippians. For the opening, conclusion, and final blessing, write down his actual words. For the thanksgiving and both parts of the message, write down the chapter and verse numbers where each section begins and ends.

- **Probably written by Paul**: Colossians and Ephesians.
- **Probably not written by Paul**: 1–2 Timothy, Titus, and Hebrews.

In addition to the genuine letters of Paul in the New Testament, we know that Paul wrote other letters. 1 Corinthians 5:9 refers to an earlier letter he had written to Corinth. 2 Corinthians 2:3–4 talks about a "letter of tears" which was written after 1 Corinthians but before 2 Corinthians. Further, some of the letters of Paul may combine two or more originally separate letters. For example, Chapter 16 of Romans may originally have been a separate letter to the church in Ephesus. Corinthians may include parts of several other letters as well.

By knowing which New Testament letters best represent Paul's own thoughts, we can be sure we're hearing his voice when we read them. By knowing Paul's style, we can notice when he makes certain points to a particular community. Such careful study helps us to understand Paul's meaning.

Have You Considered?

1. Why do you suppose Paul included Greek and Jewish elements in his greeting?
2. Based on what you know about how books were written in the ancient world, is it surprising that some letters not written by Paul were attributed to him? Why or why not?

◆ The Nature of Paul's Letters

Some people who read Paul's letters expect them to be like a careful philosophical essay, where all ideas are explained, all terms defined, and everything develops in a logical manner. Although this style might be boring, it would make everything easy to understand. Paul's letters, however, are never boring. They are usually written in response to a crisis in the local community, and they show all the signs of being hasty, spur-of-the-moment compositions. Even though his letters represent his best thinking about Christianity and the Church, Paul just didn't have time to pursue every argument or define every term. Knowing this about the letters makes a big difference in how we read them.

Addressed to Specific Situations

Paul's letters are "slices of life," reflecting his relationship with various churches. Paul speaks from his own experience and his knowledge of the Gospel, addressing issues faced by his communities. His words are meant to be immediately applied to people's problems, mistakes, and doubts. Paul's letters are never formal or abstract; they are concrete and immediate.

The letters are part of an ongoing conversation between Paul and his communities. Sometimes this creates problems for us, because Paul refers to ideas

Paul did most of his travel using the famous Roman roads. Paul most likely traveled on foot, although he could have traveled on horseback, by donkey, or in a carriage.

or events familiar to his community but not to us. For example, 2 Thessalonians reminds the reader of Paul's teaching about a "man of lawlessness." Unfortunately, we don't know what he taught, so it's hard to know what Paul meant.

A more frequent difficulty is with Paul's writing style. Paul wrote (or dictated) spontaneously and with great passion. These qualities make his letters seem alive even today, but they can sometimes be frustrating to read. Paul doesn't always follow a line of thought carefully, and sometimes he'll mix up one argument with something entirely different. His language can be difficult to understand, because he sometimes uses unfamiliar terms, and other times he gives terms his own unique meanings without fully explaining what they are.

Moreover, in his letters, Paul often defends himself or his message from attacks. We don't know what these attacks were, since all we have is Paul's response to them. However, Paul isn't impossible to understand; in most cases, Paul speaks clearly and directly. We simply have to pay careful attention to make sure we understand what Paul is saying.

The Letters Give General Principles

It will help our understanding if we remember that Paul wrote in a different time and place, with different cultural rules and assumptions. This creates problems when people attempt to apply what Paul says to our own time. We have to look for the general principle in what Paul says rather than his specific instructions.

For example, Paul says in 1 Corinthians 11:4–6 that at church meetings, a man must always pray with his head uncovered, while a woman must have her head covered. This rule actually has nothing to do with the value of prayer. Instead, it reflects the culture of Paul's day. People considered it immodest and provocative for a woman's head to be uncovered in public. Paul's point was not that it is necessary for a woman to cover her head to be heard by God. Rather, he means that Christians should not upset their neighbors by behaving in ways that will offend them. Today, Western society no longer finds it offensive for women's hair to be visible (although many Islamic cultures still follow this practice), so it's not important whether it's covered in church or not.

The principle found in this passage is that Christians should respect other's feelings. This principle is timeless and applies equally well in any cultural situation. The concrete instruction Paul derives from this principle, however, does not. We need to look for these general principles in Paul and not be distracted by specific rules that no longer make sense in our own culture.

Written under the inspiration of the same Holy Spirit that guided the growth of the early Church, Paul's letters are relevant to Christians of every generation. Through careful study, we can hear in these letters the voice of the apostle, sharing the Gospel and inviting us to join him on a journey of faith. Paul's letters can also help us in very practical ways to become better Christians and better people. When we read these letters, we recapture the excitement and sense of discovery of the early Christians, and in so doing, renew our own faith and our commitment to living a life centered on the Gospel.

Have You Considered?

1. Imagine hearing only one side of a telephone conversation. What would the problems be in understanding what was said?
2. Describe a time when you had to write an important letter to someone. What was the situation? How did things turn out?
3. The general principle we found in the passage from 1 Corinthians is that Christians should behave in ways that don't offend their neighbors. What would be a specific application of that principle be today?

Paul's Timeless Themes

Paul's letters were addressed to communities experiencing very concrete struggles. To answer those specific situations, Paul offered basic themes on (a) how Christians should live, (b) the need for unity among Christians, (c) freedom from the Law and from sin, and (d) the grace given through Jesus' death.

These themes run through all of Paul's writings, and they are as important for us today as they were for his missionary communities almost 2,000 years ago. In this section, you'll study these themes as they appear in Paul's letters to four churches: Thessalonians, Galatians, Corinthians, and Romans.

Learning Objectives for Section Two

By the end of this section, you will be able to:

- Explain Paul's views on Christian living.
- Discuss Paul's teaching on the Law.
- Explain what Paul says about right relations with God.
- Understand the relevance of Paul's themes to Christian living.

◆ The Thessalonian Letters

Paul's earliest letter is 1 Thessalonians, probably written in 51 C.E. Both 1 and 2 Thessalonians reflect the situation in the Thessalonian church, and give us a glimpse of Paul's relationship with this community. In these letters, we see Paul's first important theme: the need for Christians to live moral lives.

The Church in Thessalonica

Thessalonica was a seaport in the north of Greece and the capital of the province of Macedonia. Geographically, it was important because it was situated on the *Via Egnatia*, the main road connecting the eastern portion of the empire to the west. Paul's visit there probably lasted several months.

Paul shows great affection for the community at Thessalonica. He says:

For what is our hope or joy or crown to boast of in the presence of our Lord Jesus at his coming if not you yourselves? For you are our glory and joy.
(1 Thessalonians 2:19–20)

In this spirit of mutual love, Paul reminds the Thessalonians that his assistant Timothy has just brought news to him of their faith and love. Paul tells the Thessalonians that he longs to see them.

The Parousia

This does not mean that things were perfect among the new Christians in Thessalonica. Disputes had come up, and Paul was needed to settle them. One important controversy was over the second coming of Jesus, a doctrine called the *parousia* (a Greek word which means "presence").

Early Christians believed that Jesus would come again soon to judge people and to establish the kingdom of God in all its fullness. This idea was an important part of early Christian preaching. New Christians looked forward to the parousia with eagerness and excitement. They hoped for the end of this age, when they were a small, persecuted minority. More importantly, they looked forward to meeting Jesus. Soon, the idea of the second coming began to dominate the Thessalonian Church. Questions and disagreements about it, however, began to divide the church. Paul addressed this conflict.

What About the Dead? The Thessalonians worried about what would happen to the members of their community who had already died. Would they be included in the kingdom? Paul assured them that both the living and the dead will join Jesus on the great day to come.

> *For the Lord himself, with a word of command, with the voice of an archangel and with the trumpet of God, will come down from heaven, and the dead in Christ will rise first. Then we who are alive, who are left, will be caught up together with them in the clouds to meet the Lord in the air. Thus we shall always be with the Lord. Therefore, console one another with these words.*
>
> (1 Thessalonians 4:16–17)

Through these vivid images, Paul reassured the community that all its members, living and dead, share in the love of Christ. In fact, death makes no difference at all; once joined to Christ, a person belongs to him forever.

When Will Jesus Return? Excited by Paul's description of the coming day, many Thessalonians wanted to know when to expect Jesus' return. Paul told them that no one knows the precise date, but that God's purposes are certain. The important thing is knowing that it will happen. Not satisfied, some Thessalonians concluded that the parousia was coming any day, and quit their jobs to wait. The second letter has to lay down the law: "if anyone was unwilling to work, neither should that one eat." (2 *Thessalonians* 3:10).

Moral Living

Paul said that the proper way to prepare for the parousia is to live a life worthy of approval by Christ. To do that, Christians should always live moral, loving lives. Our energies should go into preparing for Jesus, rather than worrying about when he will come.

Many Gentiles found this to be an unfamiliar message, since Greek and Roman religion generally did not make any connection between one's religious belief and moral behavior. Paul stressed repeatedly that being Christian meant living a life centered on the Gospel.

> *This is the will of God, your holiness: that you refrain from immorality, that each of you know how to acquire a wife for himself in holiness and honor, not in lustful passion as do the Gentiles who do not know God; not to take advantage of or exploit a brother in this matter, for the Lord is an avenger in all these things, as we told you before and solemnly affirmed. For God did not call us to impurity but to holiness. Therefore, whoever disregards this, disregards not a human being but God, who [also] gives his holy Spirit to you.*
>
> (1 Thessalonians 4:3–8)

Paul urged the Thessalonians to do good, because God wills it and in preparation for Jesus' return. This message is as important for us today as it was for the Thessalonians. Paul reminds us that being Christian is not just a matter of going to Church. It also means living responsible moral lives, centered first on love of God and next on love of others.

Unknown, Bacchus, Second Century B.C.E.?

Moral conduct was not a part of the Greek or Roman religions. The Romans, in fact, worshipped the god Bacchus by drinking great amounts of wine and overeating.

Have You Considered?

1. Using your imagination, what do you think the parousia will be like? How do you envision judgment taking place?
2. Suppose you met someone who had just become a Christian, and she asked you what Paul meant by saying that Christians must lead moral lives. What would you say?

◆ The Letter to the Galatians

In Galatians, we see a very different side of Paul's personality. In the Thessalonian letters, Paul was like a proud father gently urging his children to make further progress. In Galatians, Paul is clearly angry, and his words are blistering. He is responding to charges made against him after he left the community, and he can't understand how the Galatians could question him or his message so soon after his departure. In Paul's most forceful letter, the apostle firmly restates his message to refute his critics and remove any doubt the Galatians might have.

The Churches in Galatia

Unlike Thessalonians, the Letter to the Galatians is probably not directed to a single community. Instead, it is written for a group of churches in the area of Asia Minor called "Galatia." You may remember from Chapter 12 that on each of his missionary journeys, Paul passed through this area, so the communities here probably saw more of Paul than any others. This fact may account for part of Paul's anger.

The people of Galatia were actually not Greeks at all, even though they spoke the language. They were "Gauls," Germanic tribes from the north who had been accepted into the empire. They were known for their courage and enthusiasm. They also seemed to have had trouble making a lasting commitment, explaining, in part, Paul's frustration with them.

The Gentiles and the Law

After Paul had left the Galatian churches, some other Christian missionaries arrived in the area. These missionaries were apparently Jewish-Christians, perhaps members of the Pharisee party. They insisted that the Gentile Galatian converts circumcised and obey the other laws of Moses as part of their conversion to Christianity. While some Galatians were persuaded by these arguments, Paul angrily rejected them.

Paul reminded the Galatians of what had happened in 49 C.E., when he and Barnabas went to Jerusalem to meet with the other apostles. He tells them that the apostles approved making Gentiles full members of the Christian community without forcing them to obey the Jewish law (See Acts 15:1–21).

Paul then tells of another incident not recorded in Acts. Paul says that after the Council, Peter went to Antioch and ate with the Gentile Christians there. When Jewish-Christians from Jerusalem arrived and complained about the practice, Peter pulled back. Paul then rebuked Peter:

> *If you who are a Jew are living according to Gentile ways rather than Jewish, by what logic do you force the Gentiles to adopt Jewish ways?*
>
> (Galatians 2:14)

Paul asserts throughout Galatians that both Jews and Gentiles have salvation because of Jesus' death on the cross, not because of the Law. For that reason, Paul asserts, it is unnecessary for Gentiles to become Jewish. Jews may follow the Law, because it is their custom, but they have no right to force it on the Gentiles.

Unknown, *Sacrifice to the Gods*, First Century C.E.

In Roman worship, animals sacrificed to the gods were then eaten by the worshippers. Whether or not Christians could eat food sacrificed to the gods was a question addressed by Paul in 1 Corinthians 8.

Scripture Workshop

The Letter to the Galatians

Review the format for Paul's letters covered earlier in this chapter. Then, read Galatians 1. Answer the following questions:

- Which element of the format is missing?
- With what does Paul replace it?
- What does this tell you about the tone of the letter?

Abraham, the Father of the Gentiles

Paul uses the example of Abraham to make his case that the Gentiles are justified before God, apart from the Law. His Jewish-Christian opponents would of course have to admit that Abraham, the father of the Hebrew people, was someone who was acceptable to God. Paul then posed the question, Was Abraham justified through the Law? Obviously, the answer had to be "No," since Abraham lived hundreds of years before Moses and the gift of the Law on Mount Sinai. Paul says that if Abraham could enter a relationship with God apart from the Law, then so can the Gentiles.

Paul further asserts that the Old Testament predicted that Abraham would become the father of the Gentiles who are justified through faith.

Scripture, which saw in advance that God would justify the Gentiles by faith, foretold the good news to Abraham, saying "Through you shall all nations be blessed." Consequently, those who have faith are blessed along with Abraham, who had faith.

(Galatians 3:7–9)

Through all of this, Paul does not mean that the Law is not good, or that Jews are wrong to obey it. He simply insists that adhering to the Law is not necessary to be a good Christian, and therefore the Galatians are wrong to insist that the Gentiles accept it.

Slaves No Longer

Paul compares the function of the Law to that of a household slave whose responsibility was to educate and discipline children. Paul says that Christians no longer need the Law in this way, because they have been freed from it by Christ. Similarly, the Gentiles were slaves to the power of sin, but they, too, have been freed. From this point forward, Paul says, both Jew and Gentile should live as free people, no longer as slaves.

Called to a Higher Standard   Living as a free person does not mean living without rules. Paul emphasizes, as he did in Thessalonians, that Christians are called to a high standard of action. Christian freedom is the freedom to live as brothers and sisters, knowing that all are united with Jesus in faith.

For all of you who were baptized into Christ have clothed yourselves with Christ. There is neither Jew nor Greek, there is neither slave nor free person, there is not male and female; for you are all one in Christ Jesus.

(Galatians 3:27–28)

Meaning of Freedom   Christian freedom is another of Paul's great themes. Because of Jesus, Christians live in a new world, one in which sin no longer separates them from the full love of God. Christians are no longer under the power of sin, and can love one another fully and honestly.

What is Christian freedom? It is both a freedom **from** sin and a freedom **to** love. Most importantly, freedom is possible. For Paul, before Christ, human beings could not live as God asks, because the power of sin was too strong. Jesus delivered us from this power, and we now are free to love God. Despite all the forces and influences the world throws our way, Christian freedom allows us to act as children of God.

Have You Considered?

1. Put yourself in the position of Paul's Jewish-Christian opponents in Galatia. What arguments might you make to support your position that Gentile converts had to be circumcised? How does Paul, in his letter, respond to these arguments?
2. What do you suppose Paul meant when he said that before Jesus, the Gentiles had been "slaves to sin"?

◆ The Letters to Corinth

Although there are two letters to the Corinthians in the New Testament, Paul probably wrote more than that to them. Paul spent two years among the Corinthians, and the community there had a special place in his heart. The first letter is Paul's response to unhappy news about what was going on in Corinth. The love and concern he felt for the Christians there is readily apparent.

The Corinthian community faced special challenges, many stemming from the city in which they lived. Corinth was one of the largest and most important cities in the Roman Empire. It was a major center for trade, so people were constantly moving. New philosophies and religious beliefs repeatedly swept through the city. Further, Corinthian citizens had a reputation for immoral behavior. The Greek verb "to corinthize" means to engage in sexual immorality. The city had more brothels and taverns than any other city in the empire. Given these forces competing for the people's attention, it's not surprising that several problems came up.

Competing Factions

There were quarreling factions within the Corinthian church. One cause of the fights seems to have been that people were claiming intense allegiance to different Christian leaders, such as Paul or another disciple named Apollos. It would be as if today some Christians claimed to follow Mother Theresa, while others followed Oscar Romero.

Paul does not object to the Corinthians admiring good leaders, but apparently they were saying things like "I'm better because I belong to Paul," or "I'm better because Apollos baptized me." Paul frowned on such childish rivalry. If loyalty to a particular teacher distracts you from your first loyalty to Christ, your allegiance is likewise misplaced.

Claims to Wisdom

Some individuals in the community acted with superiority, claiming to have received a higher knowledge. In Greek, the term for this special knowledge is *gnosis*. "Gnostics," people who claimed to have secret knowledge about the heavens, were common in the Roman Empire. Some Corinthians had combined gnostic ideas with their faith in Jesus.

Paul didn't directly say that the gnostics were wrong. Instead, he pointed out the difference between human wisdom and the wisdom that comes from God. Paul showed that worldly wisdom is not the same as God's wisdom. He used the case of the crucifixion of Christ to make this point.

Logically, how could a crucified man do anything for anyone? According to conventional wisdom, Jesus was powerless to help anybody. Nevertheless, the Corinthians had experienced changes in their lives because of their faith in Jesus. Since Jesus was cruci-

Paul stayed with the community in Corinth for over two years. His letters back to the community addressed issues of jealousy, Gnostic beliefs, morality, the importance of the Eucharist, and the need for the community to be one.

Some of the Christians in Corinth behaved at the Eucharist as if it were a common party. In his response to this problem, Paul retells the story of the Last Supper.

fied according to the wisdom of God, Paul says that "God's folly is wiser than men" (1 *Corinthians* 1:25), and therefore arguments over which Christians are the wisest make no sense. Paul concludes:

> *God chose the foolish of the world to shame the wise, and God chose the weak of the world to shame the strong, and God chose the lowly and despised of the world, those who count for nothing, to reduce to nothing those who are something, so that no human being might boast before God. . . . "Whoever boasts should boast in the Lord."*

(1 Corinthians 1:26–28,31)

Immorality

In view of the general situation in Corinth, it's not surprising that Paul should have to reaffirm his views on moral living. For one thing, incest of varying degrees was practiced by certain Corinthian Christians, along with many other kinds of immoral behavior, including:

- Robbery
- Drunkenness
- Adultery
- Idolatry

Paul not only rejects such behavior, but says the community should be responsible for the behavior of its members. Christians should be helped by love and correction, but if they persist in wrongdoing, Paul says they should be expelled from the community.

The Eucharist

Early Christians often met together for a common meal before they celebrated the formal Eucharist. This common meal was often called the "agape," or "love feast." In Corinth, some Christians treated the agape like a common party, drinking wine until they were drunk. As a result, they could not celebrate the Eucharist properly. Then, as now, the Eucharist was intended to honor Christ, but these people were fighting, rushing to their food, and causing chaos.

In response, Paul wrote the earliest record we have of Jesus' words at the Last Supper (probably around 55 C.E.). This passage is found in 1 Corinthians 11:17–34. Given the special character of the Eucharist as a time to remember and honor Jesus, Paul demands that the Corinthians behave appropriately.

Christian Unity

Underlying all these other problems, Paul saw one major challenge: the need for Christian unity. Quarreling, boasting, immorality and poor behavior at the Eucharist were all signs that the Corinthians weren't living as a true community, working for the good of all. Paul says that Christ is present in the whole community, all the Christians together. Splitting the unity of the membership, Paul says, is a sin against Christ.

To make his point about the importance of unity, Paul uses the famous analogy of the body. The Christian community, Paul says, is the body of Christ. If the toe were gone, the whole body would be in trouble. Conversely, the toe has no life apart from the body. Therefore, the community needs each member, and each member needs the community. God gives different gifts to different people, Paul says, but all these gifts are of equal value in keeping the community whole.

Unity is the third great theme in Paul's letters. Paul says that all members of the community should make unity their highest goal:

> *If [one] part suffers, all the parts suffer with it; if one part is honored, all the parts share its joy.*

(1 Corinthians 12:26)

Have You Considered?

1. Do you think there are factions in the Church today, as in ancient Corinth? Why or why not?
2. Do you agree with Paul that unity is the answer to all the other problems of the community? Do you think that many of the world's problems would be lessened if we all lived as a community? Why or why not?

◆ The Letter to the Romans

When Paul wrote to Rome, he was writing to a community he had neither founded nor visited, although he did know some people there. In Romans 16, he greets a number of people by name, including Prisca and Aquila. Even so, this is not his community. Instead, he is expressing his joy at being able to visit them for the first time.

Since Romans is a letter of introduction rather than a response to a specific crisis, it is Paul's most carefully developed writing. He wants to explain his message to the Romans before he arrives.

Romans is a very complex letter. In it, Paul expresses his understanding of Jesus and the Christian message. Sometimes his reasoning is not easy to follow. You may have difficulty understanding it as you read it for the first time. You will want to return to Romans repeatedly in your life to gain a deeper understanding of its message.

Conflict between Gentiles and Jews

You already know about the tensions between Jewish-Christians and Gentile-Christians. Jewish-Christians in Rome continued to insist that Gentiles must obey the Law of Moses and all of its interpretations. Paul responds to this by concentrating on how a person enters into a right relationship with God. Paul used the words "righteousness," "justification," and "justice" to express this relationship.

For Jews, the answer to the question, What makes us acceptable to God? was fulfilling the demands of the Law. Paul pointed out that there are simply too many commands, and no human can keep them all perfectly.

If the Law can't make us acceptable to God, then, what can? Paul's answer is simple: God makes us acceptable through "grace" which we receive through faith in Christ.

The Grace of God

According to Paul, "All have sinned and are deprived of the glory of God" (*Romans* 3:23). For imperfect human beings, it is impossible to **earn** a right relationship with God. God must give it to us. God's gift depends, not on our behavior, but on our faith. God offers us the gift of faith, and when we accept it, we are "justified." Then we may enjoy a proper relationship with God. This justification comes to us as a free gift, and has nothing to do with whether we "deserve" it on the basis of our behavior.

This gift springs from God's unconditional love for all people. Paul saw it most clearly in Jesus who freely gave of his life. Paul called God's free gift,

Shrines and statues to all of the gods could be found in the Pantheon in Rome. It was in a similar pantheon in Athens that Paul claimed the "unnamed god" as the God which he proclaimed.

People of Note

Prisca and Aquila

Among the people Paul sends greetings to in his letter to the Romans are those who meet in the house church of Prisca and Aquila. This couple is mentioned six times in the New Testament. They worked alongside Paul in the leather trade in Corinth before moving to Rome.

Prisca and Aquila may have been slaves of a Roman family who managed to buy their own freedom. As the leaders of a house church in Rome, their worldly status had risen greatly. Under Roman law, however, freed slaves still owed loyalty to their masters, and Prisca and Aquila risked angering them by openly practicing Christianity.

Interestingly, Paul always mentions the female name, Prisca, first, suggesting that her importance in the Church surpassed that of her husband, a degree of equality unusual for that time.

"grace," meaning that it happens without cost to us. A right relationship with God is the most profound and beautiful gift possible. Paul sums up his argument this way:

> Therefore, since we have been justified by faith, we have peace with God through our Lord Jesus Christ, through whom we have gained access [by faith] to this grace in which we stand, and we boast in hope for the glory of God. . . . How much more then, since we are now justified by his blood, will we be saved through him from the wrath. Indeed, if while we were enemies, we were reconciled to God through the death of his Son, how much more once reconciled, will we be saved by his life.

(Romans 5:1–2,9–10)

Living in Grace

Paul says our behavior has nothing to do with our justification; there's nothing we can do to deserve it. Because God has chosen to freely give us justification, when we accept this gift we should respond by honoring God in the way we live. After Christians have received justification, they still grow actively in living the Gospel. The basic challenge to that growth is sin, and the way we overcome it is grace.

Sin, Paul said, came into the world through one person's disobedience (Adam), and this act brought death. Through the obedience of Christ, grace has now entered the world, bringing life. Because we now live in grace, Paul says, our actions take on a special importance. We want to strive to love God and one another totally, because God's grace offers total love to us. In fact, we are the adopted children of God, and

This plastic reconstruction of ancient Rome can be found in the Rome Museum of Civilization. Paul's missionary journeys ended in Rome where he was martyred during the persecutions of Nero in 65 C.E.

we inherit everything Christ was and has. Whatever troubles Christians may have to go through are nothing compared with the wonders they will experience when they are perfected in Christ's glory. Through the grace given by the Holy Spirit, Christians can live in total confidence that God will be with them always. Grace is Paul's fourth major theme. Paul's concept of grace sums up his understanding of God as merciful, patient, and most of all, completely loving.

We have looked at four major themes in Paul's teaching:

- The importance of moral living
- Freedom from the Law and from sin
- Christian unity
- The grace of God

Taken together, these four themes point the way to proper Christian living, and give us confidence that we can meet its demands. Paul's letters have inspired generations of Christians to deepen their faith and to grow in love of God and each other. If we read them with patience and prayer, they can do the same for us.

Have You Considered?

1. Do you agree with Paul that it is impossible for anyone to keep the Law absolutely perfectly? Why or why not?
2. Where have you heard the word "grace" before? What does it mean to you? How close is your understanding to the way Paul used the word?
3. Assume you have a friend who worries about whether she'll be saved by God. Using the idea of grace as expressed in Romans, how would you reassure her?

Spiritual Reflection

The Love of God

Paul spoke often of the love God offers us through Christ. In 1 Corinthians, Paul described what the love of God is like. For your spiritual reflection in this chapter, pray that God's love may enter you and guide you, using this passage as the focus for your prayer.

Go to a quiet place, and take a few moments to ask God to share his love with you. Then, read the following passages from 1 Corinthians.

Love is patient, love is kind. It is not jealous, [love] is not pompous, it is not inflated, it is not rude, it does not seek its own interests, it is not quick-tempered, it does not brood over injury, it does not rejoice over wrongdoing but rejoices with the truth. It bears all things, believes all things, hopes all things, endures all things.

(1 Corinthians 13:4–7)

Consider each phrase of the passage. Evaluate your own behavior using Paul's words. How can your life be changed by love?

When you are finished praying this passage, move on to the next part of 1 Corinthians.

Love never fails. If there are prophecies, they will be brought to nothing, if tongues, they will cease, if knowledge, it will be brought to nothing. For we know partially and we prophesy partially, but when the perfect comes, the partial will pass away. When I was a child, I used to talk as a child, think as a child, reason as a child; when I became a man, I put aside childish things. At present we see indistinctly, as in a mirror, but then face to face. At present I know partially; then I shall know fully as I am fully known. So faith, hope, love remain, these three; but the greatest of these is love.

(1 Corinthians 13:8–13)

As you pray this passage, ask God to reveal to you how you need to grow in love. Reflect on each verse, stopping when you feel the need. When you're finished, thank God for this time together, and then go on with your day.

Q/A

Section One

1. What was the universal language in the eastern Roman Empire?
2. How many languages were spoken by most people in the eastern empire?
3. Why was Paul equally at home with Jews and Gentiles?
4. How could Paul speak with authority about the risen Jesus?
5. What was Paul's trade?
6. What did Paul do first when he entered a new city?
7. Describe the format of Paul's letters.
8. How did books not written by Paul come to be ascribed to him?
9. Are Paul's letters careful literary works? Explain.
10. Why is it a problem for us that Paul's letters represent one side of a conversation?
11. In reading Paul's letters, should we look for general principles or specific instructions? Why?

Section Two

1. Which letter was Paul's earliest?
2. What questions did Paul answer about the parousia?
3. What is the connection between the parousia and Christian living?
4. Who were the Galatians?
5. What problems does Paul's letter to the Galatians address?
6. Describe Paul's confrontation with Peter in Antioch.
7. Explain Paul's argument about the Gentiles and Abraham.
8. What does Paul mean by "Christian freedom."
9. What were the special challenges faced by the church in Corinth?
10. What was Paul's teaching about true wisdom?
11. Explain Paul's analogy of the body.
12. What was Paul's reason for writing the letter to the Romans?
13. Define "grace."
14. According to Paul, can someone earn a right relationship with God? Why or why not?

BIBLE ACTIVITIES

1. In 1 Corinthians 14:20–33, Paul addresses an issue that has occurred in Corinth. The problem concerns glossolalia, the gift of speaking in tongues. Read this passage and answer the following questions:
   - What is the problem Paul is concerned with?
   - What does Paul say is the purpose of speaking in tongues?
   - What concerns Paul about the Corinthians' behavior?
   - How does Paul say speaking in tongues should be handled?

2. Some scholars have suggested that Chapter 16 of Romans was originally separate from the rest of the letter. Read chapters 15 and 16 of Romans together, referring to Paul's letter format as discussed in Section One of this chapter. Why might people think that Chapter 16 was a separate letter?

3. In Galatia, Paul not only had to respond to the arguments of the Jewish-Christian missionaries about Gentiles and the Law, he also had to defend himself against their charges. One such charge appears in Galatians 1:6–10. What is the charge in this passage? Based on what you know about Paul's teachings on Gentiles and the Law, why do you think this particular charge was made against him?

4. In Romans 7, Paul explains his view about the purpose of the Law. Read that passage and answer the following questions:

   - Does Paul think the Law is good or bad?
   - What negative consequences did the Law bring?
   - How did the Law bring these consequences?
   - What happened to the Law because of Christ?

GLOSSARY

- **Elders**: Local leaders left in charge of a church community after Paul left.
- **Final Blessing:** Last element in Paul's letter format.
- **Freedom:** Christian freedom is both a freedom from sin and a freedom to give oneself totally in love.
- **Gnosis:** Greek word for "knowledge."
- **Grace:** God's free gift.
- **Greeting:** First element of Paul's letter format.
- **House Church:** Meeting place for early Christians, usually the home of a wealthy members.
- **Justification:** Right relationship with God, made possible by the death of Jesus.
- **Koine:** "Common" Greek spoken by most citizens of the eastern portion of the Roman empire.
- **Pax Romana:** "Roman peace."
- **Righteousness:** A term for a right relationship with God.
- **Thanksgiving:** Element in Paul's letter format in which Paul expresses his pride and gratitude to his community.

UNDERSTANDING MORE ABOUT:

Paul and Happiness

Early Christians loved Jesus because believing in him and living his way brought them great joy—so much joy, in fact, that sometimes they went to their deaths singing. Paul's letter to the Philippians resounds with great happiness.

This letter is a thank you note that Paul wrote to his friends in Philippi *(Philippians 4:10–14)*. Paul was in jail for preaching, and the Christians in Philippi had sent him gifts. He writes to them with obvious affection. He delights in them. Then in Philippians 4:4–9, Paul encourages them to be happy, to be joyful. He reminds them not to be nervous about life, but to ask God gratefully for everything they need. Then he tells them how to think, so, that peace and happiness will be theirs:

> Whatever is true . . . honorable . . . just . . . pure . . . lovely . . . gracious; if there is any excellence . . . anything worthy of praise, think about these things. . . . Then the God of peace will be with you.
>
> (Philippians 4:8–9)

This is Paul's prescription for joy: love Christ, rejoice in the Christian life, and think about wonderful things. Happiness will be yours then, in every circumstance.

Christianity Develops Roots

Legend

● World History
● Regional History
● Biblical History
● Books written

Robert LaFollette. 1855–1925.

R obert LaFollette was a brilliant speaker; it was said that he could enter a room full of people completely opposed to everything he stood for, and before he left they'd be cheering for him at the top of their lungs. He was first a member of the United States House of Representatives, and then the Governor of Wisconsin. Later, he served as a United States Senator, and, in 1924, ran for President.

But LaFollette is best remembered for his ideas. He championed the interests of the common people—the farmers and the industrial laborers. As Governor, LaFollette based his administration on what he called the "Wisconsin Idea," a program for ensuring decent wages and protecting the rights of workers. Later, as a Senator and a presidential candidate, LaFollette argued that these policies should apply to the entire country. To accomplish this, LaFollette said the government should regulate private wealth and use it for the public good.

Millions of Americans supported LaFollette. When he found that the Republican Party did not share his ideas, LaFollette and others formed the Progressive Party. For a while, it looked as if this third political party would stand on its own and compete with the Republicans and Democrats. With LaFollette at its head, they couldn't miss! Then, unexpectedly, LaFollette died in 1925. With him, the Progressive Party died as well. An attempt was made to revive the party in 1948, but its presidential candidate got fewer than a million votes, and it faded quietly into history.

What happened? Why did the Progressive Party come to such a quick end? The problem wasn't with its ideas, because much of LaFollette's program became law under President Franklin D. Roosevelt in the 1930s. So why did the party die? Most historians think it died because the Progressives grew so rapidly, and were successful so quickly that they never took time to build an organization. They went from campaign to campaign without preparing for the future. They didn't establish any local chapters or local leaders. The entire movement depended upon LaFollette personally. The party fell apart when he died. The Progressives had assumed that LaFollette's charisma would be enough. It wasn't.

The Early Church

Like the Progressive Party, many movements fade away after early triumphs because they never prepared for the future. The movement is unprepared for difficult times and, unable to respond to the challenge, breaks apart. Movements that last recognize when it's time to organize their ideas and structure its chain-of-command in order to address any problems that occur.

At the end of the first century, Christianity faced the need to establish roots. Christian missionaries, especially Paul, had achieved spectacular successes, and Christian communities thrived everywhere in the Roman Empire. However, these communities were young and unsure of the future. There were many internal arguments about who was in charge now that the apostles had died. Arguments erupted about how to interpret the teachings they had been given. These early communities also were being persecuted by the Roman government.

For Christianity to survive, it required new leadership after the death of the apostles, and a clarification of its basic teachings. Christians facing persecution also needed hope and consolation. The last several books in the New Testament, from Hebrews to Revelation, responded to these challenges.

Building for the Future

Rome, Catacomb of Priscilla. First Century?

The destruction of the Temple in 70 C.E., caused Christianity to begin its final move away from Judaism. Arguments between Christian and Jewish groups grew angrier. Because of these arguments, Rome recognized Christianity as a new and illegal religion, different from Judaism which was legal.

These changes produced many questions in the new Christian churches: how to respond to opposition from both Jews and Romans; how to settle arguments over teaching; how to maintain unity among various Christian communities? In this section, you'll study some of the ways Christianity responded to these challenges.

Learning Objectives for Section One

By the end of this section, you will be able to:

- Explain how the early Church developed the offices of deacon, presbyter, and bishop.
- Discuss the challenge of preserving apostolic teaching.
- Describe the nature of Roman persecution.

◆ Church Offices

In its earliest days, the apostles led the Christian community. Their authority came from their closeness to Jesus: they received his teaching directly. When disputes arose, the apostles resolved them, as at the Council of Jerusalem in 49 C.E. By the end of the first century C.E., however, most of the apostles had died. Peter and Paul died in the 60s in Rome. Tradition says that John was the last of the apostles, dying in the 90s. With their passing, new leaders for the Church had to be chosen with the authority to settle disputes and guide Christianity into the future. Several offices developed in response to these needs.

Deacons

The word *deacon* comes from the Greek term "diakonos," meaning "servant." We first hear of the office of deacon in the Book of Acts. Luke says that the growth of the church in Jerusalem was so rapid that the apostles were overwhelmed with the demands on their time and attention. They asked the community to appoint seven men who would care for the poor and distribute the community's resources. Luke describes the selection of the deacons:

> *The proposal was acceptable to the whole community, so they chose Stephen, a man filled with faith and the Holy Spirit, also Philip, Prochorus, Nicanor, Timon, Parmenas, and Nicholas of Antioch, a convert to Judaism. They presented these men to the apostles who prayed and laid hands on them.*
>
> (Acts 6:5–6)

Because of their Greek names, scholars believe the first deacons were all Hellenists. As you know from Chapter 12, the Hellenists left Jerusalem and spread the Gospel after Stephen was stoned to death by people angry at his teachings about the Temple. Philip, in Chapter 8 of Acts, makes an Ethiopian convert. These events show that the role of the deacons expanded to include preaching and teaching in addition to caring for the poor.

Deacons are also mentioned several times in the letters, including references to several women deacons (See Romans 16:1 and 1 Timothy 3:11).

By the end of the first century, the office of deacon was well-established. The author of the First Letter of Timothy, a letter sometimes attributed to Paul but actually written after Paul's death, discusses the requirements and functions of the deacon. 1 Timothy mentions that the deacon:

- Must "hold fast" to the teaching of the apostles.
- Must have been married only once.
- Must be a good manager of his or her own household, before being entrusted with care of the church's resources.
- Should be put on probation before being confirmed in office.

The deacon was a leader of considerable importance within the local community. By the end of the first century C.E., however, the deacon's function was secondary to that of the presbyter and bishop.

Presbyter/Bishop

As the founding apostle, Paul held the highest position of authority in his local churches. Assisting Paul were people such as Silvanus, Timothy, and Sosthenes. They helped Paul in his missionary work, just as Paul had started out helping Barnabas. In times of trouble or conflict, these fellow workers

The Bible in Context

Married Bishops

It may surprise you to hear that the presbyter/bishops had wives and children since Roman Catholic bishops and priests today take a vow of "celibacy" and do not marry. However, many of the original apostles were married. Paul even refers to Peter's wife in 1 Corinthians 9:5. The Jewish tradition did not have a history of a celibate priesthood.

The policy of priests and bishops not marrying developed over several hundred years as the Church began to place more emphasis on the unique nature of the priest's duties. This practice was not finalized until the Middle Ages.

spoke with the voice of the apostle. Similar relationships existed between other apostles and their fellow workers. The apostles and their helpers, however, could not remain forever in the local churches, and local leaders had to emerge.

In Paul's time, a member of a local community might be called to leadership because of:

- A personal connection to Paul or another apostle or fellow worker.
- A "gift of the Spirit," such as the ability to preach, teach, heal, or speak in tongues.
- Their wealth or social position in the community.

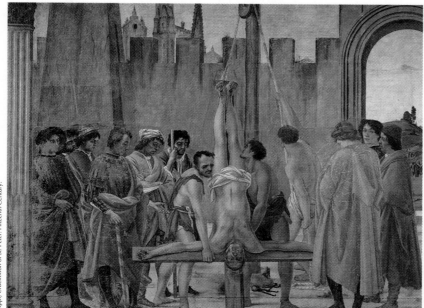

Lippi. *Crucifixion of St. Peter.* Fifteenth Century.

After the death of the apostles, new positions of leadership developed in the Church. This picture shows the death of Saint Peter. According to tradition, Peter was crucified upside-down because he did not feel worthy to die in the same way as Jesus died.

These leaders did not hold any defined office, they simply exercised authority because of their spiritual gifts, personality, or their social distinction. For example, a Christian wealthy enough to host meetings of a community in his or her home naturally assumed a position of leadership for that community. Paul may have designated certain individuals as leaders, but, more often, leadership emerged on its own.

As time went on, more definite offices began to develop. By the time of the First Letter of Timothy, at the end of the first century C.E., many local churches had a council of men, called the *presbyters*, who had the responsibility for leadership.

Presbyters were responsible for overseeing the affairs of the local church. The Greek term for an overseer is *episkopos*, usually translated into English as "bishop." In Paul's day, "presbyter" and "bishop" meant the same thing; both were terms for the leaders who guided the affairs of the local church. In the New Testament, presbyters and bishops almost always have the same functions.

The presbyter/bishop monitored the religious and ethical behavior of the local community, ensuring that people lived out their commitment to the Gospel, and did not bring shame upon the church. The presbyter/bishop also cared for the poor and sometimes presided at Christian worship. Their most important responsibility, however, was to preserve and defend the teaching of the apostles.

The author of 1 Timothy lists several requirements for anyone serving in this role. The bishop:

- Must be sensible, dignified, and moderate.
- Must be a model for other Christians, managing his own household well.
- Must be married only once, and his children must be well-behaved (the ability to guide his own family wisely was believed to be a sign that the bishop would guide the affairs of the church with wisdom).
- Must be someone respected by people outside Christianity, so that he could represent the community with confidence.
- Must be free from a love of money, not violent, and not a drinker.

In all things, the bishop must be able to command the respect of others and the obedience of his community.

The Office of Widows

Christian widows formed the final office in the early Church. In the Roman world, a widow who did not remarry was independent, but she had to live off what she inherited from her husband. If her husband had been wealthy, that could make her a very important and powerful person. Many early Christian converts were Gentile widows who were "God-fearers," or admirers of Judaism. Some of these widows were quite wealthy, and supported the Christian mission.

If a widow's husband had been poor and she had no family to support her, then the widow would have absolutely no means of support. As part of its care for the poor, Christians supported such widows with community resources. By the time of 1 Timothy, conditions were established to determine who qualified for such support.

First Timothy says that these widows:

- Had a specific duty to offer prayers.
- Must be of good character, meaning that she is hospitable and helps those in need.
- Must not engage in gossip or false teaching, giving herself "day and night" in prayer.

Along with the deacons and presbyter/bishops, the widows helped organize and expand the Christian mission in the last half of the first century.

Have You Considered?

1. Describe a club, activity, or other group to which you belong. Why is organization necessary in this group?
2. Do you think it's a good idea that a deacon had to be a good manager of his or her own household before he or she could manage the affairs of the community? Why or why not?
3. Why do you suppose it was so important to the early Christians that the bishop be someone whom those outside Christianity would respect?
4. What was the purpose of the office of Widows? What group of women today live as the letter of Timothy encourages?

◆ Defending the Faith

As long as Paul was alive, any arguments about his teaching could be settled with a letter from him. When he died, however, it was no longer clear how to resolve disputes over what Paul had said. The same was true for the other apostles. A need arose, therefore, to protect the apostolic teaching. The four gospel accounts serve this need, since they collect the shared memories of Jesus. The accounts themselves, however, were open to misinterpretation. The Church needed an office with the authority to teach the truths of the faith. This function soon became the role of the bishop.

Misinterpretation

In the first century, there were a bewildering variety of interpretations of Paul's letters. The author of 2 Peter (125 C.E.) refers to this problem:

> As our beloved brother Paul, according to the wisdom given to him, also wrote to you, speaking of these things as he does in all his letters. In them there are some things hard to understand that the ignorant and unstable distort to their own destruction, just as they do the other Scriptures.

(2 Peter 3:15–16)

The specific belief in question in 2 Peter is Paul's teaching about the parousia (the second coming of Jesus). Because of its delay, some people became convinced that it was not going to happen at all, or that it had already happened. The author urges them to remember Paul's words.

A False Knowledge

Specific teachings such as the parousia could be misunderstood by people with the best of intentions. Such misconceptions were easily addressed by the bishops. The real challenge for them came not from ordinary people struggling to understand complex teachings, but from organized groups who claimed to possess superior knowledge: the Gnostics.

Using the letters of Paul as a point of departure, the Gnostics claimed to have special insight into salvation. Specifically, they claimed to know the names of the angels and spirits who controlled the universe, and, more importantly, how to manipulate them. Gnostics began to interpret Paul as a Gnostic, and Christianity as a Gnostic system of belief.

Scripture Workshop

The Meaning of "Faith"

In the gospel accounts and in Paul, "faith" referred to the believer's trust in Christ. In the later books of the New Testament, however, faith also came to refer to the teachings that came from the apostles. The following verses show this new meaning:

- 2 Timothy 2:18, 3:8
- 1 Timothy 4:1, 6:21

Read the passages surrounding these verses. Then write a paragraph explaining what "faith" meant for the author of these two letters.

What does 1 Timothy 4:16 mean when it says: "Attend to yourself and to your teaching: persevere in both tasks, for by doing so you will save both yourself and those who listen to you."?

The letter to the Colossians (75 C.E.) refers to such beliefs when it says that all things, including "thrones or dominations, principles or powers" were made through and for Christ. "Thrones and dominations," refers to types of angels, while principles and powers express astrological and cosmological ideas. The author says that all these things exist only to serve Christ. Christians, therefore, do not need to be worried about them, for in Jesus, Christians are in contact with an infinitely greater power.

The author of 1 Timothy urged Christians to focus on the goal of their faith, which is the salvation offered by Jesus and ignore the Gnostic influences:

> guard what has been entrusted to you. Avoid profane babbling and the absurdities of so-called knowledge. By professing it, some people have deviated from the faith.

(1 Timothy 6:20–21)

Christian teaching then, is what has been handed down from the apostles. The Gnostics went wrong when they attempt to substitute their own knowledge for faith.

New Meaning of "Faith"

Gnosticism was not the only challenger to the apostolic teaching. Some Christians wanted to return to a strict obedience to the Law of Moses. This group, called the "Judaizers," were still active in the last part of the first century. Another group went to the opposite extreme and suggested getting rid of the Old Testament and Jewish traditions altogether. In the face of pressures such as these, the bishops were responsible for preserving the teaching they had inherited.

In the effort to preserve apostolic teaching, the term "faith" developed a new meaning. For the Gospel writers and for Paul, "faith" meant **being confident in the salvation offered through Jesus.** In the later part of the first century, the term also came to mean **the body of teachings handed down by the apostles.** Christians were to treasure and to preserve a body of teachings.

By the end of the first century, the Church, under the leadership of the bishops, had begun to organize the teachings that would later be expressed through the creeds (statements of belief, such as the one prayed by Catholics at Mass). The clarity of teaching became especially important when the faith came under attack, most notably by Romans who objected to Christianity as a "new religion" that seemed to threaten the empire.

◆ Facing Persecution

Christians were not persecuted by the Romans immediately. Generally, the Romans were lenient with others' religions, since people were easier to govern when they were allowed to practice their own. When Rome turned against the Christian faith, Christians experienced the power of the Empire and longed for the deliverance that only God could offer.

Christianity and the Empire

Roman law was very tolerant of non-Roman religions. In part, this was for political reasons: it made people more likely to accept Roman rule. There was also a religious reason for Roman tolerance. The Romans were afraid of offending foreign gods and bringing trouble on themselves. Before a battle, the Roman army invited the gods of the other side to join their cause. Similarly, the Romans avoided offending the gods of a conquered people, allowing them to continue honoring these gods. That tolerance extended to the Jews and the Temple in Jerusalem.

Because early Christians were thought of (and mostly thought of themselves) as Jews, Rome extended same tolerance to them. After the destruction of the Temple in 70 C.E., however, Christianity and

Have You Considered?

1. Why might Christians disagree over what Paul meant in his letters?
2. Why do you think there were so many disagreements in early Christianity about what faith means?
3. What do you think about disagreements that occur in Christianity today? How should they be resolved?
4. For Paul, faith meant being confident in the salvation offered by Jesus. How is this understanding of faith different from the later teaching that faith was the body of teachings handed down by the apostles?

The persecution of Christians began with the Emperor Nero. Christians were treated so harshly that even 30 years later the Book of Revelation remembered Nero as the hated beast.

Judaism obviously began to separate from each other. Only then did Christians begin to attract the attention of the Romans, who suspected them of worshipping a "new" god, Christ.

The Romans were conservative in matters of religion, and regarded any changes in ancient practices as threatening to the "peace of the gods" which protected the empire. Although authors such as Luke showed the Romans that Christians continued to honor the God of the Old Testament, the Romans remained suspicious.

In addition, the Romans suspected Christians of being a "secret society" because they ate and worshipped by themselves. This, too, alarmed Roman officials. Because of these suspicions, Rome sometimes punished Christians on accusations of disloyalty or creating disorder. Such occasional crackdowns, however, did not amount to "official" persecution.

Nero

Christians were first persecuted during the reign of Emperor Nero. Nero was the emperor of Rome from 54–68 C.E. Nero used his power as emperor ruthlessly. He was so cruel as to murder both his mother and his wife to prevent them from plotting against him. Nero also had a reputation for scandalous living, offending even the "liberal" citizens of Rome.

In 64 C.E., Nero, wanting to build a monument to himself in Rome, started a devastating fire that destroyed a large part of the city. Needing someone to

Unknown, Plaque honoring the Emperor Marc. Aurel. Second Century.

Christians captured by the Romans suffered greatly. The persecution of Christians increased under the Emperor Domitian.

blame for this tragedy, Nero chose the Christians. Dozens of Christians were tortured and burned during this persecution including (according to tradition) Peter and Paul. Although Christians had not been popular in Rome prior to this time, the torture inflicted by Nero made people sympathetic to them. Christians remembered the experience all too well; references to it show up in the Book of Revelation (90 C.E.) and in other writings decades later.

Domitian

Roman criminal law was largely unwritten, so the judgment of whether or not something was a crime was largely left to the *magistrate*, the government official responsible for justice. For this reason, there was probably never any law which made Christianity universally illegal, although it was not officially legalized until 311.

After the destruction of the Temple in 70 C.E., Roman magistrates tended to pay more attention to Christianity, and were more likely to punish Christians who refused to worship the spirit of the Emperor. Refusal to honor the Emperor was considered an act of political disloyalty.

---

in the Spotlight

Nero's Persecution

The Roman historian Tacitus described the persecution of Christians under Nero. He said Christians were chosen because of their "antisocial" nature (which probably refers to their celebration of evening meals with one another rather than in mixed— Christian and non-Christian—company), and their unwillingness to participate in Roman religious festivals.

Whatever the reason, Nero inflicted horrible punishments. Tacitus says that some Christians were dressed in animal skins to be torn apart by dogs, and others were used as human torches to light Nero's garden parties. The shocking brutality of these acts created sympathy among the public, and eventually the persecutions came to an end.

LEARN FROM THE MAP

Christianity at the End of the First Century

Notice all the places where Christians had established churches by the end of the first century. Given what you see on this map, why do you think the Roman emperors were so worried about Christian loyalty?

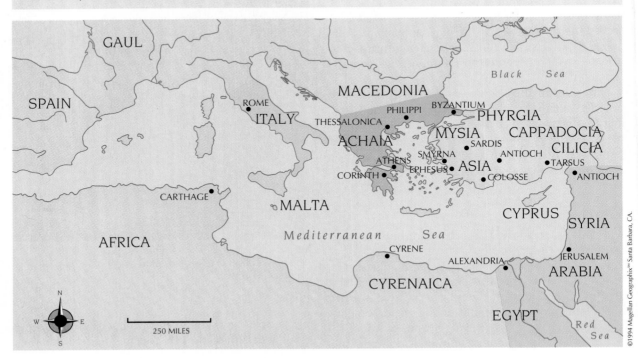

Magistrates rarely hunted Christians down. Usually, they waited until a Christian was denounced by someone else. Christians were given every opportunity to honor the Emperor, but if they refused to do so, they were put to death. Faced with this choice, some rejected their faith, while others held firmly to it.

Under the Emperor Domitian (81–96 C.E.), persecution of Christians heated up once more. Domitian viewed any potential disloyalty with suspicion. Like Nero, he targeted Christians for persecution.

Christians suffered greatly under this persecution although they were not the only ones; Domitian seemed more interested in promoting emperor worship than he was in stamping out other religions. Worship of the emperor was required of all Roman citizens. People could also worship as many other gods as they wished, as long as worship of the emperor came first. Failure to worship the emperor was a sign of treason, for which the penalty was death.

Christians and Jews both believed in the worship of Yahweh alone. They could not worship the emperor without violating the Covenant.

Such official hostility discouraged many Christians and prompted them to long for God's salvation, views expressed in the Book of Revelation. As you will see in the next section, Revelation offered a powerful message of hope to Christians facing the power of Rome.

Have You Considered?

1. Why do you think the Romans would tolerate members of "old" religions, but not members of "new" ones?
2. Given what you know about Luke's theme of salvation history, how do you think he would explain the persecution Christians faced?
3. Why do you think Christians would object to referring to the Roman Emperor as "Lord"? Do you think their refusal to do so was a political act, as the Romans felt?

Keeping the Faith

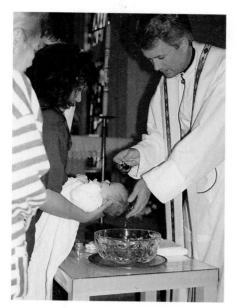

In the first section, you read about the two major challenges facing the Church in the last part of the first century: internal arguments over the faith, and external persecution from the Romans. In this section, you'll study how four New Testament authors responded to these challenges. In Hebrews, James, the letters of Peter, and the Book of Revelation, a wide variety of internal and external problems are discussed. In every case, however, the answer given by these authors is consistent: stay true to the faith, and God will not abandon you.

Learning Objectives for Section Two

By the end of this section, you will be able to:

- Explain the false teaching corrected in Hebrews, James, and the letters ⬛

- Explain how ⬛ respond to ⬛

- Discuss the ⬛

◆ The Letter to the Hebrews

Although the Letter to the Hebrews (80 C.E.) has sometimes been attributed to the apostle Paul, modern scholars generally recognize it as the product of a later author. The letter, addressed to Jewish-Christians, is a long sermon explaining the consequences of their Christian faith. In Hebrews, the author corrects a false understanding among some Jewish-Christians, who felt that it was necessary to continue making Temple sacrifices to be on good terms with God. Hebrews reminds them that Christians need nothing but the sacrifice of Jesus to be saved.

Christ the High Priest

The Letter to the Hebrews sees Jesus as the divine Son of God, the image of God in the world

No Other Sacrifices

According to the author of Hebrews, Jesus made one, perfect sacrifice for all people and all time. For this reason, no other sacrifices need to be made. Christ has accomplished the perfect sacrifice through his death. From this point forward, human beings are free from sin, and they no longer need the Temple or other rituals to restore their relationship with God.

Audience   Hebrews directs this message at Jewish-Christians who felt that God still wanted them to make sacrifices according to the Jewish law. The author tells such Christians that the death of Jesus is the only sacrifice necessary, and all Christians have to do is to accept it. To continue to rely on the traditional sacrificial system, the author says, would be a denial of the faith, suggesting that Christ's death was not sufficient to restore their relationship with God.

The belief that Christ's life and death are all Christians need is very important to the author of Hebrews. To underline this point, the author argues that God's revelation before Christ had always been partial and incomplete, while God was revealed in complete fullness through Jesus. Hebrews says:

> In times past, God spoke in partial and various ways to our ancestors through the prophets; in these last days he spoke to us through a Son, whom he made heir of all things and through whom he created the universe.
>
> (Hebrews 1:1–2)

Heroes of the Faith   Hebrews does not reject the Old Testament or Jewish traditions. In fact, Chapter 11 of Hebrews is often called the "heroes of the faith" chapter, recounting the life stories of Abel, Noah, Abraham, Sarah, Jacob, Rahab, David, and others. All of these people, the author says, are examples of lives built on faith and obedience to God.

Response in the Heart

This perfect, once-and-for-all, gift from Jesus inspires a response from the heart. The author urges the readers to take care of each other, to encourage one another, and to continue meeting for support and growth.

Hebrews also advises Christians to show hospitality, saying that some have entertained angels that way without knowing it. (See the story of Abraham in Chapter 18 of Genesis.)

Above all, the author says, Christians must cling to true teaching. No one should be allowed to lead them astray from the faith. Hebrews reinforces correct teaching and defends the faith against possible misinterpretations. The author reminds Christians that faith in Jesus is all we need.

Have You Considered?

1. Why is Jesus called the "perfect high priest"? Does this title express your understanding of Jesus? Why or why not?
2. Why might Jewish-Christians have felt that Temple sacrifices were still necessary? Based on what you know about Jewish-Christians, explain why they might think this.
3. How might our behavior towards strangers and the poor change if we regarded them as potential messengers from God? Give two or three concrete examples of things we might do differently.

◆ The Letter of James

This brief letter, written around 65 C.E., has traditionally been attributed to James, the relative of Jesus, who governed the Church in Jerusalem. You may remember James from Chapter 12; he was present at the Council of Jerusalem and made the decision about the dietary rules for Gentile converts. Although the teaching in this letter may have come from James, the actual writing was probably done by a later author.

The letter is addressed to the "twelve tribes in the diaspora," probably referring to all of the Christian communities. James is concerned with another misunderstanding of apostolic teaching, one which says that because Christians are saved by faith, it is unnecessary for them to do any good works. James reminds Christians that acts of mercy and love go hand-in-hand with salvation, and they are part of being Christian.

Endurance

James begins by recognizing that many Christians are experiencing hard times. The author may have persecution in mind, or the "trials" may simply be the isolation from loved ones and social disapproval that often came with being a Christian. James argues that trials and temptations test our faith. By passing these tests, we bring our faith to perfection, and we assure ourselves of the crown of life which Jesus has prepared for all of his loved ones.

James advises Christians experiencing difficulties to pray for the wisdom that comes from God. This prayer, however, must be offered in a spirit of trusting confidence that God will respond. One who prays in doubt must not expect anything from the Lord, James says, because such doubt shows distrust and instability. Only a heart full of faith can be open to the wisdom God offers.

An Important Christian Skill

One of the most important skills a Christian can have, according to James, is the ability to control one's tongue. "If anyone does not fall short in speech, he is a perfect man" (James 3:2).

Speech has great power. It can make another person feel wonderful. It can share about the glory and truth of God. It can express love. Speech can also cause harm through lies and gossip. As James puts it, "From the same mouth come blessing and cursing" (James 3:10).

James encourages all Christians to learn the skill of watching their tongues, so that their speech becomes like the pure fruit of a healthy tree. Everybody likes to hear good and true words. The Christian, James implies, should speak well at all times, especially when talking about another person.

The best way to learn this Christian skill is to look inside oneself and see one's own thoughts and feel-

Christians were put to death in the Colosseum in Rome as entertainment. The Letter of James encourages Christians to persevere in their faith against all hardship, even if it meant their deaths.

ings. James advises instilling wisdom and humility inside oneself. If everything inside is "pure, peaceable, gentle, compliant, and full of mercy," then one's speech will be the same.

Rich and Poor Alike

James also talks about relationships between Christians, especially between the rich and the poor. James emphasizes that everyone is welcome in the Christian assembly. In particular, no one is to be excluded because of their poverty or treated extra nicely because of their wealth.

The command for Christians is not to exclude the wealthy, but to treat rich and poor alike. No favoritism must be shown in the community based on someone's worldly status. The poor must be treated with the same decency and respect that any other member of the community enjoys.

The suffering of the poor will be rewarded in the last days, James says, while oppression and neglect of the poor will be punished. For that reason, the Christian is called to treat the poor, with special care (*James 2:1–9 and 5:1–6*).

Faith and Works

The special love Christians have for the poor is connected to one of the main themes in James: the need for Christians to perform good works. In the late first century, some Christians apparently had a distorted reading of Paul's letters. They thought that simply by repeating slogans such as "God is one" they had done enough. Instead, James insists that their faith must not be simply a matter of slogans or theories. Faith must be reflected in the Christian's daily life.

James sums the idea up this way: we must be doers of the word, not just hearers. Our faith is meaningless unless we practice it. To make this point, James uses a very down-to-earth example: If someone comes up to you and says "I am hungry, and I have nothing to wear," and all you do is say, "Goodbye, and keep warm and well-fed," what good are those words without actions? In addition to being meaningless, they're insincere, since we do nothing to help the person. James says that "faith" has no power to save anyone unless used in obedience to God's commands.

The letter of James practically summarizes good Christian living. Against the false teaching that Christian faith is simply a matter of the mind, James insists that Christianity is a way of life, an active concern for the well-being of all, including those often forgotten in society.

Christian Virtue

The Christian way of life involves more than occasional acts of mercy. It also involves making our values part of our daily living. What does this mean in practice? James mentions several things:

*The Letter of James says that Christians should be known by their good works; how a person acts **is** ultimately important.*

◆ The Letters of Peter

Two letters in the New Testament are attributed to the apostle Peter. In all likelihood, neither were written by him. The first letter was written in Rome around 65 C.E., and came at the time of the first persecutions. This persecution included social prejudice as well as actual arrest and execution. 1 Peter urges Christians to stand fast, and tries to show that Christian life will continue in such circumstances. 2 Peter was written much later by another person. It is perhaps the last book written in the New Testament (possibly written as late as 125 C.E.). This book reaffirms traditional Christian teaching about the second coming of Jesus and calls on Christians to remain true to the faith.

Christian Exile

In the face of persecution and prejudice in the Roman world, 1 Peter urges Christians to consider themselves exiles in this life. Christians are just passing through, he says, on their way to their home in the kingdom with Jesus. Their lives will always be different and perhaps more difficult than others' lives. Christians should expect this as the price of living in exile.

Despite the hardships, Christians must continue to act in goodness and accept whatever experiences come their way. They must accept suffering in the same way that Christ accepted it, as part of God's plan for the salvation of the world. Despite enduring insults and punishments for their faith, Christians need feel no shame. Instead, they should feel pride, for the degree to which Christians now share in the suffering of Christ is the degree to which they will share in his glory when he returns.

Good Examples

The author urges Christians to live blameless lives so that non-Christians will have no cause to complain about them. They should live well, so that non-Christians will learn to give glory to God. Blameless living includes shedding envy, slander, and false pride. Christians should be compassionate and humble, and not be nasty to others. In all these ways, Christian behavior should be a model for their non-Christian neighbors.

Scripture Workshop

The Man in the Mirror

A major theme in James is the importance of *doing* the word. In James 1:23–25, the author compares the Christian to a man who looks into the mirror. Read this comparison, and then answer the following questions:

- How is a person who hears the word but does not practice it like one who looks into the mirror?
- What do you think "freedom's ideal law" is?
- What does it mean to "peer" into it?

- Cultivating peacefulness (3:17–18).
- An unwillingness to judge others (4:11–12).
- Humility, and a refusal to boast of our accomplishments (3:13–14).
- Patience as we wait for the salvation promised by God (5:7–11).

James is a great help for people growing in faith and Christian living. James reminds us that Christian faith requires good actions, and that anyone who denies this is not a Christian.

Have You Considered?

1. Have you ever experienced favoritism in any group to which you belong? If so, what was done about it? Why or why not? What could have been done?
2. What does it mean to say that Christian faith must include good works? Do you think it's possible to be a Christian without acting to help others?
3. Review the list of virtues above which James says Christians should have. Which one do you think is hardest for you? Why?

Defending the Faith

1 Peter says that Christians must always be ready to defend their faith with gentleness and respect. The author reminds the presbyters that it is their duty to keep everyone on the right path. They should use their authority wisely and not abuse it in any way.

Ordinary Christians must remain solid in faith, 1 Peter says, because it is the same faith that believers are suffering for all over the world. God will give strength to those who endure, and their constancy will be rewarded when Christ returns.

The Second Coming

You already know that the *parousia*, or second coming, of Jesus had been expected by Christians from the very beginning. Many Christians, like those in Thessalonica, expected it to happen soon. As the years passed, the parousia was pushed further and further into the future. Some Christians began to doubt it was going to happen at all, and rejected the teaching altogether. 2 Peter (125 C.E.) is written to bring these Christians back to the true apostolic teaching.

Anyone who denies the parousia, according to 2 Peter, is a false teacher.

> *For talking empty bombast, they seduce with licentious desires of the flesh those who have barely escaped from people who live in error.*
>
> (2 Peter 2:18)

Christians should cling to the promises made by Jesus and not let anyone convince them to abandon hope in his return. We should wait patiently, however, because a thousand years is like a single day to the Lord. Even though Christians might want action immediately, they must trust God and be at peace.

Have You Considered?

1. When the author of 1 Peter compared Christian life to exile, what Old Testament event do you think his readers would have remembered? How might this help them endure their hardships?
2. Why would hope for the second coming of Jesus be important to Christians facing persecution?

◆ The Book of Revelation

Revelation (90 C.E.) is a book of fantastic—and sometimes horrible—visions and symbols. In it, we read about a huge red dragon with seven heads and ten horns, whose tail swept away a third of the stars; the four horsemen of the Apocalypse; and a woman wearing purple and scarlet who has become drunk on the blood of the Holy One. Some of these images sound like they come straight off the pages of a Stephen King novel!

Many of the symbols in Revelation are from the Old Testament and other Jewish literature outside the Bible. The original readers of Revelation would have recognized and understood these images immediately. Taken together, the symbols in Revelation give us a vision of Christian life and salvation. Addressed to people experiencing persecution and questioning the truth of their faith, Revelation offers hope that God's deliverance will come as promised.

Giotto, *Last Judgment*, Fourteenth Century.

Early Christians believed that Jesus would return again quickly to fulfill the kingdom. The Second Letter of Peter encourages people to stay true to the faith because Jesus would come again.

People of Note

The Beast

In general, you should not look for specific explanations for the symbols found in Revelation. They refer to events that occurred nearly 2000 years ago for which we have no evidence. We can only speculate on what they mean.

There is one case, however, where Revelation itself tells you what a symbol means. Revelation 13:8 says that the beast which forces people to be marked with its image stands for a man, and his identity can be determined from the number "666."

Ancient languages such as Greek and Hebrew did not have a system of numbers as we do, so each letter of their alphabet had a numerical value. In Hebrew, the letters in the name of the Roman Emperor Nero add up to 666, and most scholars today agree that this is the beast described. Nero had persecuted Christians, and some feared that he had escaped death and was coming back into power. The "image" of itself which the beast forced on people probably refers to Roman coins, which were stamped with the image of the Emperor.

God Is in Charge

Times are terrible, the author of Revelation says, and they're going to get worse. The violent images of destruction and chaos in the book communicate this belief. But no matter how it may appear from here, God is totally in charge. Believers in Christ, especially *martyrs*, Christians who die for their faith, will be granted a glorious life. Because deliverance is coming, however, Christians should accept these insults and injuries.

The book is written from the point of view of a *seer*, one who experiences a vision. Because this seer relates everything from God's point of view, the hearer may be sure that the present hardships are part of the divine plan. All of the difficulties Christians experience in the text have the same basic structure:

- The saints (Christians) suffer persecution.
- The coming judgment on the evil ones is described.
- A scene of salvation in heaven follows.

This structure shows the reader that the hardships Christians experience will inevitably lead to glory in heaven, so the only response is to endure with patience and confidence.

A New Jerusalem

Revelation ends with a final vision of what life will be like when the present age ends, and the kingdom comes in its fullness. The coming of the kingdom is captured in the vision of a "new Jerusalem."

Then I saw a new heaven and a new earth. The former heaven and the former earth had passed away, and the sea was no more. I also saw the holy city, a new Jerusalem, coming down out of heaven from God, prepared as a bride adorned for her husband. I heard a loud voice from the throne saying: "Behold God's dwelling is with the human race. He will dwell with them and they will be his people God himself will always be with them [as their God]. He will wipe away every tear from their eyes, and there shall be no more death or mourning, wailing or pain, [for] the old order has passed away.

(Revelation 21:1–4)

The seer goes on to describe what this New Jerusalem will be like. It will have no temple, because God will be the temple; it will have no sun or moon, for the glory of God provides the light.

For Christians experiencing harassment, punishment, and even death for their faith, this vision gave them hope to endure. The experience of these horrible things will pass away, and a new life with God awaits those who remain strong.

False Teachers

Along with the external persecution they faced, the readers of Revelation also were exposed to "false apostles and prophets" who were introducing new beliefs. The author of Revelation addresses these false teachers in the seven letters to different Christian churches which open the book. Some of these teachers claimed to have secret knowledge unavailable to ordinary Christians. Others, such as the Nicolaitians, were introducing elements of Greek and Roman religion and culture into Christian practice. The author rejects these teachings and commends his readers who have done the same.

Problems of Interpretation

The general message of Revelation is clear: Things are bad now and getting worse, but salvation is on the way. The details of the images and symbols which contain this general idea, however, can be very difficult to understand. Sometimes, people have tried to find a specific meaning for each symbol, or tried to calculate the date of the end of the world on the basis of the description in Revelation.

Read Revelation as you would any book: let the symbols and images just be there, without trying to figure them out. Read to enjoy the book, not analyze it. When people draw mistaken conclusions about the end of the world or the identity of the "anti-Christ," they can cause harm to themselves and others. Instead, read Revelation for the feelings of amazement, wonder, thanksgiving, honor to God, threat, victory, and ultimately, hope, that the symbols provoke. Try to appreciate the book just as it is.

Unknown (N. France), Apocalypse. Thirteenth Century.

The Book of Revelation uses many types of symbolism. This picture shows the opening of the second seal (Revelation 6:3–4). The red horse and rider symbolize war that will "take away peace from the earth, so that people would slaughter one another."

Have You Considered?

1. What have you heard about the book of Revelation? What images do you have of it?
2. Have you ever heard people who interpreted the symbols in Revelation as referring to people or events of today? What would you say about this kind of interpretation?
3. What images or symbols would you use to describe life in a "new world" created by God?

◆ The Importance of the Faith

Despite the different interests of the authors you have studied in this section, they all agree on one thing: Christians must hold fast to the teaching of the apostles. As you know from Section One, the apostle's teaching and belief had, by the end of the first century, become part of what it meant to have faith.

You may be surprised by this emphasis on what Christians believe. After all, isn't it how we treat others that matters? Does it make any difference what we think about the Spirit, or about Baptism? Is it really important that we all hold the same beliefs?

What Christians Believe

The authors at the end of the first century C.E. remind us that what we believe **is** important. Our beliefs shape who we are and how we think about the world. Although sometimes people use the word "Christian" simply to refer to a kind act, Christianity also includes teachings about God, Jesus, the Spirit, and the purpose of human life.

The New Testament authors have given us several reasons why it is important that we share the same beliefs:

- **Our common beliefs link us to our tradition.** They connect us to our ancestors in the faith, and they ensure that we benefit from the wisdom of those who have gone before us in the Christian life.
- **What we believe influences our values and our attitudes towards life.** Our belief in the parousia, for example, gives us an optimistic and hopeful view in the face of difficulties we encounter.
- **Unity in belief helps to bring unity to the community.** When we remain united in what we believe, we remain united in other things as well. Our common beliefs give us a shared identity and sense of purpose.

For all these reasons, Christianity must include certain basic beliefs and teachings. However, we have to recognize that a person comes to this kind of faith only gradually, by studying and honestly encountering the teachings of the Church. One's faith has to be authentic.

How Christians Live

Even though faith includes right doctrine, its most important aspect is a "yes" to the love of God in our hearts. People who say "yes" to God may have more "faith" than Christians who have all the right beliefs, but shut themselves off from the love of God and others. We can never mistake what we believe to be the whole of our faith; this was the very mistake the letter of James was written to correct. This is also echoed in the Third Letter of John

> Beloved . . . . I rejoiced greatly when some of the brothers came and testified to how truly you walk in the truth. Nothing gives me greater joy than to hear that my children are walking in truth.
>
> Beloved, you are faithful in all you do for the brothers, especially for strangers; they have testified to your love before the church. Please help them in a way worthy of God to continue their journey . . . .
>
> Beloved, do not imitate evil but imitate good. Whoever does what is good is of God; whoever does what is evil has never seen God.
>
> (3 John 2–6,11)

The author of Hebrews defined faith as "the realization of what is hoped for, and evidence of things not seen" (*Hebrews* 11:1). With confidence in the Spirit and conviction about the truths of the faith, Christians face life with hope. As 1 Peter puts it:

> Once you were "no people," but now you are God's people; you had not received mercy for you, but now you have received mercy
>
> (1 Peter 2:10)

Have You Considered?

1. Do you think holding common beliefs is an important part of Christianity? Why or why not?
2. What do you think it means for someone to "honestly encounter" a particular teaching? Describe how you think this might happen.

Spiritual Reflection

The Book of Revelation

Read Chapter 19 of Revelation. In it, you will find the author's vision of the heavenly assembly. He hears two songs of praise of God sung by the angels in the assembly.

> "Alleluia! Salvation, glory, and might belong to our God, for true and just are his judgments. He has condemned the great harlot who corrupted the earth with her harlotry. He has avenged on her the blood of his servants."
>
> (19:1–2)

> "Alleluia! The Lord has established his reign, [our] God, the almighty. Let us rejoice and be glad and give him glory. For the wedding day of the Lamb has come, his bride has made herself ready. She was allowed to wear a bright, clean linen garment."
>
> (19:6–80)

For your reflection, do the following:

- Read over these songs carefully.
- Think about what the symbols might mean, but don't get hung up on whether you're right or wrong; just let the images flow in your mind, like you might for a daydream.
- Use the words of these songs, especially the second one, as the basis of your prayer. Add your own thoughts.
- When you're finished, offer a final prayer thanking God for this time. Jot a few notes in your journal and then go back to your day.

Q/A

Section One

1. Why did the question of leadership come up in the Church in the last part of the first century?
2. Define the term "deacon." Who were the original deacons?
3. Define the term "presbyter" and the term "bishop." How are they different from each other in the New Testament?
4. What was the function of the office of widows?
5. According to 1 Timothy, what was the problem with Gnosticism?
6. What was the new meaning of "faith" at the end of the first century?
7. Why was Roman law tolerant of foreign religions?
8. Under what circumstances were Christians likely to be persecuted?

Section Two

1. What audience does the Letter to the Hebrews address?
2. According to Hebrews, what value does the Old Testament have for Christians?
3. In the Letter of James, who are the "12 tribes in the diaspora"?
4. Explain James' teaching on faith and works.
5. What virtues does James say should be in the Christian life?
6. According to 1 Peter, how should Christians respond if they are questioned about their faith?
7. How should the Book of Revelation be read?
8. What does the Third Letter of John call Christians to do? Why is that important?

BIBLE ACTIVITY

1. In Chapter 11 of the book of Hebrews, the author lists several figures from the Old Testament who serve as examples of people of faith. Make a list of the names you recognize. Next to each name, write down the action which the author points to as a sign of that person's faith. What do these actions have in common? How do you think the author of Hebrews defines "faith" based on this chapter?

2. 1 Peter 2:1–9 quotes several verses from the Old Testament to urge Christians to grow in holiness. Make a list of these verses, and find out where they appear in the Old Testament, then look them up. Compare the original in the Old Testament with the version in 1 Peter. What changes do you find? What do you think they might mean?

3. Read chapter 12 of the Book of Revelation. What do you think the woman in this chapter might symbolize? There is no right answer; use your imagination, and remember that the author of Revelation was well-versed in the Old Testament.

GLOSSARY

- **Bishop:** From the Greek word "episkopos," meaning "overseer," a bishop is one who had responsibility for guiding the affairs of the early Christian churches.
- **Christian Exile:** Idea found in 1 Peter, which says that Christians are strangers in this life, and should expect their lives to be different from others' lives.
- **Deacon:** From the Greek term for a servant, a deacon was a leader in the early Church who cared for the poor, administered community resources, and preached the Gospel.
- **Faith:** Originally an acceptance of God's offer of love through Jesus; in the late first century C.E., it also came to mean the teachings handed down from the apostles.
- **Magistrate:** Roman official responsible for administering justice; the magistrate was the person who heard complaints against Christians and ordered punishment or execution.
- **Martyr:** A person who dies for his or her faith; in many late first century C.E. Christian books, martyrs are commended and praised.
- **Widow:** Office in the early Church of prayer and service; the early Church also offered protection to widows who were left without any means of support.

UNDERSTANDING MORE ABOUT:

"An Epistle of Straw"

The Letter of James was one of the last books to be accepted into the New Testament canon. Not until after 300 C.E. was James recognized universally within the Church. The struggle over the letter did not end there, however. It began again at the time of the Protestant Reformation.

Martin Luther (1483–1546) argued that James should not have equal standing with the rest of the letters in the New Testament. Luther felt that James' attitude on works contradicted what Paul had said about salvation coming from faith alone. He assigned James to the back of the New Testament, calling it "an epistle of straw."

Today, however, most Protestant and Catholic scholars agree that this debate over James was unnecessary. James did not mean to say that salvation is impossible without good works, but rather that a proper response to God's gift of salvation must include acting for the good of others. In this way, James did not contradict Paul, but corrected a misleading interpretation of the apostle's teaching.

You and the Bible

Israel, *Dead Sea Scroll, Isaiah*. First Century B.C.E.?

Legend

● World History
● Regional History
● Biblical History
● Books written

Have you ever played the game "Marooned"? Which things would you want to have with you if you were stranded on a deserted island? A favorite CD, perhaps, or a particular movie, or even a special family member or friend. If you could have only one book, which one would it be?

When surveys have been taken that asked this question, the Bible is almost always placed at the top of the list. Why do you think this is? Before you answer, think about this true story.

> A man lived in Berlin just before World War II. He was wealthy, and his large house was filled with row upon row of books. One night the Nazis set fire to his home, and he had time to grab only a few items before he fled. The only book he packed was the Bible. When a friend asked him about his choice, he replied, "I already know what's in those other books. This book still has much to teach me."

What is it about the Bible that keeps people coming back to it? Why is it that people feel the Bible never stops challenging them, teaching them, and filling them with a sense of God's presence? Consider these reasons:

- The Bible is really 76 separate books under one cover, each with its own style and message.
- The different cultures and experiences which lie behind the Bible make its books a challenge to understand and appreciate.
- Because the Bible is the Word of God, it is not merely interesting to read; it also nourishes our faith and helps us grow in our understanding of God.
- Whatever life's problems, the Bible helps us keep hope alive. As we read about the exile of the Israelites, and the persecution of the early Christians, we know that the People of God have triumphed over hard times.
- The Bible is the book of the Church, and through the tradition of the Church, the Bible plays an important role in shaping our beliefs and worship.
- Many people feel they actually meet and know God as they know a good friend through their reading of the Bible. For some, God can be heard in the Bible's words, like a partner in conversation.
- Praying with the Bible brings inner nourishment and contentment. It strengthens and deepens people's prayer and makes it vital and alive.

The Bible is a book in which every generation finds comfort and inspiration. The Bible is the all-time best selling book in the world, because it touches people's hearts and helps them grow in faith. Listening for what the Bible has to teach is an ongoing challenge.

In this course, you've taken several important steps towards becoming a lifelong Bible reader. You've encountered the leading people, places and events of the Bible story. You've also developed some important skills for Bible study. You may be wondering, however, where you go from here. What do you do with what you've learned? In this final chapter, you'll consider how you can continue to grow in your appreciation and understanding of scripture.

Bible Study Skills

*Think about your third or fourth grade English class. What do you remember? Can you recall the specific stories and poems you read? What about the textbook you used? If you're like most people, you won't remember much at all. But you probably **are** still using the skills you learned then: how to find words in the dictionary, pronounce them properly, and use them to write a paragraph. In most cases with education, you will carry with you the skills learned better than the specific content. You apply those skills repeatedly in other classes and situations in your life, and they stay with you.*

You have learned several skills during this course. In this section, you will review the skills for Bible study you've learned.

Learning Objectives for Section One:

By the end of this section, you will be able to:

- List six skills for Bible study.
- Explain the value of these skills and give examples of how they are used.

◆ Academic Skills

Reading any literature requires certain basic skills, such as concentration, attention to the author's use of language, and an ability to follow the plot or argument. Reading and understanding the Bible requires additional skills. Once you have mastered them, you will be better equipped to read the Bible and everything else you study as well.

Reading the Bible in Context

You know that the books of the Bible were written in times and places very different from today. In order to understand what a biblical author is saying, therefore, we must know about that work's background or *context*. Scholars try to understand both the historical and literary context of a work.

- **Historical Context:** When was the book written? What was happening at that time that might have affected the author's experience and point of view?

- **Literary Context:** What other books is this author familiar with? How do those books affect what the author wrote?

Understanding a biblical book often depends on knowing its context. For example, we are able to under-

The Bible in Context

Literary Context

As you have learned, it is easier to understand an author's message if you know the books with which he or she was familiar. In the case of the New Testament authors, this means, above all, knowing the Old Testament. The New Testament authors were all Jewish, and they relied heavily on themes, images, and characters from the Jewish Scriptures. The Old Testament character Rahab, for example, appears as a model of faith in Matthew, in the Letter of James, and in the Letter to the Hebrews. If you were not familiar with the Old Testament you would not have a clue as to why Rahab is so honored.

stand the Priestly writer's Creation story because we know its authors had lived through the Exile, were familiar with the Yahwist's Creation story, and belonged to the social class of priests. Knowing this context, we can recognize the authors' message clearly.

Recognizing Diversity

The books of the Bible developed over some 2000 years, shaped by oral tradition and the contributions of many authors and editors through the inspiration of God. This means that the Bible is incredibly rich in insight and experience. It also means that the Bible expresses many different points of view. For people who think the Bible, as the Word of God, should be free of all "contradictions," this discovery is unsettling. In fact, the diversity of the Bible is one of its greatest strengths, because God's inspiration is reflected through the wisdom of many different people.

You know that each author of the four gospel accounts in the New Testament had his own understanding of who Jesus was. For Mark, Jesus was the suffering Messiah, while Matthew saw Jesus as a great teacher and founder of the Church. These are not contradictions, merely four authors examining the same subject from different points of view. When you are comfortable with this degree of diversity, you will be open to all the insights the Bible has to offer.

Scripture Workshop

Diversity in the Bible

You know that an author's point of view reflects how he or she remembers events. An example of this occurs in Acts 15 and Galatians 2. In these two passages, Luke and Paul recount the events surrounding the Council of Jerusalem, where the Church decided to admit Gentile converts without making them first become Jews.

- Read these two passages, and make a list of all the differences you note.
- Write a paragraph explaining these differences, using what you know about Luke's and Paul's reasons for writing.

The Re-Harakhte Temple in Egypt was built during the reign of Ramses II, about the time of the Exodus. The Bible was written and refined for over 2000 years. Its incredibly rich message has continued to have value to its readers for the almost 2000 years since the last book was finished.

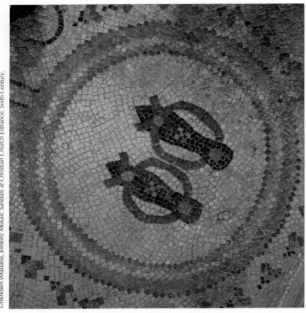

Unknown (Madaba, Jordon) Mosaic Sandals at Christian Church Entrance. Sixth Century.

In Exodus 3:4–5, God calls Moses to the burning bush and tells him, "Remove the sandals from your feet, for the place where you stand is holy ground." The same could be said about reading the Bible. To fully appreciate its gift, the reader must be aware that he or she is in the presence of God and act with humility.

Recognizing Different Kinds of Truth

Another skill you have learned in this class is to distinguish between the different kinds of truth a statement may have. For example, when your mother tells you she loves you, she isn't making a scientific claim or a historical statement. She can't prove her love using logic or the scientific method, but that doesn't make it any less true. In this case, the truth of your mother's love is personal, not scientific. In the same way, the authors of the Genesis didn't intend to write historical or scientific works. They communicated God's creation of humanity and love for us in the form of a story.

Have You Considered?

1. What do you think is the main reason so many people return to the Bible throughout their lives?
2. Give an example of how knowing the context of a literary work helps the reader to understand it.

LEARN FROM THE MAP

Israel Today

When the Temple was destroyed in 70 C.E., the Jewish nation ceased to exist. The diaspora of the Jews was complete. They were spread out across most of Northern Africa, most of Europe, and into Asia. Jews continued to live in the Middle East and Palestine (as Judah became known). Jews living in the Diaspora faced hardship and persecution. Although the Holocaust during the Second World War was the most systematic attempt, Jews have been put to death for their religion for close to 2000 years.

The Jewish people were without a homeland until the modern nation of Israel was formed by United Nations mandate in 1948. Israel's borders have changed since 1948 because of wars fought with its neighbors. Gaza, the West Bank, and the Golan Heights are known as the disputed territories and are part of the peace negotiations between Israel and its neighbors. Compare this map with the map of David's kingdom in Chapter 5. Why might these areas be of historic importance to Israel?

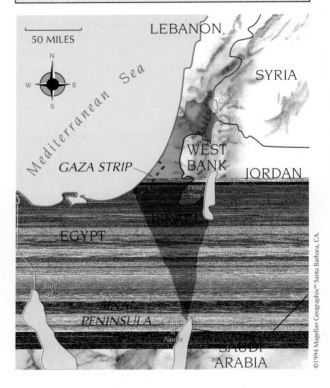

◆ Faith Skills

In order to truly understand what the Bible says, you need the academic skills discussed above. Ultimately, however, the challenge in reading the Bible is not just to understand it. Rather, the Bible's purpose is to help us grow in the love of God. The faith skills you've learned in this class will also help you to hear God's word in Scripture.

Making Moral Decisions

Paul and the other early Christian writers emphasized that being a Christian means trying to live in morally responsible ways. But how do you do this? Many people learn to make good choices by studying rules, codes, and moral principles. Others pick up values through stories which relate the experiences and choices of others. They are influenced, positively or negatively, by the examples around them.

Because the Bible contains the stories of so many faith-filled people, it is a great resource for learning values. The ultimate example for us, of course, is the life story of Jesus. By studying the choices Jesus made, and the reasons behind those choices, we begin to see the path of goodness God has marked out for us. The four gospel accounts help us follow the path through their unique interpretation of what it means to follow Jesus. As we practice following the example of Jesus in our own lives, we become moral people.

---

in the *Spotlight*

Negative Examples: Ahab

The Bible isn't just a source for positive examples. Its pages are also full of stories about those who made poor choices. Consider King Ahab from the Old Testament. (See *1 Kings 16:29 through 2 Kings 10:11.*) His fear of Assyria and Babylon (and of his wife!) prevented him from hearing the prophet Elijah. Because of his choice, Ahab was destroyed.

Ahab was afraid, and that fear paralyzed him when God called. His life story helps us learn two important lessons:

1. Our fears often keep us from making the right decisions.
2. Usually, the real consequences of wrongdoing are much worse than the imagined hardships of making the right decision.

Growing in Our Knowledge of God

A basic principle in relationships is that you can't love someone you don't know. Before you knew your best friend, you couldn't love that person. The same is true for your parents, your favorite aunt, and anyone else you love. To put it another way, getting to know people is the first step towards learning to love

"Do you not know that the runners in the stadium all run in the race, but only one wins the prize? Run so as to win. Every athlete exercises discipline in every way. They do it to win a perishable crown, but we an imperishable one" (1 Corinthians 9:24–25).

If we are willing to listen, we can learn much from our elders and from their traditions. The same is true concerning understanding the Bible. When we read the Bible we are guided by the tradition of the Church.

them. This principle holds true for God as well: we can't love God if we don't know God.

As Catholics, we learn about God from two main sources: the Bible and the tradition of the Church. In many ways, however, these two sources overlap, because the Church helps us to see God in the pages of the Bible, through its tradition of interpretation. The best way to grow in our knowledge of God, therefore, is to study the Bible in light of the tradition of Scripture study and understanding which the Church offers.

In this course, you've learned how to read the Bible for what it tells us about God. For example, you know that the gospel account of Luke and the Book of Acts are built on the theme of Salvation history. This theme tells us that God has been planning for our salvation from the beginning of time, and that God arranges the events of history to bring those plans about. The Church keeps this faith alive by helping us to see the events of our lives from the perspective of Salvation history. Knowing this, we can be confident that, in some mysterious way, things are happening as they should, and that God's love for us never fails. Reading the Bible helps us know and love God, who created us, guides us, and calls us to life in the kingdom.

Using the Bible in Prayer

Any good relationship is a two-way street, of course. Conversation is at the heart of a friendship that is alive, growing, and filled with love. Friends talk to each other constantly about everything! The same is true with our relationship with God. If we are to be friends with God, then we must talk with God. Our conversation with God occurs when we pray. Praying with the Bible is an easy way to approach God.

Some parts of the Bible are written as prayers. As you know, many of the psalms are prayers that were used in the ancient Jerusalem Temple. You can pray these same psalms directly, connecting yourself to a tradition that's 3,000 years old.

Other parts of the Bible can also help us pray. When we read stories about our ancestors in faith, we can pray that God will give us the strength to follow their example. When we read Paul's teachings about grace and the Law, we can pray that the Spirit will grant us the grace to live as God requests.

Have You Considered?

1. Name one character from the Bible you think serves as a good example. What values or lessons do you learn from this person?
2. What do you think is the most important thing you've learned about God in this course? How did the Bible help you learn this?

Applying Your Skills

If you've ever played a sport or participated in the arts, you know that practice is the key to success. Behind that dramatic single in the bottom of the ninth inning are hours spent in the batting cage; that record-breaking lap comes from countless miles run around the track after school. The life-like statue or the perfectly rendered piano concerto reveal a dedication to practice. Reading the Bible requires no less dedication: the more you practice, the better you get.

The skills reviewed in the last section can be used to improve your understanding of the Bible and to grow in faith. In this section, you'll look at ways in which you can improve your Bible study skills.

Learning Objectives for Section Two

By the end of this section, you will be able to:

- Demonstrate your mastery of the six basic Bible study skills.
- Discuss several ways to apply these skills.
- Examine how the Bible is a part of the living tradition of the Church.

◆ The Bible in Society

One of the most consistent themes in the Bible is that how we live our faith affects society as well as our own spiritual lives. Amos, you will recall, said that religious ritual is useless unless people live justly. The Law of Moses contained provisions ensuring that the poor were cared for and that people had a chance to escape from debt. In the New Testament, Luke stresses the special love God has for the poor and those forgotten by society. As Christians, therefore, we should search the Bible for what it can tell us about the social problems we face today. Your Bible study skills can help you do this.

No Specific Solutions

Many of the problems we face today are unique to modern society. The Bible has nothing directly to say, for example, about nuclear war, since nuclear power was unknown in the time of the biblical authors. Problems such as poverty and homelessness are timeless, yet in neither case does the Bible offer specific solutions.

The Bible does not tell us how to run our economy or what our policies on taxes or foreign relations should be. The policies described in the Bible were appropriate for their time and place, and these circumstances have changed over time. We must develop our own solutions for every situation, guided by the principles offered in the Bible.

The Bible Offers Religious and Moral Values

The Bible provides directions and values which pertain to our problems. The Bible upholds the dignity of people living in poverty for example. Any proposal or program that treats the poor as objects or threatens their well-being is contrary to that biblical value. Similarly, the Bible upholds the sacred nature of human life. This value should influence the way we look at society and shape our political decisions. By carefully studying the various books of the Bible, we

People of Note

Caesar Chavez

Caesar Chavez was a modern prophet, someone who read the Bible intensely and applied the insights and strength he found there to the needs of his people. Chavez was the founder of the United Farm Workers of America, a union devoted to improving the working conditions and benefits of agricultural laborers.

Many of these workers speak little English, and often don't understand their rights. As a result, they can be mistreated and taken advantage of. Chavez helped the farm workers to organize to resist these abuses. One of his tactics was to protest unfair treatment of the workers with hunger strikes. The Eucharist was always the first food he would receive when he ended one of these fasts. Caesar Chavez died in 1993, a model for us of someone who was inspired by the Bible to address the injustices he saw.

Caeser Chavez, shown here with Senator Robert Kennedy, was inspired by the Bible to act for justice.

can discover the basic values they contain, and then apply these values in our own context.

Applying Your Skills

All too often, people jump to conclusions about what "the Bible says." Using your skills, you can carefully avoid this error. The following four points summarize what you've learned about reading the Bible.

1. **The Bible is to be read in context.** When biblical authors speak, their words are directed toward a specific historical, literary, and social situation.

2. **The Big Picture must be seen.** The Bible is multifaceted. To understand the real issues being discussed, read what a variety of authors have to say.

3. **The Bible teaches by example.** Biblical stories can shape our lives by their examples. These models can show us how people of faith reacted in situations similar to our own.

4. **The Bible is a book of prayer.** To discern what the Bible has to say on a particular subject, pray over it carefully, asking the Spirit to lead you in truth and consult the teaching of the Church, to be sure that you are staying on track.

Being Prophets

You have read the stories of many of Israel's prophets: Elijah, Elisha, Isaiah, Jeremiah, and Ezekiel. As you know, these courageous servants of Yahweh spoke God's word to the leaders of their society, calling the people back to their basic Covenant values. By applying your Bible study skills, you can hear God in Scripture. Once you have heard, you can proclaim God's message to others. In so doing, you can be a prophet for our age.

Our world needs prophets. We need people who can carefully discern the values of Scripture, and speak those values clearly and compassionately. Sometimes we are so overwhelmed by problems, that the situation seems hopeless. Prophets remind us that with God, there is always hope.

Whatever your situation, your Bible study skills can help you analyze the situations you experience, discover the important values at stake, and think about the choices you can make. In this way, the Bible can help you to discover and share God's word where it is most needed.

Have You Considered?

1. Name one social problem we face today, and describe how you would study the Bible to find out what it has to say about that problem.

2. Describe a situation in which you could imagine yourself acting as a prophet.

◆ The Bible in the Life of the Church

As Catholics, we encounter the Bible in a variety of situations: in Mass, in the sacraments, during the Liturgical year, and in prayer. Another great application of the Bible study skills you have developed in this class is to participate more deeply in the life of the Church. If you do, the rituals and seasons of the Church will become more interesting and understandable.

At Mass

Mass is an important expression of the faith of the Church. Your Bible study skills can help you become a more informed and sensitive participant in the Mass. Knowing the Bible can revitalize your experience of the Mass and make it more enjoyable.

The Bible plays an important role in the Mass. The first major division of the Mass, called the *Liturgy of the Word*, is primarily taken from the Bible:

- A reading taken from the Old Testament
- A response, usually a psalm
- A reading from the New Testament, either from Acts or one of the letters
- A reading of the Gospel from one of the four accounts

Because many people don't know much about the Bible, they often don't appreciate the Liturgy of the Word. They wait for the priest's homily for things to make sense. The readings for each Mass were carefully selected to present a common theme. The

Scripture Workshop

The Readings for Mass

Find out what the readings are for this week's Sunday Mass, then, do the following:

- Look up each passage and read it. You may find the passage more understandable if you also read the entire chapter that contains the assigned passage.
- Try to identify the historical and literary context involved. Write a paragraph explaining your understanding of the passage.
- Reflect on what each reading says about God and yourself. Put these ideas into a paragraph also.
- After Mass, evaluate your work to see if this process helps your appreciation of the Liturgy of the Word.

Lectionary, the book containing the readings for Mass, has been organized so that a theme or an issue is seen in each set of readings and develops over the course of a few weeks.

One way to apply your biblical skills would be to study the Sunday readings in advance. Figure out what the authors were saying, and how their words help point us to God. Then put the readings together and try to determine the theme the Church saw in putting these particular selections together.

The Other Sacraments

Although the Eucharist is the sacrament that Catholics experience most often, other sacraments are also based on biblical teaching. The rite of baptism is based on actions performed by the disciples of Jesus (*John* 4:1–2), and our understanding of it has been shaped by Paul's teaching. Similarly, the rite of Holy Orders has been influenced by Luke's description of the coming of the Holy Spirit in Acts (*Acts* 2:1–41). The same passage in Acts is also part of the sacrament of Confirmation.

The Advent Wreath is used to celebrate the Liturgical season of Advent. The Liturgical year is organized around a three year cycle of readings from the Bible.

Just like the Mass, our interest in these sacraments, and our appreciation for them, will be enhanced if we reflect on the biblical passages that lie behind them. Maybe your own Confirmation is approaching, or your niece is being baptized soon. Maybe a friend or member of the family is being married or ordained. Whatever the case, you will get more out of the ritual surrounding the sacraments if you have used your Bible study skills to prepare.

Holy Days and Seasons

In the Catholic tradition, the Church year is divided into several seasons, each of which has a special importance in the life of the Church. The season of Advent, the four weeks before Christmas, opens the Church year. It is a time of preparation for the coming of Jesus. Christmas is then followed by the Christmas season. Later, the Church observes the season of Lent, leading up to Holy Week and Good Friday, followed by Easter Sunday and the Easter Season. In all of these periods, the Church focuses on specific aspects of the biblical story. How can your skills with the Bible help you to better appreciate these seasons?

Because Lent is a period of self-discipline and repentance leading up to the death and resurrection, you might prepare for it by reading the Bible stories that tie into this theme. Read the story of David's sin against Uriah and his sorrow when Nathan pointed out his evil deed in 2 Samuel 11 and 12. Read Psalm 51, often said to be David's prayer of repentance. Or you could read Jesus' comments on sin and forgiveness in the Gospel. Again, you would use your academic skills to figure out what these passages are saying. Then use your faith skills to hear God speaking to you through them.

The Church in Prayer

Catholics pray in many different ways. The rosary is a biblical prayer used by countless millions of Catholics every day. Maybe your family prays the rosary together. Catholics also pray at Mass, before meals, and in a wide variety of other situations. The formal prayers Catholics use are often formed around biblical passages and themes.

You already know that the Our Father is from the words of Jesus in the New Testament as they appear in Matthew 6:9–15 and Luke 11:2–4. Did you know that the Hail Mary is also biblical? The opening words of the prayer are from Luke 1:28, when the angel Gabriel appears to Mary and announces to her that she will give birth to Jesus. Elizabeth responds to Mary's visit with the next phrases of the prayer (*Luke* 1:42).

Sharing What You Know

Part of what makes us Catholic is our membership in the larger Church community. As you grow in your knowledge of the Bible, and use it to participate more deeply in the sacraments, seasons, and prayer of the Church, you should also share what you know with others.

- Take a few minutes to talk with your family about the Bible readings before you go to Mass.
- Explain the origins of the Hail Mary before you say the rosary together.
- During Lent, talk about the passion stories in the four gospel accounts.

Whatever the situation, when you share your skills with others, you respond to Jesus' call to focus on others first. You'll also keep coming back to Scripture because you're comfortable reading it.

The rosary is a vehicle for prayer and a source of great comfort for many Catholics. The rosary is based upon events mentioned in the Gospel and so is a biblical prayer.

Have You Considered?

1. Do you think you would participate better at Mass if you knew more about the Bible readings? Why or why not?
2. Describe a way in which using your Bible study skills would make Lent, Advent, or Easter more meaningful to you.

◆ The Book of the Church

The relationship between the Bible and the Church is not a one-way street. It's not just that the Bible helps us to understand the Church; the Church also helps us to better understand the Bible. In fact, the Bible is the Church's book, and only through the tradition of the Church can we fully understand the message of Scripture.

The Church Gives Us the Bible

The Bible is the "book of the Church" in many senses. As you have seen, the Bible is central to the ritual and prayer of the Church. But there is another important way in which the Bible is the Church's book: the Church gave us the Bible. This statement is true in two ways:

1. The Bible was written by members of a faith community, who were writing on behalf of that community. The New Testament was written by early Christians and its contents reflect the beliefs and practices of those early communities.
2. Later, the Church decided which books deserved to be included in the Bible and which should be excluded. The list of books approved for the Bible is called the **canon.** The Church decided what the canon of the Old and New Testaments would be.

Taken together, these two points mean that the Bible originated in the Church and has been given its present form by the Church. In other words, the Church came before the Bible and the Church gave the Bible its importance.

The Church Interprets the Bible

Catholics recognize two primary ways in which God's will is revealed: (1) through Scripture and (2) through the tradition of the Church. Just as God inspired the authors of the Bible, we believe that God has also inspired the Church, and that both Bible and tradition are valid sources of revelation.

We have already seen that the Bible is a highly diverse collection of literature, containing many different points of view. How are we to know which points of view are valid for us today, and which have to be revised in light of new experience? Our personal prayer and reflection are an important part of the answer, but an even more important source of guidance is the teaching of the Church.

Through the authority of the Pope and the bishops, the Church interprets the Bible for every generation. Because the Bible was given to us by the Church, it is only in light of the Church that we can truly understand its contents.

As Catholics, we believe that there is more to interpreting Scripture than our own, personal reaction; we are also members of a believing community, and our understanding of the Bible needs to be shaped by that community. As this process goes on, the Holy Spirit is with the Church, guiding it and protecting it. The second letter of Peter addresses this idea:

> *Know this first of all, that there is no prophecy of Scripture that is a matter of personal interpretation, for no prophecy ever came through human will; but rather human beings moved by the Holy Spirit spoke under the influence of God.*
>
> (2 Peter 1:20–21)

In other words, the biblical authors were not writing merely as individuals. Their efforts were guided by the Holy Spirit. To understand their work, we also need the guidance of the Spirit. This guidance is fully available through the Church.

The Dogmatic Constitution on Divine Revelation from the Second Vatican Council says,

> *The Tradition that comes from the apostles makes progress in the Church, with the help of the Holy Spirit. There is a growth in insight into the realities and words that are being passed on. This comes about in various ways. . . . Thus, as the centuries go by, the Church is always advancing towards the plenitude of divine truth, until eventually the words of God are fulfilled in her.*
>
> (Dei Verbum II, 8)

Have You Considered?

1. Which do you think is the most important sense in which the Bible is the "Book of the Church?" Why?
2. Give an example of how the Church helps us to understand the Bible.

◆ Personal Study and Prayer

This emphasis on the Church as the interpreter of Scripture does not mean that your personal Bible study is unimportant. Far from it! You can and should return to the Bible throughout your life to hear God speaking and to think and pray about how you want to respond.

Life Situations

All of us face difficult moments of choice. What ever your situation, choices require thought and prayer. They also require input from others. Here the Bible can help provide models; people who have overcome difficulty.

Consider the story of Ruth, who made the difficult choice to stay with her mother-in-law Naomi rather than return to her native country. Using your academic skills, you can figure out how to use this biblical situation to resolve an issue of your own. You can make a good decision grounded in prayer.

Of course, real life situations are not always filled with drama. Most of life requires that we make minor decisions and avoid insignificant obstacles. Through every choice we make, however, we develop our *character*. As a result, even seemingly minor choices we make are important.

Here, too, the Bible can help. Read something from the Bible every day, if only a few verses. Reflect on what they might mean. Think about those verses for the day. Decide on a goal you want to strive for in your behavior and your relationships with others. Over time, you will find that you have formed a character grounded in the Scripture and in the love of others.

Prayer

Your most important relationship is the one that holds you close to God. As we said above, this relationship cannot grow without conversation, and prayer is how conversation happens.

Many people today question the importance of prayer. They say, it seems weird to talk to someone (God) who doesn't talk back, and anyway, it's hard to know what to say. These feelings are natural, but they're also easy to avoid. You already know that God does speak to us—through Scripture. To hear God, however, you have to read the Bible carefully, using all of your skills to understand clearly and richly. Prayer is your chance to respond.

Pick a story or passage, and begin by using your academic skills to understand it. Then, use your faith skills to hear God's voice coming through the reading. Finally, respond in prayer in a way that makes sense for you. There's no one right way to do this. The important thing is simply to pray honestly and openly, whether you do it using words, or you just offer to God the thoughts and feelings you have inside. The Bible is the best way to develop a prayer life, and for that reason, it's the best way for you to grow in holiness and in faith.

The Bible is above all a book of prayer. We are called to pray constantly so that we might be prepared for what lies ahead of us. How can you use the Bible in your prayer?

Through this study you have gained the skills you need to use the Bible fully for the rest of your life. You can only grow in those skills through practice.

The Word of the Lord

The three uses for your Bible study skills we have covered in this chapter are not the only ways to apply what you have learned. As you grow in your appreciation of Scripture, other uses will reveal themselves. Keep coming back. Understanding and applying the Bible is a lifelong adventure. The Bible is a source of hope, comfort, inspiration, and challenge. Ultimately, Scripture is God's gift to you.

Now, it's up to you to use this gift!

Have You Considered?

1. Describe a situation in your life in which you think Bible study might help.
2. Why do you think many people have difficulty with prayer? How can the Bible help one deal with those problems?

Spiritual Reflection

Words of Encouragement

Praying with the Bible is more than just gaining an understanding of it. It is savoring the words, just as you like to take your time enjoying the taste of your favorite food. It is repeating the words that touch your heart or wake you up inside—repeating them so they really sink in. Sometimes people like to memorize favorite verses that they discover. That, too, is prayer.

Prayer is reading the words as if they were being spoken directly to you. Listen to them well, then, act. Sometimes no physical action is called for, but only a response from your heart—in feelings, words, or thoughts.

When you read the Bible, use it as a springboard for prayer.

As you finish this course, your situation is similar to that of those early communities founded by Paul. You have the basis you need to grow in faith, but you have work to do in order to master it. Use this time to thank God for this start, and to ask for help along the rest of the way.

- Read Paul's words of encouragement to his community at Philippi in Philippians 1:3–11.
- Take this message personally, and ask God to help you finish the work you have started.

Q/A

Section One
1. Why do people return to the Bible throughout their lives?
2. Describe two aspects of studying the context of the Bible.
3. Why is diversity in the Bible not a problem?
4. In which different ways could a part of the Bible be "true"?
5. Why is it important to know these different kinds of truth?
6. How can you use the Bible in making moral decisions?
7. How does the Bible help us to know God?
8. How can the Bible shape our prayer lives?

Section Two
1. Why is it necessary to practice your Bible study skills?
2. How does the Bible emphasize social issues?
3. How does the Bible offer specific solutions to these problems?
4. How can we apply the Bible to social problems?
5. How can the Bible help us to better appreciate the Mass?
6. What is the connection between the Bible and the seasons of the Church year?
7. How can you use the Bible in real life situations?
8. How does one form character?
9. Is there one right way to use the Bible in prayer? Why or why not?

BIBLE ACTIVITIES

1. Select one chapter from any Old Testament book, and one from any New Testament book. Practice your academic skills by doing the following:

- Write down the author of the book.
- Find out what was going on at the time. Write down how that history influences what the chapter means.
- Read the chapter to see if there are references to any other literary works. List them if there are, and write down what each reference means.
- See if there is more than one point of view in the chapter. If so, write down why and what they are.
- What kind(s) of truth does this chapter have? Write down your explanation of each.

2. Use these same two chapters and apply your faith study skills. Do the following:

- Write down how each chapter could help you in moral decisions. What principles or values does the chapter uphold? What positive or negative examples does it provide?
- What does each chapter tell you about God? How does each author view God and God's involvement with us? Write down your answer.
- How could you use this chapter in prayer? Write down 1 or 2 ideas.

You now have a completed study of two biblical chapters. Save them, and return to them now and then as reminders of how to use the skills you have developed.

GLOSSARY

- **Advent:** The four weeks leading up to Christmas; a season of preparation for the coming of Jesus.
- **Biblical Truth:** The sense that the Bible is correct in what it says. Different parts of the Bible are true in different ways, such as historical, scientific, mythological, personal, or moral truth.
- **Canon:** List of books approved by the Church for inclusion in the Bible.
- **Character:** A moral identity built on choices made in a person's life.
- **Diversity:** The different ideas and points of view in the Bible because of the different authors who have contributed to it.
- **Historical Context:** The events happening at the time a Biblical book was written which influenced its content and point of view.
- **Lectionary:** The Church book which contains the biblical readings for the Mass.
- **Lent:** The season of Ash Wednesday to sundown on Holy Thursday. Lent is a time of self-discipline and repentance, commemorating the suffering, death and resurrection of Jesus.
- **Literary Context:** The earlier works of literature which influenced the content of a later biblical book.
- **Liturgy of the Word:** The first of the two major divisions of the Mass; it focuses on selected readings from the Bible, especially the four gospel accounts.
- **Social Context:** The social conditions in which the author of the biblical book lived and how those conditions influenced the author's point of view.

UNDERSTANDING MORE ABOUT:

Chiasm

Authors who wrote in ancient Greek used literary devices to embellish their writing. As someone familiar with Greek literature, Paul frequently used these techniques. One such device is called *chiasm:* the elements in one line or passage are flipped in the second.

An example of this is: **Moving too fast, too scared to stop.** "Moving" goes with "to stop," and "too fast" goes with "too scared." Their positions in the lines are switched around, however, which the Greeks believe sounded better.

Many Bible scholars believe that Paul's Letter to Philemon is an extended chiasm, made up of pairs like the one above. Much of the Gospel according to John also follows this pattern, especially John 13–17, though in John the chiasm is more difficult to follow. See if you can match up the 25 verses in the Letter to Philemon in this fashion. Hint:the pairs start at the beginning and end of the letter, and work their way into the middle.

Review

Catching Your Breath

The six chapters which make up this unit have introduced you to the major people, themes, and events of the New Testament. At the center of the New Testament is Jesus, who filled his followers with a sense of God's love and blessing. The New Testament tells us about the life of Jesus, as seen from the faith perspectives of four different writers: Matthew, Mark, Luke, and John. The New Testament also includes Luke's story of the growth of Christianity, and Paul's letters to the mission communities he founded. We also read later letters which reflect the growing emphasis on doctrine and organization in the Church. All of this material helps us to grow in our knowledge and love of God.

Review Questions

1. What is the difference between the "Jesus of History" and the "Christ of Faith"?
2. Why were the gospel accounts written?
3. Explain the two dimensions of the kingdom.
4. What is kingdom life like?
5. Who were the different kinds of followers of Jesus?
6. What was Jesus' attitude towards the Law?
7. Describe the main interests of the four gospel accounts.
8. Define "agape."
9. Who is the most important figure in the book of Acts?
10. Why was the conversion of the Gentiles controversial in early Christianity?
11. Describe what happened on Pentecost.
12. How do we see the gifts of the Holy Spirit in the Book of Acts?
13. Why were first-century conditions in the Roman Empire ideal for Paul's missionary work?
14. Why did conflicts and confusion arise in Paul's communities?
15. What does it mean to say that Paul's letters are only one side of a conversation?
16. List and define four important themes in the letters of Paul.
17. Why did the question of leadership arise in the Church in the late first century?
18. Describe the key offices in the early Church.
19. Based on the book of James, what are the important virtues in the Christian life?
20. Why is it important for Christians to hold common basic beliefs?
21. Why is understanding Scripture a lifelong process?
22. Why is it never possible to simply answer "yes" or "no" when someone asks whether a particular passage in the Bible is "true"?
23. How does the Bible help us to grow in the love of God?
24. What does it mean to say that the Bible is the "gift of the Church"?

Review

Bible Activities

Matthew's Genealogy

You know that genealogies, or "family trees," are important to the Bible. Matthew opens with a genealogy of Jesus, showing his descent from Abraham. Matthew normally mentions only the father's name, but five times he breaks this pattern and gives the mother's name as well.

- List the five women Matthew includes in his genealogy.
- Four of the five are from the Old Testament; look up their stories and summarize them.
- What do all five have in common?
- Why do you think Matthew mentions these women in his genealogy?

Paul and the Olive Tree

Read Paul's Letter to the Romans 11:11–24. This passage contains Paul's famous comparison to the olive tree. See if you can understand its meaning.

- What does the "root" of the tree symbolize?
- Who are the "branches"?
- What does it mean to be "grafted in" to the tree?

Revelation

As you know, the book of Revelation is highly symbolic. Among other things, the numbers in the book are not meant to be taken literally. They are symbolic, as are the beast, the seven seals, and the four horsemen. To get a sense of how this symbolism works, do the following:

- Read Chapter 21 of Revelation.
- Write down all the numbers that appear in this chapter.
- Which number appears most frequently? What do you think is its symbolic importance?

Praying With the Bible

Every day, members of the Catholic Church around the world pray a special set of prayers known as the Liturgy of the Hours. They include:

- Luke 1:46–50, the **Canticle of Mary.** The Canticle of Mary is sometimes called the "Magnificat."
- Luke 1:68–79, the **Canticle of Zechariah.** It is also called the "Benedictus."
- Luke 2:29–32, the **Canticle of Simeon.** The prayer is also called the "Nunc Dimittis."

Over the centuries, Christians have prayed these hymns in praise of God's gift of Jesus to humanity.

For your prayer experience, use these three hymns. Divide the class into three groups. Take a few moments of silent reflection. Then, do the following:

- Have the first group read Luke's infancy account up to the **Magnificat** (1:1–45). Each member of the group can take turns reading 1–2 verses.
- When you come to the Magnificat, have everyone in class recite it together.
- The next group will read up to the **Benedictus** (1:56–66).
- Again, the entire class will recite the prayer together.
- The third group will read up to the **Nunc Dimittis** (1:80–2:28). Again, all will recite the prayer in unison.
- Have one person finish reading chapter two aloud.
- Finish the experience by reflecting on the events of Jesus' life that follow. Allow a few minutes of quiet time for this to happen.

Finish the prayer experience by saying:

May the Lord bless us, protect us from all evil, and bring us to everlasting life. Amen.

Index